Bill Bryson's bestselling travel books
include *The Lost Continent, Notes from a Small
Island, A Walk in the Woods* and *Down Under. A
Short History of Nearly Everything,* was shortlisted
for the Samuel Johnson Prize, and won the
Aventis Prize for Science Books and the Descartes
Science Communication Prize. His latest
bestsellers are *Shakespeare* (in the Eminent Lives
Series) and *The Life and Times of the Thunderbolt
Kid*.

www.billbryson.co.uk

Bill Bryson's opening lines were:
'*I come from Des Moines. Someone had to*'.

This is what followed:

The Lost Continent

A road trip around the puzzle that is small-town America introduces the world to the adjective 'Brysonesque'.

> '*A very funny performance, littered with wonderful lines and memorable images*' LITERARY REVIEW

Neither Here Nor There

Europe never seemed funny until Bill Bryson looked at it.

> '*Hugely funny (not snigger-snigger funny but great-big-belly-laugh-till-you-cry funny)*' DAILY TELEGRAPH

Made in America

A compelling ride along the Route 66 of American language and popular culture gets beneath the skin of the country.

> '*A tremendous sassy work, full of zip, pizzazz and all those other great American qualities*' INDEPENDENT ON SUNDAY

Notes from a Small Island

A eulogy to Bryson's beloved Britain captures the very essence of the original 'green and pleasant land'.

> '*Not a book that should be read in public, for fear of emitting loud snorts*' THE TIMES

A Walk in the Woods

Bryson's punishing (by his standards) hike across the celebrated Appalachian Trail, the longest footpath in the world.

'This is a seriously funny book' SUNDAY TIMES

Notes from a Big Country

Bryson brings his inimitable wit to bear on that strangest of phenomena – the American way of life.

'Not only hiliarious but also insightful and informative' INDEPENDENT ON SUNDAY

Down Under

An extraordinary journey to the heart of another big country – Australia.

'Bryson is the perfect travelling companion … When it comes to travel's peculiars the man still has no peers' THE TIMES

A Short History of Nearly Everything

Travels through time and space to explain the world, the universe and everything.

'Truly impressive … It's hard to imagine a better rough guide to science' GUARDIAN

The Life and Times of the Thunderbolt Kid

Quintessential Bryson – a funny, moving and perceptive journey through his childhood.

'He can capture the flavour of the past with the lightest of touches' SUNDAY TELEGRAPH

DOWN UNDER

Bill Bryson

BLACK SWAN

TRANSWORLD PUBLISHERS
61–63 Uxbridge Road, London W5 5SA
A Random House Group Company
www.rbooks.co.uk

DOWN UNDER
A BLACK SWAN BOOK: 9780552997034

First published in Great Britain
in 2000 by Doubleday
a division of Transworld Publishers
Black Swan edition published 2001

Addresses for Random House Group Ltd companies outside the UK
can be found at: www.randomhouse.co.uk
The Random House Group Ltd Reg. No. 954009

The Random House Group Limited supports The Forest Stewardship
Council (FSC), the leading international forest certification organisation
All our titles that are printed on Greenpeace approved FSC certified paper
carry the FSC logo. Our paper procurement policy can be found at:
www.rbooks.co.uk/environment

Typeset in 11/14 Giovanni Book by
Falcon Oast Graphic Art Ltd.

Printed in the UK by CPI Cox & Wyman, Reading, RG1 8EX.

To David, Felicity, Catherine and Sam

Acknowledgements

Among the many people to whom I am indebted for help in the preparation of this book, I wish to express particular thanks to Alan Howe and Carmel Egan for so generously sharing their time and hospitality even knowing that I was about to put them in one of my books; Deirdre Macken and Allan Sherwin for their astute observations and sporting participation in what follows; Patrick Gallagher of Allen & Unwin and Louise Burke of the Australian National University for the very generous and thoughtful provision of books and other research materials; and Juliet Rogers, Karen Reid, Maggie Hamilton and Katie Stackhouse of Random House Australia for their conscientious and ever-cheerful help.

I am also much indebted in Australia to Jim Barrett, Steve Garland, Lisa Menke, Val Schier, Denis Walls, Stella Martin, Joel Becker, Barbara Bennett, Jim Brooks, Harvey Henley, Roger Johnstone, Ian Nowak, the staff of the State Library of New South Wales in Sydney, and the late, dear Catherine Veitch.

Further afield, I am especially grateful to Professor Danny Blanchflower of Dartmouth College for much statistical assistance; my longtime friend and agent Carol Heaton; and the kindly, peerless talents at Transworld Publishers in London, among whom I must mention Marianne Velmans, Larry Finlay, Alison Tulett, Emma Dowson, Meg Cairns and Patrick Janson-Smith, who remains the best friend and mentor any writer could ask for. Above all, and as always, my profoundest thanks to my dear, patient, incomparable wife, Cynthia.

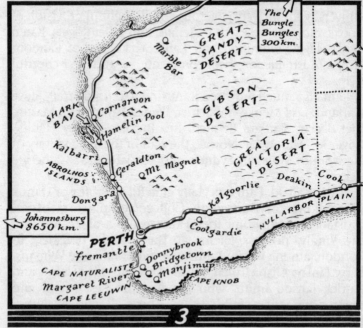

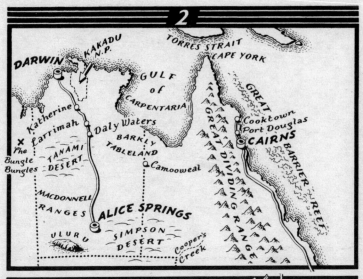

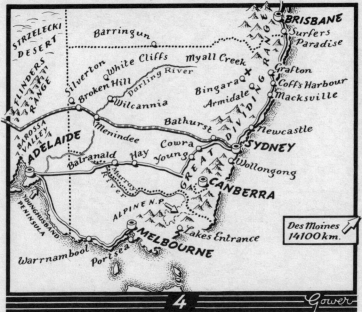

Part One

INTO THE OUTBACK

ONE

I

Flying into Australia, I realized with a sigh that I had forgotten again who their Prime Minister is. I am forever doing this with the Australian PM – committing the name to memory, forgetting it (generally more or less instantly), then feeling terribly guilty. My thinking is that there ought to be one person outside Australia who knows.

But then Australia is such a difficult country to keep track of. On my first visit, some years ago, I passed the time on the long flight from London reading a history of Australian politics in the twentieth century, wherein I encountered the startling fact that in 1967 the Prime Minister, Harold Holt, was strolling along a beach in Victoria when he plunged into the surf and vanished. No trace of the poor man was ever seen again. This seemed doubly astounding to me – first that Australia could just *lose* a Prime Minister (I mean, come on) and second that news of this had never reached me.

The fact is, of course, we pay shamefully scant attention to our dear cousins Down Under – though not entirely without reason, I suppose. Australia is, after all, mostly empty and a long way away. Its population, about 19 million, is small by world standards – China grows by a larger amount each year – and its place in the world economy is consequently peripheral; as an economic entity, it is about the same size as Illinois. From time to time it sends us useful things – opals, merino wool, Errol Flynn, the boomerang – but nothing we can't actually do without. Above all, Australia doesn't misbehave. It is stable and peaceful and good. It doesn't have coups, recklessly overfish, arm disagreeable despots, grow coca in provocative quantities or throw its weight around in a brash and unseemly manner.

But even allowing for all this, our neglect of Australian affairs is curious. As you might expect, this is particularly noticeable when you are resident in America. Just before I set off on this trip I went to my local library in New Hampshire and looked up Australia in the *New York Times Index* to see how much it had engaged attention in my own country in recent years. I began with the 1997 volume for no other reason than that it was open on the table. In that year, across the full range of possible interests – politics, sport, travel, the coming Olympics in Sydney, food and wine, the arts, obituaries and so on – the *New York Times* ran 20 articles that were predominantly on or about Australian affairs. In the same period, for purposes of comparison, it found space for 120 articles on Peru, 150 or so on Albania and a similar number on Cambodia, more than 300 on each of the Koreas, and well over 500 on

Israel. As a place that attracted American interest Australia ranked about level with Belarus and Burundi. Among the general subjects that outstripped it were balloons and balloonists, the Church of Scientology, dogs (though not dog sledding), and Pamela Harriman, the former ambassador and socialite who died in February 1997, a calamity that evidently required recording twenty-two times in the *Times*. Put in the crudest terms, Australia was slightly more important to Americans in 1997 than bananas, but not nearly as important as ice cream.

As it turns out, 1997 was actually quite a good year for Australian news in the United States. In 1996 the country was the subject of just nine news reports and in 1998 a mere six. Elsewhere in the world the news coverage may be more attentive, but with the difference, of course, that no one actually reads it. (Hands up, all those who can name the current Australian Prime Minister or say in which state you will find Melbourne or answer pretty much any antipodean question at all not involving cricket, rugby, Mel Gibson or *Neighbours*.) Australians can't bear it that the outside world pays so little attention to them, and I don't blame them. This is a country where interesting things happen, and all the time.

Consider just one of those stories that did make it into the *New York Times* in 1997, though buried away in the odd-sock drawer of Section C. In January of that year, according to a report written in America by a *Times* reporter, scientists were seriously investigating the possibility that a mysterious seismic disturbance in the remote Australian outback almost four years earlier had been a nuclear explosion set off by members of the Japanese doomsday cult Aum Shinrikyo.

It happens that at 11.03 p.m. local time on the night of

17

28 May 1993 seismograph needles all over the Pacific region twitched and scribbled in response to a very large-scale disturbance near a place called Banjawarn Station in the Great Victoria Desert of Western Australia. Some long-distance lorry drivers and prospectors, virtually the only people out in that lonely expanse, reported seeing a sudden flash in the sky and hearing or feeling the boom of a mighty but far-off explosion. One reported that a can of beer had danced off the table in his tent.

The problem was that there was no obvious explanation. The seismograph traces didn't fit the profile for an earthquake or mining explosion, and anyway the blast was 170 times more powerful than the most powerful mining explosion ever recorded in Western Australia. The shock was consistent with a large meteorite strike, but the impact would have blown a crater hundreds of feet in circumference, and no such crater could be found. The upshot is that scientists puzzled over the incident for a day or two, then filed it away as an unexplained curiosity – the sort of thing that presumably happens from time to time.

Then in 1995 Aum Shinrikyo gained sudden notoriety when it released extravagant quantities of the nerve gas sarin into the Tokyo underground, killing twelve people. In the investigations that followed, it emerged that Aum's substantial holdings included a 500,000-acre desert property in Western Australia very near the site of the mystery event. There, authorities found a laboratory of unusual sophistication and focus, and evidence that cult members had been mining uranium. It separately emerged that Aum had recruited into its ranks two nuclear engineers from the former Soviet Union. The group's avowed aim was the destruction of the world, and it appears that the event in the desert may have been a dry run for blowing up Tokyo.

You take my point, of course. This is a country that loses a Prime Minister and that is so vast and empty that a band of amateur enthusiasts could conceivably set off the world's first non-governmental atomic bomb on its mainland and almost four years would pass before anyone noticed. Clearly this is a place worth getting to know.

And so, because we know so little about it, perhaps a few facts would be in order.

Australia is the world's sixth largest country and its largest island. It is the only island that is also a continent, and the only continent that is also a country. It was the first continent conquered from the sea, and the last. It is the only nation that began as a prison.

It is the home of the largest living thing on earth, the Great Barrier Reef, and of the most famous and striking monolith, Ayers Rock (or Uluru to use its now official, more respectful Aboriginal name). It has more things that will kill you than anywhere else. Of the world's ten most poisonous snakes, all are Australian. Five of its creatures – the funnel-web spider, box jellyfish, blue-ringed octopus, paralysis tick and stonefish – are the most lethal of their type in the world. This is a country where even the fluffiest of caterpillars can lay you out with a toxic nip, where seashells will not just sting you but actually sometimes *go* for you. Pick up an innocuous coneshell from a Queensland beach, as innocent tourists are all too wont to do, and you will discover that the little fellow inside is not just astoundingly swift and testy, but exceedingly venomous. If you are not stung or pronged to death in some unexpected manner, you may be fatally chomped by sharks or crocodiles, or carried helplessly out to sea by irresistible currents, or left to stagger to an unhappy death in the baking outback. It's a tough place.

And it is old. For 60 million years, since the formation of the Great Dividing Range, Australia has been all but silent geologically, which has allowed it to preserve many of the oldest things ever found on earth – the most ancient rocks and fossils, the earliest animal tracks and riverbeds, the first faint signs of life itself. At some undetermined point in the great immensity of its past – perhaps 45,000 years ago, perhaps 60,000, but certainly before there were modern humans in the Americas or Europe – it was quietly invaded by a deeply inscrutable people, the Aborigines, who have no clearly evident racial or linguistic kinship to their neighbours in the region, and whose presence in Australia can be explained only by positing that they invented and mastered ocean-going craft at least 30,000 years in advance of anyone else in order to undertake an exodus, then forgot or abandoned nearly all that they had learned and scarcely ever bothered with the open sea again.

It is an accomplishment so singular and extraordinary, so uncomfortable with scrutiny, that most histories breeze over it in a paragraph or two, then move on to the second, more explicable invasion – the one that begins with the arrival of Captain James Cook and his doughty little ship HMS *Endeavour* in Botany Bay in 1770. Never mind that Captain Cook didn't discover Australia and that he wasn't even a captain at the time of his visit. For most people, including most Australians, this is where the story begins.

The world those first Englishmen found was famously inverted – its seasons back to front, its constellations upside down – and unlike anything any of them had seen before, even in the near latitudes of the Pacific. Its creatures seemed to have evolved as if they had misread the manual. The most characteristic of them didn't run or lope or canter, but *bounced* across the landscape, like dropped balls. The continent teemed with unlikely life. It contained a fish that could climb trees; a fox that flew (it was actually a very large bat); crustaceans so big that a grown man could climb inside their shells.

In short, there was no place in the world like it. There still isn't. Eighty per cent of all that lives in Australia, plant and animal, exists nowhere else. More than this, it exists in an abundance that seems incompatible with the harshness of the environment. Australia is the driest, flattest, hottest, most desiccated, infertile and climatically aggressive of all the inhabited continents. (Only Antarctica is more hostile to life.) This is a place so inert that even the soil is, technically speaking, a fossil. And yet it teems with life in numbers uncounted. For insects alone, scientists haven't the faintest idea whether the total number of species is 100,000 or more than twice that. As many as a third of those species remain entirely unknown to science. For spiders, the proportion rises to 80 per cent.

I mention insects in particular because I have a story about a little bug called *Nothomyrmecia macrops* that I think illustrates perfectly, if a bit obliquely, what an exceptional country this is. It's a slightly involved tale but a good one, so bear with me please.

In 1931 on the Cape Arid peninsula in Western Australia, some amateur naturalists were poking about in the scrubby wastes when they found an insect none had seen before. It looked vaguely like an ant, but was an unusual pale yellow and had strange, staring, distinctly unsettling eyes. Some specimens were collected and these

21

found their way to the desk of an expert at the National Museum of Victoria in Melbourne, who identified the insect at once as *Nothomyrmecia*. The discovery caused great excitement because, as far as anyone knew, nothing like it had existed on earth for a hundred million years. *Nothomyrmecia* was a proto-ant, a living relic from a time when ants were evolving from wasps. In entomological terms, it was as extraordinary as if someone had found a herd of triceratops grazing on some distant grassy plain.

An expedition was organized at once, but despite the most scrupulous searching no one could find the Cape Arid colony. Subsequent searches came up equally empty-handed. Almost half a century later, when word got out that a team of American scientists was planning to search for the ant, almost certainly with the kind of high-tech gadgetry that would make the Australians look amateurish and underorganized, government scientists in Canberra decided to make one final, pre-emptive effort to find the ants alive. So a party of them set off in convoy across the country.

On the second day out, while driving across the South Australia desert, one of their vehicles began to smoke and sputter, and they were forced to make an unscheduled overnight stop at a lonely pause in the road called Poochera. During the evening one of the scientists, a man named Bob Taylor, stepped out for a breath of air and idly played his torch over the surrounding terrain. You may imagine his astonishment when he discovered, crawling over the trunk of a eucalyptus beside their campsite, a thriving colony of none other than *Nothomyrmecia*.

Now consider the probabilities. Taylor and his colleagues were 800 miles from their intended search site. In the almost three million square miles of emptiness that is Australia, one of the handful of people able to identify it had just found one of the rarest, most sought-after insects on earth – an insect seen alive just once, almost half a century earlier – and all because their van had broken down where it did. *Nothomyrmecia*, incidentally, has still never been found at its original site.

You take my point again, I'm sure. This is a country that is at once staggeringly empty and yet packed with stuff. Interesting stuff, ancient stuff, stuff not readily explained. Stuff yet to be found.

Trust me, this is an interesting place.

II

Each time you fly from North America to Australia, and without anyone asking how you feel about it, a day is taken away from you when you cross the international dateline. I left Los Angeles on 3 January and arrived in Sydney fourteen hours later on 5 January. For me there was no 4 January. None at all. Where it went exactly I couldn't tell you. All I know is that for one twenty-four-hour period in the history of Earth, it appears I had no being.

I find that a little uncanny, to say the least. I mean to say, if you were browsing through your ticket folder and you saw a notice that said: 'Passengers are advised that on some crossings twenty-four-hour loss of existence may occur' (which is of course how they would phrase it, as if it happened from time to time) you would probably get up and make enquiries, grab a sleeve and say, 'Excuse me.' There is, it must be said, a certain metaphysical comfort in knowing that you can cease to have material form and it doesn't hurt at all, and, to be fair, they do give you the day back on the return journey when you cross the dateline in the opposite direction and thereby manage somehow to arrive in Los Angeles before you left Sydney, which in its way, of course, is an even neater trick.

Now I vaguely understand the principles involved here. I can see that there has to be a notional line where one day ends and the next begins, and that when you cross that line temporal oddities will necessarily follow. But that still doesn't get away from the fact that on any trip between America and Australia you will experience something that would be, in any other circumstance, the starkest impossibility. However hard you train or concentrate or watch your diet, no matter how many steps you take on the Stairmaster, you are never going to get so fit that you can cease to occupy space for twenty-four hours or be able to arrive in one room before you left the last one.

So there is a certain sense of achievement just in arriving in Australia – a pleasure and satisfaction to be able to step from the airport terminal into dazzling antipodean sunshine and realize that all your many atoms, so recently missing and unaccounted for, have been reassembled in an approximately normal manner (less half a pound or so of brain cells that were lost while watching a Bruce Willis action movie). In the circumstances, it is a pleasure to find yourself anywhere; that it is Australia is a positive bonus.

Let me say right here that I love Australia – adore it immeasurably – and am smitten anew each time I see it. One of the effects of paying so little attention to Australia is that it is always such a pleasant surprise to find it there. Every cultural instinct and previous experience tells you that when you travel this far you should find, at the very least, people on camels. There should be unrecognizable lettering on the signs, and swarthy men in robes drinking coffee from thimble-sized cups and puffing on hookahs, and rattletrap buses and potholes in the road and a real possibility of disease on everything you touch – but no, it's not like that at all. This is comfortable and clean and familiar. Apart from a tendency among men of a certain age to wear knee-high socks with shorts, these people are just like you and me. This is wonderful. This is exhilarating. This is why I love to come to Australia.

There are other reasons as well, of course, and I am pleased to put them on the record here. The people are immensely likeable – cheerful, extrovert, quick-witted and unfailingly obliging. Their cities are safe and clean and nearly always built on water. They have a society that is prosperous, well ordered and instinctively egalitarian. The food is excellent. The beer is cold. The sun nearly always shines. There is coffee on every corner. Rupert Murdoch no longer lives there. Life doesn't get much better than this.

This was my fifth trip and this time, for the first time, I was going to see the real Australia – the vast and baking interior, the boundless void that lies between the coasts. I have never entirely understood why, when people urge you to see their 'real' country, they send you to the empty parts where almost no sane person would choose to live, but there you are. You cannot say you have been to Australia until you have crossed the outback.

Best of all, I was going to do it in the swankiest possible way: on the fabled Indian Pacific railway from Sydney to Perth. Running for 2,720 pleasantly meandering miles across the bottom third of the country, through the states of New South Wales, South Australia and Western Australia, the Indian Pacific is the queen of the southern hemisphere trainwise. From Sydney it climbs gently through the Blue Mountains, chunters across endless miles of big-sky sheep country, traces the Darling River to the Murray and the Murray on towards Adelaide, and finally crosses the mighty Nullarbor Plain to the goldfields around Kalgoorlie before sighing to a well-earned halt in distant Perth. The Nullarbor, an almost inconceivable expanse of murderous desert, was something I particularly longed to see.

The colour magazine of the *Mail on Sunday* was doing a special issue on Australia, and I had agreed to file a report. I had been planning for some time anyway to come out to write a book, so this was in the nature of a bonus trip – a chance to get the measure of the country in an exceedingly comfortable way at someone else's expense. Sounded awfully good to me. To that end, I would be travelling for the next week or so in the company of a young English photographer named Trevor Ray Hart, who was flying in from London and whom I would meet for the first time the next morning.

But first I had a day to call my own, and I was inordinately pleased about that. I had never been to Sydney other than on book tours, so my acquaintance with the city was based almost entirely on cab journeys through unsung districts like Ultimo and Annandale. The only time I had seen anything at all of the real city was some years before, on my first visit, when a kindly sales rep from my local publisher had taken me out for the day in his car, with his wife and two little girls in the back, and I had disgraced myself by falling asleep. It wasn't from lack of interest or appreciation, believe me. It's just that the day was warm and I was newly arrived in the country. At some unfortunate point, quite early on, jet lag asserted itself and I slumped helplessly into a coma.

I am not, I regret to say, a discreet and fetching sleeper.

Most people when they nod off look as if they could do with a blanket; I look as if I could do with medical attention. I sleep as if injected with a powerful experimental muscle relaxant. My legs fall open in a grotesque come-hither manner; my knuckles brush the floor. Whatever is inside – tongue, uvula, moist bubbles of intestinal air – decides to leak out. From time to time, like one of those nodding-duck toys, my head tips forward to empty a quart or so of viscous drool onto my lap, then falls back to begin loading again with a noise like a toilet cistern filling. And I snore, hugely and helplessly, like a cartoon character, with rubbery flapping lips and prolonged steam-valve exhalations. For long periods I grow unnaturally still, in a way that inclines onlookers to exchange glances and lean forward in concern, then dramatically I stiffen and, after a tantalizing pause, begin to bounce and jostle in a series of whole-body spasms of the sort that bring to mind an electric chair when the switch is thrown. Then I shriek once or twice in a piercing and effeminate manner and wake up to find that all motion within 500 feet has stopped and all children under eight are clutching their mothers' hems. It is a terrible burden to bear.

I have no idea how long I slept in that car other than that it was not a short while. All I know is that when I came to there was a certain heavy silence in the car – the kind of silence that would close over you if you found yourself driving around your own city conveying a slumped and twitching heap from one unperceived landmark to another.

I looked around dumbly, not certain for the moment who these people were, cleared my throat and pulled myself to a more upright position.

'We were wondering if you might like some lunch,' my guide said quietly when he saw that I had abandoned for the moment the private ambition to flood his car with saliva.

'That would be very nice,' I replied in a small, abject voice, discovering in the same instant, with a customary inward horror, that while I had dozed a 400-pound fly had evidently been sick over me. In an attempt to distract attention from my unnatural moist sheen and at the same time re-establish my interest in the tour, I added more brightly: 'Is this still Neutral Bay?'

There was a small involuntary snort of the sort you make when a drink goes down the wrong way. And then with a certain strained precision: 'No, this is Dover Heights. Neutral Bay was' – a microsecond's pause, just to aerate the point – 'some time ago.'

'Ah.' I made a grave face, as if trying to figure out how we had managed between us to mislay such a chunk of time.

'Quite some time ago, in fact.'

'Ah.'

We rode the rest of the way to lunch in silence. The afternoon was more successful. We dined at a popular fish restaurant beside the pier at Watsons Bay, then went to look at the Pacific from the lofty, surf-battered cliffs that stand above the harbour mouth. On the way home the drive provided snatched views of what is unquestionably the loveliest harbour in the world – blue water, gliding sailboats, the distant iron arc of the Harbour Bridge with the Opera House squatting cheerfully beside it. But still I had not seen Sydney properly, and early the next day I departed for Melbourne.

So I was eager, as you may imagine, to make amends now. Sydneysiders, as they are rather quaintly known, have an evidently unquenchable desire to show their city off to visitors, and I had yet another kind offer of guidance before me, this time from a journalist on the *Sydney Morning Herald* named Deirdre Macken. An alert and cheerful lady of early middle years, Deirdre met me at my hotel with a young photographer named Glenn Hunt, and we set off on foot to the Museum of Sydney, a sleek and stylish new institution, which manages to look interesting and instructive without actually being either. You find yourself staring at artfully underlit displays – a caseful of immigrant artifacts, a room wallpapered with the pages of popular magazines from the 1950s – without being entirely certain what you are expected to conclude. But we did have a very nice latte in the attached café, at which point Deirdre outlined her plans for our busy day.

In a moment we would stroll down to Circular Quay and catch a ferry across the harbour to the Taronga Zoo wharf. We wouldn't actually visit the zoo, but instead would hike around Little Sirius Cove and up through the steep and jungly hills of Cremorne Point to Deirdre's house, where we would gather up some towels and boogie boards, and go by car to Manly, a beach suburb overlooking the Pacific. At Manly we would grab a bite of lunch, then have an invigorating session of boogie boarding before towelling ourselves down and heading for—

'Excuse me for interrupting,' I interrupted, 'but what is boogie boarding exactly?'

'Oh, it's fun. You'll love it,' she said breezily but, I thought, just a touch evasively.

'Yes, but what is it?'

'It's an aquatic sport. It's heaps of fun. Isn't it heaps of fun, Glenn?'

'Heaps,' agreed Glenn, who was, in the manner of all people whose film stock is paid for, in the midst of taking an infinite number of photographs. *Bizeet, bizeet, bizeet,* his camera sang as he took three quick and ingeniously identical photographs of Deirdre and me in conversation.

'But what does it entail exactly?' I persisted.

'You take a kind of miniature surfboard and paddle out into the sea, where you catch a big wave and ride it back to shore. It's easy. You'll love it.'

'What about sharks?' I asked uneasily.

'Oh, there's hardly any sharks here. Glenn, how long has it been since someone was killed by a shark?'

'Oh, ages,' Glenn said, considering. 'Couple of months at least.'

'Couple of months?' I squeaked.

'At least. Sharks are way overrated as a danger,' Glenn added. 'Way overrated. It's the rips that'll most likely get yer.' He returned to taking pictures.

'Rips?'

'Underwater currents that run at an angle to the shore and sometimes carry people out to sea,' Deirdre explained. 'But don't worry. That won't happen to you.'

'Why?'

'Because we're here to look after you.' She smiled serenely, drained her cup and reminded us that we needed to keep moving.

Three hours later, our other activities completed, we stood on a remote-seeming strand at a place called Freshwater Beach, near Manly. It was a big U-shaped bay, edged by low scrub hills, with what seemed to me awfully big waves pounding in from a vast and moody sea. In the middle distance several foolhardy souls in wetsuits were surfing towards some foamy outbursts on the rocky headland; nearer in a scattering of paddlers were being continually and, it seemed, happily engulfed by explosive waves.

Urged on by Deirdre, who seemed keen as anything to get into the briny drink, we began to strip down – slowly and deliberatively in my case, eagerly in hers – to the swimsuits she had instructed us to wear beneath our clothes.

'If you're caught in a rip,' Deirdre was saying, 'the trick is not to panic.'

I looked at her. 'You're telling me to drown calmly?'

'No, no. Just keep your wits. Don't try to swim against the current. Swim *across* it. And if you're still in trouble, just wave your arm like this' – she gave the kind of big, languorous wave that only an Australian could possibly consider an appropriate response to a death-at-sea situation – 'and wait for the lifeguard to come.'

'What if the lifeguard doesn't see me?'

'He'll see you.'

'But what if he doesn't?'

But Deirdre was already wading into the surf, a boogie board tucked under her arm.

Bashfully I dropped my shirt onto the sand and stood naked but for my sagging trunks. Glenn, never having seen anything quite this grotesque and singular on an Australian beach, certainly nothing still alive, snatched up his camera and began excitedly taking close-up shots of my stomach. *Bizeet, bizeet, bizeet, bizeet,* his camera sang happily as he followed me into the surf.

Let me just pause here for a moment to interpose two small stories. In 1935, not far from where we stood now, some fishermen captured a fourteen-foot beige shark and took it to a public aquarium at Coogee, where it was put on display. The shark swam around for a day or two in its new home, then abruptly, and to the certain surprise of the viewing public, regurgitated a human arm. When last seen the arm had been attached to a young man named Jimmy Smith, who had, I've no doubt, signalled his predicament with a big, languorous wave.

Now my second story. Three years later, on a clear, bright, calm Sunday afternoon at Bondi Beach, also not far from where we now stood, from out of nowhere there came four freak waves, each up to twenty-five feet high. More than 200 people were carried out to sea in the undertow. Fortunately, fifty lifeguards were in attendance that day, and they managed to save all but six people. I am aware that we are talking about incidents that happened many years ago. I don't care. My point remains: the ocean is a treacherous place.

Sighing, I shuffled into the pale green and cream-flecked water. The bay was surprisingly shallow. We trudged perhaps 100 feet out and it was still only a little over our knees, though even here there was an extraordinarily powerful current – strong enough to pull you off your feet if you weren't real vigilant. Another fifty feet on, where the water rose over our waists, the waves were breaking. If you discount a few hours in the lagoon-like waters of the Costa del Sol in Spain and an icy, instantly regretted dip once in Maine, I have almost no experience of the sea, and I found it frankly disconcerting to be wading into a rollercoaster of water. Deirdre shrieked with pleasure.

Then she showed me how the boogie board works. It was promisingly simple in principle. As a wave passed, she would leap aboard and skim along on its crest for many yards. Then Glenn had a turn and went even further. There is no question that it looked like fun. It didn't look too hard either. I was tentatively eager to have a try.

I positioned myself for the first wave, then jumped aboard and sank like an anvil.

'How'd you do that?' asked Glenn in wonder.

'No idea.'

I repeated the exercise with the same result.

'Amazing,' he said.

There followed a half hour in which the two of them watched first with guarded amusement, then a kind of astonishment, and finally something not unlike pity, as I repeatedly vanished beneath the waves and was scraped over an area of ocean floor roughly the size of Polk County, Iowa. After a variable but lengthy period, I would surface, gasping and confused, at a point anywhere from four feet to a mile and a quarter distant, and be immediately carried under again by a following wave. Before long, people on the beach were on their feet and placing bets. It was commonly agreed that it was not physically possible to do what I was doing.

From my point of view, each underwater experience was essentially the same. I would diligently attempt to replicate the dainty kicking motions Deirdre had shown me and try to ignore the fact that I was going nowhere and mostly drowning. Not having anything to judge this against, I supposed I was doing rather well. I can't pretend I was having a good time, but then it is a mystery to me how anyone could wade into such a merciless environment and expect to have fun. But I was resigned to my fate and knew that eventually it would be over.

Perhaps it was the oxygen deprivation, but I was rather lost in my own little world when Deirdre grabbed my arm just before I was about to go under again and said in a husky tone: 'Look out! There's a bluey.'

Glenn took on an immediate expression of alarm. 'Where?'

'What's a bluey?' I asked, appalled to discover that there was some additional danger I hadn't been told about.

'A bluebottle,' she explained and pointed to a small jellyfish of the type (as I later learned from browsing through a fat book titled, if I recall, *Things That Will Kill You Horridly in Australia: Volume 19*) known elsewhere as a Portuguese man-of-war. I squinted at it as it drifted past. It looked unprepossessing, like a blue condom with strings attached.

'Is it dangerous?' I asked.

Now before we hear Deirdre's response to me as I stood there, vulnerable and abraded, shivering, nearly naked and half drowned, let me just quote from her subsequent article in the *Herald*:

While the photographer shoots, Bryson and boogie board are dragged 40 metres down the beach in a rip. The shore rip runs south to north, unlike the rip further out which runs north to south. Bryson doesn't know this. He didn't read the warning sign on the beach.* Nor does he know about the bluebottle being blown in his direction – now less than a metre away – a swollen stinger that could give him 20 minutes of agony and, if he's unlucky, an unsightly allergic reaction to carry on his torso for life.

'Dangerous? No,' Deirdre replied now as we stood gawping at the bluebottle. 'But don't brush against it.'

'Why not?'

'Might be a bit uncomfortable.'

---

* The statement is inarguable. However, the author would like the record to show that he did not have his glasses on; he trusted his hosts; he was scanning a large area of ocean for sharks; and he was endeavouring throughout not to excrete a large housebrick into his pants.

I looked at her with an expression of interest bordering on admiration. Long bus journeys are uncomfortable. Slatted wooden benches are uncomfortable. Lulls in conversations are uncomfortable. The sting of a Portuguese man-of-war – even people from Iowa know this – is *agony*. It occurred to me that Australians are so surrounded with danger that they have evolved an entirely new vocabulary to deal with it.

'Hey, there's another one,' said Glenn.

We watched another one drift by. Deirdre was scanning the water.

'Sometimes they come in waves,' she said. 'Might be an idea to get out of the water.'

I didn't have to be told twice.

There was one more thing that Deirdre felt I needed to see if I was to have any understanding of Australian life and culture, so afterwards, as late afternoon gave way to the pale blush of evening, we drove out through the glittering sprawl of Sydney's western suburbs almost to the edge of the Blue Mountains to a place called Penrith. Our destination was an enormous sleek building, surrounded by an even more enormous, very full car park. An illuminated sign announced this as the Penrith Panthers World of Entertainment. The Panthers, Glenn explained, were a rugby league club.

Australia is a country of clubs – sporting clubs, workingmen's clubs, Returned Servicemen's League clubs, clubs affiliated to various political parties – each nominally, and sometimes no doubt actively, devoted to the well-being of a particular segment of society. What they are really there for, however, is to generate extremely large volumes of money from drinking and gambling.

I had read in the paper that Australians are the biggest gamblers on the planet – one of the more arresting statistics I saw was that the country has less than 1 per cent of the world's population but more than 20 per cent of its slot machines – and that between them Australians spend $11 billion* a year, or $2,000 per person, on various games of chance. But I had seen nothing to suggest such risky gusto until I stepped inside the World of Entertainment. It was vast and dazzling and immensely well appointed. The club movement in Australia is huge. In New South Wales alone, clubs employ 65,000 people, more than any other industry, and create an additional 250,000 jobs indirectly. They pay over $2 billion in wages and $500 million in gaming taxes. This is huge business and it is nearly all based on a type of slot machine popularly called a pokie.

I had assumed that we would have to bend the rules to get admitted – it was a club, after all – but in fact I learned that all Australian clubs allow instant membership to anyone, so keen are they to share the diverting pleasures of the poker machine. You just sign a temporary members' book by the door and in you go.

Surveying the crowds with a benign and cheerful eye was a man whose badge identified him as Peter Hutton, Duty Manager. In the manner of nearly all Australians, he was an easygoing and approachable sort. I quickly learned from him that this particular club has 60,000 members, of whom 20,000 will turn up on busy nights, like New Year's eve. Tonight the figure would be more like 2,000. The club contained bars and restaurants almost beyond counting,

* Unless otherwise indicated, all dollar signs refer to Australian dollars. As of early 2000, $1 was worth roughly 40 British pence (or £1 sterling to $2.50 Australian).

sports facilities, a children's play area, and nightclubs and theatres. They were just about to build a thirteen-screen cinema and a crèche big enough to hold 400 infants.

'Wow,' I said, for I was impressed. 'So is this the biggest club in Sydney?'

'Biggest in the southern hemisphere,' Mr Hutton said proudly.

We wandered into the vast and tinkling interior. Hundreds of pokies stood in long straight lines, and at nearly every one sat an intent figure feeding in the mortgage money. They are essentially slot machines, but with a bewildering array of illuminated buttons and flashing lights that let you exercise a variety of options – whether to hold a particular line, double your stake, take a portion of your winnings, and goodness knows what else. I studied from a discreet distance several people at play, but couldn't begin to understand what they were doing, other than feeding a succession of coins into a glowing box and looking grim. Deirdre and Glenn were similarly unacquainted with the intricacies of pokies. We put in a $2 coin, just to see what would happen, and got an instant payout of $17. This made us immensely joyful.

I returned to the hotel like a kid who had had a very full day at the county fair – exhausted but deeply happy. I had survived the perils of the sea, been to a palatial club, helped to win $15 and made two new friends. I can't say I was a great deal closer to feeling that I had actually seen Sydney than I had been before, but that day would come. Meanwhile, I had a night's sleep to get and a train to catch.

Chapter

TWO

I believe I first realized I was going to like the Australian outback when I read that the Simpson Desert, an area bigger than some European countries, was named in 1932* after a manufacturer of washing machines. (Specifically, Alfred Simpson, who funded an aerial survey.) It wasn't so much the pleasingly unheroic nature of the name as the knowledge that an expanse of Australia more than 100,000 miles square didn't even *have* a name until less than seventy years ago. I have near relatives who have had names longer than that.

But then that's the thing about the outback – it's so vast and forbidding that much of it is still scarcely charted. Even Uluru was unseen by anyone but its Aboriginal care-

* According to the Australian historian Geoffrey Blainey; but 1929 according to *National Geographic* magazine. There's hardly a fact about Australia that isn't significantly contradicted somewhere in print by somebody.

takers until only a little over a century ago. It's not even possible to say quite where the outback is. To Australians anything vaguely rural is 'the bush'. At some indeterminate point 'the bush' becomes 'the outback'. Push on for another 2,000 miles or so and eventually you come to bush again, and then a city, and then the sea. And that's Australia.

And so, in the company of the photographer Trevor Ray Hart, an amiable young man in shorts and a faded T-shirt, I took a cab to Sydney's Central Station, an imposing heap of bricks on Elizabeth Street, and there we found our way through its dim and venerable concourse to our train.

Stretching for a third of a mile along the curving platform, the Indian Pacific was everything the brochure illustrations had promised – silvery sleek, shiny as a new nickel, humming with that sense of impending adventure that comes with the start of a long journey on a powerful machine. Carriage G, one of seventeen on the train, was in the charge of a cheerful steward named Terry, who thoughtfully provided a measure of local colour by accompanying every remark with an upbeat Aussie turn of phrase.

Need a glass of water?

'No worries, mate. I'll get right on 'er.'

Just received word that your mother has died?

'Not a drama. She'll be apples.'

He showed us to our berths, a pair of singles on opposite sides of a narrow panelled corridor. The cabins were astoundingly tiny – so tiny that you could bend over and actually get stuck.

'This is it?' I said in mild consternation. 'In its entirety?'

'No worries,' Terry beamed. 'She's a bit snug, but you'll find she's got everything you need.'

39

And he was right. Everything you could possibly require in a living space was there. It was just very compact, not much larger than a standard wardrobe. But it was a marvel of ergonomics. It included a comfy built-in seat, a hide-away basin and toilet, a miniature cupboard, an overhead shelf just large enough for one very small suitcase, two reading lights, a pair of clean towels and a little amenity bag. In the wall was a narrow drop-down bed, which didn't so much drop down as fall out like a hastily stowed corpse as I, and I expect many other giddily experimental passengers, discovered after looking ruminatively at the door and thinking: 'Well, I wonder what's behind *there*?' Still, it did make for an interesting surprise, and freeing my various facial protuberances from its coiled springs helped to pass the half hour before departure.

And then at last the train thrummed to life and we slid regally out of Sydney Central. We were on our way.

Done in one fell swoop, the journey to Perth takes nearly three days. Our instructions, however, were to disembark at the old mining town of Broken Hill to sample the outback and see what might bite us. So for Trevor and me the rail journey would be in two parts: an overnight run to Broken Hill and then a two-day haul across the Nullarbor. The train trundled out through the endless western suburbs of Sydney – through Flemington, Auburn, Parramatta, Doonside and the adorably named Rooty Hill – then picked up a little speed as we entered the Blue Mountains, where the houses thinned out and we were treated to long end-of-afternoon views over steep-sided vales and hazy forests of gum trees, whose quiet respirations give the hills their eponymous tinge.

I went off to explore the train. Our domain, the first class section, consisted of five sleeping carriages, a dining carriage in a plush and velvety style that might be called *fin de siècle brothelkeeper*, and a lounge bar in a rather more modern mode. This was provisioned with soft chairs, a small promising-looking bar and low but relentless piped music from a twenty-volume compilation called, at a guess, 'Songs You Hoped You'd Never Hear Again'. A mournful duet from *Phantom of the Opera* was playing as I passed through.

Beyond first class was the slightly cheaper holiday class, which was much the same as ours except that their dining area was a buffet car with bare plastic tables. (These people apparently needed wiping down after meals.) The passage beyond holiday class was barred by a windowless door, which was locked.

'What's back there?' I asked the buffet car girl.

'Coach class,' she said with a shudder.

'Is this door always locked?'

She nodded gravely. 'Always.'

Coach class would become my obsession. But first it was time for dinner. The tannoy announced the first sitting. Ethel Merman was belting out 'There's No Business Like Show Business' as I passed back through the first class lounge. Say what you will, the woman had lungs.

For all its air of cultivated venerability, the Indian Pacific is actually an infant as rail systems go, having been created as recently as 1970 when a new standard-gauge line was built across the country. Before that, for various arcane reasons mostly to do with regional distrust and envy, Australian railway lines employed different gauges. New South Wales had rails 4 feet 8½ inches apart. Victoria opted for a more commodious 5 feet 3 inches. Queensland and Western Australia economically decided on a standard of 3 feet

6 inches (a width not far off that of amusement park rides; people must have ridden with their legs out of the windows). South Australia, inventively, had all three. Five times on any journey between the east and west coasts passengers and freight had to be offloaded from one train and redeposited on another; a mad and tedious process. Finally, sanity was mustered and an all-new line was built. It is the second longest line in the world, after Russia's Trans-Siberian.

I know all this because Trevor and I sat at dinner with a pair of quiet middle-aged teachers from rural north Queensland, Keith and Daphne. This was a big trip for them on teachers' salaries, and Keith had done his homework. He talked with enthusiasm about the train, the landscape, the recent bush fires – we were passing through Lithgow where hundreds of acres of bush had been scorched and two firefighters had lost their lives recently – but when I asked about Aborigines (the question of land reforms had been much in the news) he grew suddenly vague and flustered.

'It's a problem,' he said, staring hard at his food.

'At the school where I teach,' Daphne went on, hesitantly, 'the Aboriginal parents, well, they get their dole payment and spend it on drink and then go walkabout. And the teachers have to . . . well, *feed* the children. You know, out of their own pockets. Otherwise the children wouldn't eat.'

'It's a problem,' Keith said again, still fixed on his food.

'But they're lovely people really. When they're not drinking.'

And that pretty well killed the conversation.

After dinner Trevor and I ventured into the lounge carriage. While Trevor went to the bar to order I sank into an

42

easy chair and watched the dusky landscape. It was farming country, vaguely arid. The background music, I noted with idle interest, had gone from 'Much Loved Show Tunes' to 'Party Time at the Nursing Home'. 'Roll Out the Barrel' was just finishing when we arrived and was swiftly succeeded by 'Toot Toot Tootsie Goodbye'.

'Interesting choice of music,' I observed drily to the young couple opposite me.

'Yes, lovely!' they replied with simultaneous enthusiasm.

Suppressing an urge to shriek, I turned to the man beside me – an educated-looking older man in a suit, which was striking because everyone else on the train was in casual wear. We chatted about this and that. He was a retired solicitor from Canberra on his way to visit a son in Perth. He seemed a reasonable and perceptive sort, so I mentioned to him, in a confiding tone, my puzzling conversation with the schoolteachers from Queensland.

'Ah, Aborigines,' he said, nodding solemnly. 'A great problem.'

'So I gather.'

'They want hanging, every one of them.'

I looked at him, startled, and found a face on the edge of fury.

'Every bloody one of them,' he said, jowls trembling, and without another word took his leave.

Aborigines, I reflected, were something I would have to look into. But for the moment I decided to keep the conversation to simple matters – weather, scenery, popular show tunes – until I had a better grasp of things.

The great if obvious feature of a train, as compared with a hotel room, is that your view is ever changing. In the morning I awoke to a new world: red soil, scrubby vegetation, huge skies and an encircling horizon broken only by an occasional skeletal gum tree. As I peered blearily from my narrow perch, a pair of kangaroos, flushed by the train, bounded across the foreground. It was an exciting moment. We were definitely in Australia now!

We arrived at Broken Hill just after eight and stepped blinking from the train. An airless heat hung over the land – the kind of heat that hits you when you open an oven door to check a roasting turkey. Waiting for us on the platform was Sonja Stubing, a good-natured young lady from the regional tourist office who had been sent to collect us from the station and take us to pick up a rental car for a drive around the outback.

'How hot does it get here?' I asked, breathing out hard.

'Well, the record's forty-eight.'

I thought for a minute. 'That's one hundred and eighteen degrees!' I said.

She nodded serenely. 'It was forty-two yesterday.'

Another brief calculation: 107 degrees. 'That's very hot.'

She nodded. 'Too hot.'

Broken Hill was a positively delightful little community – clean, trim, cheerfully prosperous. Unfortunately this was not at all what we wanted. We wanted proper outback: a place where men were men and sheep were nervous. Here there were cafés and a bookstore, travel agents offering enticing packages to Bali and Singapore. They were even doing a Noel Coward play at the civic centre. This wasn't the outback at all. This was Guildford with the heat turned up.

Things took a more hopeful turn when we went to Len Vodic Vehicle Hire to pick up a four-wheel drive for a two-day jaunt into the baking wilderness. The eponymous Len was a wiry old guy, energetic and friendly, who looked as

44

if he had spent every day of his life doing tough stuff in the out of doors. He jumped behind the wheel and gave us the kind of swift, thorough rundown that people give when they assume they are dealing with intelligent and capable listeners. The interior presented a bewildering assortment of dials, levers, knobs, gauges and toggles.

'Now say you get stuck in sand and need to increase your offside differential,' Len was saying on one of the intermittent occasions I dipped into the lecture. 'You move this handle forward like so, select a hyperdrive ratio of between twelve and twenty-seven, elevate the ailerons and engage both thrust motors – but *not* the left-hand one. That's very important. And whatever you do, watch your gauges and don't go over one hundred and eighty degrees on the combustulator, or the whole thing'll blow and you'll be stuck out there.'

He jumped out and handed us the keys. 'There's twenty-five litres of spare diesel in the back. That should be more than enough if you go wrong.' He looked at us again, more carefully. 'I'll get you some more diesel,' he decided.

'Did you understand any of that?' I whispered to Trevor when he had gone.

'Not past the putting the key in the ignition part.'

I called to Len: 'What happens if we get stuck or lost?'

'Why, you die of course!' Actually, he didn't say that, but that's what I was thinking. I had been reading accounts of people who had been lost or stranded in the outback, like the explorer Ernest Giles who spent days wandering waterless and half dead before coming fortuitously on a baby wallaby that had tumbled from its mother's pouch. 'I pounced upon it,' Giles related in his memoirs, 'and ate it, living, raw, dying – fur, skin, bones, skull and all.' And this was one of the happier stories. Believe me, you don't want to get lost in the outback.

I began to feel a tremor of foreboding – a feeling not lightened when Sonja gave a cry of delight at the sight of a spider by our feet and said: 'Hey, look, a redback!' A redback, if you don't know already, is death on eight legs. As Trevor and I whimperingly tried to climb into each other's arms, she snatched it up and held it out to us on the tip of a finger.

'It's all right,' she giggled. 'It's dead.'

We peered cautiously at the little object on her fingertip, a telltale red hourglass shape on its shiny back. It seemed unlikely that something so small could deliver instant agony, but make no mistake, a single nip from a redback's malicious jaws can result within minutes in 'frenzied twitching, a profuse flow of body fluids and, in the absence of prompt medical attention, possible death'. Or so the literature reports.

'You probably won't see any redbacks out there,' Sonja reassured us. 'Snakes are much more of a problem.'

This intelligence was received with four raised eyebrows and expressions that said: 'Go on.'

She nodded. 'Common brown, western puff pastry, yellow-backed lockjaw, eastern groin groper, dodge viper . . .' I don't remember what she said exactly, but it was a long list. 'But don't worry,' she continued. 'Most snakes don't want to hurt you. If you're out in the bush and a snake comes along, just stop dead and let it slide over your shoes.'

This, I decided, was the least-likely-to-be-followed advice I had ever been given.

Our extra diesel loaded, we climbed aboard and, with a grinding of gears, a couple of bronco lurches and a lively but inadvertent salute of windscreen wipers, took to the open road. Our instructions were to drive to Menindee, 110 kilometres to the east, where we would be met by a man named Steve Garland. In the event, the drive to Menindee was something of an anticlimax. The landscape was shimmering hot and gorgeously forbidding, and we were gratified to see our first willy-willy, a column of rotating dust perhaps a hundred feet high moving across the endless plains to our left. But this was as close to adventure as we got. The road was newly paved and relatively well travelled. While Trevor stopped to take pictures, I counted four cars pass. Had we broken down, we wouldn't have been stranded more than a few minutes.

Menindee was a modest hamlet on the Darling River: a couple of streets of sun-baked bungalows, a petrol station, two shops, the Burke and Wills Motel (named for a pair of nineteenth-century explorers who inevitably came a cropper in the unforgiving outback) and the semi-famous Maidens Hotel, where in 1860 the aforementioned Burke and Wills spent their last night in civilization before meeting their unhappy fate in the barren void to the north.

We met Steve Garland at the motel and, to celebrate our safe arrival and recent discovery of fifth gear, crossed the road to Maidens and joined the noisy hubbub within. Maidens' long bar was lined from end to end with sun-leathered men in shorts and sweat-stained muscle shirts and wide-brimmed hats. It was like stepping into a Paul Hogan movie. This was more like it.

'So which window do they eject the bodies through?' I asked the amiable Steve when we were seated, thinking that Trevor would probably like to set up his equipment for a shot at chucking-out time.

'Oh, it's not like that here,' he said. 'Things aren't as wild in the outback as people think. It's pretty civilized really.' He looked around with what was clearly real fondness, and exchanged hellos with a couple of dusty-looking characters.

Garland was a professional photographer in Sydney until his partner, Lisa Menke, was appointed chief warden of Kinchega National Park up the road. He took a job as the regional tourism and development officer. His territory covered 26,000 square miles, an area half the size of England but with a population of just 2,500. His challenge was to persuade dubious locals that there are people in the world prepared to pay good money to holiday in a place that is vast, dry, empty, featureless and ungodly hot. The other part of his challenge was to find such people.

Between the merciless sun and the isolation, outback people are not always the most gifted of communicators. We had heard of one shopkeeper who, upon being asked by a smiling visitor from Sydney where the fish were biting, stared at the man incredulously for a long moment and replied: 'In the fucking river, mate, where do you think?'

Garland only grinned when I put the story to him, but conceded that there was a certain occasional element of challenge involved in getting the locals to see the possibilities inherent in tourism.

He asked us how our drive had been.

I told him that I had expected it to be a little more harsh.

'Wait till tomorrow,' he said.

He was right. In the morning we set off in mini convoy, Steve and his partner Lisa in one car, Trevor and I in the other, for White Cliffs, an old opal-mining community

250 kilometres to the north. Half a mile outside Menindee the asphalt ended and the surface gave way to a hard earthen road full of potholes, ruts and cement-hard corrugations, as jarring as driving over railway sleepers.

We jounced along for hours, raising enormous clouds of red dust in our wake, through a landscape brilliantly hot and empty, over tablelands flecked with low saltbush and spiky spinifex, the odd turpentine bush and weary-looking eucalypt. Here and there along the roadside were the corpses of kangaroos and the occasional basking goanna, a large and ugly type of monitor lizard. Goodness knows how any living things survive in that heat and aridity. There are creekbeds out there that haven't seen water in fifteen years.

The supreme emptiness of Australia, the galling uselessness of such a mass of land, was something it took the country's European settlers a long time to adjust to. Several of the earliest explorers were so convinced that they would encounter mighty river systems, or even an inland sea, that they took boats with them. Thomas Mitchell, who explored vast tracts of western New South Wales and northern Victoria in the 1830s, dragged two wooden skiffs over 3,000 miles of arid scrub without once getting them wet, but refused to the last to give up on them. 'Although the boats and their carriage had been of late a great hindrance to us,' he wrote with a touch of understatement after his third expedition, 'I was very unwilling to abandon such useful appendages to an exploring party.'

Reading accounts of early forays, it is clear that the first explorers were often ludicrously out of their depths. In 1802, in one of the earliest expeditions, Lieutenant Francis Barrallier described a temperature of 82.5 degrees F. as 'suffocating'. We can reasonably assume that he was recently arrived in the country. His men tried for days without success to hunt kangaroos before it occurred to them that they might stalk the creatures more effectively if they first removed their bright red jackets. In seven weeks they covered just 130 miles, an average of about one and a half miles a day.

In expedition after expedition the leaders seemed wilfully, almost comically, unable to provision themselves sensibly. In 1817, John Oxley, the surveyor-general, led a five-month expedition to explore the Lachlan and Macquarie Rivers, and took only 100 rounds of ammunition – less than one shot a day from a single gun – and hardly any spare horseshoes or nails. The incompetence of the early explorers was a matter of abiding fascination for the Aborigines, who often came to watch. 'Our perplexities afforded them an inexhaustible fund of merriment and derision,' wrote one chronicler glumly.

It was into this tradition of haplessness that Burke and Wills improvidently stepped in 1860. They are far and away the most famous of Australian explorers, which is perhaps a little curious since their expedition accomplished almost nothing, cost a fortune and ended in tragedy.

Their assignment was straightforward: to find a route from the south coast at Melbourne to the Gulf of Carpentaria in the far north. Melbourne, at that time much larger than Sydney, was one of the most important cities in the British Empire, and yet one of the most isolated. To get a message to London and receive a reply took a third of a year, sometimes more. In the 1850s, the Philosophical Institute of Victoria decided to promote an expedition to find a way through the 'ghastly blank', as the interior was poetically known, which would allow the establishment of a telegraph line to connect Australia first to the East Indies and then onward to the world.

They chose as leader an Irish police officer named Robert O'Hara Burke, who had never seen real outback, was famous for his ability to get lost even in inhabited areas, and knew nothing of exploration or science. The surveyor was a young English doctor named William John Wills, whose principal qualifications seem to have been a respectable background and a willingness to go. A notable plus was that they both had outstanding facial hair.

Although by this time expeditions into the interior were hardly a novelty, this one particularly caught the popular imagination. Tens of thousands of people lined the route out of Melbourne when, on 19 August 1860, the Great Northern Exploration Expedition set off. The party was so immense and unwieldy that it took from early morning until 4 p.m. just to get it moving. Among the items Burke had deemed necessary for the expedition were a Chinese gong, a stationery cabinet, a heavy wooden table with matching stools, and grooming equipment, in the words of the historian Glen McLaren, 'of sufficient quality to prepare and present his horses and camels for an Agricultural Society show'.

Almost at once the men began to squabble. Within days, six of the party had resigned, and the road to Menindee was littered with provisions they decided they didn't need, including 1,500 pounds (let me just repeat that: 1,500 *pounds*) of sugar. They did almost everything wrong. Against advice, they timed the trip so that they would do most of the hardest travelling at the height of summer.

With such a burden, it took them almost two months to traverse the 400 miles of well-trodden track to Menindee; a letter from Melbourne normally covered the same ground in two weeks. At Menindee, they availed themselves of the modest comforts of Maidens Hotel, rested their horses and reorganized their provisions, and on 19 October set off into a blank ghastlier than they could ever have imagined. Ahead of them lay 1,200 miles of murderous ground. It was the last time that anyone in the outside world would see Burke and Wills alive.

Progress through the desert was difficult and slow. By December, when they arrived at a place called Cooper's Creek, just over the Queensland border, they had progressed only 400 miles. In exasperation Burke decided to take three men – Wills, Charles Gray and John King – and make a dash for the gulf. By travelling light he calculated that he could be there and back in two months. He left four men to maintain the base camp, with instructions to wait three months for them in case they were delayed.

The going was much tougher than they had expected. Daytime temperatures regularly rose to over 140 degrees F. It took them two months rather than one to cross the interior, and their arrival, when at last it came, was something of an anticlimax: a belt of mangroves along the shore kept them from reaching, or even seeing, the sea. Still, they had successfully completed the first crossing of the continent. Unfortunately, they had also eaten two-thirds of their supplies.

The upshot is that they ran out of food on the return trip and nearly starved. To their consternation, Charles Gray, the fittest of the party, abruptly dropped dead one day. Ragged and half delirious, the three remaining men pushed on. Finally, on the evening of 21 April 1861, they stumbled into base camp to discover that the men they had left behind, after waiting four months, had departed only that day. On a coolibah tree was carved the message:

They dug and found some meagre rations and a message telling them what was already painfully evident – that the base party had given up and departed. Desolate and exhausted, they ate and turned in. In the morning they wrote a message announcing their safe return and carefully buried it in the cache – so carefully, in fact, that when a member of the base party returned that day to have one last look, he had no way of telling that they had made it back and had now gone again. Had he known, he would have found them not far away, plodding over rocky ground in the impossible hope of reaching a police outpost 150 miles away at a place called Mount Hopeless.

Burke and Wills died in the desert, far short of Mount Hopeless. King was saved by Aborigines, who nursed him for two months until he was rescued by a search party.

Back in Melbourne, meanwhile, everyone was still awaiting a triumphal return of the heroic band, so news of the fiasco struck like a thunderbolt. 'The entire company of explorers has been dissipated out of being,' the *Age* reported with frank astonishment. 'Some are dead, some are on their way back, one has come to Melbourne, and another has made his way to Adelaide . . . The whole expedition appears to have been one prolonged blunder throughout.'

When the final tally was taken, the cost of the entire undertaking, including the search to recover Burke's and Wills' bodies, came to almost £60,000, more than Stanley had spent in Africa to achieve far more.

*   *   *

Even now, the emptiness of so much of Australia is startling. The landscape we passed through was officially only 'semi-desert', but it was as barren an expanse as I had ever seen. Every twenty or twenty-five kilometres there would be a dirt track and a lonely mailbox signalling an unseen sheep or cattle station. Once a light truck flew past in a bouncing hell-for-leather fashion, spraying us with gravelly dinks and a coating of red dust, but the only other lively thing was the endless shaking flubbity-dubbing of the axles over the corduroy road. By the time we reached White Cliffs, in mid-afternoon, we felt as if we had spent the day in a cement mixer.

Seeing it today, it is all but impossible to believe that White Cliffs, a small blotch of habitations under a hard clear sky, was once a boom town, with a population of nearly 4,500, a hospital, a newspaper, a library and a busy core of general stores, hotels, restaurants, brothels and gaming houses. Today central White Cliffs consists of a pub, a launderette, an opal shop, and a grocery/café/petrol station. The permanent population is about eighty. They exist in a listless world of heat and dust. If you were looking for people with the tolerance and fortitude to colonize Mars this would be the place to come.

Because of the heat, most houses in town are burrowed into the faces of the two bleached hills from which the town takes its name. The most ambitious of these dwellings, and the principal magnet for the relatively few tourists who venture this far, is the Dug-Out Underground Motel, a twenty-six-room complex cut deep into the rocks on the side of Smith's Hill. Wandering through its network of rocky tunnels was like stepping into an early James Bond movie, into one of those subterranean complexes where the loyal minions of SMERSH are preparing to take over the world by melting Antarctica or hijacking the White House with the aid of a giant magnet. The attraction of burrowing into the hillside is immediately evident when you step inside – a constant year-round temperature of 67 degrees. The rooms were very nice and quite normal except that the walls and ceilings were cavelike and windowless. When the lights were off, the darkness and silence were total.

I don't know how much money you would have to give me to persuade me to settle in White Cliffs – something in the low zillions, I suppose – but that evening as we sat on the motel's lofty garden terrace with Leon Hornby, the proprietor, drinking beer and watching the evening slink in, I realized that my fee might be marginally negotiable. I was about to ask Leon – a city man by birth and, I would have guessed, inclination – what possessed him and his pleasant wife Marge to stay in this godforsaken outpost where even a run to the supermarket means a six-hour round trip over a rutted dirt road, but before I could speak a remarkable thing happened. Kangaroos hopped into the expansive foreground and began grazing picturesquely, and the sun plonked onto the horizon, like a stage prop lowered on a wire, and the towering western skies before us spread with colour in a hundred layered shades – glowing pinks, deep purples, careless banners of pure crimson – all on a scale that you cannot imagine, for there was not a scrap of intrusion in the forty miles of visible desert that lay between us and the far horizon. It was the most extraordinarily vivid sunset I believe I have ever seen.

'I came up here thirty years ago to build reservoirs on the sheep stations,' Leon said, as if anticipating my question, 'and never expected to stay, but somehow the place gets to you. I'd find these sunsets hard to give up, for one thing.'

I nodded as he got up to answer a ringing phone.

'Used to be even nicer once, a long time ago,' said Lisa, Steve's partner. 'There's been a lot of overgrazing.'

'Here or all over?'

'All over – well, nearly. In the 1890s there was a really bad drought. They say the land's never really recovered, and probably never will.'

Later, Steve, Trevor and I went down the hill to the White Cliffs Hotel, the local hostelry, and the appeal of the little town became more evident still. The White Cliffs was as nice a pub as I have ever been in. Not to look at, for Australian country pubs are nearly always austere and utilitarian places, with linoleum floors, laminated surfaces and glass-doored coolers, but rather for the congenial and welcoming atmosphere. Much of this is a tribute to the owner, Graham Wellings, a chipper man with a firm handshake, a matinee-idol hairstyle and a knack for making you feel as if he settled here in the hope that one day some folks like you would drop by.

I asked him what had brought him to White Cliffs. 'I was an itinerant sheep shearer,' he said. 'Came here in '59 to shear sheep and just never left. It was a lot more remote back then. Took us eight hours from Broken Hill, the roads were that bad. You can do it in three now, but back then the roads were rough as guts every inch of the way. We tumbled in here gasping for a cold beer, and of course there were no coolers in those days. Beer was room temperature – and room temperature was 110 degrees. No air conditioning either, of course. No electricity at all, unless you had your own generator.'

'So when did you get electricity in White Cliffs?'

He thought for an instant. 'Nineteen ninety-three.'

I thought I had misheard him. 'When?'

'Just about five years ago. We have telly now, too,' he added suddenly and enthusiastically. 'Got that two years ago.'

He seized a remote control unit and pointed it at a television mounted on the wall. When it warmed to life, he ran through their choice of three channels, turning to us at each with an expression that invited staggered admiration. I have been in countries where people still ride waggons and gather hay with forks, and countries where the per capita gross domestic product would not buy you a weekend at a Holiday Inn, but nowhere before had I been invited to regard television as a marvel.

He switched off and put the remote back on the shelf as if it were a treasured relic.

'Yeah, it was a different world,' he said musingly.

Still is, I thought.

Chapter

THREE

In the morning Steve and Lisa escorted us back along the lonely dirt track to the paved highway at Wilcannia, where we parted ways – they to go left to Menindee, Trevor and I to go right to Broken Hill, 197 kilometres away down a straight and empty road, thus completing a large and irregular circle.

We had an afternoon in Broken Hill and spent it seeing the sights. We drove out to Silverton, once a rowdy mining town, now virtually derelict but for a big pub, which is said to be the most photographed and filmed in Australia. It's not that there is anything wildly special about the pub; it's more that it gives the appearance of being in the middle of nowhere while actually being conveniently handy to the air-conditioned amenities of Broken Hill. It's been used as a film location 142 times – in *A Town like Alice*, *Mad Max 2* and about every Australian beer commercial ever made. It now gets by, evidently, on the visits of film crews and of occasional tourists like us.

Broken Hill has had tough times, too. Even by Australian standards, it is a long way from anywhere – 750 miles from Sydney, the state capital, where all the decisions are made – and its citizens have an understandable tendency to think of themselves as neglected. As recently as the 1950s it had 35,000 people, against just 23,000 now. Its history dates from 1885, when a boundary rider checking fences chanced upon a lode of silver, zinc and lead in sumptuous proportions. Almost overnight Broken Hill became a boom town and gave birth along the way to Broken Hill Proprietary Ltd, still Australia's mightiest industrial colossus.

At its peak in 1893 Broken Hill had sixteen mines employing 8,700 miners. Today there is just one mine and 700 workers, which is the main reason for the population decline. Even so, that one mine produces more ore than all sixteen mines together at their peak. The difference is that whereas before you had thousands of men crawling about in poky shafts, today a handful of engineers with explosives blow out cathedral-sized chambers up to 300 feet high and the size of a football pitch and, when the dust has settled and everyone's ears have stopped ringing, a team of workers on giant bulldozers come along and scoop up all the ore. It's so vastly efficient that in only a decade or so all the ore will be gone, and quite what will become of Broken Hill is anyone's guess.

Meanwhile, it's a nice little town with an air of busyness and prosperity that brings to mind one of those establishing shots you'd see in a 1940s Hollywood movie featuring Jimmy Stewart or Deanna Durbin. Its main street is lined with handsome buildings in a modestly exuberant

Victorian style. Seeking refreshment, Trevor and I ventured into one of the many imposing hotels – and I should just note that in an Australian context 'hotel' can signify many things: a hotel, a pub, a hotel *and* pub – that stand on nearly every corner. This one was called Mario's Palace Hotel, and it was very grand from without – it covered half a block and had a large wraparound balcony employing a lot of intricate ironwork – though inside it had an under-lit and musty air. The bar seemed to be open – a TV was playing silently in the corner, the signs were illuminated – but there was no one in attendance and no sounds of anyone nearby. Leading off the bar were several large rooms – a ballroom, a dining room, perhaps another ballroom – all looking as if they had been decorated at considerable expense in 1953 and not used since.

A door led out into a hallway with a grand stairway. From the ground to the distant ceiling, a good three storeys above us, the stairwell walls were divided into panels of different sizes by strips of wood and some artist had filled each of them – scores in all – with a mural, some of them several feet across, some much smaller. They consisted entirely of romantic and idealized land-scapes showing herds of kangaroos sipping at billabongs or swagmen gathered around a lonely coolibah tree. They were undeniably hokey, but charming even so and without question from a gifted hand. Almost invol-untarily, we found ourselves advancing slowly up the stairs, moving with silent absorption from one image to the next.

'Good, eh?' came a voice after a minute and we turned to see a young man looking up at us and apparently not at all perturbed that we were making our way into the depths of his building. He was wiping his forearms with a cloth, as if he had been engaged in some large task like cleaning out a cauldron.

'They were done by a blackfella named Gordon Waye,' he went on. 'Pretty amazing bloke. He didn't sketch anything out or anything, didn't have any kind of a plan. He just picked up his paints and a brush and did it straight off. At the end of the day there'd be a finished painting. Then he'd collect his pay from the owner and clear off. Go walkabout, you know? Some time later – maybe a week or two, maybe a few months – he'd come back and knock off another one, collect some more money and clear off again, until eventually he'd done them all. Then he cleared off for good.'

'What became of him?'

'No idea. Don't think anyone knows. So where you fellas come from?'

'America and Britain,' I said, pointing appropriately.

'Long way to come. Expect you'll be wanting a cold beer then.'

We followed him into the bar, where he drew us two schooners of Victoria Bitter.

'Nice hotel,' I said, not really meaning it.

He looked at me faintly dubiously. 'Well, you can have it if you want. It's on the market.'

'Oh, yeah? How much for?'

'One million seven hundred and fifty thousand dollars.'

It took me a moment to form the words. 'That's a *lot* of money.'

He made a look of agreement. 'More than most people around here have got, that's for sure.' Then he disappeared with a crate through the door behind him.

We wanted to ask him more, and after a few minutes we wanted another beer, but he never did come back.

* * *

The following morning we caught the second of the twice-weekly Indian Pacifics to Perth. In the deliciously air-chilled bar car of the train, Trevor and I spread out a map of Australia and discovered with astonishment that for all our hours of driving over the previous days we had covered only the tiniest fraction of land surface – a freckle, almost literally, on the face of Australia. It is such an immense country, and we still had 3,227 kilometres of it to get through before we reached Perth. There was nothing to do but sit back and enjoy it.

After the heat and dust of the outback, I was glad to be back in the clean, regulated world of the train, and I fell into its gentle routines with gratitude and relish. Train life, I decided, takes some beating. At some point in the morning, generally when you have gone for breakfast, your bed vanishes magically into the wall, and in the evening just as magically reappears, crisply made with fresh sheets. Three times a day you are called to the dining car, where you are presented with a thoroughly commendable meal by friendly and obliging staff. In between times there is nothing to do but sit and read, watch the endlessly unfurling scenery or chat with your neighbour. Trevor, because he was young and full of life and unaccountably had failed to bring any of my books to make the hours fly, felt restless and cooped up, but I wallowed in every undemanding minute of it.

With all your needs attended to and no real decisions to make, you soon find yourself wholly absorbed with the few tiny matters that are actually at your discretion – whether to have your morning shower now or in a while, whether to get up from your chair and pour yourself another complimentary cup of tea or be a devil and have a bottle of Victoria Bitter, whether to stroll back to your cabin for the book you forgot or just sit and watch the landscape for emus and kangaroos. If this sounds like a living death, don't be misled. I was having the time of my life. There is something wonderfully lulling about being stuck for a long spell on a train. It was like being given a preview of what it will be like to be in your eighties. All those things eighty-year-olds appear to enjoy – staring vacantly out of windows, dozing in a chair, boring the pants off anyone foolish enough to sit beside them – took on a special treasured meaning for me. This was the life!

Our new complement of passengers seemed a livelier bunch. There was Phil, a printmaker from Newcastle in New South Wales; Rose and Bill, a sweet, quiet couple from England who were on their way to see their son, a mining engineer in Kalgoorlie; three white-haired guys from a lawn bowling club in Neutral Bay, who drank like sailors on shore leave; and a wonderful, rake-thin, chain-smoking, perpetually wobbly-drunk lady whose name no one seemed to know and whose response to any pleas-antry of any type directed at her – 'Good morning,' 'Sleep well?', 'I'm Bill and this is Trevor' – was to cry 'Yes!' and give a prolonged, demented laugh, and take a sip of Shiraz. In such a crowd, the evenings tended to be nicely festive – so much so that my notes for the relevant periods are on matchbooks and the backs of beer mats, and show a certain measure of elevated incoherence ('G. attacked by camel in men's lav. Alice Springs 1947 – great!!!'). Still, my recollection is of having a jolly nice time and that is of course the main thing.

On our second day out from Broken Hill, we entered the mighty Nullarbor. Many people, even Australians, assume Nullarbor is an Aboriginal term, but in fact it is a corruption of the Latin for 'no trees', and the name could not be more apt. For hundreds of miles the landscape is as flat as a calm sea and unrelievedly barren – just glowing red soil, tussocky clumps of bluebush and spinifex, and scattered rocks the colour of bad teeth. In an area four times the size of Belgium there is not a scrap of shade. It is one of the most forbidding expanses on earth.

Just after breakfast, we entered the longest straight stretch of railway line in the world – 297 miles without a hint of deviation – and in mid-morning we heaved into Cook, a community that makes White Cliffs look accessible and urbane. Five hundred miles from any real town to east or west, a hundred miles from the nearest paved highway to the south and over a thousand to the north, Cook (pop. 40) exists solely to water, fuel and otherwise service the trains that pass through. Beside the track stood a sign that said: 'No Food or Fuel for Next 862 Kilometres' – rather a daunting thought, what?

We had two hours to kill in Cook – goodness knows why so long – and everyone was allowed to get off and look around. It was agreeable to move about without having to steady yourself against a swaying wall every couple of paces, but the thrill of Cook swiftly palls. There was nothing much to it – a railway station and post office, a couple of dozen prefabricated bungalows standing on dusty ground, a little shop whose shelves were mostly bare, a shuttered community centre, an empty school (it was the middle of school holidays), a small open-air swimming pool (also closed), and an airstrip with a limp windsock. The heat was terrific. On every side desert lapped at the town like floodwater.

I was standing there with a map of Australia, surveying the emptiness and trying to absorb the ungraspable fact that if I walked north from here I wouldn't come to a paved surface for 1,100 miles, when Trevor trotted up and told me we had been given permission to travel for an hour in the locomotive, so that he could take photos. This was a rare treat, and exciting news. Just before the train resumed its journey, we climbed aboard the locomotive with two replacement drivers, Noel Coad and Sean Willis, who would take the train on to Kalgoorlie.

They were genial and laid-back, in their late twenties or early thirties. Their cab was snug and comfy – homey even in a high-tech sort of way. It featured a fancy console with lots of switches and toggles, three shortwave radios and two computer screens, but also a number of domestic comforts: a kettle, a small refrigerator, an electric hotplate for cooking. Coad drove. He flipped a couple of switches, moved a gear lever a fraction of an inch, and we were off. Within a couple of minutes we were up to our cruising speed of 100 kilometres an hour.

I sat quite still, fearful of touching anything that would get us on the evening news, and enjoyed the novel perspective of looking straight ahead. And what an ahead it is on the boundless Nullarbor. Before us stretched a single-line track, two parallel bars of shining steel, dead straight and painfully shiny in the sunshine, and hatched with endless rungs of concrete sleepers. Somewhere in the vicinity of a preposterously remote horizon the two gleaming lines of steel met in a shimmery vanishing point. Endlessly, monotonously, we hoovered up sleepers as we progressed, but however much we pressed onward the vanishing point stayed always in the same place. You couldn't look at it – well, I couldn't look at it – without getting a headache.

'How far is it to the next curve?' I asked.

'Three hundred and sixty kilometres,' Willis answered.

'Don't you go crazy out here?'

'No,' they replied in unison and with evident sincerity.

'Do you ever see anything to break the monotony – animals and so forth?'

'A few 'roos,' Coad said. 'A camel from time to time. Once in a while somebody on a motorbike.'

'Really?'

'On that.' He indicated a rough dirt maintenance road that ran alongside the track. 'Very popular with the Japanese for some reason. Something to do with an initiation into a club or something.'

'We saw a bloke on a bicycle the other week,' Willis volunteered.

'No kidding?'

'Japanese bloke.'

'Was he all right?'

'Out of his mind if you ask me, but he seemed all right. He waved.'

'Isn't it awfully risky out there?'

'Nah – not if you keep to the track. There's fifty or sixty trains a week along this line, and nobody's going to leave you out here if you're in bother.'

We had arrived at a siding called Deakin, where the Indian Pacific had to pull over to let a freight train through, and where Trevor and I were to return to the passenger section. We hopped down from the locomotive and walked briskly back along the train towards the passenger carriages. (And you would walk briskly too, believe me, if you were outside a train with its motor running in the middle of a desert.) At the door of the first passenger carriage, David Goodwin, the train manager, was waiting for us.

He helped us up – it's a long way up onto a train when

you haven't got a platform to start with – and we half fell in. Looking up, I discovered with a start that we were in the forbidden coach section. I have never felt so stared at in my life. As we followed David through the two coach carriages, 124 pairs of sunken eyes sullenly followed our every move. These were people who had no dining carriage, no lounge bar, no cosy berths to crawl into at night. They had been riding upright for two days since leaving Sydney, and still had twenty-four hours to go to Perth. I am almost certain that if we had not had the train manager as an escort they would have eaten us.

We arrived in Perth at first light and stepped from the train, glad to be back on solid ground and feeling disproportionately pleased with our achievement. I know that all that was required of us to get there was to sit passively for a total of seventy-two hours, but still we had done something that lots of Australians never do – namely, cross Australia.

It is a lame and obvious conclusion to draw, but Australia truly does exist on a unique scale. It's not just a question of brute distance – though goodness knows, there is plenty enough of that – but of the incredible emptiness that lies within all that distance. Five hundred miles in Australia is not like 500 miles elsewhere, and the only way to appreciate that is to cross the country at ground level.

I couldn't wait to see more.

Part Two

CIVILIZED AUSTRALIA

(The Boomerang Coast)

Chapter

FOUR

You wouldn't think that something as conspicuous, as patently *there*, as Australia could escape the world's attention almost to the modern age, but there you are. It did. Less than twenty years before the founding of Sydney it was still essentially unknown.

For nearly 300 years explorers had been looking for a conjectured southern continent, *Terra Australis Incognita* – some commodious mass that would at least partly counterbalance all that land that covered the northern half of the globe. In every instance one of two things happened: either they found it and didn't know they had or they missed it altogether.

In 1606, a Spanish mariner named Luis Vaez de Torres sailed across the Pacific from South America and straight into the narrow channel (now called the Torres Strait) that separates Australia from New Guinea without having the faintest idea that he had just done the nautical equivalent of threading a needle. Thirty-six years later the Dutchman

Abel Tasman was sent to look for the fabled South Land and managed to sail 2,000 miles along the underside of Australia without detecting that a substantial land mass lay just over the left-hand horizon. Eventually he bumped into Tasmania (which he called Van Diemen's Land after his superior at the Dutch East India Company), and went on to discover New Zealand and Fiji, but it was not a successful voyage. In New Zealand, Maoris captured and ate some of his men – not the sort of thing that looks good in a report – and he failed to find anything in the way of riches. On the way home he passed within sight of the north coast of Australia, but, disheartened, accorded it no importance and sailed on.

That isn't to say that Australia had never felt a European footprint. From the early seventeenth century onwards mariners occasionally fetched up on its northern or western shores, often after running aground. These early visitors left a few names on maps – Cape Leeuwin, the Dampier Archipelago, the Abrolhos Islands – but saw no reason to linger in such a barren void and moved on. They knew there was something there – possibly a biggish island like New Guinea, possibly a mass of smaller islands like the East Indies – and they called this amorphous entity New Holland, but none equated it with the long-sought southern continent.

Because of the random and casual nature of these visits, no one knows when Australia first fell under a European gaze. The earliest recorded visit was in 1606, when a party of Dutch sailors under a Willem Jansz, or Janszoon, stepped briefly ashore in the far north (and as hastily retreated under a hail of Aboriginal spears), but it is evident that others had been there earlier still. A pair of Portuguese cannons, dating from no later than 1525, were found in 1916 at a place called Carronade Island on the north-west coast. Whoever left them would have been among the first Europeans to stray this far from home, but of this epochal visit not a thing is known. Even more intriguing is a map, drawn by a Portuguese hand and dating from roughly the same period, that shows not only a large land mass where Australia stands, but an apparent familiarity with the jogs and indentations of Australia's east coast – something supposedly not seen by outsiders for another two and a half centuries.

So when in April 1770 Lieutenant James Cook and his crew aboard HMS *Endeavour* sighted the south-east corner of Australia and followed the coast 1,800 miles north to Cape York, it wasn't so much a discovery as a confirmation.

Though Cook's voyage was unquestionably heroic, its first purpose was mundane. He had been sent halfway around the world, to Tahiti, to measure a transit of Venus across the sun. Combined with measurements taken at the same time elsewhere, this would permit astronomers to calculate the distance of the earth from the sun. It wasn't an especially complicated procedure but it was important to get it right. An attempt during the last transit eight years earlier had failed, and the next one wasn't due for another 105 years. Happily for science and for Cook, the skies stayed clear and the measurements were taken without setback or complication.

Cook was now free to go off and fulfil the second part of his assignment – to explore the lands of the South Seas and bring home anything that looked scientifically interesting. To this end, he had with him a brilliant and wealthy young botanist named Joseph Banks. To say that Banks was a dedicated collector is to indulge in the drollest understatement. In the course of the *Endeavour*'s three-year voyage, he gathered up some 30,000 specimens, including at least 1,400 plants never seen before – at a stroke increasing the world's stock of known plants by about a quarter. Banks brought back so many items that the Natural History Museum in London has whole drawers full of objects that, 220 years later, await cataloguing. The same voyage also made the first successful circumnavigation of New Zealand, confirming that it was not part of the fabled southern continent, as Tasman had optimistically concluded, but two islands. By any measure, it had been a good voyage and we can assume an air of satisfaction as the *Endeavour* turned at last for home.

So when, on 19 April 1770, three weeks out from New Zealand, Lieutenant Zachary Hicks cried 'Land ahoy!' at the sight of what turned out to be the extreme south-east tip of Australia, the *Endeavour* and its crew were already on something of a roll. Cook named the spot Point Hicks (it's now called Cape Everard) and turned the ship north.

The land they found was not only larger than had been supposed but more promising. For the whole of its length, the east coast was lusher, better watered and more congenially provisioned with harbours and anchorages than anything that had been reported elsewhere in New Holland. It presented, Cook recorded, a 'very agreeable and promising aspect . . . with hills, ridges, plains and valleys, with some grass but for the most part . . . covered with wood'. This was nothing like the barren and savage wastes that others had met.

For four months they headed up the coast. They stopped at a place Cook named Botany Bay, ran disastrously aground on the Great Barrier Reef, and finally, after making some urgent repairs, rounded the northernmost tip of the continent at Cape York. On the evening of 21 August, almost as an afterthought, he stepped ashore at a place he called Possession Island, planted a flag and claimed the east coast for Great Britain.

It was a remarkable achievement for a man who had been born a labourer's son in inland Yorkshire, hadn't been to sea until he was eighteen, and had joined the Navy only thirteen years before at the advanced age of twenty-seven. He would return twice more to the Pacific on even greater voyages – on the next he would sail 70,000 miles – before being murdered (and possibly eaten himself) by natives on a beach in Hawaii in 1779. Cook was a brilliant navigator and a conscientious observer, but he made one critical mistake on his first voyage: he took Australia's wet season for its dry one, and concluded that the country was more hospitable than it was.

The significance of this misapprehension became evident when Britain lost its American colonies, and, deciding it needed a new place to send its less desirable subjects, plumped for Australia. Remarkably, the decision was taken without any attempt at reconnoitring. When Captain Arthur Phillip at the head of a squadron of eleven ships – known reverentially ever after as the First Fleet – set sail from Portsmouth in May 1787, he and the 1,500-odd people in his care were heading off to start a colony in a preposterously remote, virtually unknown place that had been visited just once, briefly, seventeen years before and had not seen a European face since.

Never before had so many people been moved such a great distance at such expense – and all to be incarcerated. By modern standards (by any standards really), their punishments were ludicrously disproportionate. Most were small-time thieves. Britain wasn't trying to rid itself of a body of dangerous criminals so much as thin out an underclass. The bulk were being sent to the ends of the earth for stealing trifles. One famously luckless soul had been caught taking twelve cucumber plants. Another had unwisely pocketed a book called *A Summary Account of the Flourishing State of the Island of Tobago*. Most of the crimes smacked either of desperation or of temptation unsuccessfully resisted.

Generally, the term of transportation was seven years, but since there was no provision for their return and few could hope to raise the fare, passage to Australia was effectively a life sentence. But then this was an unforgiving age. By the late eighteenth century Britain's statute books were plump with capital offences; you could be hanged for any of 200 acts, including, notably, 'impersonating an Egyptian'. In such circumstances, transportation was quite a merciful alternative.

The voyage from Portsmouth took 252 days – eight months – and covered 15,000 miles of open sea (more than would seem strictly necessary, but they crossed the Atlantic in both directions to catch favourable winds). When they arrived at Botany Bay, they found it wasn't quite the kindly refuge they had been led to expect. Its exposed position made it a dangerous anchorage, and a foray ashore found nothing but sandflies and marsh. 'Of the natural meadows which Mr Cook mentions near Botany Bay, we can give no account,' wrote a puzzled member of the party. Cook's descriptions had made it sound almost like an English country estate – a place where one might play a little croquet and enjoy a picnic on the lawn. Clearly he had seen it in a different season.

As they stood surveying their unhappy situation, there happened one of those coincidences in which Australian history abounds. On the eastern horizon two ships appeared and joined them in the bay. They were in the command of an amiable Frenchman, Count Jean-François de La Pérouse, who was leading a two-year journey of exploration around the Pacific. Had La Pérouse been just a little faster, he could have claimed Australia for France and saved the country 200 years of English cooking. Instead, he accepted his unlucky timing with the grace that marked the age. La Pérouse's expression when it was explained to him that Phillip and his crew had just sailed 15,000 miles to make a prison for people who had stolen lace and ribbons, some cucumber plants and a book on Tobago, must have been one of the great looks in history, but alas there is no record of it. In any case, after an uneventful rest at Botany Bay, he departed, never to be seen again. Soon afterwards his two ships and all aboard were lost in a storm off the New Hebrides.

Meanwhile, Phillip, seeking a more amenable location, sailed up the coast to another inlet, which Cook had noted but not explored, and ventured through the sandstone heads that form its mouth. There he discovered one of the great harbours of the world. At the point where Circular Quay now stands, he anchored his ships and started a city. It was 26 January 1788. The date would live for ever as Australia Day.

Among the many small and interesting mysteries of Australia in its early days is where so many of its names come from. It was Cook who called the eastern coast New South Wales, and no one now has any idea why. Did he mean to signify that this would be a new Wales of the South or merely a new version of South Wales? If the latter, why just South Wales and not the whole of it? No one can say. What is certain is that he had no known connection to that verdant principality, southerly or otherwise.

Sydney likewise is a curious appellation. Phillip intended the name only to apply to the cove. He meant for the town to be known as Albion, but that name never took. We know for whom Sydney was named: Thomas Townshend, first Baron Sydney, who was Home and Colonial Secretary and therefore Phillip's immediate master. What we don't know is why Townshend, when he was ennobled, chose Sydney as his title. The reason died with him, and the title didn't last much longer; it was extinct by 1890. The harbour itself was called Port Jackson (it is officially still so known) after an admiralty judge, one George Jackson, who later abandoned his birth name in order to secure an inheritance from an eccentric relation and finished his life as Duckett.

Of the roughly one thousand people who shuffled ashore, about 700 were prisoners and the rest were marines and officers, officers' families and the governor and his staff. The exact numbers of each are not known,* but it hardly matters. They were all prisoners now.

They were, to put it mildly, a curious lot. The complement included a boy of nine and a woman of eighty-two – hardly the sort of people you would invite to help you through an ordeal. Though it had been noted in London that certain skills would be desirable in such a remote situation, no one had actually acted on that observation. The party included no one proficient in the natural sciences,

---

* For the record, Captain Watkin Tench, who was there, recorded the numbers as 751 convicts and 211 marines landed, with 25 fatalities en route. Hughes in *The Fatal Shore* puts the number of convicts landed as 696 and the total number of fatalities as 48; he doesn't specify the number of marines. A *National Geographic* article I read put the number of prisoners at 775; a Penguin *Concise History* made it 529. I could go on and on.

no master of husbandry, not a soul who had the faintest understanding of growing crops in hostile climes. The prisoners were in nearly every practical respect woeful. Among the 700 there was just one experienced fisherman and no more than five people with a working knowledge of the building trade. Phillip was by all accounts a kindly man of even temper and natural honesty, but his situation was hopeless. Confronted with a land full of plants he had never seen and knew nothing about, he recorded in despair: 'I am without one botanist, or even an intelligent gardener.'

Gamely, they made the best of things: they had no choice. Parties were sent into the countryside to see what they could find (essentially nothing); a government farm was set up on ground overlooking the harbour where the Botanic Gardens now stand; and attempts were made to establish friendly relations with the natives. The 'Indians', as they were at first generally called, were bewilderingly unpredictable. Generally friendly, they would none the less opportunistically attack settlers who ventured out of camp to fish or forage. In the first year, seventeen colonists were picked off in this way and scores more wounded, including Governor Phillip himself, who approached an Aborigine at Manly Cove in an attempt to converse and, to his consternation, had a spear thrust into his shoulder and out the back. (He recovered.)

Nearly everything was against them. They had no waterproof clothes to keep out the rain and no mortar to make buildings; no ploughs with which to till fields and no draught animals to pull the ploughs that they didn't have. The ground everywhere seemed cursed with an 'unconquerable sterility'. Such crops as managed to push through the soil were, more often than not, stolen under cover of darkness – by marines as often as by prisoners. For years, both groups would want not just for food but for nearly every basic commodity one could name: shoes, blankets, tobacco, nails, paper, ink, groundsheets, saddlery – whatever, in short, required manufacture. The soldiers did their best to evaluate their resources, but most had little idea of what they were looking for when they went after it, or at when they found it. The historian Glen McLaren quotes one report from a soldier sent to the Hunter River valley to see what might be there. 'The soil is black,' the soldier wrote hopefully, 'but mixed with a sort of sand or marly substance. Fish also are plenty, and I suppose, from their leaping, are of the trout kind.'

Development was further set back by the need to rely on prisoners, who clearly lacked any basis for devotion beyond self-interest. The cannier ones soon learned to lie their way to softer duties. One fellow named Hutchinson, coming across some scientific apparatus that had been packed away in one of the holds, persuaded his superiors that he knew all there was to know about dyestuffs, and spent months conducting elaborate experiments with beakers and scales, until it gradually became apparent that he didn't have the faintest idea what he was doing. When they couldn't fool their masters the prisoners could often fool their fellows. For years there existed an illicit commerce in which newly arrived convicts were sold maps showing them how to walk to China. Up to sixty at a time fled their captivity in the belief that that magically accommodating land lay just the other side of a vaguely distant river.

By 1790, the government farm had been abandoned and, with no sign of relief from England, they were desperately dependent on their dwindling supplies. It wasn't just that the food was short, but by now years old and barely edible, the rice so full of weevily grubs that 'every grain . . . was a moving body', as Watkin Tench queasily noted. At the height of their crisis they awoke one morning to find that half a dozen of their remaining cattle had wandered off, not to be seen again. These were seriously at-risk settlers.

There was at times a kind of endearing quality to their hopelessness. When Aborigines killed a convict named McEntire, Governor Phillip in an uncharacteristic fury (this was not long after he had been speared himself) dispatched a band of marines on a punitive expedition with orders to bring back six heads – any six. The marines tramped about in the bush for a few days, but managed to capture just one Aborigine, and he was released when it was realized he was a friend. In the end they captured no one and the matter seems to have been quietly forgotten.

Exhausted by the stresses, Phillip was called home after four years, and retired to Bath. Apart from founding Sydney, he had one other notable achievement. In 1814, he managed to die by falling from a wheelchair and out of an upstairs window.

II

It is impossible in the frappaccino heaven that is modern Sydney to get the slightest sense of what life was like in those early years. Partly this is for the obvious reason that things have moved on a bit. Where, 200 years ago, there stood rude huts and sagging tents, today there rises a great and comely city, a transformation so total that it is impossible to see both ends at once, as it were. But there is also the consideration that the nature of Australia's beginnings is, even now, a tiny bit fudged, if not actually suppressed.

Nowhere in the city will you find a monument to the First Fleet. Go to the National Maritime Museum or Museum of Sydney and you will certainly get an impression that some of the early residents experienced privations – you might even deduce that their presence was not completely voluntary – but the idea that they arrived in chains is somewhat less than manifest. In his majestic history of the country's early years, *The Fatal Shore*, Robert Hughes notes that until as late as the 1960s Australia's convict beginnings were not deemed worthy of scholarly attention, and certainly not taught in school. John Pilger, in *A Secret Country*, writes that in his Sydney boyhood in the 1950s even among the family one never made reference to 'The Stain', the curiously menstrual euphemism by which convict antecedents were acknowledged. I can personally affirm that to stand before an audience of beaming Australians and make even the mildest quip about a convict past is to feel the air conditioning immediately elevated.

Personally, I think Australians ought to be extremely proud that from the most awkwardly unpropitious beginnings, in a remote and challenging place, they created a prosperous and dynamic society. That is exceedingly good going. So what if dear old gramps was a bit of a sticky-fingered felon in his youth? Look what he left behind.

And so once more to Circular Quay in Sydney, where Governor Phillip and his straggly, salt-encrusted band stepped ashore two centuries ago. I was back in Australia after a trip home to fulfil some other commitments and I was feeling, I have to say, pretty perky. The sun was gorgeously plump, the city coming to life – shutters were rattling open, chairs being set out at cafés – and I was basking in that sense of wonder and delight that comes with being freed from a sealed aeroplane and finding myself once again Down Under. I was about to see Sydney at last.

Life cannot offer many places finer to stand at eight thirty on a summery weekday morning than Circular Quay in Sydney. To begin with, it presents one of the world's great views. To the right, almost painfully brilliant in the sunshine, stands the famous Opera House with its jaunty, severely angular roof. To the left, the stupendous and noble Harbour Bridge. Across the water, shiny and beckoning, is Luna Park, a Coney Island-style amusement park with a maniacally grinning head for an entrance. Before you the spangly water is crowded with the harbour's plump and old-fashioned ferries, looking for all the world as if they have been plucked from the pages of a 1940s children's book with a title like *Thomas the Tugboat*, disgorging streams of tanned and lightly dressed office workers to fill the glass and concrete towers that loom behind.

An air of cheerful industriousness suffuses the scene. These are people who get to live in a safe and fair-minded society, in a climate that makes you strong and handsome, in one of the world's great cities – *and* they get to come to work on a boat from a children's story book, across a sublime plane of water, and each morning glance up from their *Heralds* and *Telegraphs* to see that famous Opera House and inspiring bridge and the laughing face of Luna Park. No wonder they look so damned happy.

It is the Opera House that gets all the attention, and you can understand why. It's so startlingly familiar, so hey-I'm-in-Sydney, that you can't stop looking at it. Clive James once likened the Opera House to 'a portable typewriter full of oyster shells', which is perhaps a tad severe. In any case, the Opera House is not about aesthetics. It's about being an icon.

That it exists at all is a small miracle. It's difficult to conceive now just what a backwater Sydney was in the 1950s, forgotten by the world and overshadowed even by Melbourne. As late as 1953, there were just 800 hotel rooms in the city, barely enough for one medium-sized convention, and not a thing to do in the evenings; even the bars closed at 6 p.m. The city's capacity for mediocrity cannot be better illustrated than by the fact that where the Opera House now stands, on as fine a situation as water and land afford, was then the site of a municipal tram garage.

Then two things happened. Melbourne was awarded the 1956 Summer Olympics – a call to action for Sydney if ever there was one – and Sir Eugene Goossens, head of the Sydney Symphony Orchestra, began to agitate for a concert hall in a city that didn't have a single decent orchestral space. Thus goaded, the city decided to tear down the ramshackle tram shed and build something glorious in its place. A competition was held for a suitable design and a panel of local worthies convened to select a winner. Unable to reach a consensus, the judges sought the opinion of the Finnish-born American architect Eero Saarinen, who sifted through the offerings and selected a design that the jurors had rejected. It was by a little-known 37-year-old Danish architect named Jørn Utzon. Possibly to the panel's relief, certainly to its credit, it deferred to Saarinen's opinion and Utzon was cabled with the news.

'The plan', in the words of John Gunther, 'was bold, unique, brilliantly chosen – and trouble – from its inception.' The problem was the famous roof. Nothing so daringly inclined and top-heavy had ever been built before and no one was sure that it could be. In retrospect, the haste with which the project was begun was probably its salvation. One of the lead engineers later noted that if anyone had realized at the outset how nearly impossible a challenge it would be, it would never have received the go-ahead. Just working out the principles necessary to build the roof took five years – the whole project had been intended to last no more than six – and construction in the end dragged on for almost a decade and a half. The final cost came in at a weighty $102 million, fourteen times the original estimate.

Utzon, interestingly, has never seen his prized creation. He was effectively dismissed in 1966 after an election brought in a change of state government, and has never been back. He also never designed anything else remotely as celebrated. Goossens, the man who started it all, like-wise failed to see his dream realized. In 1956, while passing through customs at Sydney Airport, he was found to be carrying a large and diversified collection of porno-graphic material, and he was invited to take his sordid continental habits elsewhere. Thus, by one of life's small ironies, he was unable to enjoy, as it were, his own finest erection.

The Opera House is a splendid edifice and I wish to take nothing away from it, but my heart belongs to the Harbour Bridge. It's not as festive, but it is far more domi-nant – you can see it from every corner of the city, creeping into frame from the oddest angles, like an uncle who wants to get into every snapshot. From a distance it has a kind of gallant restraint, majestic but not assertive, but up close it is all might. It soars above you, so high that you could pass a ten-storey building beneath it, and looks like the heaviest thing on earth. Everything that is in it – the stone blocks in its four towers, the latticework of girders, the metal plates, the six million rivets (with heads like halved apples) – is the biggest of its type you have ever seen. This is a bridge built by people who have had an Industrial Revolution, people with mountains of coal and ovens in which you could melt down a battleship. The arch alone weighs 30,000 tons. This is a great bridge.

From end to end, it stretches 1,650 feet. I mention this not just because I walked every foot of it now, but because there is a certain poignancy in the figure. In 1923, when the city burghers decided to throw a bridge across the harbour, they determined to build not just any bridge, but the longest single-arch span ever constructed. It was a bold enterprise for a young country and it took longer to construct than expected – almost ten years. Just before it was completed, in 1932, the Bayonne Bridge in New York quietly opened and was found to be 25 inches – 0.121 per cent – longer.*

After such a long spell in an aeroplane I was eager to stretch my shapely limbs, so I crossed the bridge to Kirribilli and plunged into the old, cosily settled neighbourhoods of the lower north shore. And what a wonderful area it is. I wandered past the little cove where my hero, the aviator Charles Kingsford Smith (about whom much more anon), once impossibly took off in an

* This was not a good period for Australian pride vis-à-vis America. Just over two weeks after the bridge opened and was found to be tragically short of superlative, Phar Lap, the greatest racehorse in Australian history, died in mysterious circumstances in California. There are still Australians who say we poisoned it. Australians are hugely proud of this horse, and will not thank you for pointing out that actually it was bred in New Zealand.

aeroplane, and into the shaded hills above, through quiet neighbourhoods of cottagey homes buried in flowering jacaranda and fragrant frangipani (and in every front garden cobwebs like trampolines, in the centre of each the sort of spider that would make a brave man gasp). At every turn there was a glimpse of blue harbour – over a garden wall, at the bottom of a sloping road, suspended between close-set houses like a sheet hung to dry – and it was all the finer for being furtive. Sydney has whole districts filled with palatial houses that seem to consist of nothing but balconies and plate glass, with scarcely a leaf to block the beating sun or interrupt the view. But here on the north shore, wisely and nobly, they have sacrificed large-scale vistas for the cool shade of trees, and every resident will, I guarantee, go to heaven.

I walked for miles, through Kirribilli, Neutral Bay and Cremorne Point, and on through the prosperous precincts of Mosman, before at last I came to Balmoral with a sheltered beach overlooking Middle Harbour and a splendid waterfront park shaded with stout Moreton Bay figs, the loveliest tree in Australia by far. A sign by the water's edge noted that if you were eaten by sharks it wasn't because you hadn't been warned. Apparently shark attacks are much more likely inside the harbour than out. I don't know why. I had also read in Jan Morris's engaging and cheery book *Sydney* that the harbour teems with lethal goblinfish. What is notable about this is that in all my reading I never came across a single other reference to these rapacious creatures. This isn't to suggest, I hastily add, that Ms Morris was being inventive; merely that it isn't possible in a single lifetime to read about all the dangers that lurk under every wattle bush or ripple of water in this wondrously venomous and toothy country.

These thoughts took on a certain relevance some hours later in the dry heat of afternoon when I returned to the city dog tired and pasted with sweat, and impulsively popped into the grand and brooding Australian Museum beside Hyde Park. I went not because it is fabulous, but because I was half crazed from the heat and it looked to be one of those old buildings that are dimly lit and gratifyingly cool inside. It was both of those, and fabulous as well. It is a vast and old-fashioned place – I mean that as the most admiring compliment; I know of no higher for a museum – with lofty galleried halls full of stuffed animals and long cases of carefully mounted insects, chunks of luminous minerals or Aboriginal artefacts. In a country such as Australia, every room is a wonder.

As you can imagine, I was particularly attracted to all those things that might hurt me, which in an Australian context is practically everything. It really is the most extraordinarily lethal country. Naturally, they play down the fact that every time you set your feet on the floor something is likely to jump out and seize an ankle. Thus my guidebook blandly observed that 'only' fourteen species of Australian snakes are seriously lethal, among them the western brown, desert death adder, tiger snake, taipan and yellow-bellied sea snake. The taipan is the one to watch out for. It is the most poisonous snake on earth, with a lunge so swift and a venom so potent that your last mortal utterance is likely to be: 'I say, is that a sn—'

Even from across the room you could see at once which was the display case containing the stuffed taipan, for it had around it a clutch of small boys held in rapt silence by the frozen gaze of its beady, lazily hateful eyes. You can kill it and stuff it and put it in a case, but you can't take away

88

the menace. According to the label, the taipan carries a venom fifty times more deadly than that of the cobra, its nearest challenger. Amazingly, just one fatal attack is on record, at Mildura in 1989. But *we* knew the real story, my attentive little friends and I – that once you leave this building the taipans aren't stuffed and behind glass.

At least the taipan is five feet long and thick as a man's wrist, which gives you a reasonable chance of spotting it. What I found far more appalling was the existence of lethal small snakes, like the little desert death adder. Just eight inches long, it lies lightly buried in soft sand so that you have no hope of seeing it before setting your weary butt on its head. Even more worrying was the Point Darwin sea snake, which is not much larger than an earthworm but packs venom enough if not to kill you at least to make you very late for dinner.

But all of these are as nothing compared with the delicate and diaphanous box jellyfish, the most poisonous creature on earth. We will hear more of the unspeakable horrors of this little bag of lethality when we get to the tropics, but let me offer here just one small story. In 1992, a young man in Cairns, ignoring all the warning signs, went swimming in the Pacific waters at a place called Holloways Beach. He swam and dived, taunting his friends on the beach for their prudent cowardice, and then began to scream with an inhuman sound. It is said that there is no pain to compare with it. The young man staggered from the water, covered in livid whip-like stripes wherever the jellyfish's tentacles had brushed across him, and collapsed in quivering shock. Soon afterwards emergency crews arrived, inflated him with morphine, and took him away for treatment. And here's the thing. Even unconscious and sedated he was still screaming.

Sydney has no box jellyfish, I was pleased to learn. The famous local danger is the funnel-web spider, the most poisonous insect in the world with a venom that is 'highly toxic and fast-acting'. A single nip, if not promptly treated, will leave you bouncing around in the grip of seizures of an incomparable liveliness; then you turn blue; then you die. Thirteen deaths are on record, though none since 1981 when an antidote was devised. Also poisonous are white-tailed spiders, mouse spiders, wolf spiders, our old friend the redback ('hundreds of bites are reported each year . . . about a dozen known deaths') and a reclusive but fractious type called the fiddleback. I couldn't say for sure whether I had seen any of these in the gardens I had passed earlier in the day, but then I couldn't say I hadn't since they all looked essentially the same. No one knows, incidentally, why Australia's spiders are so extravagantly toxic; capturing small insects and injecting them with enough poison to drop a horse would appear to be the most literal case of overkill. Still, it does mean that everyone gives them lots of space.

I studied with particular alertness the funnel-web since this was the creature that I was most likely to encounter in the next few days. It was about 1.5 inches long, plump, hairy and ugly. According to the label, you can identify a funnel-web by 'the mating organ on the male palp, deeply curved fovea, shiny carapace and lower labium studded with short blunt spines'. Alternatively, of course, you can just let it sting you. I carefully copied all this down before it occurred to me that if I were to awake to find any large, furry creature advancing crablike across the sheets I was unlikely to note any of its anatomical features, however singular and telling. So I put away my notebook and went off to look at minerals, which aren't so exciting but do have the compensating virtue that almost never will they attack you.

I spent four days wandering around Sydney. I visited the principal museums with dutiful absorption and spent an afternoon in the admirably welcoming State Library of New South Wales, but mostly I just went wherever there was water. Without question, it is the harbour that makes Sydney. It's not so much a harbour as a fjord, sixteen miles long and perfectly proportioned – big enough for grandeur, small enough to have a neighbourly air. Wherever you stand, the people on the far shore are almost never so distant as to seem remote; often you could hail them if you wished. Because it runs through the heart of the city from east to west it divides Sydney into more or less equal halves, known as the northern and eastern suburbs. (And never mind that the eastern suburbs are actually in the south, or that many of the northern suburbs are decidedly eastern. Australians, never forget, started life as Britons.) To note that it is sixteen miles long barely hints at its extent. Because it constantly wanders off into arms that finish in the serenest little coves, the most gently scalloped bays, the harbour shoreline actually extends to 152 miles. The consequence of this wandering nature is that one moment you are walking beside a tiny sheltered cove that seems miles from anywhere, and the next you round a headland to find before you an open expanse of water with the Opera House and Harbour Bridge and clustered skyscrapers gleaming in airy sunshine and holding centre stage. It is endlessly and unbelievably beguiling.

On my last day I hiked out to Hunter's Hill, a treasured and secretive district about six miles from the city centre on a long finger of land overlooking one of the quieter inner reaches of the harbour. I chose it because Jan Morris had made it sound so delightful in her book. I dare say she reached it by water, as any sensible person would. I decided to walk out along Victoria Road, which may not be the ugliest road in Australia but must be the least agreeable to walk along.

I strode for shadeless miles through zones of factories, warehouses and railway lines, then miles more of marginal commercial districts of discount furnishers, industrial wholesalers and dingy pubs offering surreally unappealing inducements ('Meat Raffles 6–8 pm'). By the time I reached a small sign pointing down a side road to Hunter's Hill my expectations were flagging. Imagine then my satisfaction at discovering that Hunter's Hill was worth every steaming step – a lovely, hidden borough of plump stone mansions, pretty cottages and picturesquely clustered shops of an often impressive venerability. There was a small but splendid town hall dating from 1860 and a chemist's shop that had been in business since 1890, which must be a record in Australia. Every garden was a treasure and somewhere in almost every backdrop lurked a glimpse of harbour view. I could not have been more charmed.

Reluctant to retrace my steps, I decided to push on further, through Linley Point, Lane Cove, Northwood, Greenwich and Wollstonecraft, and rejoin the known world at the Harbour Bridge. It was a long way round and the day was sultry, but Sydney is such a constantly rewarding place and I was feeling ambitious. I suppose I walked for about an hour before it dawned on me that this was actually *quite* ambitious – I had barely penetrated Linley Point and was still miles from the central business district

– but then I noticed on the map what appeared to be a worthwhile short cut through a place called Tennyson Park.

I followed a side road down to a residential street and about halfway along came to the entrance to the park. A wooden sign announced that what lay beyond was preserved bush land and politely requested users not to stray from the path. Well, this seemed a splendid notion – an expanse of native bush in the heart of a great city – and I ventured in eagerly. I don't know what image 'bush' conjures up in your mind, but this was not the brown and semi-barren tract I would have expected, but a wooded glade with a sun-dappled path and tinkling brook. It appeared to be scarcely used – every few yards I would have to duck under or walk around big spider webs strung across the path – which lent the whole enterprise a sense of lucky discovery.

I guessed it would take about twenty minutes to cut through the park – or 'the reserve', as Australians call these things – and I was probably about halfway along when from an indeterminate distance off to the right there came the bark of a dog, tentative and experimental, as if to say: 'Who's that?' It wasn't very close or intimidating, but it was clearly the bark of a big dog. Something in its timbre said: meat eater, black, very big, not too many generations removed from wolf. Almost in the same instant it was joined by the bark of a companion dog, also big, and this bark was decidedly less experimental. This bark said: 'Red alert! Trespasser on our territory!' Within a minute they had worked themselves up into a considerable frenzy.

Nervously I quickened my pace. Dogs don't like me. It is a simple law of the universe, like gravity. I am not exaggerating when I say that I have never passed a dog that didn't act as if it thought I was about to help myself to its Pedigree Chum. Dogs that have not moved from the sofa in years will, at the sniff of me passing outside, rise in fury and hurl themselves at shut windows. I have seen tiny dogs, no bigger than a fluffy slipper, jerk little old ladies off their feet and drag them over open ground in a quest to get at my blood and sinew. Every dog on the face of the earth wants me dead.

And now here I was alone in an empty wood, which suddenly seemed very large and lonely, and two big and angry-sounding dogs had me in their sights. As I pushed on, two things became increasingly apparent: I was definitely the target and these dogs were not messing around. They were coming towards me, at some speed. Now the barking said: 'We are going to have you, boy. You are dead meat. You are small, pulpy pieces.' You will note the absence of exclamation marks. Their barks were no longer tinged with lust and frenzy. They were statements of cold intent. 'We know where you are,' they said. 'You cannot make it to the edge of the woods. We will be with you shortly. Somebody call forensic.'

Casting worried glances at the foliage, I began to trot and then to run. It was now time to consider what I would do if the dogs burst on to the path. I picked up a rock for defence, then discarded it a few yards further on for a stick that was lying across the path. The stick was ludicrously outsized – it must have been twelve feet long – and so rotten that it fell in half just from being picked up. As I ran, it lost another half, and another, until finally it was no more than a soft spongy stub – it would have been like defending myself with a loaf of bread – so I threw it down and picked up a big jagged rock in each hand, and quickened my pace yet again. The dogs now seemed to be moving parallel to me, as if they couldn't find a way through, but at a distance of no more than forty or fifty yards. They were furious. My unease expanded, and I began to run a little faster.

In my stumbling haste, I rounded a bend too fast and ran headlong into a giant spider's web. It fell over me like a collapsing parachute. Ululating in dismay, I tore at the cobweb, but with rocks in my hands only succeeded in banging myself on the forehead. In a small, lucid corner of my brain I remember thinking: 'This really is very unfair.' Somewhere else was the thought: 'You are going to be the first person in history to die in the bush in the middle of a city, you poor, sad schlubb.' All the rest was icy terror.

And so I trotted along, wretched and whimpering, until I rounded a bend and found, with another small and disbelieving wail, that the path abruptly terminated. Before me stood nothing but impenetrable tangle – a wall of it. I looked around, astounded and appalled. In my panic – doubtless while I was scraping the cobwebs from my brow with the aid of lumps of granite – I had evidently taken a wrong turn. In any case, there was no way forward and nothing behind but a narrow path leading back in the direction of two surging streaks of malice. Glancing around in desperation, I saw with unconfined joy, at the top of a twenty-foot rise, a corner of rotary clothesline. There was a home up there! I had reached the edge of the park, albeit from an unconventional direction. No matter. There was a civilized world up there. Safety! I scrambled up the hill as fast as my plump little pins would carry me – the dogs were very close now – snagging myself on thorns, inhaling cobwebs, straining with every molecule of my being not to become a headline that said: 'Police find writer's torso; head still missing.'

At the top of the hill stood a brick wall perhaps six feet high. Grunting extravagantly, I hauled myself on to its flat summit and dropped down on the other side. The transformation was immediate, the relief sublime. I was back in the known world, in someone's much-loved back garden. There was a set of old swings that didn't look as if they had been used in some years, flower beds, a lawn leading to a patio. The garden appeared to be fully enclosed by brick wall on three sides and a big comfortable-looking house on the fourth, which I hadn't quite anticipated. I was trespassing, of course, but there wasn't any way I was going back into those woods. Part of the view was obscured by a shed or summerhouse. With luck there would be a gate beyond and I could let myself out and slip back into the world undetected. My most immediate concern was that there might be a big mean dog in here as well. Wouldn't that be richly ironic? With this in mind, I crept cautiously forward.

Now let us change the point of view just for a moment. Forgive me for getting you up, but I need to put you at the window beside the kitchen sink of this tranquil suburban home. You are a pleasant middle-aged homemaker going about your daily business – at this particular moment filling a vase with water to hold some peonies you have just cut from the bed by the drawing-room windows – and you see a man drop over your back wall and begin to move in a low crouch across your back garden. Frozen with fear and a peculiar detached fascination, you are unable to move, but just stand watching as he advances stealthily across the property in a commando posture, with short, frenzied dashes between covering objects, until he is crouched beside a concrete urn at the edge of your patio only about ten feet away. It is then that he notices you staring at him.

'Oh, hello!' says the man cheerfully, straightening up and smiling in a way that he thinks looks sincere and ingratiating, but in fact merely suggests someone who has failed to take his medication. Almost at once your thoughts go to a police mugshot you saw in the evening paper earlier in the week pertaining, if you recall, to a breakout at an institution for the criminally insane at Wollongong. 'Sorry to crash in on you like this,' the man is saying, 'but I was desperate. Did you hear all the racket? I thought they were going to *kill* me.'

He beams foolishly and waits for you to reply, but you say nothing because you are powerless to speak. Your eyes slide over to the open back door. If you both moved for it now, you would arrive together. All kinds of thoughts start to run through your head.

'I didn't actually *see* them,' the man goes on in a judicious but oddly pumped-up tone, 'but I know they were after me.' He looks as if he has been living rough. Smudges of dirt rim his face and one of his trouser legs is torn at the knee. 'They always go for me,' he says, earnest now, and puzzled. 'It's as if there's some kind of conspiracy to get me. I can be just walking down the street, you know, minding my own business, and suddenly from out of nowhere they just *come* for me. It's very unsettling.' He shakes his head. 'Is your gate unlocked?'

You haven't been listening to any of this because your hand has been moving almost imperceptibly towards the drawer containing the steak knives. As the question dawns on you, you find yourself giving a small, tight, almost involuntary nod.

'I'll just let myself out then. Sorry to have disturbed you.'

At the gate he pauses. 'Take it from me,' he says, 'you don't ever want to go back in those woods alone. Something terrible could happen to you back there. I love your delphiniums by the way.' He smiles in a way that freezes your marrow, and says: 'Well, bye then.'

And he is gone.

Six weeks later you put the house on the market.

Chapter

FIVE

I

When Australians get hold of a name that suits them they tend to stick with it in a big way. We can blame this unfortunate custom on Lachlan Macquarie, a Scotsman who was governor of the colony in the first part of the nineteenth century, and whose principal achievements were the building of the Great Western Highway through the Blue Mountains, the popularizing of Australia as a name (before him the whole country was indifferently referred to as either New South Wales or Botany Bay) and the world's first nearly successful attempt to name every object on a continent after himself.

You really cannot move in Australia without bumping into some reminder of his tenure. Run your eye over the map and you will find a Macquarie Harbour, Macquarie Island, Macquarie Marsh, Macquarie River, Macquarie Fields, Macquarie Pass, Macquarie Plains, Lake Macquarie, Port

Macquarie, Mrs Macquarie's Chair (a lookout point over Sydney Harbour), Macquarie's Point and a Macquarie town. I always imagine him sitting at his desk, poring over maps and charts with a magnifying glass, and calling out from time to time to his first assistant: 'Hae we no' got a Macquarie Swamp yet, laddie? And look here at this wee copse. It has nae name. What shall we call *it*, do ye think?'

And that's just some of the Macquaries, by the way. Macquarie is also the name of a bank, a university, the national dictionary, a shopping centre, and one of Sydney's principal streets. That's not to mention the forty-seven other Roads, Avenues, Groves and Terraces in Sydney that, according to Jan Morris, are named for the man or his family. Nor have we touched on the Lachlan River, Lachlan Valley or any of the other first-name variations that sprang to his tireless mind.

You wouldn't suppose there would be much left after all that, but one of Macquarie's successors as governor, Ralph Darling, managed to get his name all over the place too. In Sydney you will find a Darling Harbour, Darling Drive, Darling Island, Darling Point, Darlinghurst, and Darlington. Elsewhere Darling's modest achievements are remembered in the Darling Downs and Darling Ranges, a slew of additional Darlingtons, and the important Darling River. What isn't called Darling or Macquarie is generally called Hunter or Murray. It's awfully confusing.

Even when the names aren't exactly the same, they are often very similar. There is a Cape York Peninsula in the far north and a Yorke Peninsula in the far south. Two of the leading explorers of the nineteenth century were called Sturt and Stuart and their names are all over the place, too, so that you have constantly to stop and think, generally at busy intersections where an instant decision is required, 'Now did I want the Sturt Highway or the *Stuart* Highway?' Since both highways start at Adelaide and finish at places 3,994 kilometres apart, this can make a difference, believe me.

I was thinking about all this – the confusion of place names and monuments to Lachlan Macquarie – the following morning because I spent much of it in the grip of the first while in pursuit of the second. I was in a rental car, you see, trying to find my way out of the endless, bewildering sprawl of Sydney. According to the local telephone directory, there are 784 suburbs and other named districts in the city, and I believe I passed through every one of them as I sought in vain for a corner of Australia not covered by bungalows. Some neighbourhoods I visited twice, at opposite ends of the morning. For a time I thought about just abandoning the car at the kerb in Parramatta – I rather liked the name and people were beginning to wave to me familiarly – but eventually I shot out of the city, like a spat bug, pleased to find myself on the correct heading for Lithgow, Bathurst and points beyond, and filled with that sense of giddy delight that comes with finding yourself at large in a new and unknown continent.

My intention over the next couple of weeks was to wander through what I think of as Civilized Australia – the lower right-hand corner of the country, extending from Brisbane in the north to Adelaide in the south and west. This area covers perhaps 5 per cent of the nation's land surface but contains 80 per cent of its people and nearly all its important cities (specifically Brisbane, Sydney, Melbourne, Canberra and Adelaide). In the whole of the vast continent this is pretty much the only part that is conventionally habitable. Because of its curving shape, it is sometimes called the Boomerang Coast, though in fact my interest was largely internal. I was headed in the first instance for Canberra, the nation's interesting, parklike and curiously much scorned capital; thence I would cross 800 miles of lonely interior to distant Adelaide before finally fetching up, dusty but ever indomitable, in Melbourne, where I was to meet some old friends who would hose me down and take me off for a long-promised tour of the snake-infested, little-visited but gorgeously rewarding Victorian bush. There was much to see along the way. I was very excited.

But first I had to make my way through the Blue Mountains, the scenic and long-impassable hills lying just to Sydney's west. On approach the Blue Mountains don't look terribly challenging; they rise to no great height and everywhere wear a softening cloak of green. But in fact they are rent with treacherous gorges and bouldered canyons, some with walls rising sheer hundreds of feet, and that lovely growth proves on closer inspection to be of an unusually tangled and obscuring nature. For the first quarter of a century of European occupation, the Blue Mountains stood as an impenetrable barrier to expansion. Expeditions tried repeatedly to find a way through but were always turned back. Even if progress could be gained through the lacerating undergrowth, it was nearly impossible to maintain one's bearings amid the wandering gorges. Watkin Tench, a leader of one party, reported with understandable exasperation how he and his men struggled for hours to find a route to the top of one impossibly taxing defile, only to discover when they attained the summit that they were exactly opposite where they expected to be.

Finally, in 1813, three men, Gregory Blaxland, William Charles Wentworth and William Lawson, broke through – exhausted, tattered and 'ill with Bowel Complaints', as Wentworth glumly noted, then and on any occasion that anyone would listen for the rest of his long life. It had taken them eighteen days, but as they stepped onto the airy heights of Mount York they were rewarded with a view of pastoral splendour never before seen by European eyes. Below them, for as far as the gaze could reach, stretched a sunny, golden Eden, a continent of grass – enough, it seemed, to support a population of millions. Australia would be a mighty country. The news, when they returned to Sydney, was electrifying. In less than two years a road was cut through the wilderness and the westward peopling of Australia had begun.

Today the Great Western Highway, as it is grandly and romantically known, follows almost exactly the route taken by Blaxland and his companions nearly 200 years ago. It certainly feels venerable. The route goes up and through the mountains and for much of the way passes along such confined spaces that there is no room for a big modern road. So the Great Western has the tight bends and unyielding width of a road designed for an age when motorists clapped goggles over their eyes and started their cars with a crank. I had been through here not long before on the Indian Pacific, but the views from the train weren't good – glimpsed vistas seen through a picket fence of gum trees and then, each time, an abrupt veering away into denser woodland – and anyway I had been preoccupied with exploring the train. So I was eager now to see the mountains up close, in particular the famous, dreamy views from the little town of Katoomba.

Alas, luck was not with me. As I followed the tortuous

road up into the distant hills, the windscreen became speckled with drizzle and a chill, swirling fog began to fill the spaces between the coachwood and sassafras trees that loomed up on every side. Very quickly the fog thickened to the density of woodsmoke. I had never been out in such fog. Within minutes, it was like piloting a small plane through cloud. There was a bonnet in front of me, and then just white. It was all I could do to keep the car affixed to its lane – the road was almost preposterously narrow and twisting, and with the visibility so low every sudden curve was received with a whoop of surprise.

At length I reached Katoomba where the fog was, if anything, worse. The town was reduced to spooky shapes that loomed out of the murk from time to time, like frights at a funfair ride. Twice, at no more than two miles an hour, I nearly drove into the backs of parked cars. I have no idea why I bothered but, having come this far, I found my way to a lookout spot called Echo Point, parked and got out. Not surprisingly, I was the only person there. I went and grasped the railing and gazed out, the way you do at a lookout point. Before me there stood nothing but depthless white and that peculiar twitchy stillness that fog brings. To my surprise, from out of the milky vapours there emerged an elderly couple, dapper and doddery and bundled up as if for a long winter. The man walked with a particularly unsteady gait, propped by a cane on one side and his wife on the other.

As they drew level he looked at me in surprise. 'You won't see anything today!' he barked as if I was wasting his time as well as my own. I guessed from the volume that he might be a little deaf. 'This won't clear for thirty-six hours.' More confidingly he added: 'Depression over the Pacific.

Often happens.' He nodded sagely and joined me in con-templating the nothingness.

His wife gave me a tiny smile that was at once apolo-getic, long-suffering and a little wistful. 'It might clear after a bit,' she speculated hopefully.

He looked at her as if she had just announced an inten-tion to have a shit on the pavement. '*Clear*? It's never going to *clear*. There's a depression over the Pacific.' He looked for a moment as if he might swipe her with his cane.

Her optimism was not lightly deflected, however. 'Don't you remember how it came out all lovely that time at Bunbury?' she said.

'Bunbury?' he replied incredulously. '*Bunbury*? That's the other side of the country. It's a different bloody ocean. What are you talking about? You're *mad*. You want putting away.' Suddenly I recognized the accent. He was a Yorkshireman, or at least once had been.

'It didn't look like it was going to turn out fine,' she went on to me, expecting a more sympathetic hearing, 'and then it *did* turn out—'

'It's a different ocean, woman! Are you deaf as well as mad?' It was clear that this was, at least in the funda-mentals, a conversation that they had been having for years. 'You get a quite different set of meteorological con-ditions in the Indian Ocean – quite different. Any fool knows that.' He was quiet for half a second, and then said: 'I thought we were going for a cup of tea.'

'We are, dear. I just thought we'd have a little stroll.' Deftly she set him in motion again.

'A stroll? What *for*? There's bugger all to see. Are you blind as well as deaf and mad? This won't clear for thirty-six hours.'

'I know, dear, but—'

Within moments they were just voices floating out of a veil of white and then they were gone altogether.

Reluctant to leave the area, I spent the night in Blackheath, a pretty village in the woods a dozen miles further down the highway. My last view from my motel window before turning in was of a car passing slowly on the highway, its headlamps like searchlights, and the world settled under a thick eiderdown of murk. It didn't look terribly promising.

So you may imagine my surprise when I awoke in the morning to find bright sunshine spilled across my bed and filling the tops of the trees outside. I opened the door to a golden world, so bright it made me blink. Birds were singing in the exotic tones of the bush. I wasted not a moment getting back to Katoomba.

The view when I returned to Echo Point was outstanding – a broad vale of very green forest broken at intervals by square-topped outcrops and fractured pinnacles, the whole filled with a vast and imposing silence. The sky was a rich and all but cloudless blue. Even at nine in the morning you could tell it was going to be a really hot day. I spent ninety minutes or so walking along the clifftop, enjoying the view from various angles; I had a look at Katoomba Falls and the stranded sandstone uprights known as the Three Sisters, and at length, entirely satisfied, wandered back into town for coffee.

In the 1930s and 1940s, Katoomba was a popular retreat for people of a genteel and discriminating nature. It was much less raffish than Bondi or the other beach outposts, where there was always the danger that young Bruce and Noelene might be exposed to more flesh than was healthy at their ages or overhear strong language – men saying 'jeezums' and 'strewth' and so on. Katoomba offered more refined pursuits: strolls through the woods, a therapeutic dip in a hydro pool, orchestral dancing in the evenings. Today Katoomba clings, with a slight air of desperation, to its bygone glory. Its main street had a generous sprinkling of art deco buildings, notably a wonderful old movie house, though several, including the movie house, were closed.

I bought a morning newspaper and found my way into a café. It always amazes me how seldom visitors bother with local papers. Personally, I can think of nothing more exciting – certainly nothing you could do in a public place with a cup of coffee – than to read newspapers from a part of the world you know almost nothing about. What a comfort it is to find a nation preoccupied by matters of no possible consequence to oneself. I love reading about scandals involving ministers of whom I have never heard, murder hunts in communities whose names sound dusty and remote, features on revered artists and thinkers whose achievements have never reached my ears, whose talents I must take on faith. I love above all to venture into the colour supplements and see what's fashionable for the beach in this part of the world, what's new for the kitchen, what I might get for my money if I had $400,000 to spare and a reason to live in Dubbo or Woolloomooloo. There is something about all this that feels privileged, almost illicit, like going through a stranger's drawers. Where else can you get this much pleasure for a trifling handful of coins?

At this time I was following with some devotion a libel trial in which two government ministers were suing a publisher over a book containing scurrilous and, as it proved, groundless allegations implying sexual indiscretions in times gone by. With each passing day the trial had taken on the most exhilarating air of farce. Just recently a former leader of the opposition had taken the stand and, for no reason that any sane person could deduce, had begun recounting lively stories of alleged sexual improprieties by other ministers who were not remotely connected to the book or trial. But what had attracted me to the case in the first place, and what made it all seem particularly special, was the simple happy coincidence that the two ministers at the heart of the affair were named Abbott and Costello.

So I was sitting happily absorbed in this when I heard a familiar voice say, quite loudly and in a discontented tone: 'This isn't strawberry jam. It's blackcurrant.'

I looked up to see my two little old friends from the day before. They were looking much smaller and frailer with their hats and coats and scarves off. These items, neatly folded, were stacked high on the chairs beside them, as if awaiting transfer to a linen cupboard. I wondered if perhaps they wore all those clothes not so much for warmth as because all the dressing and undressing helped them fill their days.

'They haven't got strawberry, dear,' said the wife in a quieter voice. 'The lady explained. They only have blackcurrant or marmalade.'

'Well, I don't want either.'

'Then don't have either.' This said with just a hint of weariness.

'But it's on my toast.'

'No, dear, that's my toast. I ordered you a jam doughnut.'

'Jam doughnut? *Jam doughnut?* Are you mad? I don't like jam doughnuts. This tea is cold.'

I lowered myself back into my paper, but on the way out

I stopped to bid my elderly friends good day. The man clearly didn't have any very real notion who I was. The jam doughnut, I noticed, had been devoured; only a small purple dollop gleamed on the plate before him.

'It's the young man from Echo Point,' the woman explained, but her husband was too busy chasing the dollop of jam with a spoon to pay me any heed.

'I see the weather's cleared,' I observed cheerfully.

'Often happens like that,' the man said in a small shout, without looking up. 'I said it wouldn't last thirty-six hours.'

'We had an experience just like it at Bunbury once,' the wife said to me. 'Terrible fog and then all of a sudden it came out all lovely and clear. Do you remember that, dear?'

'Quite,' said the old man distractedly. Coaxing the elusive jam aboard with a forefinger, he lifted the spoon and bunged it in his mouth with a look of immense satisfaction. 'Quite.'

And so once more to the wandering road. Beyond Blackheath the highway began a steep and curvaceous descent towards Lithgow, where it skirted along the hem of the mountains before striking off cross country through grassy plains, towards the country town of Bathurst. I was now in the rural heartlands, in an area known to geology as the Murray-Darling Basin. The fields on all sides were filled with tall blond grass, which waved in a languid manner, and there were buttercups in the verges, the whole bathed in the sweetest, brightest sunlight. Here and there stately trees shaded a white farmhouse. There wasn't a gum tree in sight. I could almost have been in the American Midwest.

The welcoming world I was passing into now wasn't

quite as virginal as Blaxland and his cronies had supposed when they first gazed down on it from the heights behind me. When the first settlers stepped from the wooded mountains they were startled to find herds of cows, numbering in the hundreds, grazing contentedly on the tall grasses – all offspring of the ones that had wandered off from Sydney Cove all those years before. The cows, it transpired, had gone *around* the mountains, through an open pass to the south. Why it had not occurred to a human being in twenty-five years to try to do likewise is a question that is rarely asked and has yet to be satisfactorily answered.

Nor were the fertile plains quite as boundless as had at first been supposed. Good grazing land extended only a few score miles inland from the coast and even that was subject to the dispiriting vagaries of nature. It still is. A hundred miles or so north of where I was driving now, on the edge of this grassy zone, stands the little town of Nyngan. In 1989, 1990, 1992, 1995, 1996 and 1998 it was devastated by torrential flash floods. For five years during this same period, while Nyngan was repeatedly inundated, the town of Cobar, just eighty miles to the west, recorded not a drop of rain. This is, if I haven't made it clear already, one tough country.

And yet the striking thing about this area was how thoroughly delightful and accommodating it appeared. The farms were neat and trim, and the towns I passed through gave every appearance of a comfortable prosperity. It was impossible to believe that a metropolis of four million people lay just over the hills behind. I felt as if I had stumbled into some forgotten, magically self-contained world. There were things out here I hadn't seen in years. Petrol stations with old-fashioned pumps and no canopies over the forecourt, so that you pumped your petrol in full sun, as I am sure God intended it. Metal pinwheel windmills of the sort that used to stand in every Kansas farm field. Little towns with people in them – people going about their business, greeting each other with a smile and a nod. It all had a familiarity about it, but the familiarity of something half forgotten. Gradually it dawned on me that I *was* in the American Midwest – but it was the American Midwest of long ago. I was, in short, in the process of making the marvellous and heart-warming discovery that outside the cities it is still 1958 in Australia. Hardly seems possible, but there you are. I was driving through my childhood.

Partly it was to do with that dazzling light. It was the kind of pure, undiffused light that can come only from a really hot blue sky, the kind that makes even a concrete highway painful to behold and turns every distant reflective surface into a little glint of flame. Do you know how sometimes on very fine days the sun will shine with a particular intensity that makes the most mundane objects in the landscape glow with an unusual radiance, so that buildings and structures you normally pass without a glance suddenly become arresting, even beautiful? Well, they seem to have that light in Australia nearly all the time. It took me a while to recognize that this was precisely the light of Iowa summers from my boyhood, and it was a shock to realize just how long it was since I had seen it.

Partly, too, it was to do with the road. Almost all Australian highways are still just two lanes wide, and what a difference that makes. You're not cut off from the wider world, as you are on a motorway, but part of it, intimately connected. All the million details of the landscape are there beside you, up close, not blurred into some distant, tediously epic backdrop. It changes your whole outlook.

There's no point in hurrying when all it's going to do is put you in the feathery wake of that old chicken truck half a mile ahead. Might as well hold back and enjoy the scenery. So there's none of that mad, pointless urgency – gotta pass this guy, gotta keep pushing, gotta make some miles – that makes any drive on a motorway such an exhausting and unsatisfying business. When you come to a town on such a road it is an event. You don't fly through at speed, but slow down and *glide* through, in a stately manner, like a float in a parade, slow enough to nod to pedestrians if you wish and to check out the goods in the windows on Main Street. 'Oh, that's a good price on men's double-knit shirts,' you observe in a thoughtful tone, or 'Those lawn chairs were cheaper in Bathurst,' for, needless to say, you are talking to yourself by now. Sometimes – quite often, in fact – you stop for a coffee and a browse round the shops.

Afterwards you return to the open road and naturally at first you go a little too fast, for speed is an instinct, but then – whoops! – you round a bend to find yourself fast approaching the back of a tip lorry kicking out smoke and labouring heavily up a slope. So you drop back and take it easy. You lean an arm on the windowsill, lay a finger on the wheel and cruise. You haven't done this for years. You haven't been on a drive like this since you were a kid. You'd forgotten motoring could be fun. I loved it.

As if to underscore the agreeably retro nature of the driving experience in Australia, I began to discover that radio stations in country towns specialize in songs from yesteryear. I don't mean songs from the sixties and seventies, but much earlier. This may be the last country in the world where you can turn on a car radio and stand a more than passing chance of hearing Peggy Lee or Julie London, possibly even Gisele McKenzie, whose popularity in the 1950s can only be attributed to a winning smile and the luck to live in an undiscriminating age. It would be intemperate to make a sweeping generalization about rural Australian radio stations because I listened to no more than six or seven thousand hours of them in the time I was there, so I might have missed something good, but I will say this: when our modern monuments have crumbled to dust, when the careless hand of time has worn away all traces of the twentieth century, you can be certain that somewhere in an Australian country town there will be a disc jockey saying: 'And that was Doris Day with her classic hit "Que Sera Sera".' I even loved that too.

For a week or so.

And so by such happy means did I proceed through Lithgow, Bathurst, Blayney and Lyndhurst, and finally, in mid-afternoon, fetched up in Cowra, a compact and tidy community of 8,207 people in the Lachlan Valley on the Lachlan River – both named, of course, for our old friend Mr Macquarie. I knew nothing about Cowra, but I quickly learned that it is well known to Australians as the site of the infamous Cowra breakout.

During the Second World War, a large prisoner-of-war camp stood just outside Cowra. One side held 2,000 Italian POWs; on the other were 2,000 Japanese. The Italians were model prisoners. Overcoming the mortifica- tion of finding themselves taken from the front lines and transported to a distant, sunny land far from the roar of guns, they settled down and made the best of things. So gamely did they cover their disappointment that one might almost have thought they welcomed their new situ- ation. They worked on local farms and were only lightly guarded. Their officers – I just love this – weren't guarded at all. They were free to come and go as they pleased, and asked only to close the door behind them to keep out the flies. Regularly they could be seen strolling into Cowra for cigarettes and newspapers, possibly an aperitif at the Lachlan Hotel.

The Japanese presented a sombre contrast. They refused to undertake work or offer any measure of cooperation. Most gave false names, so painful was the shame of capture. Ridiculously and tragically, in August 1944, in the middle of the night, 1,100 of them staged a suicidal mass breakout, bursting from their barracks with a banzai cry and charging en masse at the guard tower clutching baseball bats, chair legs and whatever other weapons they could contrive. The startled guards poured bullets into the mass but were quickly overwhelmed. Within minutes, 378 prisoners had escaped into the countryside. Quite what they expected to do out there is anyone's guess. It took nine days to round them all up. The furthest any of them had got was fifteen miles. The Japanese casualties were 231 killed and 112 wounded. The Australians suffered three killed on the night, and a fourth during the hunt afterwards.

All this is commemorated in photographs and other displays at Cowra's visitors' centre, which in itself was excellent, but in a room at the back was a small audio-visual theatre that was one of the most enchanting things I believe I have ever seen – certainly ever seen in a small country town in the middle of nowhere.

Behind glass on a kind of small stage were objects saved from the POW camp: some books and diaries, a couple of framed photographs, a baseball bat and glove, a medicine bottle, a Japanese board game. As I entered, the lights automatically dimmed in the room. A little introductory music played and then – this was the enchanting part – a young woman about six inches high stepped *out* of one of the framed photographs and began moving around among the objects and talking about Cowra in the 1940s and the prison breakout. My mouth fell open. She didn't just move about but interacted with the objects – stepped around books, idly leaned on a shell casing – as she went through her presentation. As you can imagine, I got up and had a closer look and I can tell you that no matter how close you got to the glass (and I had my head pressed up against it the way children do when they wish to be amusing) you couldn't see the artifice. She was a perfectly formed, full-colour, charmingly articulate, rather dishy three-dimensional person right in front of me and only six inches high. It was the most captivating thing I had seen in years. It was obvious that it was a film projected in some way from beneath, but there wasn't a stutter or bump, no scratchy lines or wriggly hairs. It was as real as an image can get. She was a perfect little hologram. The narrative, it is worth noting, was sympathetic and informative – a model of its type. I watched it three times and couldn't have been more impressed.

'Good, eh?' beamed a lady at the reception desk, seeing the amazed look on my face when I emerged.

'I'll say!'

Anticipating my questions, she passed me a laminated card that explained how it was all done. The display was created by a company in Sydney, employing an optical trick that has been around for well over a century. It was all to do with projecting an image onto a glass plate artfully positioned in such a way as to become invisible to the spectator. Beyond that the only real trick was taking fastidious care that the actress hit her marks exactly. It must have taken months. It was simply brilliant.

And I will say this. When they figure a way to get the little person to lap dance, they will make a *fortune*.

I ended the day at Young, a farming town in plum and cherry country forty miles down the Olympic Highway from Cowra in the direction of Canberra. I got a room in a motel on a side street not far from the town centre. The owner, a fit-looking fellow in shorts and a short-sleeved shirt, read my name off the registration card and said: 'G'day, Bill. Welcome to Young,' and gave my hand a powerful shake as if inducting me into a secret society. The friendliness of Australians – all of it quite sincere and spontaneous, as far as I could ever tell – never ceases to amaze or gratify. I had never had a motelier pump my hand before or act so pleased that fate had thrown us together. 'Glad to have you,' he went on, still pumping away. 'My name's Bruce' – or whatever it was, for I was too disarmed, in every sense, to catch it.

'Well, g'day, Bruce,' I stammered uncertainly. 'I'm Bill.'

'Yes, Bill, we've established that,' he said and dropped my hand abruptly. 'You're in room six.'

I took my key to my room, opened the door and stepped in. The room was, in every tiny particular, from 1958. I don't mean that it had not been decorated since 1958 or anything remotely disrespectful. I mean that inside that room it was 1958. The walls were panelled in knotty pine. The TV had a UHF dial on it. The toilet seat had been gift-wrapped with a 'sanitized for your convenience' wrapper. In a drawer in the bedroom were two complimentary postcards featuring views of the motel and a paper bag into which I was urged, for my further convenience, to place unflushable objects. The bag bore a drawing of a lady (to tip us off, presumably, that it was intended for female 'personal' things rather than, say, corn cobs or small engine parts). I could not have been happier. I dumped my stuff and walked into town through the baking end-of-day heat. Now I saw the 1950s everywhere. Even the 'children crossing' signs in Australia, I noticed, show kids in 1950s attire – a little girl in a party dress, a boy in short trousers.

Superficially, Young didn't look terribly much like the towns I had grown up with. The exceptionally wide streets (they love really wide streets in Australian country towns), the red tin roofs, the metal awnings that run like hat brims around every commercial building – all this was indubitably Australian. But in the way it worked, and what it contained, Young was uncannily familiar. This was a place where, when you had an errand to run, you drove into town, not out of it, and parked in an angled slot on Main Street. This alone was enough to hold me transfixed for some minutes. I had forgotten that there was a time when a little parking along Main Street was all a community needed. I walked around in a state of the profoundest admiration. Except for the banks and a supermarket, the businesses were locally owned, with all the peculiarities of taste and presentation that that implies. There were shops here of types I hadn't seen in years – fix-it shops and little electrical shops, bakeries, cobblers, tea rooms – and sometimes they sold the most extraordinary combinations of goods. At the far end of the main street, I came across one place so exceptional in this respect that it stopped me in my tracks.

It was a shop that sold pet supplies and pornography. I am quite genuine. I stood back to stare at the sign, then peered through the window and finally stepped inside. It was a smallish shop and I was the only customer. On a raised platform about halfway back sat a man beside a cash register, reading a newspaper. He didn't say hello or make any acknowledgement, which seemed odd – very un-Australian – until I realized he was being discreet. I imagine most of his customers do what I was doing now: wander around showing an unwonted interest in catnip and flea powders, pausing from time to time to study the labels on canisters of fish flakes and the like, before ending up, entirely by accident, at the back of the shop, in the heavy breathing section. Remarkably, this is what happened to me now. The adult section was partitioned into a little compound, with admission through a wooden gate. As I stood there, the gate made a small electronic buzzing sound – the kind of buzz that is made in office buildings when a door is opened from a remote location – and swung to in a provocative manner. I looked around, surprised. The man was still to all appearances absorbed in his newspaper. He seemed unaware that I was even in his shop, much less on the threshold of porno heaven. I grinned foolishly and thought about approaching him to explain that he had just made a quite understandable but nonetheless comical error – that I, far from being a desperate pervert in need of pictorial nutrition, was in fact a respectable travel writer drawn to his shop by the unusual juxtaposition of its contents. Then we would have a good laugh and possibly strike up a correspondence.

But then it occurred to me that if I *did* buy something – I am not suggesting for a moment that I would, but on the other hand I still had nothing for the kids – I probably wouldn't want my business card pinned to his bulletin board. It also occurred to me that I had a certain duty to find out if there was some unexpected connection between the two strands of his business. Perhaps *petting* had a whole different meaning in rural Australia. To say nothing of *dog fancier*. For all I knew the racks beyond the barrier were full of publications with frisky, animalistic titles – *Prime Mounts*, *Whip and Collar*, *Sheep Dip Frolics*. Who could say? Clearly I had a duty to find out, so I resumed my expression of sober perusal and stepped inside.

I had never actually been in one of these places before – and by that I don't mean a pet-supply porno parlour. I mean any kind of adult enclosure, and frankly I was shocked. The participants were human, not animal. More than that I am unwilling to specify. It certainly wasn't 1958 at the back of the pet-food shop in Young. That's all I'm saying.

II

Gratified though I was to find a pornographic pet-supply store in Young (or indeed anywhere), my business there was of a slightly more elevating nature. I had come to see the famous Lambing Flat Museum, which commemorates the town's days of glory as a gold-mining outpost. It was too late to visit the museum that afternoon, but I presented myself at the front door at 9 a.m. the next morning only to find that the museum didn't open till ten.

Never one to waste a living moment, I decided to repair to a town centre café for breakfast and prepare myself with a little background reading. Thus I was to be found ten minutes later sitting in a mostly empty establishment on Young's main drag, drinking coffee, waiting for eggs and bacon, and delving through a hefty one-volume paperback history of Australia by the noted historian Manning Clark, which I had purchased a few days earlier in Sydney.

The history of gold in Australia is a lively and generally heart-warming tale. It begins with a fellow named Edward Hargraves, who in 1849 travelled from Sydney to the California goldfields hoping to make his fortune. In two years of digging he found nothing but dirt, but he did notice an uncanny similarity between the gold-bearing terrain of California and the land of New South Wales beyond the Blue Mountains – the countryside I had just been driving through.

Hastening back to Australia before anyone else was struck by a similar thought, Hargraves began to hunt in the creekbeds around Orange and Bathurst, and very quickly found gold in payable quantities. Within a month of his discovery a thousand people were swarming through the district turning over rocks and banging away with picks. Once they knew what to look for, they began to find gold everywhere. Australia was swimming in the stuff. An Aboriginal farmworker tripped over one lump that yielded nearly eighty pounds of precious ore, an almost inconceivable amount to be found in one place. It was enough to ensure a life of princely splendour – or would have been except that as an Aborigine he wasn't allowed to keep it. The rock went instead to the property's owner.

Scarcely had this rush got under way than gold was found in even more luscious quantities over the border in the newly created colony of Victoria. Australia became seized with a gold fever that made the California rush seem almost pale and indecisive. Cities and towns became visibly depopulated as workers left to seek their fortunes. Shops lost all their clerks. Policemen walked off their posts. Wives came home to find a note on the table and the waggon gone. Before the year was out, it was estimated that half the men in Victoria were digging for gold, and thousands more were pouring into the country from abroad.

The gold rush transformed Australia's destiny. Before it, people could scarcely be induced to settle there. Now a stampede rose from every quarter of the globe. In less than a decade, the country took in 600,000 new faces, more than doubling its population. The bulk of that growth was in Victoria, where the richest goldfields were. Melbourne became larger than Sydney and for a time was probably the richest city in the world per head of population. But the real effect of gold was to put an end to transportation. When it was realized in London that transportation was seen as an opportunity rather than a punishment, that convicts *desired* to be sent to Australia, the notion of keeping the country a prison became unsustainable. A few boatloads of convicts were sent to Western Australia until 1868 (they would find gold there as well, in equally gratifying quantities) but essentially the gold rush of the 1850s marked the end of Australia as a concentration camp and its beginning as a nation.

Despite all the wealth that was to be found, things weren't always so easy for the diggers. In the hope of giving everyone a fair crack, prospectors were allowed to stake out only very modest claims – an area of just a few square yards – and here was where the problems began. When, in April 1860, gold was found at Lambing Flat, as Young was then known, fortune seekers turned up in quantity. By 1861, 22,000 people, among them 2,000 Chinese, were digging away, each on a plot of land about the size of a large throw rug. Inevitably most weren't finding much. Many of the miners began to cast resentful glances at the

Chinese, who seemed to bear the heat and privations more cheerfully than their European counterparts, and who cooperated in a way that was felt to give them an unfair advantage. Also they seemed to be finding more gold. Also they were Chinese.

The upshot is that the white diggers decided to go and beat up the Chinese. That would make things much better surely. So in the middle of 1861 a substantial minority of the white miners – somewhere between 2,000 and 3,000, it appears – got together and staged a riot. It was a curiously organized affair. To begin with, the rioters brought in a brass band, which played 'Rule Britannia' and 'The Marseillaise' among other rousing songs deemed suitable for a civil disturbance. They also made and carried a large banner, which has since become something of an icon in Australian history. So, as the band played the kind of tunes normally heard at a Sunday afternoon park concert, the miners moved through the Chinese area beating people up with pickaxe handles or worse, robbing them and setting their tents alight. Then, just to make a day of it, they went on to burn down the courthouse. Afterwards, eleven of the rioters were tried but none was convicted. Obviously not Australia's proudest moment.

What was the immediate outcome of all this I can't tell you. Manning Clark, who is – I just have to say this – a most exasperating historian, mentions that one European miner was killed in the fray, but gives no hint as to how many Chinese died or were injured. Nor does he say what became of them afterwards – whether they were driven permanently from the site or whether things settled down and they returned to work. What is certain is that the Lambing Flat riot led to the adoption of what became known as the White Australia Policy, which essentially forbade the immigration of any non-European people until the 1970s. It would – and I really don't mean a pun here – colour nearly every aspect of Australian life for over a century.

The Lambing Flat Museum was a large, old, single-storey brick building on a side street. I was there for the opening of the front door – an event that seemed to involve a great deal of unbolting and fiddling with a set of keys by someone on the inside. I began to suspect that it wasn't quite as popular or important an institution as I had supposed, for when the door swung open the lady nearly jumped out of her skin – 'Oh, you gave me such a start!' she said, chuckling merrily as if I had played a waggish joke on her – which left me with the impression that visitors were perhaps somewhat occasional. Anyway, she seemed glad to have me and, after accepting my $3 admission, urged me to take my time and come straight to her if I had any questions.

The museum was quite large and filled with the most extraordinary collection of stuff – flat irons, boot lasts, a buggy, old lanterns, odd fragments of machinery. Except for the absence of cobwebs, I could have been in my grandfather's barn. In a corner of the main room I found the centrepiece of the museum's collection – the large banner that the rioters carried in 1861. It is known as 'the roll-up flag' because neatly embroidered across it are the words: 'Roll Up. Roll Up. No Chinese.' In his book *A Secret Country*, which I had read before coming to Australia, the Australian journalist John Pilger suggests that the Lambing Flat Museum rather glorifies the event and offers nothing in the way of contrition. If that was true when Pilger visited – his book was published in 1991 – it no longer is. The labels give a balanced and thoughtful account of the riots, though again with a curious blankness regarding casualty numbers on either side.

The museum went on and on, and seemed to contain everything that everyone in Young had ever acquired and no longer wanted – sewing machines, adding machines, rifles, wedding albums, christening gowns. On a table was a large jar filled with small shiny black spheres, thousands of them. I peered at it, trying to figure out what it was.

'Canola seeds,' said a voice, quite near – so near it made me jump. I turned to find the lady who had let me in.

'Oh! You made me jump,' I said and she smiled in a way that made me suspect that that had been her intention. Perhaps, it occurred to me, that was how people passed the time in Young.

'Are you finding everything?' she asked.

I looked at her with interest. How would I know if I was or not? But I replied: 'Yes, I am,' then added politely: 'It's very interesting.'

'Yes, there's a lot of history in Young,' she agreed, and looked around as if thinking perhaps there was too much.

My gaze returned to the jar of seeds. 'Do you grow a lot of canola around here?' I asked.

'No,' she said simply.

I considered this and tried to think of something more to say. 'Well, you've got the seeds if you decide to start,' I observed helpfully.

'Some people call it . . . *rape*,' she said, all but whispering the last word and raising her eyebrows significantly.

'Yes,' I agreed in what I believe was a concerned tone.

'I prefer canola.'

'Me, too.' I don't know why I said that. I have no position on seed names, however emotive, but it seemed prudent to agree with her.

Mercifully, just then a bell went – the kind of bell that sounds when someone comes in a shop entrance – and she excused herself. I waited half a dozen beats then followed her out, for I had seen all I needed to and I wanted to get a move on.

In the front hallway a middle-aged couple were in the process of buying tickets. The space was confined and I had to wait for them to step aside to let me out, and I thanked the white-haired lady as I passed.

'You enjoyed it, did you?' she asked.

'Very much,' I lied.

'Here on holiday?' asked the lady customer, presumably picking up on my accent.

'Yes, I am,' I lied again.

'How are you enjoying Australia?'

'I love it.' This was not a lie, but she looked at me doubtfully. 'Honestly,' I added.

Then a rather strange thing – well, I thought it was strange. The female customer placed a hand on my forearm and said, with a touch of real anxiety: 'I hope everyone is nice to you.'

I looked at her.

'Of course they will be,' I said. 'Australians are always nice.'

She gave me a look of imploring earnestness. 'Do you really think so?' Now don't get me wrong. Australians are the most wonderful people, but when they grow introspective it's sometimes a little strange.

I nodded. 'Really,' I said reassuringly. 'Australians are always nice.'

'Course they are, Maureen!' barked her husband. 'Salt of the earth. Now let the poor man go. I'm sure he has places he wants to be.' He was clearly from the other, heartier school of Australian archetypes – the one that thinks that any bloke not lucky enough to be born in Australia is tragically ill-favoured by fate and probably has a tiny dick as well, poor bastard.

And he was right, of course – about having places to be, I mean. It was time to move on to Canberra.

I

Before Australia's six colonies federated in 1901, they were, to an almost ludicrous degree, separate. Each issued its own postage stamps, set clocks to its own time, had its own system of taxes and levies. As Geoffrey Blainey notes in *A Shorter History of Australia*, a pub owner in Wodonga, in Victoria, who wished to sell beer brewed in Albury, on the opposite bank of the Murray River in New South Wales, paid as much duty as he did on beer shipped from Europe. Clearly this was madness. So in 1891, the six colonies (plus New Zealand, which nearly joined, but later dropped out) met in Sydney to discuss forming a proper nation, to be known as the Commonwealth of Australia. It took some years to iron everything out, but on 1 January 1901 a new nation was declared.

Because Sydney and Melbourne were so closely matched in terms of pre-eminence, it was agreed in a spirit of compromise to build a new capital somewhere in the bush. Melbourne, meanwhile, would serve as interim capital.

Years were consumed with squabbles about where the capital should be sited before the selectors eventually settled on an obscure farming community on the edge of the Tidbinbilla Hills in southern New South Wales. It was called Canberra, though the name by then was often anglicized to Canberry. Cold in the winter, blazing hot in the summer, miles from anywhere, it was an unlikely choice of location for a national capital. About 900 square miles of surrounding territory, most of it pastoral and pretty nearly useless, was ceded by New South Wales to form the Australian Capital Territory, a federal zone on the model of America's District of Columbia.

So the young nation had a capital. The next challenge was what to call it, and yet more periods of passion and rancour were consumed with settling the matter. King O'Malley, the American-born politician who was a driving force behind federation, wanted to call the new capital Shakespeare. Other suggested names were Myola, Wheatwoolgold, Emu, Eucalypta, Sydmeladperbrisho (the first syllables of the state capitals), Opossum, Gladstone, Thirstyville, Kookaburra, Cromwell and the ringingly inane Victoria Defendera Defender. In the end, Canberra won more or less by default. At an official ceremony to mark the decision, the wife of the Governor-General stood up before a gathering of dignitaries and, 'in a querulous voice', announced that the winning name was the one that had been in use all along. Unfortunately, no one had thought to brief her, and she mispronounced it, placing the accent emphatically on the middle syllable rather than lightly on the first. Never mind. The young nation had a site for a capital and a name for a capital, and it had taken them just eleven years since union to get there. At this blistering pace, all being well, they might get a city going within half a century or so. In fact, it would take rather longer.

Although Canberra is now one of the largest cities in the nation and one of the most important planned communities on earth, it remains Australia's greatest obscurity. As national capitals go, it is still not an easy place to get to. It lies forty miles off the main road from Sydney to Melbourne, the Hume Highway, and is similarly spurned by the principal railway lines. Its main road to the south doesn't go anywhere much and the city has no approach at all from the west other than on a dirt track from the little town of Tumut.

In 1996 the Prime Minister, John Howard, caused a stir after his election by declining to live in Canberra. He would, he announced, continue to reside in Sydney and commute to Canberra as duties required. As you can imagine, this caused an uproar among Canberra's citizens, presumably because they hadn't thought of it themselves. What made this particularly interesting is that John Howard is by far the dullest man in Australia. Imagine a very committed funeral home director – someone whose burning ambition from the age of eleven was to be a funeral home director, whose proudest achievement in adulthood was to be elected president of the Queanbeyan and District Funeral Home Directors' Association – then halve his personality and halve it again, and you have pretty well got John Howard. When a man as outstandingly colourless as John Howard turns his nose up at a place you know it must be worth a look. I couldn't wait to see it.

You approach Canberra along a dual carriageway

129

through rural woodland, which gradually morphs into a slightly more urban boulevard, though still in woodland, until finally you arrive at a zone of well-spaced but significant-looking buildings and you realize that you are there – or as near there as you can get in a place as scattered and vague as Canberra. It's a very strange city, in that it's not really a city at all, but rather an extremely large park with a city hidden in it. It's all lawns and trees and hedges and a big ornamental lake – all very agreeable, just a little unexpected.

I took a room in the Hotel Rex for no other reason than that I happened upon it and had never stayed in a hotel named for a family pet. The Hotel Rex was exactly what you would expect a large hotel built of concrete and called the Rex to be. But I didn't care. I was eager to stretch my legs and gambol about in all that green space. So I checked in, dumped my bags and returned at once to the open air. I'd passed a visitors' centre on the way in, and recollected it as being a short walk away, so I decided to start there. In the event, it was a long way – a very long way, as things in Canberra invariably prove to be.

The visitors' centre was almost ready to close when I got there, and in any case was just an outlet for leaflets and brochures for tourist attractions and places to stay. In a side room was a small cinema showing one of those desperately upbeat promotional films with a title like *Canberra – It's Got It All!* – the ones that boast how you can water ski and shop for an evening gown *and* have a pizza all in the same day because this place has . . . *got it all*! You know the kind I mean. But I watched the film happily because the room was air conditioned and it was a pleasure to sit after walking so far.

It was just as well that I didn't require an evening gown

or a pizza or water skiing when I returned to the street because I couldn't find a thing anywhere. My one tip for you if you ever go to Canberra is don't leave your hotel without a good map, a compass, several days' provisions and a mobile phone with the number of a rescue service. I walked for two hours through green, pleasant, endlessly identical neighbourhoods, never entirely confident that I wasn't just going round in a large circle. From time to time I would come to a leafy roundabout with roads radiating off in various directions, each presenting an identical vista of antipodean suburban heaven, and I would venture down the one that looked most likely to take me to civilization only to emerge ten minutes later at another identical roundabout. I never saw another soul on foot or anyone watering a lawn or anything like that. Very occasionally a car would glide past, pausing at each intersection, the driver looking around with a despairing expression that said: 'Now where the fuck is my house?'

I had it in mind that I would find a handsome pub of the type that I had so often enjoyed in Sydney – a place filled with office workers winding down at the end of a long day, so popular at this hour that there would be an overspill of happy people on the pavement. This would be followed by dinner in a neighbourhood bistro of charm and hearty portions. But diversions of this or any other type seemed signally lacking in the sleepy streets of Canberra. Eventually, and abruptly, I turned a corner and was in the central business district. Here at last were stores and restaurants and all the other commercial amenities of a city, but all were closed. Downtown Canberra was primarily a series of plazas wandering between retail premises, and devoid of any sign of life but for a noise of slap and clatter that I recognized after a moment as the sound of skateboards. Having nothing better to do, I followed the sounds to an open square where half a dozen adolescents, all in backward-facing baseball caps and baggy shorts, were honing their modest and misguided skills on a metal railing. I sat for a minute on a bench and with morbid interest watched them risking compound fractures and severe testicular trauma for the fleeting satisfaction of sliding along a banister for a distance of from zero inches to a couple of feet before being launched by gravity and the impossibility of maintaining balance into space in the direction of an expanse of unyielding pavement. It seemed a remarkably foolish enterprise.

If there is anything more half-witted than asking six adolescents in backward-facing baseball caps for a dining recommendation then it doesn't occur to me just at the moment, but I'm afraid this is what I did now.

'Are you an American?' asked one of the kids in a tone of surprise that I wouldn't necessarily have expected to encounter in a world capital.

I allowed that I was.

'There's a McDonald's just around the corner.'

Gently I explained that it was not actually a condition of citizenship that I eat the food of my nation. 'I was thinking of maybe a nice Thai restaurant,' I suggested.

They looked at me with that flummoxed, dead-end expression that you have to be fourteen years old to produce with conviction.

'Or perhaps an Indian?' I offered hopefully and got the same no-one-home look. 'Indonesian?' I went on. 'Vietnamese? Lebanese? Greek? Mexican? West Indian? Malaysian?'

As the list grew, they shifted uncomfortably, as if fearing

that I was going to hold them individually accountable for the inadequacies of the local culinary scene.

'Italian?' I said.

'There's a Pizza Hut on Lonsdale Street,' piped up one with a look of triumph. 'They do an all-you-can-eat buffet on Tuesdays.'

'Thanks,' I said, realizing this was getting me nowhere, and started to leave, but then turned back. 'It's Friday today,' I pointed out.

'Yeah,' the kid agreed, nodding solemnly. 'They don't do it on Fridays.'

I found my way back to the Rex, but got only as far as the front entrance when I realized that I did not want to dine in my own hotel. It is such a tame and lonely thing to do – an admission that one has no life. As it happened, I had no life, but that wasn't quite the point. Do you know what is the most melancholy part of dining alone in your hotel? It's when they come and take away all the other place settings and wine glasses, as if to say: 'Obviously no one will be joining *you* tonight, so we'll just whip away all these things and seat you here facing a pillar, and in a minute we'll bring you a very large basket with just one roll in it. Enjoy!'

So I lingered by the entrance of the Rex for the merest moment, then returned to the street. I was on a boulevard built on an important scale, though it had almost no traffic and was mostly lined with darkened office buildings lurking in dense growth. Several hundred yards further on I came to a hotel not unlike the Rex. It contained an Italian restaurant with its own entrance, which was probably as good as I was going to get. I went in and was taken aback to realize that it was full of locals, dressed up as if for an occasion. Something in their familiar manner with the waiters, and with the surroundings generally, bespoke a more than transient relationship with the place. When locals eat in the restaurant of a big glass and concrete hotel, you know that the community must be in some measure wanting.

The waiter took away all the other place settings, but he brought me six breadsticks – enough to share if I made a friend. It was quite a jolly place with everyone around me getting comprehensively refreshed – the Australians do like a drink, bless them – and the food was outstanding, but it was nonetheless evident that we were dining in a hotel. Canberra has quite a lot of this, as I was to discover – eating and drinking in large, characterless hotels and other neutral spaces, so that you spend much of the time feeling as if you are on some kind of long layover at an extremely spacious international airport.

Afterwards, bloated with pasta, three bottles of Italian lager and all six of the breadsticks (I never did make a friend), I went for another exploratory amble, this time in a slightly contrary direction, certain that somewhere in Canberra there must be a normal pub and possibly a convivial restaurant for the following evening, but I passed nothing and once again found myself eventually on the threshold of the Rex. I looked at my watch. It was only nine thirty in the evening. I wandered into the cocktail lounge, where I ordered a beer and took a seat in a deep-backed chair. The lounge was empty but for a table with three men and a lady at it, getting boisterously merry, and a lone gent hunched over a tumbler at the bar.

I drank my beer and pulled out a small notebook and pen and placed them on the table in front of me in case I was taken with a sudden important observation, then followed that with a book I had bought at a second-hand bookshop in Sydney. Called *Inside Australia* and published in 1972, it was by the American journalist John Gunther, a name that once towered in the annals of travel journalism but is now, I fear, largely forgotten. It was his last book; it just about had to be as he died while preparing it, poor man.

I opened it to the chapter on Canberra, curious to see what he had to say about the place back then. The Canberra he describes is a small city of 130,000 people with the 'pastoral feeling of a country town' – an easygoing place with few traffic lights, little nightlife, a modest sprinkling of cocktail lounges and about 'half a dozen good' restaurants. In a word, it appeared actually to have gone backwards since 1972. I was proud to see that the Rex Hotel was singled out as a stylish address for visitors – always nice to see one's choices validated even when they are nearly thirty years out of date – and that its cocktail bar was adjudged one of the liveliest in the city. I looked up from my book and shrank at the thought that very possibly it still was.

At length I turned to the chapter on Australian politics – my reason for buying the book in the first place. Apart from the scoring of Australian Rules Football and the appeal of a much-esteemed dish called the pie floater (think of something unappetizing and brown floating on top of something unappetizing and green and you pretty well have it) there is nothing in Australian life more complicated and bewildering to the outsider than its politics. I had tried once or twice to wade through books on Australian politics written by Australians, but all these had started from the novel premise that the subject is interesting – a bold position, to be sure, but not a very helpful one – so I was hoping that the detached observations of a

135

fellow American might be more instructive. Gunther gave it a game stab, I must say, but it was a challenge beyond even his talents for lucid compression. Here, for instance, is just a snippet of his attempt to explain Australia's system of preference voting:

> If, after the second-preference votes are added to the first, there is still no candidate with a majority of the total ballots cast, the process is repeated: the ballots of the candidate trailing at this stage of the computation are divided up on the basis of second preference. If he inherited some second preference votes from the first man eliminated, these are now redistributed on the basis of third preference. And so on.

I particularly liked that casual concluding 'And so on.' It's a deft piece of work because it seems to say: 'I understand all this perfectly, but I see no need to tax you with the details,' whereas of course what he is really saying is: 'I haven't the faintest idea what any of this means and frankly I don't give two tiny mouse droppings because, as I pen these words, I am sitting in the lounge bar of a bush mausoleum called the Rex Hotel and it's a Friday night and I am half cut and bored out of my mind and now I am going to go and get another drink.' The uncanny thing was I knew the feeling exactly.

I glanced at my watch, appalled to realize it was only ten minutes after ten, and ordered another beer, then picked up the notebook and pen and, after a minute's thought, wrote: 'Canberra awfully boring place. Beer cold, though.' Then I thought for a bit more and wrote: 'Buy socks.' Then I put the notebook down, but not away, and tried without much success to eavesdrop on the conversation among the lively foursome across the room. Then I decided to come up with a new slogan for Canberra. First I wrote: 'Canberra – There's Nothing to It!' and then 'Canberra – Why Wait for Death?' Then I thought some more and wrote: 'Canberra – Gateway to Everywhere Else!', which I believe I liked best of all. Then I ordered another beer and drew a little cartoon. It showed two spawning salmon, halfway up a series of lively cascades, resting exhausted in a pool of calm water, when one turns to the other and says: 'Why don't we just stop here and have a wank?' This amused me very much and I put the page in my pocket against the day I learn to draw objects that people can actually recognize. Then I eavesdropped on the people some more, nodding and smiling appreciatively when they appeared to make a quip in the hope that they would see me and invite me over, but they didn't. Then I had another beer.

I think the last beer might have been a mistake because I don't remember much after that other than a sensation of supreme goodwill towards anyone who passed through the room, including a Filipino lady who came in with a hoover and asked me to lift my legs so that she could clean under my chair. My notes for the evening show only two other entries, both in a slightly unsteady hand. One says: 'Victoria Bitter – why called??? Not bitter at all. But quite nice!!!' The other said: 'I tell you, Barry, he was farting sparks!' I believe this was in reference to a colourful Aussie turn of phrase I overheard from the people at the next table rather than to any actual manifestation of flatulence of an electrical nature.

But I could be wrong. I'd had a few.

In the morning I woke to find Canberra puddled under a dull, persistent rain. My plan was to stroll across the main bridge over Lake Burley Griffin, to a district of museums and government buildings on the other side. It was a rotten morning, a foolish day to be out on foot, made more wretched by the slow-dawning realization, once I had set off from the hotel, that I was embarked on an expedition even more epic than the one the afternoon before. Canberra really is the most amazingly spacious city. On paper it looks quite inviting, with its serpentine lake, leafy avenues and 10,000 acres of parks (for purposes of comparison, Hyde Park in London is 340 acres), but at ground level it is simply a great deal of far-flung greenness, broken at distant intervals by buildings and monuments.

It is worth considering how it got this way. In 1911, with the capital site chosen, a competition was held for a design for it, which was won by Walter Burley Griffin of Oak Park, Illinois, a disciple of Frank Lloyd Wright. Griffin's design was unquestionably the best, but that doesn't necessarily mean a great deal. Another leading entrant, a Frenchman named Alfred Agache, failed to read the briefing notes carefully, or possibly at all, and placed Parliament and many other important buildings on a flood plain, guaranteeing that legislators would have to spend part of the year treading water while debating. Also, for reasons that can only invite wondered speculation, he placed the municipal sewage works in the very heart of the city, as a kind of centrepiece. Despite these quirky shortcomings, his entry came third. Second prize went to Eliel Saarinen, father of Eero, the man who later persuaded the Opera House judges to choose the bold design of Jørn Utzon. The elder Saarinen's design was perfectly workable, but it had a kind of brutal grandeur about it – a sort of proto-Third Reichish quality – that unsettled the Australian judges.

Griffin's plan, by contrast, was instantly engaging. It

envisaged a garden city of 75,000 people, with tree-lined avenues angling through it and an ornamental lake at its heart. Handsome and confident, majestic but not imperious, it ideally suited the modest yearnings for respectability without fuss that marked the Australian character. Moreover, Griffin had an advanced understanding of the importance of presentation. His submissions were not modest sketches that looked as if they had been scribbled on the back of a cocktail napkin, but a series of large panoramic tableaux, exquisitely drafted on the finest stretched linen. In this he was assisted inestimably – totally, in fact – by his new bride, Marion Mahony Griffin, who was without doubt one of the great architectural artists of this century.

The drawings, all done by Marion, show a silhouetted skyline full of comely shapes – a dome here, a ziggurat there – but with surprisingly little in the way of committing details. They are tantalizing impressions – ethereal, cunningly distant. These are drawings you could gaze at for hours with pleasure, but turn your back for a moment and you cannot remember a thing that was in them, other than a vague sense of a pleasing composition. Although Griffin and his wife had never been to Australia (they worked from topographic maps) the drawings show an almost uncanny affinity for the landscape – an appreciation of its simple uncluttered beauty and big skies that you would swear was based on the closest acquaintance-ship. Take nothing away from Walter: he was a gifted, occasionally even inspired, architect; but Marion was the genius of the outfit.

The Griffins had a decidedly bohemian bent – he liked big floppy hats and velvety ties; she had an unfortunate fondness for dancing through woodland glades in diaphanous gowns, in the manner of Isadora Duncan – and this no doubt counted against them in the rough and ready world of Australian politics in the second decade of the century. In any case, they found little in the way of funds or enthusiasm awaiting them when they arrived in Australia in 1913, and the outbreak of the First World War the following year made both scarcer still. Once on site, Griffin seemed unable to get to grips with things. He had no experience of managing a big project and clearly it did not suit his temperament. By 1920, no work at all had been done beyond a cursory staking out of the main roads. At the end of the year, more or less by mutual agreement, he left the project.

Griffin stayed in Australia another fifteen years and became one of the country's most illustrious architects, but nearly all the buildings he designed either were never built or have since been torn down. Increasingly beset by financial difficulties, he moved to India in 1935. There, in 1937 he contracted peritonitis after falling from some scaffolding and died, aged sixty. He was buried in an unmarked grave. Today almost all that remains from a long and busy career are Newman College at the University of Melbourne, a couple of municipal incinerators, and Canberra – and Canberra isn't really his at all.

Only the floor plan, so to speak, is his – the avenues, the roundabouts, the lake that cuts the city in half. The component parts fell to scores of other hands, none working together. An entirely new city was built on his layout, but it has none of the coherence that his design implied. It's really just a scattering of government buildings in a man-made wilderness. Even the lake, which winds a serpentine way between the commercial and parliamentary halves of the city, has a curiously dull, artificial feel. On a sloping promontory on its wooded north shore was a modestly sized building called the National Capital Exhibition, and I called there first, more in the hope of drying off a little than from any expectation of extending my education significantly.

It was quite busy. In the front entrance, two friendly ladies were seated at a table handing out free visitors' packs – big, bright yellow plastic bags – and these were accepted with expressions of gratitude and rapture by everyone who passed.

'Care for a visitors' pack, sir?' called one of the ladies to me.

'Oh, yes please,' I said, more thrilled than I wish to admit. The visitors' pack was a weighty offering, but on inspection it proved to contain nothing but a mass of brochures – the complete works, it appeared, of the visitors' centre I had visited the day before. The bag was so heavy that it stretched the handles until it was touching the floor. I dragged it around for a while, and then thought to abandon it behind a pot plant. And here's the thing. There wasn't room behind the pot plant for another yellow bag! There must have been ninety of them back there. I looked around and noticed that almost no one in the room still had a plastic bag. I leaned mine against the wall beside the plant and as I straightened up I saw that a man was advancing towards me.

'Is this where the bags go?' he asked gravely.

'Yes, it is,' I replied with equal gravity.

In my momentary capacity as director of internal operations I watched him lean the bag carefully against the wall. Then we stood for a moment together and regarded it judiciously, pleased to have contributed to the important work of moving hundreds of yellow bags from the foyer to a mustering station in the next room. As we stood, two more people came along. 'Place them just there,' we suggested, almost in unison, and indicated where we were sandbagging the wall. Then we exchanged satisfied nods and moved off into the museum.

The National Capital Exhibition was excellent. These things in Australia generally are. It wasn't a large building, but it gave a good grounding in the history and development of Canberra. What surprised me was how very recent most of it is. Several of the walls had blown-up photographs of Canberra as it was in times past, and most of these were arresting when compared with the present. Lake Burley Griffin,* for instance, wasn't filled until 1964. Before that, for many years, it was just a muddy depression between the two halves of the city. On another wall a pair of matched aerial photographs showed Canberra in 1959 (pop. 39,000) and Canberra now (pop. 330,000). Apart from the addition of a few large buildings in what is known as the Parliamentary Zone and the filling of the lake, what was remarkable was how little changed the city looked.

Thus briefed, I was eager now to see it all with my own eyes, so I left the building and ventured along the wooded lakeside to the Commonwealth Avenue Bridge and set off for the distant and, as it were, official side of the city. The rain had stopped, but Lake Burley Griffin contains an engineering wonder (the wonder being why they bothered) called the Captain Cook Memorial Jet, a plume of water that shoots a couple of hundred feet into the air in a dazzlingly unarresting manner, then catches the prevailing

---

* Whoever named the lake evidently didn't realize that Burley was Walter's middle name, not part of his surname.

breeze and drifts in a fine but drenching spray over the bridge and whatever is on it. Sighing, I pushed through it and emerged on the other side into an area of the most extravagantly spacious lawns, punctuated at distant intervals with government buildings and museums, each as remote as objects viewed through the wrong end of a telescope.

Even the National Capital Authority, the governing body for the city, admits in a promotional fact sheet that 'many people believe the Parliamentary Zone has an empty and unfinished character, where the vast distances between the institutions and other facilities discourage pedestrian movement and activity.' I'll say. It was like walking around the site of a very large world's fair that had never quite got off the ground.

I called first at the National Library because I wanted to see the *Endeavour* Journal, Captain Cook's famous diary of his voyage. Cook naturally took the journal home with him after his epic trip of discovery, but it was lost soon after his death and remained lost for almost one hundred and fifty years before it turned up unexpectedly at a Sotheby's auction in London in 1923. The Australian government hurriedly bought it for £5,000 (almost double what it was prepared to pay for the design of the city in which it sits) and it is now treated with the sort of reverence we in America reserve for ancient treasures like the Constitution and Nancy Reagan. Unfortunately, as I discovered when I presented myself at the information desk, it isn't out on display, but rather is shown just once a week by appointment.

I stared at the man in dismay. 'But I've travelled eight thousand miles,' I blurted.

'I'm sorry,' he said and seemed to mean it.

'I spent a night in the Rex,' I said, thinking surely that would clinch it, but he was powerless to help. He did, however, direct me to a leaflet in which I could see a picture of the journal and encouraged me to have a look round the public galleries. As it happened, these were splendid. One room held paintings showing Australians of note (well, of note to other Australians) and in another was an exhibition of the original drawings for the Sydney Opera House. These included not only Utzon's winning sketches, but the second and third place entries – both radiantly undistinguished. Second place went to a fat cylinder with a harlequin-style pattern in stainless steel. Third place looked like a large supermarket. In a glass case was a wooden model made by Utzon showing that the sails of the Opera House roof were not meant to echo the sailboats in the harbour (an assertion that is made over and over in books and articles, inside Australia and out) but are simply sections of a sphere.

Then it was across another thousand acres of un-developed veldt to the National Gallery, a surprisingly big museum in a fortress-like building. It was airy and various and generally very good. I was particularly taken with the outback paintings of Arthur Streeton, of whom I had not heard, and with the large collection of Aboriginal paint-ings, mostly done on curled bark or other natural surfaces and covered in colourful dots and squiggles. It is a fact little noted that the Aborigines have the oldest continu-ously maintained culture on earth, and their art goes back to the very roots of it. Imagine if there were some people in France who could take you to the caves at Lascaux and explain in detail the significance of the paintings – why this bison is bolting from the herd, what these three wavy lines mean – because it is as fresh and sensible to them as if it were done yesterday. Well, Aborigines can do that. It is an unparalleled human achievement, scarcely appreciated, and I think that is worth a mention here, don't you agree?

I had intended to go on to Parliament House, but I emerged from the National Gallery to find that the afternoon was almost gone. I would have to leave that for the next day. I started back down the gentle slope towards the lake and bridge. The skies were clearing at last and on the far-off hills lay patches of silvery light. Now that the clouds had ceased their low-level assault and retired to fluffier heights, the view was really quite fine. Canberra is a city of memorials, most of them fairly grand and nearly all with a private avenue of trees, and from here I could take them in with a single panning motion of my head. It reminded me less of a city – much less – than of, say, a preserved battlefield. There was that sense of spaciousness and respectful greenness that you would expect to find at Gettysburg or Waterloo.

It was impossible to believe that 330,000 people were tucked into that view and it was this thought – startling when it hit me – that made me change my perception of Canberra completely. I had been scorning it for what was in fact its most admirable achievement. This was a place that had, without a twitch of evident stress, multiplied by a factor of ten since the late 1950s and yet was still a park.

I imagined some sweet little American community such as Aspen, Colorado, trying to absorb 300,000 additional residents in forty years and thought of the miles of random, carelessly dribbled infrastructure that that would require – the shopping malls and parking lots, the eight-lane roads stretching off into a forest of bright signs and elevated hoardings, the vast graded acres of housing (bye, woods! bye, farm!), the distant plazas of supermarkets and box stores, the tangled ganglia of motels, petrol stations and fast food places. Well, there is virtually none of this in Canberra. What an accomplishment that is. My feeling for the place was transformed entirely.

Still, I must say a decent pub or two wouldn't go amiss.

II

Now here is why you will never understand Australian politics. In 1972, after twenty-three years of rule by the conservative Liberal Party, Australia elected a Labor government under the leadership of the dashing and urbane Gough Whitlam. At once Whitlam's government embarked on a programme of ambitious reforms – it gave Aborigines rights they had not previously enjoyed, began to disengage Australian troops from Vietnam, made university education free, and much more. But, as sometimes happens, the government gradually lost its majority and by 1975 Parliament was in a deadlock from which neither Whitlam nor the leader of the opposition, Malcolm Fraser, would budge.

Into this impasse stepped the Governor-General, Sir John Kerr, the Queen's official representative in Australia. Using a reserve privilege not before invoked, he dissolved Whitlam's government, placed Fraser in control and ordered a general election. The outrage and indignation Australians felt at this high-handed interference can scarcely be described. The country was thrown into a fury of resentment. Before they had had any real chance to sort out their differences themselves, an unelected representative of a government on the other side of the planet had taken the matter out of their hands. It was a humiliating reminder that Australia was still at root a colony, constitutionally subordinate to the United Kingdom.

Nonetheless, as required, the Australians held a general election at which the voters overwhelmingly – overwhelmingly – turned Whitlam out of office and brought in Fraser. In other words, the electorate calmly endorsed the action that had so exercised the nation only a month before.

And that, as I say, is why you will never understand Australian politics.

Part of the problem, of course, is that it is nearly impossible to track Australian politics from abroad because so little news of the country's affairs leaks out into the wider world. But even when you are there and dutifully trying to follow it, you find yourself mired in a density of argument, a complexity of fine points, a skein of tangled relationships and enmities, that thwarts all understanding. Give Australians an issue and they will argue it so passionately and in such detail, from so many angles, with the introduction of so many loosely connected side issues, that it soon becomes impenetrable to the outsider.

At the time of my visit the big national issue was whether Australia was to become a republic – whether it was going to snip its last colonial ties to Britain and take the steps necessary to ensure that no future John Kerr ever similarly humbled the nation again. It seemed to me no issue. Surely any nation would want to have control of its own destiny? You would expect, at the very least, that the decision would be a straightforward one.

Yet for two years to my certain knowledge Australians had been tying themselves in knots over every possible objection to such a change. Who will be the new president under such a system and how can we guarantee that he

147

never does anything he shouldn't do? What becomes of all those names like 'Royal Australian Air Force' and 'Royal Flying Doctor Service' if we're not actually royal any longer? What words shall we put in the new preamble to the constitution? Shall we refer to the Australian quality of 'mateship' as John Howard would like or shall we recognize that that is a fundamentally vacuous and embarrassing concept? Oh dear, this is awfully complicated. Maybe it would be better if we just left things as they are, and hope the British are good to us.

I don't mean to suggest that these are not important issues, of course. But it is an exhausting process to witness, and you do rather come away with two interlinked impressions – that Australians love to argue for argument's sake and that basically they would rather just leave everything as it is. In the end, of course, they voted against a republic, though at the time of my visit that seemed an extremely unlikely outcome. Yet another reason why outsiders will never understand Australian politics.

On the other hand, and what makes up for a lot, is that Australians have the best and most entertaining parliamentary debates anywhere. American and even British television news coverage would be vastly enlivened if it provided a nightly report from Australia's parliamentary chambers. You wouldn't have to explain what it was all about – it generally surpasses understanding anyway – but just allow the audience to savour the rich thrust and parry of Australian insult.

In his book *Among the Barbarians*, the Australian writer Paul Sheehan records an exchange in Parliament between a man named Wilson Tuckey and the then Prime Minister Paul Keating of which the following is a small part:

> *Tuckey: 'You are an idiot. You are just a hopeless nong . . .'*
> *Keating: 'Shut up! Sit down and shut up, you pig . . . Why*
> *do you not shut up, you clown? . . . This man has a crim-*
> *inal intellect . . . this clown continues to interject in*
> *perpetuity.'*

This was actually a fairly tame exchange for the linguistically versatile Mr Keating. Among the epithets that have taken flight from his tongue during the course of public debate, and are to be found gracing the pages of whatever is the Australian equivalent of *Hansard*, have been *scumbags, pieces of criminal garbage, sleazebags, stupid foul-mouthed grubs, piss-ants, mangy maggots, perfumed gigolos, gutless spivs, boxheads, immoral cheats,* and *stunned mullets.* And that was just to describe his mother. (I'm joking, of course!) Not all parliamentary invective is quite so ripe, but it is nearly all pretty good.

I had watched this sort of thing with the greatest of pleasure during my various Australian visits, so you can imagine the eagerness with which I parked my car in the visitors' area on Parliament Hill the next morning and proceeded across the manicured lawns for a quick look round before moving on to Adelaide.

Parliament House is a new building, which replaced an older, more modest Parliament House in 1988. It is a rather arrestingly horrible edifice, crowned with a ridiculous erection that looks like nothing so much as a very big Christmas-tree stand. On the way in, I stopped beside a large ornamental pool to have a look at the rooftop erection.

'Largest aluminium structure in the southern hemisphere,' declared, with evident pride, a man with a camera around his neck who saw me studying it.

'And are there many other aluminium structures competing for the honour?' I asked before I could stop myself.

The man looked flustered. 'Why, I don't know,' he said. 'But if there are they're smaller.'

I hadn't meant to offend. 'Well, it's certainly very . . . striking,' I offered.

'Yes,' he agreed. 'I think that's the word for it. Striking.'

'How much aluminium is in it?' I asked.

'Oh, I've no idea. But a great deal, you can be sure of that.'

'Enough to wrap a lot of sandwiches!' I suggested brightly.

He looked at me as if I were dangerously stupid. 'I don't know about that,' he said and, after a moment's befuddled hesitation, took his leave.

As it was a Sunday morning, I hadn't expected Parliament House to be open to visitors, but it was. I had to submit to a security inspection and had a small pocket-knife taken away from me and twenty minutes later was sawing away on a scone in the cafeteria with something far more lethal. The whole of Parliament House is rather like that – superficially grave and security-conscious, in keeping with the trappings of an important nation, but at the same time really quite relaxed, as if they know that no international terrorists are going to come storming over the parapets and that visitors are mostly just people like you and me who want to see where it all happens and then have a nice cup of tea and a cautiously flavourful treat in the cafeteria afterwards.

Inside it was much handsomer than the bland exterior had suggested, with a lot of native woods covering the floors and walls. Best of all, you weren't herded round in a group but left to explore on your own. I have never been in America's Capitol Building, but I dare say they don't just leave you to wander as whimsy takes you. I felt here as if I could go anywhere – that if I had known which was the right door I could have slipped into the Prime Minister's office and scribbled a note on his blotter or perhaps left my salmon cartoon to brighten his day. A couple of times I furtively tried door handles. They were always locked, but no alarms went off and no security people crashed through the windows to smother me with nets and take me away for interrogation. In the areas where security people were posted, they were always friendly and happy to answer any questions. I was very impressed.

Australia's Parliament is divided into two chambers, the House of Representatives and the Senate (interesting, in a very low-grade sort of way, that they use the British term for the institution and the American terms for the chambers), and both of these were open for inspection from the visitors' galleries. Both were quite small, but handsomer than I had expected. On television the green of the House of Representatives has a decidedly bilious look, as if the members are debating inside someone's pancreas, but in person it was much more tasteful and restrained. The Senate, which I had never seen on television (I believe because the Senators don't actually *do* anything – though I will check my John Gunther and get back to you on this), was in a restful ochre tone.

In a large upstairs foyer was a gallery containing portraits in oil of all the Prime Ministers, which I toured with interest. I had been doing quite a lot of reading, as you can imagine, so there was a real pleasure – a genuine oh-I've-heard-so-much-about-you quality – in seeing their faces at last. Here was kindly old Ben Chifley, a Labor PM just after the war and so much a man of the people that when in Canberra he stayed in the modest Kurrajong Hotel at a cost to the taxpayer of just six shillings a day, and could be found each morning strolling in his dressing gown to the communal bathroom to shave and wash with the other guests. Then there was the grand and leonine Robert Menzies, who was Prime Minister for twenty years but thought of himself as 'British to the bootstraps' and dreamed of retiring to a cottage in the English countryside, evidently happy to turn his back on his native soil for ever. And poor old Harold Holt whose fateful plunge into the sea in 1967 earned him my permanent devotion.

It's quite a small club. Since 1901 Australia has had just twenty-four Prime Ministers, and I was startled to realize how many of them remained unfamiliar to me. Of the twenty-four, I counted fourteen of whom I knew essentially nothing, including eight – exactly one third – of whom I had not even heard. These included the festively named Sir Earle Christmas Grafton Page, who was, to be fair, Prime Minister for less than a month in 1939, but also William McMahon, who held the office for almost two years in the early 1970s and whose existence was until this moment quite unsuspected by me.

I would have felt worse about this except that only the day before I had read an article in the papers reporting a government study that had found that Australians themselves were essentially as ignorant of these men as I was – that indeed more people in Australia could identify and discuss the achievements of George Washington than could provide similar service for their own first elected head of state, Sir Edmund Barton.

And with that sobering thought to ponder, I left the nation's capital and set off for distant Adelaide.

Chapter

SEVEN

It is 800 miles from Canberra west to Adelaide, most of it along a lonely, half-forgotten road called the Sturt Highway. The highway was named for Captain Charles Sturt, who explored the region in a series of expeditions between 1828 and 1845. Apart from charting the languid course of the Murray River and its tributaries, Sturt's principal distinction was in being the first of the early explorers to show a measure of competence. He knew, for instance, to secure his horses at night. This might seem a self-evident requirement for anyone hundreds of miles into a desolate void, but it was a skill indifferently applied before him. John Oxley, the leader of a slightly earlier expedition, failed to keep his horses tethered and woke up one morning to find them all gone. He and his men spent five days, mostly on foot, rounding them all up. Soon after, the horses wandered off again. Nonetheless, Oxley is commemorated with a highway of his own in northern New South Wales. Australians are very generous in this respect.

The Sturt Highway begins near Wagga Wagga, a hundred miles or so west of Canberra, and crosses broad, flat, dust-brown sheep country known as the Riverina, an area of plains cut by the fidgety meanderings of the Murrumbidgee River. It provides a perfect demonstration in three dimensions of how swiftly you can be in the middle of nowhere in Australia. One minute I was in a comely world of paddocks, meadows and pale green hills, with little country towns scattered at reliably accommodating intervals, and the next I was alone in an almost featureless nowhere – a disc of brown earth under a dome of blue sky, with only an occasional gum interposed between the two. Such habitations as I passed through weren't really communities at all, but just a couple of houses and a petrol station, occasionally a pub, and eventually even they all but ceased. Between Narrandera, the last outpost of civilization, and Balranald, the next, lay 200 miles of highway without a town or hamlet on it. Every hour or so I would pass a lonely roadhouse – a petrol station with an attached café of the sort known in the happy vernacular of Australia as a chew and spew – and occasionally an earthen track bumping off to a distant, unseen sheep station. Otherwise nothing.

As if to emphasize the isolation, all the area radio stations began to abandon me. One by one their signals faltered, and all those smoky voices so integral to Australian airwaves – Vic Damone, Mel Torme, Frank Sinatra at the mindless height of his doo-bee-doo phase – faded away, as if being drawn by some heavy gravity back into the hole from which they had escaped. Eventually the radio dial presented only an uninterrupted cat's hiss of static, but for one clear spot near the end of the dial. At first I thought that's all it was – just an empty clear spot – but then I realized I could hear the faint shiftings and stirrings of seated people, and after quite a pause a voice, calm and reflective, said:

'Pilchard begins his long run in from short stump. He bowls and . . . oh, he's out! Yes, he's got him. Longwilley is caught leg-before in middle slops by Grattan. Well, now what do you make of that, Neville?'

'That's definitely one for the books, Bruce. I don't think I've seen offside medium slow fast pace bowling to match it since Baden-Powell took Rangachangabanga for a maiden ovary at Bangalore in 1948.'

I had stumbled into the surreal and rewarding world of cricket on the radio.

After years of patient study (and with cricket there can be no other kind) I have decided that there is nothing wrong with the game that the introduction of golf carts wouldn't fix in a hurry. It is not true that the English invented cricket as a way of making all other human endeavours look interesting and lively; that was merely an unintended side effect. I don't wish to denigrate a sport that is enjoyed by millions, some of them awake and facing the right way, but it is an odd game. It is the only sport that incorporates meal breaks. It is the only sport that shares its name with an insect. It is the only sport in which spectators burn as many calories as players (more if they are moderately restless). It is the only competitive activity of any type, other than perhaps baking, in which you can dress in white from head to toe and be as clean at the end of the day as you were at the beginning.

Imagine a form of baseball in which the pitcher, after

155

each delivery, collects the ball from the catcher and walks slowly with it out to centre field; and that there, after a minute's pause to collect himself, he turns and runs full tilt towards the pitcher's mound before hurling the ball at the ankles of a man who stands before him wearing a riding hat, heavy gloves of the sort used to handle radioactive isotopes, and a mattress strapped to each leg. Imagine moreover that if this batsman fails to hit the ball in a way that heartens him sufficiently to try to waddle sixty feet with mattresses strapped to his legs he is under no formal compulsion to run; he may stand there all day, and, as a rule, does. If by some miracle he is coaxed into making a misstroke that leads to his being put out, all the fielders throw up their arms in triumph and have a hug. Then tea is called and everyone retires happily to a distant pavilion to fortify for the next siege. Now imagine all this going on for so long that by the time the match concludes autumn has crept in and all your library books are overdue. There you have cricket.

But it must be said there is something incomparably soothing about cricket on the radio. It has much the same virtues as baseball on the radio – an unhurried pace, a comforting devotion to abstruse statistics and thoughtful historical rumination, exhilarating micro-moments of real action – but stretched across many more hours and with a lushness of terminology and restful elegance of expression that even baseball cannot match. Listening to cricket on the radio is like listening to two men sitting in a rowing boat on a large, placid lake on a day when the fish aren't biting; it's like having a nap without losing consciousness. It actually helps not to know quite what's going on. In such a rarefied world of contentment and inactivity, comprehension would become a distraction.

'So here comes Stovepipe to bowl on this glorious summer's afternoon at the MCG,' one of the commentators was saying now. 'I wonder if he'll chance an offside drop scone here or go for the quick legover. Stovepipe has an unusual delivery in that he actually leaves the grounds and starts his run just outside the Carlton & United Brewery at Kooyong.'

'That's right, Clive. I haven't known anyone start his delivery that far back since Stopcock caught his sleeve on the reversing mirror of a number 11 bus during the third test at Brisbane in 1957 and ended up at Goondiwindi four days later owing to some frightful confusion over a changed timetable at Toowoomba Junction.'

After a very long silence while they absorbed this thought, and possibly stepped out to transact some small errands, they resumed with a leisurely discussion of the England fielding. Neasden, it appeared, was turning in a solid performance at square bowel, while Packet had been a stalwart in the dribbles, though even these exemplary performances paled when set beside the outstanding play of young Hugh Twain-Buttocks at middle nipple. The commentators were in calm agreement that they had not seen anyone caught behind with such panache since Tandoori took Rogan Josh for a stiffy at Vindaloo in '61. At last Stovepipe, having found his way over the railway line at Flinders Street – the footbridge was evidently closed for painting – returned to the stadium and bowled to Hasty, who deftly turned the ball away for a corner. This was repeated four times more over the next two hours and then one of the commentators pronounced: 'So as we break for second luncheon, and with 11,200 balls remaining, Australia are 962 for two not half and England are four for a duck and hoping for rain.'

I may not have all the terminology exactly right, but I believe I have caught the flavour of it. The upshot was that Australia was giving England a good thumping, but then Australia pretty generally does. In fact, Australia pretty generally beats most people at most things. Truly never has there been a more sporting nation. At the 1996 Olympics in Atlanta, to take just one random but illustrative example, Australia, the fifty-second largest nation in the world, brought home more medals than all but four other countries, all of them much larger (the countries, of course, not the medals). Measured by population, its performance was streets ahead of anyone else. Australians won 3.78 medals per million of population, a rate more than two and a half times better than the next best performer, Germany, and almost five times the rate of the United States. Moreover, Australia's medal-winning tally was distributed across a range of sports, fourteen, matched by only one other nation, the United States. Hardly a sport exists at which the Australians do not excel. Do you know, there are even forty Australians playing baseball at the professional level in the United States, including five in the Major Leagues – and Australians don't even *play* baseball, at least not in any particularly devoted manner. They do all this on the world stage *and* play their own games as well, notably a very popular form of loosely contained mayhem called Australian Rules Football. It is a wonder in such a vigorous and active society that there is anyone left to form an audience.

No, the mystery of cricket is not that Australians play it well, but that they play it at all. It has always seemed to me a game much too restrained for the rough-and-tumble Australian temperament. Australians much prefer games in which brawny men in scanty clothing bloody each other's noses. I am quite certain that if the rest of the world vanished overnight and the development of cricket was left in Australian hands, within a generation the players would be wearing shorts and using the bats to hit each other.

And the thing is, it would be a much better game for it.

In the late afternoon, while the players broke for high tea or fifth snack or something – in any case, when the activity on the field went from very slight to non-existent – I stopped at a roadhouse for petrol and coffee. I studied my book of maps and determined that I would stop for the night in Hay, a modest splat in the desert a little off the highway a couple of hours down the road. As it was the only community in a space of 200 miles, this was not a particularly taxing decision. Then, having nothing better to do, I leafed through the index and amused myself, in a very low-key way, by looking for ridiculous names, of which Australia has a respectable plenitude. I am thus able to report that the following are all real places: Wee Waa, Poowong, Burrumbuttock, Suggan Buggan, Boomahnoomoonah, Waaia, Mullumbimby, Ewlyamartup, Jiggalong and the supremely satisfying Tittybong.

As I paid, the man asked me where I was headed.

'Hay,' I replied, and was struck by a sudden droll thought. 'And I'd better hurry. Do you know why?'

He gave me a blank look.

'Because I want to make Hay while the sun shines.'

The man's expression did not change.

'I want to make Hay while the sun shines,' I repeated with a slight alteration of emphasis and a more encouraging expression.

The blank look, I realized after a moment, was probably permanent.

'Aw, you won't have any trouble with that,' the man said after a minute's considered thought. 'It'll be light for hours yet.'

Hay was a hot and dusty but surprisingly likeable little town off the Sturt Highway across an old bridge over the muddy Murrumbidgee. In the motel, I dumped my bag and reflexively switched on the TV. It came up on the cricket, and I sat on the foot of the bed and watched it with unwonted absorption for some minutes. Needless to say, very little was happening on the pitch. An official in a white coat was chasing after a blown piece of paper and several of the players were examining the ground by the stumps, evidently looking for something. I couldn't think what, but then one of the commentators noted that England had just lost a wicket, so I supposed it was that. After a time a lanky young man in the outfield, who had been polishing a ball on his trouser leg as if about to take a bite from it, broke into a loping run. At length he hurled the ball at the distant batsman, who insouciantly lifted his bat an inch from the ground and putted it back to him. These motions were scrupulously replicated three times more, then the commentator said: 'And so at the end of the four hundred and fifty-second over, as we break for afternoon nap, England have increased their total to seventeen. So still quite a lot of work for them to do if they're going to catch Australia before fourth snack.'

I went out for a stroll over the terrestrial hotplate that is inland New South Wales in summer. The day was extravagantly warm. Every leaf on the kerbside trees was limp, like a tongue hanging out. I wandered up and down both sides of Lachlan Street, the main drag, and then some way out into the country to enjoy the sunset – an event always of calm and golden glory in the bush – and in the hope, ever unfulfilled, of seeing some kangaroos hopping picturesquely into frame. Kangaroos are commoner in Australia now than they were before Europeans came because all the rural improvements – the encouragement of grassland, the creating of ponds and so on – have benefited them in the same way they have sheep and cattle. Nobody knows how many kangaroos the country holds, but the number is generally assumed to be over 100 million, making them not much less numerous than sheep. But could I find even one out here? I could not.

So I strolled back into town and passed the evening in my usual gracious style – lager cocktails in a forlorn and nearly empty pub, dinner of steak and salad in a restaurant next door, another stroll to the edge of town to look, in vain, for kangaroos by moonlight. I was back in my room by about nine thirty. I switched on the TV and was impressed to see that play was still going on. Give the cricketers their due. It may be light work but they put in the hours. The man in the white coat was still chasing paper, though it wasn't possible to tell if it was the same piece. England, according to the commentator, had lost another three wickets, which seemed rather absent-minded of them. At this rate they would soon run out of equipment altogether and have to call it a day.

Perhaps, I decided as I switched the TV off, that was what they were hoping for.

In the morning I treated myself to a big breakfast to fortify myself for another long day's drive. Breakfast is, of course, our most savage event in western society (if you hesitate to agree, then I urge you to name me another occasion – any occasion at all – when you would happily devour an embryo), and Australians seem to have a good fix on this. A lot of it comes down to a mastery of bacon. Unlike the curled shoe tongues that are consumed in Britain or the boringly crisp, regimented strips we go for in America, Australian bacon has a rough, meaty, fair dinkum heartiness. It looks as if it was taken off the pig while it was trying to escape. You can almost hear the squeal in every bite. Lovely. Also, they cut their toast thick. In short, the Australians know what they are about with breakfasts.

And so, radiant with cholesterol and contentment, I returned to the lonesome road. Beyond Hay, the landscape was even more impossibly flat, brown, empty and dull. The monumental emptiness of Australia is not easy to convey. It is far and away the most thinly peopled of nations. In Britain the average population density is 632 people per square mile; in the United States the average is 76; across the world as a whole it is 117. (And, just for interest, in Macau, the record holder, it is a decidedly snug 69,000 people per square mile.) The Australian average, by contrast, is six people per square mile. But even that modest figure is wildly skewed because Australians overwhelmingly live in a few clustered spots along the coast and leave the rest of the country undisturbed. Indeed, the proportion of people in Australia who live in urban areas is, at 86 per cent, about as high as in Holland and nearly as high as in Hong Kong. Out here if you found six people occupying the same square mile it would be either a family reunion or an Aum Shinrikyo planning session.

From time to time I passed through long miles of mallee scrub – low shrubs just bushy enough and high enough to strangle any view – and very occasionally, in the open plains, I would spy a low line of vivid green on the right-hand horizon, which I presumed marked an irrigated zone along the Murrumbidgee. Otherwise nothing. Just hard earth that strained to support a little dry grass and the odd thorny acacia or bent eucalypt.

It wasn't always so. Although inland Australia has never been exactly verdant, much of the marginal land once experienced periods of relative lushness, sometimes lasting years, occasionally lasting decades, and it enjoyed a natural resiliency that let it spring back after droughts. Then in 1859 a man named Thomas Austin, a landowner in Winchelsea, Victoria, a little south of where I was now, made a big mistake. He imported twenty-four wild rabbits from England and released them into the bush for sport. It is hardly a novel observation that rabbits breed with a certain keenness. Within a couple of years they had entirely overrun Austin's property and were spreading into neighbouring districts. Fifty million years of isolation had left Australia without a single predator or parasite able even to recognize rabbits, much less dine off them, and so they proliferated amazingly.

Collectively their appetite was essentially insatiable. By 1880, two million acres of Victoria had been picked clean. Soon they were pushing into South Australia and New South Wales, advancing over the landscape at a rate of seventy-five miles per year. Until the rabbits came, much of the countryside where I was driving now was characterized by lush groves of emu bush, a shrub that grew to a height of about seven feet and was in flower for most of the year. It was by all accounts a beauty and its leaves a boon to nibbling creatures. But rabbits fell on the emu bush like locusts, devouring every bit of it – leaves, flowers, bark, stems – until none was to be found. The rabbits ate so much of everything that sheep and other livestock were forced to extend both their range and their diet, punishing yet wider expanses. As sheep yields fell, farmers perversely compensated by increasing stocking levels, adding to the general devastation.

The problem would have been acute enough, but in the 1890s, after forty unusually green years, Australia fell into a murderous, decade-long drought – the worst in its recorded history. As the earth cracked and turned to dust, the topsoil – already the thinnest in the world – blew away, never to be replenished. In the course of the decade, some 35 million sheep, more than half the nation's total, perished; 16 million went in a single pitiless year, 1902.

The rabbits, meanwhile, hopped on. By the time science finally came up with a solution, almost a century had passed since Thomas Austin tipped his twenty-four bunnies out of the bag. The weapon deployed against the rabbits was a miracle virus from South America called myxomatosis. Harmless to humans and other animals, it was phenomenally devastating to rabbits, with a mortality rate of 99.9 per cent. Almost at once the countryside filled with twitching, stumbling, very sick rabbits, and then with tens of millions of little corpses. Although just one rabbit in a thousand survived, those few that did were naturally resistant to myxomatosis, and it was resistant genes that they passed on when they began to breed again. It took a while for things to get rolling, but today Australia's rabbit numbers are back up to 300 million and climbing fast.

At all events, the damage to the landscape, much of it irreversible, had already been done. And all so some clown could have something to pot at from his veranda.

Just as you plunge into emptiness with startling abruptness in Australia, so you plunge out of it again. Shortly after crossing into South Australia in mid-afternoon, I found myself entering rolling hills of orange groves. It was so startling I got out and had a look. On one side lay arid emptiness – a plain of stretched hessian spattered with clumps of mallee. But before me, filling the view to the distant horizon, spread a biblical-looking promised land – citrus groves and vineyards and vegetable patches in every lush shade of green. As I pushed on, the balance between orchards and vineyards tipped increasingly in favour of the latter until eventually there was nothing but vineyards and I realized I had reached the Barossa Valley, a quite spectacularly pretty corner of South Australia, with rolling hills of abundant green that gave it, literally and metaphorically, a Mediterranean air.

It was mostly settled by German farmers, who started Australia's wine industry here. Today Australians are among the most wine-savvy people on earth, but that development is quite recent. A story often recounted is how the British wine expert Len Evans, on a visit to the country in the 1950s, asked for a glass of wine in a country hotel. The hotelier regarded him narrowly for a long moment and asked: 'What are you, some kind of poof?' Even now the wines for which the Barossa is celebrated – Chardonnay, Cabernet Sauvignon and Shiraz – are all recent arrivals. Into the 1980s, the government was paying growers to uproot Shiraz vines and produce sticky sweet Rieslings. I've never quite understood why tourists from the more prosperous end of the market are so drawn to wine-growing areas. They wouldn't, presumably, want to go and see cotton before it became Gap slacks or caviar being gutted from sturgeon, but give them a backdrop of vines and they appear to think they have found heaven. Having said that, the Barossa Valley *is* awfully appealing, particularly after a couple of days on the lonely and far-flung Sturt Highway.

I stopped for the night in Tanunda, a handsome and well-touristed little town, mostly built along one very long street, fetchingly shadowed with leafy trees. Given its popularity with tourists and its Germanic beginnings, I had rather feared that Tanunda would be themed accordingly, but apart from one or two restaurants with 'Haus' in their titles and the odd mention of wurst in shop windows, there was mercifully little attempt to exploit its heritage. It was the eve of Australia Day, the big national holiday, and Tanunda was busy with people who had come for a mini-break.

I found a room, not without some difficulty, then wandered to the main street for a stroll before dinner. It was crowded with people who, like me, were trying to fill that empty hour between the shops' closing and the moment when one might with propriety start to drink. I walked among them, happy to be back in civilization – happy, above all, to be able to eavesdrop on conversations that didn't involve sheep dip, temperamental machinery, new wells or land clearance. (Or rumps, sumps, pumps and stumps, as I had begun to think of it.) It was clear from the conversations that I had landed in Yuppieville. Most were engaged in the interesting middle-class pastime of identifying all the objects in shop windows that looked like objects belonging to people they knew. Wherever I lingered I could hear someone observing, 'Oh, look. Sarah's got a bowl just like that,' or 'Your mother used to have a tea service like that one. I wonder whatever became of it. You don't suppose she gave it to Samantha, do you?' A few couples were playing a slightly edgier version of this game, which involved supplementary comments like 'No, the one *you* broke was *much* nicer' and 'But how many pairs of pearl earrings do you *need*, for God's sake?' and 'Well, if she did give it to Samantha, I'm going to be extremely pissed off, frankly, because she promised it to me. You'll just have to have a word with her.' These were the people, I guessed, who had driven the furthest to get here and most needed a drink. Or possibly were just assholes.

I liked Tanunda and had a very pleasant evening there, but there was absolutely nothing exceptional or eventful in the experience, so I am going to tell you instead a little story related to me by a lovely woman named Catherine Veitch.

Catherine Veitch was my oldest friend in Australia, both in the sense that she was my first chum there and also that she was just about old enough to be my mother. I met her at the Melbourne Writers' Festival in 1992. I can't remember the circumstances now other than that she approached me after a reading either to set me straight with regard to some mistake I had made in one of my books on language – she was of a scholarly bent and impatient with sloppiness – or to enlighten me concerning some aspect of Australian life on which I had imprudently commented in the question and answer session. The upshot is that we had a cup of tea in the cafeteria and the next day I took a tram to her house in St Kilda for lunch, where I met most of her family. Her children, of whom she seemed to have a large but indeterminate number, were all grown and living away, but most of them called in at various points in the afternoon, to borrow a tool or check for messages or burrow in the fridge. It was just the kind of household I had always longed to grow up in – happy, comfortable, nicely chaotic, full of shouted conversations of the 'Try looking in the cupboard at the top of the stairs' type. And I liked Catherine very much. She was kind and funny and thoughtful and direct.

So we became great friends – though it was a friendship based almost entirely on correspondence. She had never been to America, and I went to Australia once a year if I was lucky, and not always to Melbourne. But three or four times a year she would send me long, wonderfully discursive letters hammered out on a jumpy and wilful typewriter. These letters seldom took less than an hour to read. In a single page they could range over a galaxy of subjects – her childhood in Adelaide, the inadequacies of certain politicians (actually, of most politicians), why Australians lack confidence, what her children had been up to. Generally she stuck in a wad of cuttings from the *Age*, the Melbourne newspaper. Much of what I know about Australia I learned from her.

I loved those letters. They came from so far away – just getting an envelope from Australia still seemed to me a faintly wondrous event – and described events and experiences that were unexceptional to her but breathtakingly exotic to me: taking a tram into the city, suffering through a heatwave in December, attending a lecture at the Royal Melbourne Institute, shopping for curtains at David Jones, the big local department store. I can't explain it except to say that, without giving up any part of the life I had already, I wanted intensely to have all that in my life as well. So it was through her letters, more than from almost anything else, that I consolidated my fixation with Australia.

Her letters were always happy, but the last one I received from her was especially sunny. She and John, her husband, were about to sell the house in St Kilda and move to the

Mornington Peninsula, south of Melbourne, to take up a life of gracious retirement beside the sea, fulfilling a dream of many years' duration. Just after she sent that letter, to the shock of everyone who knew her, she suffered a sudden heart attack and died. I'd have been on my way to visit her now. Instead all I can offer is my favourite of the many stories she told me.

In the 1950s, a friend of Catherine's moved with her young family into a house next door to a vacant lot. One day some builders arrived to put up a house on the lot. Catherine's friend had a three-year-old daughter who naturally took an interest in all the activity going on next door. She hung around on the margins and eventually the builders adopted her as a kind of mascot. They chatted to her and gave her little jobs to do and at the end of the week presented her with a little pay packet containing a shiny new half crown, or something.

She took this home to her mother who made all the appropriate cooings of admiration and suggested that they take it to the bank the next morning to deposit it in her account. When they went to the bank, the cashier was equally impressed and asked the little girl how she had come by her own pay packet.

'I've been building a house this week,' she replied proudly.

'Goodness!' said the cashier. 'And will you be building a house next week, too?'

'I will if we ever get the fucking bricks,' answered the little girl.

Chapter

EIGHT

South Australians are very proud that theirs is the only Australian state that never received convicts. What they don't often mention is that it was planned by one. In the early 1830s, Edward Gibbon Wakefield, a man of independent means and unsavoury inclinations, was in Newgate Prison in London, on a charge of abducting a female child for sweaty and nefarious purposes, when he hatched the idea to found a colony of freemen in Australia. His plan was to sell parcels of land to sober, industrious people – farmers and capitalists – and use the funds raised to pay the passage of labourers to work for them. The labourers would gain ennobling employment; the investors would acquire a workforce and a market; everyone would benefit. The scheme never worked terribly well in practice, but the result was a new colony, South Australia, and a delightful planned city, Adelaide.

Whereas Canberra is a park, Adelaide is merely full of them. In Canberra you have the sense of being in a very large green space you cannot ever quite find your way out of; in Adelaide you are indubitably in a city, but with the pleasant option of stepping out of it from time to time to get a breath of air in a spacious green setting. Makes all the difference. The city was laid out as two distinct halves facing each other across the green plain of the Torrens River, with each half fully enclosed by parks. On a map, therefore, central Adelaide forms a large, plump, somewhat irregular figure of eight, with parks creating the figure and the two inner halves of the city filling the holes. It works awfully well.

I had no special destination in mind, but the next morning as I drove into the city from Tanunda I passed through North Adelaide, the handsome and prosperous zone inside the top half of the figure eight, spotted an agreeable-looking hotel and impetuously threw the car at the kerb. I was on O'Connell Street, in a neighbourhood of old, well-preserved buildings with lots of trendy restaurants, pubs and cafés. After Canberra, I wasn't going to let a slice of urban heaven like this slip past. So I procured a room and lost not a moment getting back into the open air.

Adelaide is the most overlooked of Australia's principal cities. You could spend weeks in Australia and never suspect it was there, for it rarely makes the news or gets a mention in anyone's conversation. It is to Australia essentially what Australia is to the world – a place pleasantly regarded but far away and seldom thought about. And yet it is unquestionably a lovely city. Everyone is agreed on that, including millions who have never been there.

I had been just once myself, on a book tour a few

months before. What remained from that experience was an impression of physical handsomeness coupled with an oddly pleased sense of doom on the part of the inhabitants. Remark to anyone in Adelaide what an agreeable place it is, and you will be told at once, with a kind of eager solemnity: 'Yes, but it's dying, you know.'

'Is it?' you say in a tone of polite concern.

'Oh yes,' confides your informant, nodding with grim satisfaction. Then, if you are very unlucky, the person will tell you all about the collapse of the Bank of South Australia, an event of fiscal carelessness that took years to conclude and is nearly as long in the telling.

Adelaide's problem, it appears, is geographical. The city stands on the wrong edge of civilized Australia, far from the vital Asian markets and with nothing on its own doorstep but a great deal of nothing. To the north and west lie a million-odd square miles of searing desert; to the south nothing but open sea all the way to Antarctica. Only to the east are there any cities, but even Melbourne is 450 miles away and Sydney nearer a thousand. Why would anyone build a factory in Adelaide when it is so far from its markets? It is a reasonable question, but somewhat undermined by the consideration that Perth is even more remote – 1,700 miles more remote in its lonely outpost on the Indian Ocean – yet has a far more vibrant economy. At all events, the bottom line is that Adelaide seems stuck in an unhappy place, in every sense of the word.

Yet to the casual observer it seems quite as affluent as any other big city in Australia, possibly even more so. Its central shopping district is better looking and at least as well used as the equivalent zones in Sydney or Melbourne, and its pubs, restaurants and cafés appear to be as bustling and lively as any entrepreneur could wish. It has an outstanding stock of Victorian buildings, an abundance of parks and comely squares, and constant small touches – an ornate lamp-post here, a stone lion there – that give it a dash of classiness and respectful venerability that Sydney and Melbourne all too often discarded for the sequined glitter of skyscrapers. It feels rather like an urban version of a gentlemen's club – comfortable, old-fashioned, quietly grand, slightly drowsy by mid-afternoon, redolent of another age.

As I strolled downhill past Pennington Gardens, one of the central parks, I became gradually and then over-whelmingly aware of the tide of human activity all moving in a single direction – thousands and thousands of people converging on a stadium in the park. I asked two young men what was going on and was told there was a cricket match between England and Australia at the Oval.

'What – here in Adelaide? Today?' I said in surprise.

He considered the question with the bemusement it merited. 'Well, either that,' he replied drily, 'or thirty thou-sand people have made one pretty amazing bloody mistake, wouldn't you say?' Then he smiled to show that he wasn't being aggressive or anything. It appeared that he and his partner had stopped for a gallon or two of refresh-ment en route.

'Do you know, are there still tickets left?' I asked.

'Nah, mate, sold out. Sorry.'

I nodded and watched them go. That was another very British thing I'd noticed about Australians – they apolo-gized for things that weren't their fault.

I found my way along North Terrace, the city's grandest thoroughfare, to the South Australian Museum, a stately pile devoted to natural and anthropological history. I was interested to see if it displayed a fossil called *Spriggina*, named for a minor hero of mine called Reginald Sprigg. In 1946, Sprigg, then a young government geologist, was poking around in the blisteringly inhospitable Ediacaran hills of the Flinders Ranges, some 300 miles north of Adelaide, when he made one of those miraculous discoveries in which Australian natural history almost impossibly abounds. You will recall from an earlier chapter the case of the strange and long-lost proto-ant *Nothomyrmecia macrops* found unexpectedly at a dusty hamlet in the middle of nowhere. Well, Sprigg's find was in much the same general area and, in its way, no less remarkable.

His special moment came when he clambered a few yards up a rocky slope to find a piece of shade and a comfortable rock to lean against to have his lunch. As he sat eating his sandwiches he idly stretched out a toe and turned over a hunk of sandstone. Sprigg left no informal account of the event, but I think we can safely imagine him pausing in his chewing – pausing for a long moment, mouth slightly open – to stare at what he had just turned over, then slowly creeping nearer to have a closer look. What he had just found, you see, was something that wasn't thought to exist.

For almost a century, since the time of Charles Darwin, scientists had been puzzled by an evolutionary anomaly – that 600 million years ago complex life forms of an improbable variety had suddenly burst forth on earth (the famous Cambrian explosion), but without any evidence of earlier, simpler forms that might have paved the way for such an event. Sprigg had just found that missing link, a piece of rock swimming in delicate pre-Cambrian fossils. He was looking, in effect, at the dawn of visible life – at something no one had ever seen before or ever expected to see. It was a moment of supreme geological significance. And if he had sat anywhere else – anywhere at all in the infinite baking expanse that is the Australian outback – it would not have been made, certainly not then, possibly not ever.

That's the thing about Australia, you see. It teems with interesting stuff, but at the same time it's so vast and empty and forbidding that it generally takes a remarkable stroke of luck to find it.

Unfortunately, in 1946 the world scientific community paid little heed to news from Australia, and Sprigg's reports of his findings, duly recorded in the *Transactions of the Royal Society of South Australia*, languished for two decades before their significance became generally appreciated. But never mind. In the end, credit fell where it was due: Sprigg was immortalized with the name of a fossil, and the epoch he uncovered became known as the Ediacaran, after the hills through which he had tramped.

Alas, the museum was not open when I passed by – closed for the national holiday, I supposed – and so my hopes of glimpsing the dawn of life were dashed. Wandering on through shady side streets, however, I found a second-hand bookshop open and was happy to take that as a consolation prize. Probably because new books have always been expensive in Australia, the country has outstanding second-hand bookshops. These always have a large section devoted to 'Australiana' and these sections never fail to amaze, if only because they show you what a remarkably self-absorbed people the Australians are. I don't mean that as a criticism. If the rest of the world is going to pay them no attention, then they must do it themselves surely. That seems fair enough to me. But you do find in any trawl through the jumbled stacks the most wondrous titles. One of the first I took down now was called *That's Where I Met My Wife: A Story of the First Swimming Pool in the National Capital at Canberra*. Nearby was a plump volume entitled *A Sense of Union: A History of Sydney University Football Club*. Beside that was a history of the South Australia Ambulance Service. There were hundreds of titles like this – books about things that could never possibly have been of interest to more than a handful of people. It's quite encouraging that these books exist, but somehow faintly worrying as well.

Among them, however, you will often find the most rewarding surprises. This was so now when I took down a photographic history of Surfers Paradise, the famous Queensland beach resort, which caught my eye because I was heading there shortly. The book covered the story of the resort's development from the 1920s, when it was a fly-blown coastal hamlet of neither fame nor consequence, to the early 1970s, when it abruptly burst forth as a kind of Miami Beach of the southern hemisphere. What particularly captivated me were the photographs of it during its intermediate phase, in the 1940s and 50s, when it was much closer in spirit and appearance to Coney Island or Blackpool. It is odd to be filled with a nostalgic longing for a place you have never known, but I was with Surfers Paradise and its innocent holidaymakers. I gazed enraptured at page after page of crisp black and white photographs showing happy people at play – strolling in groups along the Esplanade, jitterbugging in dance halls, sitting with drinks at surfside bars. How I envied them their snazzy outfits. I realize I may be in a minority here, but I would give almost anything to live in an age when I could put on two-tone shoes, red socks, a lively cotton shirt with a repeating pattern based on, say, baggage labels, hoist my baggy brown pants to *just* level with my nipples, drop a felt hat on my head and have people walking past look at me twice and think: '*Stylish guy!*'

There was something so marvellously innocent, so irretrievably lost, about the world back then. You could see it in the easy, confident gait and sun-drenched smiles of the holidaymakers in every photograph. These people were *happy*. I don't mean they were happy. They were *happy*. They were living at a good time in a lucky country and they knew it. They had good jobs, good homes, good families, good prospects, good holidays in cheerful, sunny places. I wouldn't suggest for an instant that Australians are unhappy people now – anything but, in fact – but they don't have that happiness in their faces any more. I don't think anybody does.

It was, it must be said, an age of the most dazzling primness. In the 1950s, Australia was probably the least confident nation in the English-speaking world. It was so far from everywhere that the authorities didn't seem to know quite what was acceptable, so essentially they played it safe and allowed nothing. One of the photographs in the Surfers Paradise book showed a souvenir emporium that had a very large billboard on its roof. The ad on the billboard was the famous Coppertone suntan lotion ad in which a small girl is having her swimsuit pulled down by an impish puppy, exposing an inch or two of sweet little bottom. And here's the thing. Someone had got out a ladder, climbed up with a bucket of paint and carefully painted panties over the little girl's crack. (Well, can't have people masturbating on the Esplanade, after all.) It wasn't just suntan lotion ads that were censored, but movies, plays, magazines and books in numbers unbelievable.

One thing you won't find much in Australian second-hand bookshops are 1950s or earlier editions of lots of books – *The Catcher in the Rye*, *A Farewell to Arms*, *Animal Farm*, *Peyton Place*, *Another Country*, *Brave New World* and hundreds and hundreds of others. The reason for this is simple: they were banned. Altogether, at its peak, 5,000 titles were forbidden to be imported into the country. By the 1950s this had fallen to a couple of hundred, but it still featured some extraordinary exclusions – *Childbirth Without Pain*, for instance, whose unflinching candour in describing where babies come from was considered a little too rich for Australian sensibilities. This was just conventional titles, by the way. The total doesn't include smutty stuff, which was of course banned outright. It wasn't just that you couldn't get certain books. You couldn't even find out which ones you couldn't get because the list of proscribed books was itself a secret.

It was Adelaide, interestingly, that put an end to all this. For decades it had been one of the more arrestingly unprogressive of Australian cities. The blame for this can be dropped in the lap of one Sir Thomas Playford, who for thirty-eight years, from the 1930s to the 1960s, was South Australia's Premier. Playford was a man so parochial that once during a commodities crisis he suggested that the state might have to 'import wheat from Australia', and on another occasion remarked to the Vice Chancellor of the University of Adelaide that he couldn't see any point in universities at all. As you can imagine, he did not notably enrich the intellectual vigour of South Australia. Then in 1967 the state elected a youthful and charismatic Labor Premier named Don Dunstan, and almost at once Adelaide and South Australia underwent a transformation. The city became a haven for artists and intellectuals. The

Adelaide Festival blossomed into the nation's pre-eminent cultural event. Books that were still banned elsewhere in Australia – *Portnoy's Complaint* and *Naked Lunch*, for example – were freely available in Adelaide. Nude bathing beaches were allowed. Homosexuality was legalized. For one giddy decade or so, Adelaide was the hippest city in the country – the San Francisco of the Antipodes.

In 1979, Dunstan's wife died and he abruptly retired from politics. Adelaide lost its momentum and began a gentle descent into obscurity. The artists and intellectuals drifted away; even Dunstan moved to Victoria. Under Playford South Australia had been backward but interestingly so. Under Dunstan it was racy and exhilaratingly so. The real problem with Adelaide these days, I suspect, is that it has just stopped being interesting.

Still, it's a lovely place for an amble on a summer's day. I made a couple of small purchases in the bookshop – an old hardback called *Australian Paradox*, which I bought for no more solid reason than that I rather liked the cover and it was attractively priced at $2, and a more recent volume entitled *Crocodile Attack in Australia*, which was nearly ten times dearer but had the compensating virtue of containing a great many gruesome anecdotes – then wandered off for a hike through the city's green and commodious parks.

Central Adelaide boasts almost 1,800 acres of parks, less than Canberra but a great deal more than most other cities of its size. As so often in Australia, they reflect an effort to recreate a familiarly British ambience in an antipodean setting. Of all the things people longed for when they first came to Australia, an English backdrop was perhaps the most outstanding. It is notable, when you look at early paintings of the country, how awkward, how strikingly un-Australian, the landscape so often appears. Even the gum trees look unusually lush and globular, as if the artists were willing them to take on a more English aspect. Australia was a disappointment to the early settlers. They ached for English air and English vistas. So when they built their cities, they laid them out with rolling English-style parks arrayed with stands of oak, beech, chestnut and elm in a way that recalled the dreamily bucolic efforts of Humphry Repton or Capability Brown. Adelaide is the driest city in the driest state on the driest continent, but you would never guess it from wandering through its parks. Here it is forever Sussex.

Unfortunately, such arrangements are out of fashion in the horticultural world. Since many of the original plantings are now coming to the end of their natural lives, the park authorities have instituted plans to sweep away the intruder species and recreate a riverine landscape dominated by mallee scrub and red river gums of the sort that existed here naturally before Europeans came along. Heart-warming though it is to see Australians taking pride in their native flora, the plan seems unfortunate to say the least. To begin with, Australia has several hundred thousand square miles of landscape featuring mallee scrub and red river gums; it is not as if this is a threatened environment. Worse, the parks as they are now are unusually fine, among the best in the world, and it would be a tragedy to lose them wherever they were. If you accept the logic that they are inappropriate because they are in a European style then clearly you would have to get rid of all of Adelaide's houses, streets, buildings and European-derived people. Unfortunately, as so often in a short-sighted world, no one asked me about any of this.

Still, the parks remain lovely for the moment and I was happy to pass into them now. They were packed with large family groups enjoying Australia Day, picnicking and playing cricket with tennis balls. Adelaide has miles of good beaches in its western suburbs, so it surprised me that such numbers of people had forsaken the shore to come into the city. It gave the day an engagingly old-fashioned air. This is how we spent the Fourth of July when I was a kid in Iowa – in parks, playing ball games. It seemed odd, too – but again pleasing – that in a country of so much space people chose to crowd together to relax. Perhaps it's all that intimidating emptiness that makes Australians such social creatures. The parks were so crowded, in fact, that it was often impossible to tell which ball game belonged to which group of onlookers, or even sometimes which fielders belonged to which ball game. When a ball bounced into a neighbouring party, as seemed to happen quite regularly, there was always an exchange of apologies on the one hand and a call of 'No worries' on the other as the ball was tossed back into play. It was effectively all one very large picnic, and I felt almost ridiculously pleased to be part of it even in such a marginal way.

It took about three hours, I suppose, to do the complete circuit of the parks. Quite often a roar would rise from the Oval. Cricket was obviously a livelier spectacle in person than on the radio. At length I emerged onto a street called Pennington Terrace, where a row of neat bluestone houses with shady lawns overlooked the Oval. At one a family had essentially moved its living room onto the front lawn. I know it can't have been so, but in my recollection they had brought out everything – floor lamps, coffee table, rug, magazine basket, coal scuttle. They had certainly brought out a sofa and a television on which they were watching the cricket. Behind the television, a couple of hundred yards away across open parkland, stood the Oval, so that whenever anything dramatic happened on their screen it was accompanied in real time by a roar from the stadium just beyond.

'Who's winning?' I called as I walked past.

'Bloody poms,' the man said, inviting me to share his amazement.

I trudged on uphill past the imposing hulk of St Peter's Cathedral. I was heading in a general way towards my hotel, intending to have a shower and a change of clothes before setting off to look for a pub and dinner. Out of the shade of the parks it was a blisteringly hot afternoon, and I was by now quite footsore, but I found myself drawn helplessly into the residential streets of North Adelaide. It was an area of quiet prosperity, settled under a Sunday serenity, with street after street of old houses, each buried under roses and frangipani, and every little plot a model of meticulously managed floral abundance.

At length I arrived at a place called Wellington Square, an open space overlooked by a grand pub of venerable aspect. I went straight over. Inside, it was cool and convivial, with gleaming fittings and a lot of burnished pale wood – nothing like the austere pubs of the bush. This was a place for cocktails, for talking about one's investment portfolio. It was busy, too, though most of the customers were eating rather than drinking – or at least eating as well as drinking. At nearly every table, they were hunched over steaks or battered portions of fish so hearty that they hung over the edge of the plates. On a large pulldown screen the cricket was showing, but with the sound turned down. I had found my home for the evening. I ordered a pint of Cooper's Draught and retired with it to a table overlooking the square. And there I sat for a good few minutes doing nothing at all, not even touching my glass, just savouring the pleasure of sitting down and finding myself in a far country with a glass of beer and cricket on the TV and a roomful of people enjoying the fruits of a prosperous age. I could not have been happier.

After a while I remembered my purchases from the second-hand bookshop and pulled them out for examination. I turned first to *Australian Paradox*, an account of a year-long stay in the country in 1959–60 written by an English journalist named Jeanne MacKenzie, and cracked it open, interested to see how Australia today compared with the Australia of forty years ago.

Well, what a different world it was. The Australia Ms MacKenzie describes is a place of boundless prosperity, full employment, twinkling wholesomeness and infinite optimism. In 1959–60, Australia was the third wealthiest country on the planet – I hadn't realized this – exceeded only by the United States and Canada. But what was particularly interesting was how modest were the components of material well-being back then. With admiration bordering on amazement, Ms MacKenzie notes that by the end of the 1950s three-quarters of city dwellers in Australia had a refrigerator and almost half had a washing machine (there wasn't yet enough electricity in most rural areas to run big appliances, so they didn't count). Nearly every home in the nation, she went on, had 'at least one radio' – gosh! – and 'most homes have other electrical appliances such as vacuum cleaners, irons and electric jugs'. Oh, to live in a world in which the ownership of an electric jug is a source of pride.

I spent a good hour reading through the book at random, spellbound by the simplicity of the age she described. In 1960, television was still an exciting novelty (it didn't reach Australia until 1956, and then only in

183

Sydney and Melbourne at first), colour television a distant dream. In Melbourne on Sundays there were no newspapers, and cinemas and pubs were shut by law. Perth was still at the end of a very long dirt road and would remain so for many years. Adelaide was just half the size it is now and its famous festival was then brand new. Queensland was backward. (Still is!) Even in the best restaurants, chicken Maryland and beef stroganoff were dishes of exotic distinction, and oysters were served with ketchup. For most people, foreign cuisine began and ended with spaghetti out of tins. Cheese came in two varieties – 'sharp' and 'tasty'. Supermarkets were a new and exciting concept. Five per cent of university-age kids in 1959 were actually in university – this also reported with admiration – up from 1.56 per cent twenty years before. It was, in every way, a different world.

What struck me in all this was not how much better off Australians are today, but how much worse they feel. One of the oddest things for an outsider to do is watch Australians assessing themselves. They are an extraordinarily self-critical people. You encounter it constantly in newspapers and on television and radio – a nagging conviction that no matter how good things are in Australia, they are bound to be better elsewhere. A curiously large proportion of books on Australian life and history bear grave, pessimistic titles: *Among the Barbarians*, *The Future Eaters*, *The Tyranny of Distance*, *This Tired, Brown Land*, *Fatal Impact*, *The Fatal Shore*. Even when the titles are neutral (they are never positive), they often contain the oddest, most startling conclusions. In *A Shorter History of Australia*, a thoughtful and unexceptionable survey of the country's considerable achievements over the past 200 years, the author, Geoffrey Blainey, finishes by noting that Australia has nearly completed its first century under peaceful federation. Then, out of the blue, he concludes with these words: 'Whether it will last for two centuries is not certain. In the sweep of human history no political boundary is permanent.'

Now is that very strange or what? You could understand a Canadian writing those words, or a Belgian or a South African. But an Australian? Please. This is a country that has never had a serious civil disturbance, never jailed a dissident, never shown the tiniest inclination to fray at the edges. Australia is the Norway of the southern hemisphere. And yet here is the country's foremost living historian suggesting that its continuation as a sovereign nation is by no means assured. Extraordinary.

If Australians lack one thing in their lonely eminence Down Under, it is perspective. For four decades they have watched in quiet dismay as one country after another – Switzerland, Sweden, Japan, Kuwait and many others – has climbed over them on the per capita GDP table. When news came out in 1996 that Hong Kong and Singapore had also squeezed ahead, you'd have thought from the newspaper editorials that Asian armies had come ashore somewhere around Darwin and were fanning out across the country, appropriating consumer durables as they went. Never mind that most of these countries were only marginally ahead and that much of it was to do with relative exchange rates. Never mind that when you take into account quality-of-life indicators such as cost of living, educational attainments, crime rates and so on Australia bounds back up near the top. (It ranks seventh on the United Nations' Human Development Index, a little behind Canada, Sweden, the United States and one or two others, but comfortably ahead of Germany, Switzerland,

Austria, Italy and several other countries with stout economies and higher GDPs.) At the time of my visit, Australia was booming as never before. It was enjoying one of the fastest rates of economic growth in the developed world, inflation was invisible and unemployment was at its lowest level in years. Yet according to a study by the Australian Institute, 36 per cent of Australians felt life was getting worse and barely a fifth saw any hope of its getting better.

These days, it is true, in terms of gross dollars accumulated per head, Australia is no longer near the top. It comes in at number twenty-one, in fact. But I ask you, which would you rather be – third richest and thrilled because you have an electric jug and at least one radio, or twenty-first richest and living in a world where you can have everything a person could reasonably want?

On the other hand, in very few of these other countries do you run the slightest risk of being eaten by an estuarine crocodile, a thought that occurred to me now as I pulled out my second purchase, *Crocodile Attack in Australia* by Hugh Edwards, and waded chest deep into its 240 pages of gruesome, violent attacks by this most cunning and unsporting of creatures.

The saltwater crocodile is the one animal that has the capacity to frighten even Australians. People who would calmly flick a scorpion off their forearm or chuckle fearlessly at a pack of skulking dingoes will quake at the sight of a hungry croc, and I had not ventured far into the pages of Mr Edwards's chilling chronicles before I began to understand why. Consider this tale of an afternoon at play in north-western Australia:

In March 1987, a motorcruiser with five people aboard was making its way along the Kimberley coast when it detoured up the Prince Regent River to visit Kings Cascade, a remote beauty spot where a tropical waterfall spills picturesquely over a granite outcrop. There they moored and went off variously to clamber over the cascades or have a swim. One of the swimmers was a young American model named Ginger Faye Meadows. As she and another young woman stood waist deep on a rock ledge under the waterfall, one of them noticed the cold, steady eyes and half-submerged snout of a crocodile coming towards them. Now imagine it. You are standing with your back to a rock wall much too steep and slippery to climb, with nowhere to retreat, and one of the deadliest creatures on earth is coming towards you – a creature so perfectly engineered to kill that it has scarcely changed in 200 million years. You are, in short, about to be killed by something from the age of the dinosaurs.

One of the two women took off a plastic shoe and threw it at the crocodile. It bounced off his head, causing him to blink and hesitate. In the same instant, Meadows decided to make a break for it. She dived into the water and tried to swim the twenty-five yards to safety. The friend stayed put. Meadows swam with strong strokes, but the crocodile followed on a line designed to intercept her. About halfway across it caught her round the middle and jerked her beneath the water.

According to the boat's skipper, Meadows stayed under for several seconds, then surfaced with 'her hands in the air and a really startled look on her face . . . She was looking right at me . . . but she didn't say a word.' Then she went under again and was seen no more. The next day would have been her twenty-fifth birthday.

This is probably the most famous crocodile attack in Australia in the last twenty-five years because it involved a well-known beauty spot, a luxury cruiser and a victim from America who happened to be young and very good looking. But here's the thing: there have been *lots* of others. What's more, Meadows's death was atypical because she saw it coming. For most people a crocodile attack comes completely unexpectedly. The chronicles of crocodile killings are full of stories of people standing in a few inches of water or sitting on a bank or strolling along an ocean beach when suddenly the water splits and, before they can even cry out, much less enter into negotiations, they are carried away for leisurely devouring. That is what is so scary about them.

Now I ask you. Who gives a stuff how much money people are making in Hong Kong or Singapore when you've got matters like that to worry about? That's all I'm saying.

Chapter

NINE

I

I would happily have stayed another day or two in Adelaide, but I had tracks to make. It was almost time to meet my friends in Melbourne, but first I had a promise to myself of long standing to visit the Mornington Peninsula, a coastal area of beauty and charm just south of Melbourne. As ever in Australia, it would take some getting to. I left Adelaide early and was dismayed to discover, within an hour or so of setting off, that I was facing yet another long day of driving on empty roads through a featureless expanse. This seemed particularly unfair because, in the first place, I had supposed that I was heading back into civilization and, second, I had had quite enough of this sort of thing already and, third, I had intentionally chosen a slightly longer route along a coastal highway to avoid the prospect of overland visual tedium.

The road I was on was called the Princes Highway. The

map showed it running in a graceful arc along the edge of a vast bay identified as the Younghusband Peninsula, and indeed it did present hours of sunny coastal views, but the tide was miles out, leaving the sea as a distant thread of bright blue on the far side of a million painfully reflective acres of saltpans. The inland side presented an equally featureless blankness filled with a single, infinitely repeated species of low shrub. For 146 kilometres the road was perfectly empty.

To pass the time, I sang Australia's unofficial national anthem, 'Waltzing Matilda'. It is an interesting song. It was written by Banjo Paterson, who was not only Australia's greatest poet of the nineteenth century but also the only one named for a stringed instrument. It goes (and I think the record should show that these are the words precisely as set down by Paterson):

Oh! there once was a swagman camped in the Billabong
Under the shade of a Coolibah tree
And he sang as he looked at his old billy boiling
Who'll come a-waltzing Matilda with me.

The main distinguishing feature of 'Waltzing Matilda', you will notice, is that it makes no sense. Obviously it makes no sense to anyone not familiar with bush lingo – that part was intentional – but even when you understand the words it makes no sense. A *billabong*, for instance, is a waterhole. So a question that immediately arises, before you have even concluded the first line, is: Why was the swagman camped *in* it? I would camp beside it myself. You see what you are up against? The only possible conclusion is that Paterson had had a few when he grabbed his inkpot and dashed off the words. Anyway, just to keep you fully informed, a *swagman* in Australian parlance is an itinerant traveller. The term comes from the rolled blanket, or *swag*, that he carried. Another name for a swag was a *Matilda*, evidently from the German *Mathilde*. (Don't ask me; my interest in this goes only so far.) A *billy* is a can for boiling water and a *coolibah tree* is a coolibah tree. There you have the terms. Why the swagman is a-waltzing with his bedroll and why above all he desires someone or something (in the second verse it's a sheep, for goodness' sake) to join him in this bizarre and possibly depraved activity are, of course, questions that cannot be answered.

On the other hand, it has a lovely tune (it's borrowed from an old Scottish air, 'Thou Bonnie Wood O' Craigielea'), which I render particularly melodically, if I say so myself, especially with my head out of the window to achieve that warbly effect that comes from singing into an onrush of air at speed. The problem with knowing only one verse, of course, is that it gets a trifle repetitive after a time. So you may conceive my satisfaction when I realized that if you changed 'billy boiling' to 'willy boiling' it put an entirely new slant on things, and I was able to come up with approximately forty-seven new stanzas, which not only extends the song to a length suitable for long bus journeys, but brings to it a dimension of coherence that it has lacked for almost a century.

I might have got the verse total even higher except that as I rounded the last sweep of bay and followed the road inland through a stretch of scrub, I came upon a sign announcing 'The Big Lobster' and in the excitement I abandoned my musical interests. The Big Lobster, you see, was something – or more properly a species of something – that I had longed to see ever since I had hit the road.

One of the more cherishable peculiarities of Australians is that they like to build big things in the shape of other things. Give them a bale of chicken wire, some fibreglass and a couple of pots of paint and they will make you, say, an enormous pineapple or strawberry or, as here, a lobster. Then they put a café and a gift shop inside, erect a big sign beside the highway (for the benefit of people whose acuity evidently does not extend to spotting a fifty-foot-high piece of fruit standing beside an otherwise empty highway), then sit back and wait for the money to roll in.

Some sixty of these objects are scattered across the Australian landscape, like leftover props from a 1950s' horror movie. You can, if you have sufficient petrol money and nothing approaching a real life, visit a Big Prawn, a Big Koala, a Big Oyster (with searchlights for eyes, apparently), a Big Lawnmower, a Big Marlin, a Big Orange and a Big Merino Ram, among many others. The process, I am patriotically proud to tell you, was started by an American named Landy who built a Big Banana at Coff's Harbour, on the New South Wales coast, which proved so magically attractive to passing vehicles that it made Mr Landy, as it were, the big banana of the business.

Generally these objects are cannily set along a stretch of highway so astoundingly void and dull that you will stop for almost anything – as of course I did now when the road bent once again and I found looming before me a monstrously large, reddish pink, commendably lifelike lobster rearing up beside the road as if about to dine on a morsel of passing traffic. Owing to the peculiar shape of a lobster, the owners had decided (I imagine after quite a lot of thought) not to try to accommodate a gift shop and café inside, so the Big Lobster sat on the front lawn, secured with guy wires, while the retail facilities were in a separate building behind. I got out and approached for a closer look. It was impressively outsized. I learned from subsequent enquiry that it is fifty-six feet from the ground to the tip of its feelers – a good size even in the ambitious world of giant objects.

I was looking at it from various angles when I realized that I had wandered into someone's photograph.

'Oh, sorry!' I called.

'No worries, mate,' he replied with an easygoing air. 'You help to give it scale.'

He came up and stood beside me. He was in his early thirties and looked vaguely sad and dorky, like someone who worked in a low-grade job and still lived at home. He was dressed as if for a vacation, in shorts and a T-shirt that said 'Noosa' in large letters. Noosa is a Queensland resort. Together we stood and for quite a period silently admired the lobster.

'Big, isn't it?' I remarked at last, for very little escapes me in the world of fibreglass crustaceans.

'You wouldn't get a snap of me in front of it, would you?' he said in that curiously circular way in which Australians beg a favour.

'Of course.'

He went and stood beside it, a hand perched affectionately on a foreleg.

'You can tell people it's an engagement photo,' I suggested.

He liked that idea. 'Yeah!' he said keenly. 'Meet the fiancée. She's not much for looks or conversation, but jeez can she scuttle!'

I decided I liked this guy.

'So do you visit these things a lot?' I said, handing him back the camera.

'Only if I'm passing, you know. It's a pretty good one, though. Better than the Big Koala at Moyston.'

I didn't feel there was a great deal I could say to this.

'At Wauchope there's a Big Bull,' he added.

I raised my eyebrows in a way that said: 'Oh yes?'

He nodded fondly. 'Its testicles swing in the breeze.'

'It has testicles?' I said, impressed.

'I'll say. If they fell on you, you wouldn't get up in a hurry.'

We took an extended moment to savour this image. 'It would make an interesting insurance claim, I suppose,' I observed at last.

'Yeah!' He liked this idea, too. 'Or a newspaper headline: "Man crushed by falling bollocks."'

'"By falling bullock's bollocks",' I offered.

'Yeah!'

We were getting on like a house on fire. I hadn't had a conversation this long in days. What am I saying – I hadn't had this much *fun* in days. Unfortunately, neither of us could think of anything more to say, and so we just stood awkwardly for a while.

'Well, nice meeting you,' he said at last and with a shy smile shuffled off.

'Nice meeting *you*,' I said and meant it.

I went inside and bought a fridge magnet and about fifteen Big Lobster postcards, and returned to the road in a mellow frame of mind. I headed the car towards Warrnambool and the famous Great Ocean Road and drove some minutes in thoughtful silence. Then abruptly I thrust my head out of the window, and in a sweet but robust voice sang:

Forgetting that spoons stir hot liquids much better
The swagman immersed his tool in his tea
And he sighed as he spied his old willy boiling
Now I can't bugger you, so will you bugger me?

II

I spent the night in Port Fairy, and drove on the next day to the Mornington Peninsula along the Great Ocean Road, a tortuous, spectacularly scenic coastal highway built after the First World War as a make-work scheme for veterans. It took fourteen years to construct and you can see why at once because for most of its 187 miles it swoops along an impossibly challenging coastline in a hair-raising manner, barrelling around rocky headlands and clinging to the edges of sheer and crumbly cliffs. So demanding of attention are the endless hairpin bends that you scarcely have a moment to notice the views, but I figured an occasional glimpsed view was better than none. Here and there in the water stand pinnacles of rock created by the tireless erosive might of the sea. There used to be a natural rock arch called London Bridge over which you could stroll to stand above the sea, but in 1990 it collapsed, sending tons of debris into the surf below and stranding two startled but miraculously unharmed tourists on the seaward stub. London Bridge is now London Stacks.

The drive was as gorgeous as the guidebooks had promised: on one side the steep, wooded, semi-tropical hills of the Otway Range plunging straight into the sea, on the other foamy surf rolling onto long, curving beaches framed at either end by rocky outcrops. This stretch of Victoria is famous for two things: surfing and shipwrecks.

With its wild currents and famous fogs, the south Victorian coast was long notorious to mariners. If you took all the water away, you would see 1,200 ships lying broken on the seabed, more than almost anywhere else in the world. I stopped from time to time to get out and take in the views – it really was the only way for a solitary driver to see them – and poked about in one or two of the sweetly old-fashioned little resort communities that lay along the way. These were surprisingly quiet, considering that it was the height of the Australian summer and the day after a national holiday. It struck me, not for the first time, that there seemed to be more places in Australia for tourists to go than there were tourists to fill them.

At a place called Torquay, the Great Ocean Road rejoined the main highway towards Melbourne. Twenty miles to the west, I noticed, was Winchelsea, where Thomas Austin set free the twenty-four rabbits that transformed the Australian landscape. The countryside roundabout looked vaguely arid and unpromising – it reminded me of Oklahoma or western Kansas – but I had no way of knowing, of course, how much of this could be attributed to the voracity of rabbits. Now you would think that people might have learned a lesson from Austin's experience, but amazingly no. At the very moment that rabbits were eating their way across the countryside, influential people were introducing other species of animals in great numbers – sometimes for sport, sometimes by accident, but mostly in an effort to liven things up a little. Precisely the same impulse that led people to build English-style parks in places like Adelaide led them to try to manipulate the countryside as well. Australia was deemed biologically deficient, its semi-arid plains too monotonous, its forests too silent. Gradually there arose acclimatization societies that made scores of eager introductions to fulfil a longing for the familiar. Before long it occurred to the societies that there was no reason to stop with British or even European animals. They began to dream of creating an African veldt in Australia, with giraffes, springboks and buffalo grazing the sunny plains. Their aspirations took on an almost surreal quality. In 1862, Sir Henry Barkly, governor of Victoria, called for the introduction of monkeys into the colony's forests 'for the amusement of wayfarers, whom their gambols would delight'. Before this could be acted on, Barkly had been replaced as governor by Sir Charles Darling, who said he didn't want monkeys but would be very pleased to see boa constrictors. He didn't get his way either, but scores of others did.

'Acclimatization was one of the most foolish and dangerous ideas ever to infect the thinking of nineteenth-century men,' writes Tim Low in the improbably gripping *Feral Future: The Untold Story of Australia's Exotic Invaders*, but infect them it did. Victoria, for some reason, became the hotbed of all this. Despite the experience with rabbits, dozens of other foolish introductions were made. In the 1860s the Ballarat Acclimatization Society loosed foxes into the landscape and they quickly became a scourge, a position from which they have not yet retreated. Other animals escaped or were abandoned and went wild. Camels were used to build the railway from Adelaide to Alice Springs, but were set free when the work was completed. Today 100,000 of them roam the central and western deserts, the only place in the world where one-humped dromedaries exist in the wild. Across the country there are up to five million wild donkeys, a million or more wild horses (called brumbies) and large numbers of water buffalo, cows, goats, sheep, pigs, foxes and dogs. Feral pigs have been caught in Melbourne suburbs. There are so many introduced species, in fact, that the red kangaroo, once the largest animal on the continent, is now only the thirteenth biggest.

The consequences for native species have often been devastating. About 130 mammals in Australia are threatened. Sixteen have become extinct – more than in any other continent. And guess what is the mightiest killer of all? According to the National Parks and Wildlife Service, it is the common cat. Cats love the Australian wild. There are 12 million of them out there, inhabiting every niche in the landscape from the driest deserts to the tallest mountains. With the fox they have driven many of Australia's smallest, cutest and most vulnerable native animals to the edge of extinction – numbats, bettongs, quolls, potoroos, bandicoots, rock wallabies, platypuses and many others. Since most of these creatures are nocturnal and rarely seen, most people don't notice their absence, but they are going fast.

As with animals, so with plants. In the 1850s, Victoria was unfortunate to have as chief botanist a dedicated acclimatizer with the imposing name of Baron Ferdinand Jacob Heinrich Von Mueller. As with animal acclimatizers, Von Mueller couldn't abide what he viewed as the impoverished nature of Australia's flora, and he spent much of his free time travelling the country sowing seeds of pumpkins, cabbages, melons and whatever else he thought might flourish. He had a special affection for blackberries, planting clumps of them all over. The blackberry is now Victoria's most pernicious weed, all but ineradicable and the bane of farmers everywhere. Where unmolested, it takes over whole landscapes. I saw some now as I drove along.

The lesson in this – that exotic species often thrive in

Australia in a way that staggers belief – is one that Australians have had a curiously hard time fully grasping. Prickly pear, a type of pulpy cactus native to America, was introduced in Queensland early in the twentieth century as a potential stock feed and quickly went crazy. By 1925, 30 million acres were overrun with impenetrable groves of prickly pear up to six feet high. It is an almost absurdly dense plant – an acre of prickly pear weighs 800 tons, as against about fifteen tons for an acre of wheat – and a nightmare to clear. For a while it looked as if much of Queensland and beyond would simply become one Europe-sized bed of prickly pear. Fortunately it could be treated effectively with pesticides and a moth whose larvae relished its leaves, but it was a close-run thing and the cost was substantial.

Altogether, according to Low, Australia is now home to more than 2,700 foreign weeds. Interestingly, botanical gardens are among the worst offenders. Three escapees from Darwin's Botanic Gardens – mimosa bush, leucaena and crutch tree – threaten Kakadu National Park, a World Heritage site, and there have been others elsewhere.

Where these things come from is often a mystery. According to Low, in recent years a biting ant, from the species *Iridomyrmex*, has infested Brisbane. It has become a common nuisance. Interestingly, no one knows where it came from or how it got there. It just one day appeared. Nor, for obvious reasons, can anyone say where it will spread or what quiet havoc it might wreak. One thing alone is certain. As so often, it appears to be doing better in Australia than wherever it came from.

The Mornington Peninsula is a spur of land just south of Melbourne. It is, I suppose, Victoria's Cape Cod, in that it is coastal and very pretty and crowded with summer homes. It even has something of the same shape, curling around in a scorpion tail that almost encloses the considerable immensity of Port Phillip Bay, across which, at a distance of some fifty miles, stands Melbourne. I had two particular reasons for wanting to be here: Catherine Veitch had made it sound so appealing in her letters and it was here that Australia's tragically submersible Prime Minister, Harold Holt, went for his final swim.

Holt's fateful dip was at Portsea, at the peninsula's far end, so it was there I directed myself the next morning after overnighting in the little town of Mornington. Though I set off in watery sunshine, of the sort that seemed to promise a fine day later on, Portsea was settled under a heavy sea mist, and the temperature when I stepped out of the car was cooler than it had been twenty miles up the road. Most of the few people out in Portsea, I noticed, were wearing cotton jumpers or jackets.

Portsea is very small – a handful of shops and cafés against a larger backdrop of big houses looking aloof and broody in the wispy fog – but famously well heeled. A beach hut had just sold at auction here for $185,000. Not a beach house, you understand, but a beach hut – a simple wooden shed with no electricity, water or any features at all other than proximity to sand and sea. The purchaser didn't even actually get to own the hut. All his $185,000 bought him was the right in perpetuity to pay the council several hundred dollars in annual rent. The huts, which only locals are allowed to acquire, are immensely prized possessions. The one that had just been sold had been in the same family for fifty years.

I had coffee to warm up before continuing on to the Mornington Peninsula National Park, which covers the last nubbin of land before it meets the sea at a hilly out-post called Point Nepean, beyond which lies a notorious swirl of water called the Rip – a narrow passage forming the entrance to Port Phillip Bay. Only recently had this land become public. For a hundred years, the whole of this area – several hundred acres of the most glorious coastal property in Victoria – was off limits to the public because it was owned by the military, which used it as a firing range. Pause with me for a moment while we put this in perspective. Here you have a country of three million square miles, nearly all of it empty and eminently bom-bable. And here, just a couple of hours' drive from the country's second city, you have a headland of rare and sumptuous beauty, and of considerable ecological impor-tance, and from this land you bar the public because you are trying to blow it to smithereens. Doesn't make much sense, what? The upshot is that after many years of wheedling and cajoling, the military was finally prevailed upon to yield a fragment of this land to form a national park. Even so, the army kept about two-thirds of the peninsula and still occasionally lofts bombs into it. In consequence, once you have acquired a ticket of admission at a visitors' centre on the edge of Portsea, you have to pass through a two-mile-long zone of military land on a road lined on both sides with tall fences bearing severe warn-ings of unexploded bombs and the folly of trespass. You can take a shuttle bus into the park or walk. I decided to walk, for the exercise, and set off through the cloaking mist. I appeared to have the place pretty much to myself.

I had gone no more than a dozen feet when I was joined by a fly – smaller and blacker than a housefly. It buzzed around in front of my face and tried to settle on my upper lip. I swatted it away, but it returned at once, always to the same spot. A moment later it was joined by another that wished to go up my nose. It also would not go away. Within a minute or so I had perhaps twenty of these active spots all around my head and I was swiftly sinking into the state of abject wretchedness that comes with a prolonged encounter with the Australian fly.

Flies are of course always irksome, but the Australian variety distinguish themselves by their very particular persistence. If an Australian fly wants to be up your nose or in your ear, there is no discouraging him. Flick at him as you will and each time he will jump out of range and come straight back. It is simply not possible to deter him. Somewhere on an exposed portion of your body is a spot about the size of a shirt button that the fly wants to lick and tickle and turn delirious circles upon. It isn't simply their persistence, but the things they go for. An Australian fly will try to suck the moisture off your eyeball. He will, if not constantly turned back, go into parts of your ears that a Q-tip can only dream about. He will happily die for the glory of taking a tiny dump on your tongue. Get thirty or forty of them dancing around you in the same way and madness will shortly follow.

And so I proceeded into the park, lost inside my own little buzzing cloud of woe, waving at my head in an increasingly hopeless and desultory manner – it is called the bush salute – blowing constantly out of my mouth and nose, shaking my head in a kind of furious dementia, occasionally slapping myself with startling violence on the cheek or forehead. Eventually, as the flies knew all along I would, I gave up and they fell upon me as on a corpse.

At length the flies and I reached the end of the military zone and the beginning of the park proper. Just inside this transition area was a signposted path leading up a medium-sized eminence called Cheviot Hill. This is what I had come to see, for it was at Cheviot Beach, on the other side, that Harold Holt went for the Swim That Needs No Towel. I followed the path upward through misty groves of low bushy trees – moonah, milkwort and tea trees, according to helpful noticeboards posted at intervals. At the top of the hill a stiff breeze was running, forceful enough to make me totter when I neglected to brace for it, and here at last the flies gave me a tiny bit of surcease. I stood with the wind full in my face, happier than I can tell you just to be left alone.

The view from the top of Cheviot Hill is said to be one of the finest in coastal Victoria, though I cannot vouch for this as I could see almost nothing. Across a grey-green vale, a mile or so distant, rose another hill at Point Nepean, covered in lazy cloud. Beyond was the notorious Rip, invisible from here. Below me, things were no less impenetrable. I appeared to be perhaps a hundred feet directly above Cheviot Beach, but it was like peering into a cauldron. All I could see through the drifting soup were some vague outlines of rocks and an indeterminate expanse of sand. Only the sounds of unseen waves flopping onto an unseen shore made it evident that I had found the sea.

Still, I felt a frisson of satisfaction at having reached the place of Holt's fateful swim. I tried to imagine the scene as it must have been, though it wasn't easy. On the day Holt waded into the surf, the weather was windy but fine. Things were not going very well for him as Prime Minister – his skills lay more in kissing babies and making the ladies tingle (he was evidently a bit of a hottie) than in running affairs of state – and we may safely assume that he was glad to be out of Canberra for the long Christmas break. Holt came to this beach because he had a weekend home at Portsea and the army let him stroll on its grounds for the sake of his privacy. So there were no lifeguards, members of the public or even security guards in attendance when, on 17 December 1967, Holt went for a breezy stroll with some friends among the rocks and pounding waves just below. Although the sea was lively and the tide dangerously high, and although Holt had almost drowned there six months earlier while snorkelling with some chums, he decided to go for a swim. Before anyone could react he had whipped off his shirt and plunged into the surf. He swam straight out from the beach a couple of hundred feet and almost instantly vanished, without fuss or commotion or even a languorous wave. He was fifty-nine years old and had been Prime Minister for not quite two years. His body was never found.

Cheviot Beach remains closed to the public, and in any case there was no way down to it from the clifftops, so I amused myself for a few minutes prowling through a complex of pillboxes and murky concrete bunkers left over from the Second World War until I walked into a large cobweb and, with an echoing shriek and a few moments of caroming about between walls, low lintels and other unyielding impedimenta, returned in subdued form to the open air. Rubbing my head and calling round the flies again, I followed the path back down to the road. At the bottom of the hill was a large and straggly cemetery, a relic from when this was a quarantine station. I tried to have a look around, but the flies would give me no peace. I had intended to stroll out to the headland where there was a nineteenth-century fort, but the thought of having the flies as my companions for another hour was more than I could endure, so I set off back along the empty road by which I had come.

At the visitors' centre I stopped in to have a look at the displays and got chatting with the park ranger. I asked him how dangerous this stretch of coastline was.

'Oh, very,' he said cheerfully. He showed me on a marine chart how the currents ran – which is to say all over the place. If they got hold of you, I gathered, they would pass you around like an unwanted parcel. Even the strongest swimmer would soon be exhausted by the fight. It was mostly to do with the Rip, where massive volumes of water rush through an opening only a few hundred yards across each time the tide rolls in or out. I hadn't realized until I saw the chart just how proximate Cheviot Beach was to this zone of watery turmoil. Even on a map it looked supremely foolhardy.

'So it wasn't a good idea for Harold Holt to go swimming out there?'

'Well, I wouldn't go swimming out there,' he replied. 'You know, there's about a hundred shipwrecks just along here.' He indicated an absurdly modest stretch of shoreline in the vicinity of Cheviot and the Rip. 'I think you can take it as read that when you've got a stretch of sea that sinks a hundred ships, it's probably not the most placid environment for a dip, you know?'

'Isn't it odd that they never found his body?'

'No.' This was said without hesitation.

'Really?' I don't understand the dynamics of the sea, but if driftwood and Coke cans are anything to go by, then I thought most buoyant objects ended up on a beach somewhere.

'Not to be too blunt about it, if you die out there it doesn't take too long to become part of the food chain.'

'Ah.'

'The thing you've got to remember,' he added with a sudden thoughtful air, 'is that the only thing unusual about the Harold Holt drowning was that he was Prime Minister when it happened. If it hadn't been for that the whole thing would have been completely forgotten. Mind you, it's pretty well forgotten anyway.'

'So you don't get a lot of people coming here in a kind of pilgrimage?'

'No, not at all. Most people barely remember it. A lot of people under thirty have never even heard of it.'

He broke off to issue tickets to some new arrivals and I drifted away to look at the displays of seagrasses and life in rockpools. But as I was leaving he called to me with an afterthought. 'They built a memorial to him in Melbourne,' he said. 'Know what it was?'

I indicated that I had no idea.

He grinned very slightly. 'A municipal swimming pool.'

'Seriously?'

His grin broadened, but the nod was sincere.

'This is a terrific country,' I said.

'Yeah,' he agreed happily. 'It is, you know.'

Chapter

TEN

Throughout my childhood on Friday nights whenever my father was away, which was often (he was a sportswriter who travelled a lot for his work), my mother and I had an arrangement whereby I would take a bus downtown to meet her (she also worked for the local paper) and we would go to dinner at a cafeteria called Bishop's and then to a movie.

I don't wish to suggest that my mother abused the trust I placed in her with regard to the selection process, but it did seem uncanny that the movies I favoured had always just left town and that we ended up seeing something involving murder, passion and betrayal, usually starring Jeff Chandler, for whom my mother had a strange admiration, usually in a part that required him to spend a good deal of time bare-chested.

'Oh,' she would tut in a tone of shared chagrin, '*Twenty*

Thousand Leagues under the Sea has just gone. But the Orpheum has the new Jeff Chandler movie, *Tame Lust*. Shall we go see that?'

I don't know if through the passage of time these movies have blurred into one in my memory or whether they actually were all identical, but they seemed always to have the same elements – way too much talking, lots of steamy embraces with Lana Turner or some other hard-looking blonde, very occasional gunfire resulting in a clutched belly, a staggered walk and a disappointingly modest seepage of blood, and a part for Chandler that put him frequently on a speedboat or lifeguard's stand dressed only in swimming trunks. (Without even looking at the screen you could tell which were the swimming trunks scenes because of the avidity with which my mother would begin to suck her lemon drops.) If a Jeff Chandler movie wasn't available – and amazingly sometimes whole weeks passed in which he didn't produce a picture – we would have to see something else.

Thus it was that one week when I was about nine we went to see *The Sundowners*, a Technicolor epic starring Robert Mitchum and Deborah Kerr in the story of a lovably feisty and indomitable couple making a life for themselves in the Australian bush. It was a memorable movie in many ways, not least in that it provided the endearing spectacle of Robert Mitchum doing an Aussie accent, and that it dealt with Australia at all, which made it, in Hollywood terms, essentially unique. Nearly forty years after the event I don't recall much of the detail of the film other than that Mitchum and Kerr spent every waking moment herding armies of sheep and fighting one discommoding peril of antipodean life after another – bushfires, dust storms, drought, locust infestations and pub brawls mostly. It was also evidently very hot in Australia: Mitchum never spoke without first taking off a dusty hat and running a forearm across his brow. Since my plans for myself, even at the age of nine, were to spend my adulthood driving an open-topped sports car through Europe with Jean Seberg at my side, I concluded that Australia was of essentially zero interest and did not actively think about it again for thirty years.

In consequence, when finally I made my first trip Down Under, to attend the 1992 Melbourne Writers' Festival, I was actually able to be astounded to find it there at all. I clearly recall standing on Collins Street in Melbourne, so freshly arrived that I still smelled of (possibly even glistened from) the insecticide with which the flight attendants sprayed the plane before arrival, watching the clanging trams and swirl of humanity, and thinking: 'Good lord, there's a country here.' It was as if I had privately discovered life on another planet, or a parallel universe where life was at once recognizably similar but entirely different.

I can't tell you how exciting it was. Insofar as I had accumulated any expectations of Australia at all in the intervening years, I had thought of it as a kind of alternative southern California, a place of constant sunshine and the cheerful vapidity of a beach lifestyle, but with a slight British bent – a sort of *Baywatch* with cricket, as I thought it. But this was nothing like that. Melbourne had a settled and gracious air that was much more European than North American, and it rained, rained the whole week, which delighted me inordinately because it was so totally not what I had expected.

What's more, and here we come to the real crux of things, I liked it, straight off, without quibble or doubt, in a way I had never expected to. Something about it just agreed with me. I suppose it helped that I had spent half my life in America and half in Britain because Australia was such a comfortable fusion of the two. It had a casualness and vivacity – a lack of reserve, a comfortableness with strangers – that felt distinctly American, but hung on a British framework. In their optimism and informality Australians could pass at a glance for Americans, but they drove on the left, drank tea, played cricket, adorned their public places with statues of Queen Victoria, dressed their children in the sort of school uniforms that only a Britannic people could wear without conspicuous regret. I felt extremely comfortable with this.

Almost at once I became acutely, and in an odd way delightedly, aware of how little I knew about the place. I didn't know the names of their newspapers or universities or beaches or suburbs, knew nothing of their history or private achievements, couldn't tell a policeman from a postman. I didn't even know how to order coffee. It appeared that you had to specify a length (principally long or short), a colour (black or white) and even an angle of orientation to the perpendicular (flat or not), and these could be put together in a multitude of permutations – 'long black', 'short black', even 'long short black'. My own preference, I discovered after many happy hours of experimentation, was 'flat white'. It was a moment of the sublimest happiness.

Because my responsibilities at the festival were extremely slight – one or two stage presentations and a little light sweeping afterwards – I was free to roam through the city and I did so with the greatest enthusiasm and devotion, eavesdropping on conversations, sitting in coffee bars with all the morning newspapers and half a dozen beverages

(I was still in the experimental stage), devouring both, reading labels and hoardings and the signs in shop windows, asking questions of complete strangers: 'Excuse me, what's a Jacky Howe? What are norks? What's a Hills Hoist?'*

I loved – still do – Australian voices, the lilt and cadence, the effortlessly dry, direct way of viewing the world. At a reception for some minor awards presentation – the East Gippsland Young Farmers First Novel Award or something, which I attended because I was just so pleased to get an invitation to anything and because cocktails were promised – I was standing with two female publicists from my publisher's when some obviously self-infatuated nork breezed in.

'Oh look, it's Bruce Dazzling,' observed one and then with a kind of distant, perfectly encapsulating disdain added: 'He'd go to the opening of an envelope.'

Someone else told me the story of an English friend of his who was flying to Australia when the stewardess tonged him a hot towel, which proved upon application to be cold. So he told her – not in complaint, but simply because he thought she might want to warm them up some more. The stewardess turned to him and, smiling sweetly, with only the tiniest trace of sarcasm, said: 'Well, why don't you sit on it a bit? That should warm it up.' I knew as soon as I heard that story that I was going to like this place. I haven't stopped yet.

Because my first exposure was to Melbourne, I formed a certain slavish attachment to the place. I still find it terribly

* Respectively a singlet, a slang term for breasts (I saw it on the cover of a magazine and actually made a sales assistant blush in asking, but how else to learn?) and a type of rotary clothesline of which the Australians are mysteriously but touchingly proud.

211

exciting to arrive in Melbourne – not an emotion you will hear expressed often, but there you are – and driving now through the glossy high-rises of its central business district had something of the feeling of a homecoming. Over there was the first Australian hotel I'd stayed in, there the first coffee shop I'd tried, there the celebrated Melbourne Cricket Ground, where I once spent three hours happily bewildered by an Australian Rules Football match and dined on my first (and last) four-and-twenty pie ('made with real blackbirds', I was drolly assured). Insofar as such a statement could have meaning, this was my home in Australia.

Most people (and when I say 'most people' I mean of course me when I first got there) don't realize that for a long time Melbourne was much the most important city in Australia. Although Sydney has been slightly the bigger of the two for a century (Melbourne's population now is about 3.5 million to Sydney's 4 million), Melbourne was until relatively recently the centre of things, particularly in the realms of finance and culture. Sydney used to compensate by making up cruel but generally outstanding jokes about Melbourne's supposed lack of liveliness, like:

> 'Do you have any children?'
> 'Yes, two living and one in Melbourne.'

These days Sydney makes jokes about Melbourne *and* steals its thunder, which is naturally a little hard for Melbourne people to take. Nothing better illustrates the shift in the two cities' relative standings than that in 1956 the Olympics went to Melbourne and in 2000 they have gone to Sydney. Most things do nowadays. In 1956, Melbourne was headquarters to fifty of Australia's largest companies while Sydney had just thirty-seven. Today the proportions are almost exactly reversed. A generation ago, international companies routinely chose Melbourne for their Australian headquarters; today over two-thirds opt for Sydney. But far more galling to a city that has always viewed Sydney as having the intellectual vibrancy of, let us say, daytime television, Melbourne has had to watch as Sydney has appropriated chunks of its cultural pre-eminence – in publishing, fashion, film and television, all the performing arts. I used to visit my Australian publishers in Melbourne. Today I go to Sydney.

Having said all that, and once you strip out the huge visual advantage Sydney derives from its harbour, there is precious little to choose between the two in terms of quality of life or cultural satisfaction. Much less separates Melbourne from Sydney than separates Los Angeles from New York or Birmingham from London.

Melbourne may not have a Harbour Bridge or an Opera House like Sydney's but it has something in its way no less singular: the world's most bizarre right turns. If you are driving in central Melbourne and you wish to turn against the traffic, you don't get in the middle lane, but rather pull over to the kerb – as far as possible from where you want to be – and sit there for an indeterminate period (in my case until all the clubs and restaurants have shut and everyone has gone home for the night) and make your turn from there in a frantic moment just before the lights change. It's all to do with keeping out of the way of the trams – Melbourne's other speciality – which go down the middle of the road and can't have turning cars blocking their way. It's immensely confusing, not only to visitors from overseas but to other Australians – even, I suspect, to many Melbourne people.

But what really sets Melbourne apart is its love of Australian Rules Football, a sport little followed in Sydney or New South Wales, where rugby is the passion. It's interesting that Melburnians don't tell jokes about Sydney. They tell jokes about their beloved footy. To wit:

A man arriving for the Grand Final in Melbourne is surprised to find the seat beside his empty. Tickets for the Grand Final are sold out weeks in advance and empty seats unknown. So he says to the man on the other side of the seat: 'Excuse me, do you know why there is no one in this seat?'

'It was my wife's,' answers the second man, a touch wistfully, 'but I'm afraid she died.'

'Oh, that's terrible. I'm so sorry.'

'Yes, she never missed a match.'

'But couldn't you have given the ticket to a friend or relative?'

'Oh no. They're all at the funeral.'

I was on my way to meet an old friend named Alan Howe, who, it so happens, is the person who introduced me to the transfixing peculiarities of Australian Rules. I first met him nearly twenty years ago when I was working as a sub-editor on the business desk of *The Times* in London and he was a downy-faced recruit from Down Under. I had been there for a few months already when he arrived and was given a seat beside me on the subs' table. I don't want to say he was awfully young back then, but he was wearing a Cub Scout uniform. Anyway, I took him under my wing as a fellow colonial and taught him all I knew. Admittedly this was only three things – that Lloyd's the insurers had an apostrophe while Lloyds Bank did not; that the hyphen was oddly placed in the company name Rio Tinto-Zinc;

and that the canteen was in the basement – but in those days that was all you needed to know to work on the business desk.

He was a quick learner and he soon outstripped us all. I remember one day I was having an argument with a colleague over whether the 'p/e' in 'p/e ratio' stood for penis envy or Prince Edward, when Howe told us it was short for 'price/earnings ratio', and that it was a staple measure of an equity's perceived worth arrived at by dividing its current value by its earnings per share over the previous twelve months, and I knew then that this was a guy who was going places. He hasn't disappointed us, I must say. After a distinguished spell at *The Times* he returned to Australia, where he became a rising star in the Murdoch firmament, fetching up in the early 1990s as editor of the *Sunday Herald-Sun*, over which popular publication he still presides. When I think of him sitting there at *The Times* in his little neckerchief and blue shirt, my old heart swells with pride.

He and his wife, a kindly and placid soul named Carmel Egan, live in South Melbourne in a lovely old house that was formerly a butcher's shop, of all things. I was late in arriving owing to a little inadvertent experiment I conducted to establish whether it is possible to find your way to an address in Melbourne using a street plan for Perth, but I found it at length. It was Carmel who received me.

'Howie's out,' she said, ushering me in. 'He's gone for a run.'

'A run?' I tried not to sound too astounded, but in the years I had known him Howe's idea of a whole-body workout was to drink standing up. Besides, he was one of those restless, high-energy people who are constitutionally incapable of putting on fat. He needed to run the way I needed to increase my children's college expenses. 'It's his heart,' she added.

I stared at her. 'He's got a heart problem?'

'No, of course not,' she laughed. 'He's just, you know, discovered it.'

I understood at once. Howe has long been one of the world's great hypochondriacs. For years he has been moving from organ to organ, certain that one of them is about to maim him in a painful and costly way. He is forever standing off in corners palpating himself for mysterious lumps and adjusting his lifestyle accordingly.

So Carmel and I sat and had a nice cup of tea, and I told her fond stories about her husband in those far-off London days before she had met him: how I taught him to use soap and wear matching socks, and helped him to find the treatments that made his gonads drop – the usual sort of thing. It was at this point that the great man himself flopped into the house, extravagantly flushed, breathless and sweaty. 'Hey, mate,' he managed to breathe out in what it looked like might be his dying words.

'Are you OK?'

'Never been better.'

'What are you running for?' I said.

'Ticker, mate.'

'There's nothing wrong with your heart.'

'That's right,' he said proudly. 'And do you know why? Because I look after it.' He nodded sagely, as if I hadn't thought of that, and cast a privately thoughtful glance at my bulk.

For dinner we walked to a local restaurant, where we talked agreeably about a million things – mutual friends, work, where I had been on this trip and where I was going, all the sorts of things you talk about when you get together with friends you rarely see. At one point Howe mentioned casually that he had recently been boogie boarding at Byron Bay, in New South Wales, when he had encountered a shark.

'Truly?' I said, impressed.

He nodded. 'It was a fair size, too – nine or ten footer, I'd say.'

'So how close was it?'

'Close. I could just about have touched it.'

'So what did you do?'

'Strategically retreated. What do you think?'

'Weren't you scared?'

He made a look of sudden enthusiasm, as if I had just put my finger on something. 'Yeah,' he said, 'I was a bit.'

'A bit?'

'Oh, yeah,' he returned wholeheartedly, as if being a bit scared was the maximum permitted in Australia, which I suppose it is.

This led to a fond recollection of other near-death experiences with animals, of which Australians always have a large fund – an encounter with a crocodile in Queensland, killer snakes nearly stepped on, waking up to find a red-back abseiling on a thread towards one's face. Australians are very unfair in this way. They spend half of any conversation insisting that the country's dangers are vastly overrated and that there's nothing to worry about, and the other half telling you how six months ago their Uncle Bob was driving to Mudgee when a tiger snake slid out from under the dashboard and bit him on the groin, but that it's OK now because he's off the life-support machine and they've discovered he can communicate with eye blinks.

I was, of course, all ears for all this.

'So what's the story with the crocodile?' I asked eagerly.

Howe smiled with just a hint of sheepishness. 'Well, Carmel and I were on holiday up in Queensland, at a place called Port Douglas, when we decided' – he saw her about to correct him – 'when I decided that it would be fun to hire a boat and go out for a little fishing.'

'In a crocodile-infested estuary,' Carmel added. She turned to me. 'Alan was too cheap to pay for a big boat with a guide, so we got a little boat by ourselves. A very little boat.' She allowed him to continue.

'So we got this little boat,' he went on, with a magnanimous nod in her direction, 'with a little outboard motor on it, and we set off across this kind of estuary. The estuary was crowded with other boats, but I spotted an inlet, and I thought: "Oh, we'll try up there." Well, the inlet turns out to be a river – a really beautiful one. So we go cruising up this river and it's just wonderful, your quintessential tropical paradise – big green river, jungle backdrop, colourful birds flying through the trees. You can imagine it. Best of all, there's not a soul around. We've got it all to ourselves. So we find a nice spot and I cut the engine and we're sitting there with our fishing lines in the water having a nice relaxing time when Carmel points out a kind of muddy bare patch on the bank, and we realize it's a crocodile launching place. Couldn't be anything else. Then we notice that there are several of these launching places all along the bank. It starts to dawn on us that maybe this is why there is nobody else up here, because it's infested with crocodiles. Just as we are coming to this significant conclusion there's a splash off to one side, like something heavy going into the water, and then a line in the water moving vaguely towards us.'

'Whoa,' I said.

'My sentiments exactly, Bryson.' He grinned.

'So what did you do?'

'Well, like the good sailor I am, I hopped to the motor to get us out of there. Only the motor wouldn't start. It just would not go.'

'Meanwhile,' Carmel interjected, 'I'm sitting in the back of the boat watching this line coming towards us and saying, "Alan, the crocodile's coming. It's definitely coming our way. Let's get out of here, mate. What do you say?" '

'And I'm pulling on the cord, and pulling and pulling, and the engine is just going *putt putt putt pfffffft*. And all the while the crocodile's coming. *Finally*, miraculously, the engine catches and we're able to move off. Only we're pointing in the wrong direction, so we've got to go *up* the river, away from where we want to be, in order to turn around. Anyway, after much messing around and crashing into banks and a little affectionate discussion of how we're going to die in a minute and it's all my fault, we get turned around. Only to get out of there we've got to go towards where the crocodile is.'

'So where is the crocodile now?'

'No idea. There's no sign of him now. He's there somewhere, but we don't know where. He could be right alongside the boat for all we know. The water's so murky you can't see two inches into it. But we do know that sometimes crocodiles go for boats.'

'Especially little cheap tinny boats,' Carmel said, smiling at him.

Alan grinned happily. 'So I throw open the throttle,' he went on, 'and the boat putters along at about half a mile an hour because it is, I have to admit, a very small and cheap boat. We've got to go maybe a quarter of a mile through the crocodile's territory at crawling speed and all the while we're sitting there expecting to feel a bang against the hull and to be tipped into the water. It was a little unnerving.'

'Did you know,' I said, 'that an outboard motor engine sounds to a crocodile very like the territorial growl of another crocodile? That's why crocodiles so often go for small boats apparently.'

They looked at me with amazement. It's not often a foreigner gets to scare the crap out of Australian listeners, but I had just read the book after all.

'I'm so glad I didn't know that at Port Douglas,' Carmel said. She gave an expansive shiver.

'But you got back OK, I take it?' I asked.

Alan nodded happily. 'We went down the river, across the estuary and were out of that boat – and I mean clean out – before it touched the dock.' He looked at me with a very pleased and expectant smile. 'And how long do you think we'd had the boat out? We'd hired it for a half day, bear in mind.'

I indicated that I couldn't guess.

Howe leaned towards me, beaming all over. 'Twenty-nine minutes,' he said with the supremest pride. 'Guy told us it was a record.'

'That's splendid,' I said.

'A proud achievement for the Howe family,' he added, and you could see that he meant it.

Howe had to put out a paper the next day, but Carmel offered to show me the sights. So late the next morning we drove into the city to drop off my rental car, and to do some shopping and have a look around. We were driving down Chapel Street looking for a place to park, and Carmel was telling me about her work – she is the Melbourne correspondent for News International – when she broke off and said brightly: 'Oh look, it's Jim Cairns.' She indicated a little old man crossing the road in front of us carrying a chair and a card table. He looked a touch timeworn, but otherwise unremarkable. 'He was Deputy Prime Minister in the Whitlam government,' she informed me. I looked at her to see if she was pulling my leg, but she smiled sincerely. 'He sells his autobiography at that market over there.' She indicated the sort of covered market where you would go to buy vegetables.

I looked at her. 'He sells books – his own book – from a card table?'

She smiled, cheerfully acknowledging that this might strike an outsider as just a trifle cheesy. 'I suppose it's a way for him to make a little pocket money,' she added.

This was a man, you understand, who had not so long ago held the second highest office in the land. The equivalent in America, I suppose, would be to find Walter Mondale sitting at a card table in a mall in Minneapolis selling White House coasters and other memorabilia.

'He does this regularly?' I asked.

'Oh, he's a fixture. You want to meet him?'

'Very much.'

We found a space and parked, but when we got to the market we discovered that he had gone. Evidently we had seen him on his way home. 'I think things are sometimes a little slow for him,' Carmel said sympathetically. 'He's been selling the book for a long time.'

I nodded and reflected, not for the first time, what a strange, small, distant country Australia is.

We were headed for the Immigration Museum but our route took us past the new Crown Casino, a gaming palace that all Melbourne people either loathe because it's tacky and tempts foolish people to lose their savings, or adore because it's tacky and sometimes pays out big. 'You want to have a look at it?' Carmel asked. I hesitated – I felt I had satisfied my gambling curiosity at the Penrith Panthers club in Sydney on my first trip – but she said with unusual certitude, 'I think it'll interest you,' and we went in.

She couldn't have been more right. It was an amazing place, vast in scale – it dwarfed by far even the Penrith club – and dripping with ornate fixtures. Some kind of frantic laser show involving synthesized music and lots of drifting smoke (the better to show up the dancing beams, I guess) was taking place in a lofty outer atrium, but almost nobody was watching. The real business was in the casino beyond, which was no less extravagant in decor and went on seemingly for ever. I can say with confidence that whoever won the contract for the carpet at the Crown Casino has not had to work since. It took twenty minutes to stroll from one end of the room to the other. The amazing thing was its busyness and strange intensity. It was barely lunchtime and perhaps 2,000 gamblers were already in devoted attendance. Hardly a pit or machine wasn't in fully active service. I had never seen anything on this scale outside Las Vegas, and in Las Vegas a good chunk of the people are just fooling around and having a good time. The people here were merely intent. At one roulette table I saw a man distribute perhaps twenty chips around the baize, lose them all, then reach into a wallet and pluck out twenty $50 bills to buy more. Quite slowly – for urban Australia is such a multicultural place that you scarcely notice these things normally – it dawned on me that he and the overwhelming proportion of other patrons were Chinese. I may have misjudged his attire, but he looked like a waiter or cook – certainly not like someone who could afford to lose thousands in a session. I mentioned this to Carmel and she nodded.

'Spectacular gamblers,' she whispered. She gave a wan smile. 'It's huge business. A billion dollars a year goes through here. Victoria gets 15 per cent of all its revenues from gambling.'

I thought for a moment. That must be hundreds of millions of dollars. 'So how many casinos are there in the state?' I asked.

'You're in it,' she said.

The Immigration Museum, just over the Yarra River in a grand old edifice that was once the local Customs House, provided a calm and decidedly more cerebral contrast. It had only recently opened, and still gleamed with shiny newness. Howe had been particularly eager that I see it because in his capacity as pillar of the community he had been one of the driving forces behind its foundation. Since the immigrant experience is essentially the story of modern Australia, it was really a museum of social history and quite the best one I have seen anywhere.

In a cavernous central hall was a large walk-in display in the shape of an ocean liner and designed, with the help of replica cabins and various ephemera, to convey the flavour of shipboard life for immigrants at different periods. I was particularly taken with the 1950s portion. I suppose because I grew up a thousand miles from the sea and missed the great age of passenger liners, I have always been subject to a romantic longing for ocean travel. In any case, I found myself helplessly lingering over every trivial detail of shipboard life – studying a forty-year-old menu as if I would soon be making my choice between lamb cutlets and braised beef, imagining my own books and toiletries on the shelf beside the bunk, thinking whether for the tea dancing this afternoon I should wear my baggage label shirt or go for a wild-orchids-of-Hawaii motif.

I hadn't realized – or at least hadn't stopped to reflect in anything like an adequate manner – quite what an investment in both time and funds a trip to Australia represented in those days. Until as late as the early 1950s a round-trip aeroplane ticket from Australia to England cost as much as a three-bedroom suburban home in Melbourne or Sydney. With the introduction by Qantas of larger Lockheed Super Constellation airliners in 1954, prices began to fall, but even by the end of the decade travelling to Europe by air still cost as much as a new car. Nor was it a terribly speedy or comfortable service. The Super Constellations took three days to reach London and lacked the power or range to dodge most storms. When monsoons or cyclones were encountered, the pilots had no choice but to put on the seat-belt signs and bounce through them. Even in normal conditions they flew at a height guaranteed to produce more or less constant turbulence. (Qantas called it, without evident irony, the Kangaroo Route.) It was, by any modern measure, an ordeal.

So for nearly every immigrant throughout the 1950s, a trip to Australia meant a five-week sea cruise. Even now, of course, when you must allow yourself to be sealed into a winged canister for a full day in order to get there, Australia feels a long way away. But how infinitely remote it must have seemed when you stood on a ship's deck and watched the continents fall away one by one and measured out the distance in 12,000 miles of ship's wake. I studied the faces of the beaming people lounging on sunchairs or striding about on breezy decks. They wore expressions just like those on the faces of the people I'd seen in the Surfers Paradise book in Adelaide. These people were happy, too – radiantly so. They were on their way to a lucky country and they knew it. Awaiting them was a life of abundant sunshine and good jobs, good homes, good prospects, and electric jugs for all. They were going on a holiday and they were going *for ever.*

It was such an interesting age for Australia. It wasn't just millions of foreigners who became Australian in the 1950s but, in an odd way, Australians themselves. I had only just learned that until 1949 there was no such thing as Australian citizenship. People born in Australia were not in any technical sense Australians at all but Britons – as British as if they were from Cornwall or Scotland. They swore allegiance to king and country, and when Britain went to war they unhesitatingly went off to die in foreign fields for her. At school, they studied British history, geography and economics as assiduously as if they were growing up in Liverpool or Manchester. I remember in one of her letters Catherine Veitch remarking to me on the surreal quality of sitting in an Adelaide classroom in the 1930s looking out on blazing waratah trees and flocks of kookaburras or whatever while learning the heights of Scottish mountains or the figures for barley production in East Anglia.

The absurdity of the situation wasn't lost on Australians, but Britain was all they had. As the historian Alan Moorehead once wrote: 'Australians of my generation grew up in a world apart. Until we went abroad we had never seen a beautiful building, hardly ever heard a foreign language spoken, or been to a well-acted play, or eaten a reasonably sophisticated meal, or listened to a good orchestra.' The oddest aspect of all was that millions of

Australians, most of whom had never left the country, went through life thinking of England in some odd, ultimate sense as home. As late as 1957 in *On the Beach*, the Nevil Shute novel in which a nuclear war leaves Australia as the last inhabited place on earth, the author could have his Australian heroine lament: 'I was going home in March. To London. It's been arranged for years . . . It's so bloody unfair.' By 'home' she means a country she has never seen and now never will.

But even as Shute wrote Australia was in the process of becoming a very different country. In the Second World War it had suffered a kind of blunt trauma when, after the fall of Burma and Singapore, Britain pulled out of the Far East, leaving Australia suddenly alone and dangerously exposed. At the same time Winston Churchill, a man whose presumptuousness was never less than enthralling, asked Australia's military leaders to divert their troops to India – in effect, to abandon their wives and children and fight for the greater good of empire. The Australians decided they could not. Instead they stayed behind and fought a rearguard action to try to stop the Japanese advance across New Guinea.

Not many people outside Australia realize just how close the Japanese got. They had captured most of the Solomon Islands and much of New Guinea, just to the north, and seemed poised for an invasion. The Australian military, knowing the position was hopeless, drew up a plan to fall back to the south-east corner of the country, sacrificing nearly the whole of the continent in the hope of defending the main cities. It could have been no more than a delaying tactic. Luckily, the tide of battle moved elsewhere after the American naval victory at Midway and an Australian victory over Japan at Milne Bay. Australia was reprieved.

Australia escaped but it was left with two scars – a realization that Britain could not be counted on to come to its rescue in a crisis, and a sense of immense vulnerability to the teeming and unstable countries to the north. Both of these matters deeply influenced Australian attitudes in the post-war years – indeed still do. Australia became seized with the conviction that it must populate or perish – that if it didn't use all that empty land and fill all those empty spaces someone from outside might do it for them. So in the years after the war, the country threw open its doors. In the half century after 1945 its population soared, from seven million to 18 million.

Britain alone couldn't provide the necessary bodies, so people were welcomed from all over Europe, particularly Greece and Italy in the immediate post-war years, making the nation vastly more cosmopolitan. Suddenly Australia was full of people who liked wine and good coffee and olives and aubergines, and realized that spaghetti didn't have to be a vivid orange and come from tins. The whole warp and rhythm of life changed. Good Neighbour Councils were established everywhere to help the immigrants settle and feel welcomed, and the Australian Broadcasting Corporation offered English language courses which were enthusiastically taken up by tens of thousands. By 1970, the country could boast of 2.5 million 'New Australians', as they were known.

Of course, it wasn't perfect. In the fever to populate, some migrants were accepted with less reflection than might have been wished. At least ten thousand children, many as young as four, were dispatched from British orphanages between 1947 and 1967 by child welfare groups such as the Salvation Army, Barnardo's and the Christian Brothers. The impulse was genuinely altruistic –

it was felt that the children would have a chance of a better life in a country that was warm and sunny and needed labour – but the execution often lacked subtlety. Siblings were frequently parted, never to meet again, and many of the children had essentially no notion of what was happening to them. In his book *Orphans of the Empire*, Alan Gill notes how one little boy, seeing a sign announcing the mustering point for 'the Barnardo's party', was thrilled because he presumed 'party' meant cake and ice cream. Another enquired, as the ship made its way up the Thames, whether they would be home in time for tea. Stories don't get a great deal more poignant than that.

There was also the deep odium of the White Australia Policy, which allowed immigration officials to keep out undesirables by requiring them to pass a literacy test in any European language of the authorities' choosing (including on one famous occasion Scottish Gaelic) and to deport non-whites with little thought of compassion. In the early 1950s, Arthur Calwell, the Minister for Immigration, tried to repatriate the Indonesian-born widow and eight children of an Australian citizen. If Australians have a single radiant virtue, it is the belief in a 'fair go' – a sense of the fundamental rightness of common justice – and the case caused an outcry. The courts told Calwell to get real, and the more insensitive side of the exclusion policy swiftly began to erode. Around 1970, as Australia increasingly recognized that it was, at least geographically, an Asian nation and not a European one, the colour bar came down and hundreds of thousands of immigrants were let in from across the region. Today Australia is one of the most multicultural countries on earth. A third of the people in Sydney were born in another country; in Melbourne the four most common surnames are Smith, Brown, Jones and Nguyen. Across the country as a whole almost a quarter of people have no British antecedents on either side of their families. For millions of people it truly was a chance of a new life – one that, on the whole, was generously extended and gratefully accepted.

In a single generation, Australia remade itself. It went from being a half-forgotten outpost of Britain, provincial, dull and culturally dependent, to being a nation infinitely more sophisticated, confident, interesting and outward looking. And it did all this, by and large, without discord or disturbance or serious mistakes – indeed often with a kind of grace.

By coincidence, a few nights earlier I had watched a television documentary about the immigrant experience in the 1950s. One of the people interviewed was a man who had arrived from Hungary as a teenager after the uprising there. On his first full day in the country he had gone as instructed to the local police station and explained in halting English that he was a new immigrant who had been told to register his address. The sergeant had stared at him for a moment, then risen from his seat and come around the desk. The Hungarian recalled that for one bewildered moment he thought the policeman might be about to strike him, but instead the sergeant thrust out a meaty hand and said warmly, 'Welcome to Australia, son.' The Hungarian recalled the incident with wonder even now, and when he finished there were tears in his eyes.

I tell you sincerely. It's a wonderful country.

Chapter

Come to EAST VICTORIA

ELEVEN

Carmel grew up on a farm in eastern Victoria on the southern edge of the Great Dividing Range, in lovely country of green fields set against a backdrop of blue hills. Howe, a lifelong city boy whose notion of the bush was of a monotonous expanse filled with deathly creatures, had gone to visit the family farm out of a sense of husbandly duty and fallen for it at once – so much so that he and Carmel had bought a parcel of land high on a neighbouring hillside, trucked in a jaunty wooden cottage and placed it in a lofty spot giving views over miles of hills, woods and farms. Howe had been telling me about it with a certain repetitive rapture for years and was keen for me to see it. So the next day, after loading up with provisions, we set off in their car for the three-hour drive to their rural idyll.

'Bush' is such a vague word in Australia that I wasn't sure

what to expect, but it became obvious once we had shrugged off the outer suburbs of Melbourne that eastern Victoria was a favoured corner of the world – greener than any part of Australia I had seen before and backed by mountains that attained a wholly respectable eminence. The road wound through meadowy landscapes in a charmingly indecisive manner and through a succession of small and pleasant little towns. With strange, unshakeable pride, Howe wore an arrestingly outsized and touchingly misguided bush hat he had lately acquired, which inclined Carmel and me, when we stopped for petrol or coffee, to signal to staring strangers that he was out on a visit and we'd be taking him back to the home at the end of the week, but otherwise the journey passed without incident or embarrassment.

Alan and Carmel's house stands in glorious seclusion on the brow of a steep hill. The view, over a snug and restful valley of tobacco fields and vineyards, was expansive and charming in a way that brought to mind a children's picture book. This was, I realized after a minute, the view from high up the beanstalk.

'Not bad, eh?' said Howe.

'Much too good for anyone in a hat like that. What's this area called?'

'The King Valley. Carmel's old man used to farm over there.' He pointed to a rolling piece of land nestled against a neighbouring hill. It recalled, almost impossibly, the landscapes of the American artist Grant Wood – gumdrop hills, rolling fields, plump trees – which depicted an idealized Iowa that never actually existed. It existed here.

Howe let us into the house and he and Carmel immediately began moving about in an impressively practised manner, opening windows, putting on the water heater, packing away groceries. I helped carry stuff in from the car, watching for snakes with every step, and when that was finished ventured onto the broad deck to take in the view. Howe came out after a minute bearing two cold beers, one of which he passed to me. I don't believe I had ever seen him looking so relaxed. Mercifully he had removed the hat.

He took a sip of beer, then said in an anecdotal tone: 'When I first met Carmel, she used to talk about one day buying a piece of land out here and putting a house on it and I thought: "Yes, dear." I mean, why would you want to own a house in the middle of the bush with all the costs and dangers of bush fires and everything? And then one day we came up to visit her family, and I took one look and I said: "Right, where do I sign?" Not long after that the family sold up and moved to Ballarat. So we bought this corner of the property, which they were happy to sell because it's too steep to farm, and had the house put up.' He nodded at Carmel, humming away in the kitchen. 'She loves it here. So do I, come to that. I never thought I'd say I loved the country but jeez you know it's a nice place to get away to.'

'Are bush fires a big worry?'

'Well, they are when they happen. Sometimes they're colossal. Gum trees just want to burn, you know. It's part of their strategy. How they outcompete other plants. They're full of oil, and once they catch fire they're a bugger to put out. You get a really big bush fire moving across the landscape at fifty miles an hour with flames leaping a hundred and fifty feet in the air and it's an awesome sight, believe me.'

'How often does that happen?'

'Oh, I suppose every ten years or so you get a really big

one. There was one in 1994 that burned 600,000 hectares and threatened parts of Sydney. I was there at the time and in one direction there was this pall of black smoke that completely filled the sky. Burned for days. The biggest one ever was in 1939. People still talk about that one. It was during a heatwave so bad that department store mannequins' heads actually started to melt in the windows. Can you imagine that? That one burned up most of Victoria.'

'So how much at risk are you here?'

He shrugged philosophically. 'It's all in the lap of the gods. Could be next week, could be ten years from now, could be never.' He turned to me with an odd smile. 'You are totally at the mercy of nature in this country, mate. It's just a fact of life. But I tell you one thing.'

'What's that?'

'It sure makes you appreciate something like this when you know it could all go up in a puff of smoke.'

Howe is one of those people who can't stand to see anyone sleeping when there is daylight to be utilized, and he rousted me out early the next morning with the announcement that he had a busy day planned for us. For a terrible moment I thought he meant we were going to shingle the roof or dig up boulders or something, but then he noted that we were going to have a Ned Kelly day. Howe was immensely proud that Kelly came from this part of Victoria and wanted to show me several of the sights connected with his short and brutish life. This sounded somewhat more promising.

It is an interesting fact, and one that no doubt speaks much about the Australian character, that the nation never produced a law enforcement hero along the lines of Wyatt

Earp or Bat Masterson in America. Australian folk heroes are all bad guys of the Billy the Kid type, only here they are known as bushrangers, and the most famous of them all was Ned Kelly.

The story of Kelly is easily told. He was a murderous thug who deserved to be hanged and was. He came from a family of rough Irish settlers, who made their living by stealing livestock and waylaying innocent passers-by. Like most bushrangers he was at pains to present himself as a champion of the oppressed, though in fact there wasn't a shred of nobility in his character or his deeds. He killed several people, often in cold blood, sometimes for no very good reason.

In 1880, after years on the run, Kelly was reported to be holed up with his modest gang (a brother and two friends) in Glenrowan, a hamlet in the foothills of the Warby Range in north-eastern Victoria. Learning of this, the police assembled a large posse and set off to get him. As surprise attacks go, it wasn't terribly impressive. When the police arrived (on an afternoon train) they found that word of their coming had preceded them and that a thousand people were lined up along the streets and sitting on every rooftop eagerly awaiting the spectacle of gunfire. The police took up positions and at once began peppering the Kelly hideout with bullets. The Kellys returned the fire and so it went throughout the night. The next dawn during a lull Kelly stepped from the dwelling, dressed unexpectedly, not to say bizarrely, in a suit of home-made armour – a heavy cylindrical helmet that brought to mind an inverted bucket, and a breastplate that covered his torso and crotch. He wore no armour on his lower body, so one of the policemen shot him in the leg. Aggrieved, Kelly staggered off into some nearby woods, fell over and was captured. He was taken to Melbourne, tried and swiftly executed. His last words were: 'Such is life.'

Not exactly the stuff of legend, one would have thought, yet in his homeland Kelly is treated with deep regard. Sidney Nolan, one of Australia's most esteemed artists, did a famous series of paintings devoted to Kelly's life, and books abound on the subject. Even serious historians often accord him an importance that seems to the outsider curiously disproportionate. Manning Clark, for example, in his one-volume history of Australia, devotes just a paragraph to the design and foundation of Canberra, dispenses with federation in two pages, but gives a full nine pages to the life and achievements of Ned Kelly. He also allows Kelly some of his most florid and incoherent prose, which is saying a great deal, believe me. Manning Clark is an extraordinary stylist at the best of times – a man who would never call the moon 'the moon' when he might instead call it 'the lunar orb' – but with Kelly he was inspired to lofty allusions and cosmic musings of a rare impenetrability. Here is a small part of his description of Kelly's fateful emergence from the compound after the night-long shootout:

In the half light before that red disc [i.e., the sun] appeared again on the eastern horizon . . . a tall figure, encased in armour, came out of the mists and wisps of frosty air . . . Some thought it was a madman or a ghost; some thought it was the Devil, the whole atmosphere having stimulated in friend and foe alike a 'superstitious awe.'

Personally – and this is just a stab in the dark – I think Manning Clark was taking way too much codeine. Here's another of his well-juiced creations, this the merest fragment of a much longer passage discussing Kelly's legacy:

> *He lived on as a man who had confronted the bourgeois calm-down with all the uproar of a magnificent Dionysian frenzy, a man who had taken down the mighty from their seat and driven the rich empty away. He lived on as a man who had savaged policemen in the old convict tradition . . . and denounced the brutal barbarism of those who clothed their sadism toward the common people in the panoply of the law.*

About 2,800 milligrams talking there, I would say.

Today Glenrowan is a one-street town with a couple of pubs, a scattering of houses and a short strip of enterprises dedicated to extracting a little cash from the Kelly legend. On this hot summer's day there were perhaps a dozen visitors in town, including Alan, Carmel and me. The biggest of the commercial establishments, a place called Ned Kelly's Last Stand, was covered in painted signs of a semi-professional quality. 'This is not a place for Whimps,' said one, promisingly. Another added: 'It is absolutely absurd that after allowing yourself 10 to 20 minutes to take photos, walk up and down the street and buy some souvenirs and then have the audacity to tell your friends – "Don't go to Glenrowan, for there is nothing to see." To be quite honest most visitors to Glenrowan wouldn't know if the country shithouse fell on them . . .'

The impression one derived from further study was that Ned Kelly's Last Stand contained some kind of animatronic show. Alan, Carmel and I exchanged happy looks and knew that this was a place for us. Inside, a friendly man presided over the till. We were mildly staggered to see that they wanted $15 a head for admission.

'It's good, is it?' said Howe.

'Mister,' said the man with the greatest sincerity, 'it's like Disneyland in there.'

We bought tickets and shuffled through a door into a dim room where the spectacle was to begin. The space was designed to look like an old saloon. In the middle were benches for the audience. Before us, in a deep gloom, we could just make out the shapes of furniture and seated dummies. After a few minutes, the lights dimmed altogether, there was a sudden startling bang of gunfire and the performance began.

Well, call me a Whimp, drop a brick shithouse on me, but I can honestly say that I have seldom seen anything so wonderfully, so delightfully, so monumentally bad as Ned Kelly's Last Stand. It was so bad it was worth every penny. Actually, it was so bad it was worth more than we paid. For the next thirty-five minutes we proceeded through a series of rooms where we watched home-made dummies, each with a frozen smile and a mop of hair that brought to mind wind-blown pubis, re-enacting various scenes from the famous Kelly shootout in a random and deliriously incoherent way. Occasionally one of them would turn a stiff head or jerk up a forearm to fire a pistol, though not necessarily in sync with the narrative. Meanwhile, around each room lots of other mechanical events were taking place – empty chairs rocked, cupboard doors mysteriously opened and shut, player pianos played, a figure of a boy on a trapeze (and why not?) swung back and forth amid the rafters. Do you know those fairground stalls where you fire a rifle at assorted targets to make an outhouse door swing open or a stuffed chicken fall over? Well, this reminded me of that, only much worse. The narrative, insofar as it could be heard above the competing noises, made no sense at all.

When at last we were liberated into the sunshine, we were so delighted that we considered going in again – but $45 is a lot of money, after all, and we feared that with repeated exposure it might begin to make some sense. So instead we went and looked at a giant fibreglass Ned Kelly that stood outside one of the souvenir shops. It wasn't as big or as intimidating as the Big Lobster, and its testicles didn't swing in the breeze, but it was still a game stab at the genre. Then we had a look around a couple of the shops and bought some postcards, and returned to the car for the next part of our day's adventure.

This was to see the famous Kelly Tree at a remote spot called Stringybark Creek. This involved a long drive into a strange, spooky valley of abandoned and semi-abandoned farms, nearly all of them half buried under blackberry brambles, then up into dense and verdant rainforest, and finally into crowded groves of towering stringybark trees. Australia has some 700 varieties of eucalyptus trees and they have the most wonderfully expressive names – kakadu woollybutt, bastard tallow-wood, gympie messmate, candlebark, ghost gum – but the stringybark was the first that I could identify by sight. The bark peels off in long strips and hangs from the branches in fibrous tassels or lies in curled heaps on the ground, all the better to burn apparently. It was a handsome tree, too: tall, straight and exceptionally close-growing. Some miles into the woods we came to a parking area beside a sign announcing the Kelly Tree. We were the only visitors; it felt as if we might have been the only visitors in years. The forest was cool and noiseless, and with all the strands of bark hanging down it had a strange, unwelcoming, otherworldly feel. The Kelly Tree stood along a path through the woods, distinguished from the others by the stoutness of its trunk and by a metal plaque in the shape of Kelly's famous helmet.

'And what is the Kelly Tree exactly?' I asked.

'Well,' Alan said with a learned air, 'as the Kelly gang got more and more notorious the police started hunting them with greater determination, and so they had to hide out in increasingly remote and desperate places.'

'Such as here?'

He gave a nod. 'Can't get much lonelier than this.'

We took a moment to consider our surroundings. Because of the denseness with which the stringybarks grew beside each other, there was almost no space to stretch out or move around, and the air had a kind of dank, organic closeness. It was, I think, the least bucolic forest I have ever been in. Even the light seemed stale.

'For three years, Kelly and his gang laid low, but in 1878 four policemen tracked them here. Somehow Kelly and his men captured and disarmed the policemen. Then they murdered three of them in a slow and pretty horrible way.'

'Horrible in what way?' I asked, ever alert for the morbid detail.

'Shot them in the balls and let them bleed to death. To maximize the pain and indignity.'

'And the fourth policeman?'

'Scarpered. He hid overnight in a wombat's burrow and the next day he made his way back to civilization and raised the alarm. So it was the murder of three men here that led eventually to the shootout at Glenrowan, as so memorably depicted for us by the robotic wonders of Ned Kelly's Last Stand.'

'So how come you know so much about all this?'

He looked at me with a hint of disappointment. 'Because I know a great deal about many things, Bryson.'

'You haven't got a clue about hats, though,' said Carmel cheerfully.

He looked at her and decided that this was a comment not to be dignified with a response, then turned back to me. 'Now to Powers Lookout,' he announced with a certain resolve, and set off in a stately tramp for the car.

'And how many more Kelly sights will we be visiting?' I called, trying not to betray too much alarm as I followed him through the woods. I wish no disrespect to Australia's most treasured thug, nor to imply any disappointment at all in the Kelly Tree – quite the reverse – but we did seem to be hours from anywhere and fast approaching that time of day when one begins to think about the convivial possibilities of food and drink.

'Just one more and it's on the way home and you won't regret it, and then we'll have a pint.'

He was as good as his word. Powers Lookout was fabulous. A platform of rock hanging high in the sky, it was named for Harry Powers, another storied bushranger, who sometimes shared the view with Kelly and his gang. Some diligent crew had built sturdy wooden walkways up and around the craggy rocks, making it a simple if slightly taxing matter to get from the main body of the cliff to the rocky outcrop that was the lookout. The view was sensational: perhaps a thousand feet below spread the King Valley, a snug and tidy realm of small farms and white farmhouses. Beyond, across air of flawless clarity, rose waves of low mountains, culminating in the distinctive hump of Mount Buffalo some fifty kilometres away.

'You know, if you put this in Virginia or Vermont,' I

mused, 'there would be scores of people here, even at this hour. There'd be souvenir stands and probably an Imax screen and an adventure park.'

Howe nodded. 'It'd be the same in the Blue Mountains. It's like I've been telling you. This corner of Victoria is a great secret. Don't put it in your book.'

'Certainly not,' I replied sincerely.

'And wait'll you see what we've got for you tomorrow. It's even better.'

'Not possible,' I said.

'No, it is. It's even better.'

What he had for us the next day was a place called Alpine National Park, and in fact it was even better. Covering 2,500 square miles of eastern Victoria, it was lofty, grand, cool and green. If ever there was a portion of Australia remote from all the clichéd images of red soil and baking sun, this was it. They even skied here in winter. Alpine is perhaps a somewhat ambitious term. You will find no craggy Matterhorns here. The Australian Alps have a gentler profile, more like the Appalachians of America or the Scottish Cairngorms. But they do attain entirely respectable heights – Kosciuszko, the tallest, tops out at something over 7,000 feet.

Howe, through one of his contacts, had got hold of a friendly and helpful warden named Ron Riley, who had agreed to show us round his airy domain. A genial man with a dapper grey beard, Ron had the lean bearing and far-off gaze of someone whose world is the outdoors. We met in the little town of Mount Beauty, where we decanted into one of the park's four-wheel-drive vehicles and set off on the long, twisting drive up Mount Bogong, Victoria's highest peak at 6,500 feet. I asked him if Mount Bogong was named for the famous bogong moths, which erupt in vast, fluttery multitudes every spring and for a day or two seem to be everywhere. Along with plump witchetty grubs and long, slimy mangrove worms, they are the delicacies of the Aboriginal diet most often noted by chroniclers – noted because of course they are so unappealing to the western palate. The bogongs are roasted in hot ashes and eaten whole, or so I had read.

Ron acknowledged that this was where they came from.

'And the Aborigines really eat them?'

'Oh, yeah – well, traditionally anyway. A bogong moth is eighty-five per cent fat and they didn't get a lot of fat in their diet, so it was quite a treat for them. They used to come from miles.'

'Have you ever eaten one?'

'Once,' he said.

'And?'

'Once was enough.' He smiled.

'What did it taste like?'

He thought for a moment. 'Like a moth.'

I grinned. 'I read that it has a kind of buttery taste.'

He thought about that. 'No. It has a moth taste.'

We climbed up a steep, winding road through dense groves of an amazingly tall and beautiful tree. Ron told me they were mountain ashes.

I made an appropriately appreciative face. 'I didn't know you had ashes here.'

'We don't. They're eucalypts.'

I looked again, surprised. Everything else about it – its long, straight body, its height, its lushness – was completely at odds with the skeletal gums associated with the lowlands. It really was true that the eucalypts have filled every ecological niche in Australia. There never was a more various tree.

'Tallest tree in the world after the California redwoods,' Ron added with a nod at the ashes, causing me to make another appreciative face.

'How tall do they grow?'

'Up to three hundred feet. They average about two hundred.' Three hundred feet is about the height of a twenty-five-storey building. Big trees.

'Do you get many bush fires?'

Ron gave a regretful nod. 'Sometimes. We lost five hundred thousand hectares in this part of the Great Dividing Range in 1985.'

'Gosh,' I said, though the figure meant little to me. Later I looked in a book and discovered that 500,000 hectares is equivalent to the area covered by Yosemite, Grand Teton, Zion and Redwood National Parks in America. In other words, it was a natural disaster on a scale almost inconceivable elsewhere. (I also looked in the *New York Times Index* to see what coverage it had been given: none.) Even without being able to conceive quite what 500,000 hectares is, I knew of course that it was a lot, so I added politely: 'That must have been awful.'

Ron nodded again. 'Yeah, it was a bit,' he said.

We passed through a zone of snow gums – yet another niche dominated by the versatile eucalypts – and emerged into a sunny world of high, gently undulant plains, covered everywhere in pale grass and spongy alpine plants, with long views to distant summits. Quite a few visitors were evident, most of them with the springy step and considered apparel of the serious walker. At every group we passed, Ron slowed and called, 'G'day,' and asked if they had everything they needed in the way of information. They always did, but it seemed an unusually welcoming gesture.

And then we had the most marvellous day. Sometimes we stopped and walked a little, and the rest of the time we drove. The weather was gorgeous – cool at these heights but sunny – and Ron was droll and good-natured. He knew every leaf and bud and insect, and seemed genuinely to enjoy showing off all the secret corners of the park. We bumped along overgrown tracks through meadowy vales and skittered up near-perpendicular gravel roads to hidden firetowers. At every turn there was a point of interest or a memorable view. Alpine National Park is immense. It extends to 6,460 square kilometres – the equivalent of about seventeen Isle of Wights – but it is actually vaster still because it is contiguous along its eastern border with the even larger Kosciuszko National Park in the Snowy Mountains just over the border in New South Wales. Ron pointed out Kosciuszko – 'Kozzie', he called it – almost exactly 100 kilometres away, but I couldn't see it even with binoculars.

We finished the day at an imposing eminence called Mount McKay, where there were yet more top-of-the-world views: range upon range of steep hills rolling away to a far-off horizon. He took in the view with the assessing gaze of someone watching for a tell-tale plume of smoke.

'So how much of all this are you responsible for?' I asked.

'A hundred thousand hectares,' he replied.

'Lot of ground,' I said, thinking of the responsibility.

'Yeah,' he replied, squinting thoughtfully at the vista before us, 'I'm very lucky.'

It would of course take something extremely exceptional to match Glenrowan and Powers Lookout and Alpine

National Park, and frankly I am not sure that many other countries could have provided it, but Howe assured me that he had one last special something for us to see – something that existed nowhere else in the world but in one small corner of Victoria. Beyond that he would not be drawn. The next day, to add to the savour of pleasure deferred, we went to a sleepy, old-fashioned coastal resort called Lakes Entrance, where we stopped for the night and had a nice seafood supper and a shuffle around, and the day after set off for our mystery attraction en route to Melbourne.

For quite a spell we drove through flat, sunny, uneventful farming country. I sat in the back in a state of tranquil mindlessness until Alan abruptly steered the car off the highway beside a big sign I couldn't see well enough to read and parked in a large and mostly empty car park. I unfolded myself from the back seat and stepped blinking from the car. Beside us was a long tubular building – rather like a very large cloche, but made of concrete and painted white.

I looked questioningly at Howe.

'The Giant Worm,' he announced.

I stared at him in wonder and admiration.

'Not as in the famous giant worms of south-west Gippsland?'

'The same. You're familiar with them then?'

I gave the hollow laugh that such a question deserved. I had been reading about these behemoths of the underworld for months, albeit mostly in footnotes and other passing references. I had never expected to find a shrine to them.

Even in a land of extraordinary creatures, the giant worms of Gippsland are exceptional. Called *Megascolides australis*, they are the world's largest earthworms, growing up to twelve feet in length and more than six inches in diameter. So substantial are they that you can actually hear them moving through the earth, with a gurgling sound, like bad plumbing. What it is about this one small corner of Victoria that led to the evolution of extremely outsized worms is a question that science has yet to answer – but then, it must be said, very few of the world's best minds are drawn to questions of earthworm physiology and distribution. However, Howe promised, such knowledge as the world holds was contained within the tubular structure before us.

We procured three tickets and stepped eagerly into the display areas. On the wall facing us as we entered was a blown-up photograph, taken early in the twentieth century, showing four ridiculously pleased-looking men holding a droopy twelve-footer, little thicker than a normal earthworm but clearly ambitious in the length department. This I studied with great interest until Carmel drew my attention to a display of living giant worms. These were in a large glass panel, half an inch thick and filled with earth, rather like a very large ant farm, which hung on the wall. According to a label, the case contained a pair of giant worms. In a couple of spots where the earth had come away from the glass, we could see a millimetre or two of living giant worm, but as they weren't moving or doing anything (*Megascolides* is extremely devoted to rest, it seems) the experience was, I confess, a trifle anticlimactic. I had rather hoped there would be a petting corner or perhaps a tamer with a whip and a chair getting them to go through hoops. Alan and I tried to enliven the worm by tapping lightly on the glass, but it declined to respond.

Beside the panel were two long glass tubes filled with

formaldehyde and containing a pair of preserved giant worms, each of normal earthworm circumference but about four or five feet long – not exactly titans but long enough to impress. Worms don't preserve terribly well and the formaldehyde had horrible little bits of worm skin floating in it as if somebody had been shaking the tubes or, more probably (as Alan and I conclusively established by tapping on them), by tapping on them. It was hard to look at them without growing a little queasy.

In the next room was a short film that told all that was known about the giant earthworm, which is to say almost nothing. They are reclusive, delicate, not terribly numerous and deeply uncooperative creatures, and thus not easy to study, even assuming you had a mind to. As you may recall from childhood experiments, earthworms really don't wish to come out of their holes, and if you pull they tend to snap. Well, imagine trying to tug a twelve-foot-long worm out of its burrow. Nearly impossible.

The one thing the Giant Worm Museum establishes beyond question is that you can only get so much mileage out of giant worms. Recognizing this, the proprietors had provided many other displays. Next door were some glass cases containing live snakes, including the famous and fearsome taipan, Australia's deadliest snake. Alan and I conducted some further glass-tapping experiments, then retreated four yards together in a platonic embrace when the taipan snarled at us (or possibly just yawned), opening its jaws wide enough to swallow a human head, or so it seemed. Deciding that henceforth we would keep our hands in our pockets, we followed Carmel outdoors where there was a compound containing yet more animals – kangaroos and emus, a forlorn-looking dingo, some caged cockatoos, half a dozen curled and dozing wombats and a couple of koalas, also dozing. It was a very hot, still afternoon and evidently siesta time, so the enclosures had an air of profound inertness – even the cockatoos slept – but I strolled among them with fascination, delighted to see so much native exotica brought together in one place. I peered with particular interest at the wombats – 'a squat, thick, short-legged and rather inactive quadruped, with great appearance of stumpy strength', as the first Englishman to see one recorded in 1788 in words that could not be bettered. (The man, David Collins, was a little less reliable with the kangaroo, which he described as 'a small bird of beautiful plumage'.) Alan and Carmel looked on with the tolerant amusement with which an American might view a display of raccoons and chipmunks, for most of these were animals that they saw regularly in their natural state, but to me every one was a novelty, even the dingo, which is after all just a dog. I made two complete circuits of the menagerie, then with a look of satisfaction I gave a nod and we set off once again for Melbourne.

We went to dinner at a Vietnamese restaurant in the inner Melbourne suburb of Richmond, on a street lined seemingly for miles with exotic restaurants, and Alan made the point, with which I could not argue, that Melbourne is an infinitely better city than Sydney for dining out in. In the course of conversation Alan asked if I was going to the Great Barrier Reef, a place for which he had a special fondness. I said I wasn't on this trip, but I was when I came back in a few weeks.

'Just be careful they don't leave you out there.' He gave a thin smile.

'What do you mean?'

'There was a story here recently. An American couple were left out on the reef.'

'Left?' I said, puzzled but intrigued.

Howe nodded and speared at some pasta. 'Yeah. Somehow the boat went back to port two passengers short. Bit of a pisser for the people left behind, wouldn't you say? I mean, one minute you're swimming around looking at coral and fish, having the time of your life, and then you surface and discover that the boat has gone and you are all alone in a very large and empty ocean.'

'They couldn't swim to shore?'

He smiled tolerantly at my ignorance. 'Barrier Reef's a long way out, Bryson – something over thirty miles where they were. Long way to swim.'

'And there were no islands or anything?'

'Not where they were. They were effectively out to sea. Apparently there were a couple of things they could swim to – a big moored pontoon that the dive company used and some kind of a coral atoll, both a couple of miles away. So presumably they started swimming towards those. What they didn't know – couldn't know – was that they were swimming across a deep-water channel. And guess what lurks in deep-water channels?'

'Sharks,' I said.

He nodded at my perspicacity. 'So imagine it. You're miles out to sea, stranded. You're tired. You're swimming towards a coral outcrop and it's hard going because the tide is coming in. The light is fading. And you look around and see fins circling you, maybe half a dozen of them.' He gave me a moment to form a picture in my mind, then fixed me with a deadpan expression. 'I don't know about you, but I think I'd ask for my money back.' He laughed.

'So nobody came back to rescue them?'

'It was two days before anyone noticed they were missing,' said Carmel.

I turned to her in wonder. 'Two days?'

'By which time, of course, they were long gone.'

'Eaten by sharks?'

She shrugged. 'No way of knowing, but presumably. Anyway, they were never seen again.'

'Wow.'

We ate in thoughtful silence for a minute, then I mentioned that every time there was an odd story in Australia, it seemed to come out of Queensland. My favourite of the moment concerned a German man, recently detained outside Cairns, who had arrived on a tourist visa in 1982 and spent the past seventeen years wandering on foot through the northern deserts living almost exclusively off road kill. I was also extremely partial to the story of a group of illegal immigrants who were brought from China on an old fishing boat, which dropped them in shallow water a hundred yards off a beach near Cairns. They were caught when one of their members, carrying a suitcase, dripping water conspicuously from sodden trousers and squelching with every step, presented himself at a newsagent's shop and politely asked the proprietor if he would order a fleet of taxis to take him and some associates to the railway station at Cairns. Nearly every day, it seemed, the papers had a story of arresting improbability under a Queensland dateline.

Alan nodded in accord. 'There's a reason for that, of course.'

'What's that?'

'They're crazy in Queensland. Madder than cut snakes. You'll like it up there.'

In the morning, Alan ran me to the airport by way of his office. While he went off to hold the front page, or do whatever editors do, he left me to sit at his big desk and play in his swivel chair. When he returned he was carrying a folder, which he passed to me. 'I dug out some stuff on that American couple that disappeared. I thought it might be of use to you.'

'Thank you,' I said, quite touched.

'It should give you some tips on how not to get left on the reef. I know what a dozy bugger you are, Bryson.'

At the airport he jumped out of the car and helped me haul my bag out of the back. He shook my hand. 'And remember what I said about watching yourself up north,' he said.

'Madder than cut snakes,' I repeated, to show that I had been listening.

'Madder than a sack of them.'

He smiled, then jumped back in the car, waved and was gone.

Chapter

TWELVE

It is possible, I suppose, to construct hypothetical circumstances in which you would be pleased to find yourself, at the end of a long day, in Macksville, New South Wales – perhaps something to do with rising sea levels that left it as the only place on earth not under water, or maybe some disfiguring universal contagion from which it alone remained unscathed. In the normal course of events, however, it is unlikely that you would find yourself standing on its lonely main street at six thirty on a warm summer's evening gazing about you in an appreciative manner and thinking: 'Well, thank goodness I'm here!'

I was in Macksville owing to the interesting discovery that Brisbane is not three or four hours north of Sydney, as I had long and casually supposed, but the better part of a couple of days' drive. Well, if you look on the television weather map Brisbane and Sydney are practically neighbours, their little local suns and storm clouds all but bumping on the chart. But in Australia neighbourliness is of course a relative concept. In fact, it is almost 1,000 kilometres from Sydney to Brisbane, much of it along a cheerfully poky two-lane road. And so, in mildly confounded consequence, I was in Macksville for the night.

I don't wish to disparage a community that 2,811 people proudly call home (and what a miraculous notion that is), but as I had rather had it in mind that I would be dining on fresh-caught barramundi and watching a sunset emblazon the Pacific on Queensland's storied Gold Coast rather than stuck in an obscure backwater barely halfway there, my disappointment was real. My immediate preoccupation was that I was running out of time on this trip. I had a commitment of long standing to take part in a fund-raising hike in Syria and Jordan for a British children's charity. In three days I was to fly home from Sydney, to collect hiking gear and see how many of my children still recognized me, before flying off again to London and onward to Damascus. It was clear that I wasn't going to see as much of the northern reaches of the Boomerang Coast as I had hoped.

So my mood as I strolled into town from my motel was, let us say, restrained. Macksville wasn't so bad really. Set on the bank of the swift and muddy Nambucca River, it was essentially just a pause in the highway: a tentacle of neatly gardened bungalows and small office buildings leading to a very compact town centre. Though the road through town is the Pacific Highway, the main artery connecting Sydney and Brisbane, only two cars passed as I followed its dusty margin into town. At the heart of the modest community stood the large and fading Nambucca Hotel, and I stepped in, glad to escape the heat. It was a roomy place but nearly empty. Two older guys in singlets and battered bush hats propped up one end of the long bar. In a side room a man and a woman sat in silent absorption amid the soft, mechanical glow of pokies. I procured a beer, stood long enough to establish that no one was going to take any interest in me that might lead to a conversation, and retired to the central portion of the bar where I parked myself on a stool and idly watched the evening news on a silent TV mounted on the wall.

Somewhere police were out in the bush with a pack of straining sniffer dogs; there was no telling what the dogs were looking for, though if it was red clay soil they were doing extremely well. Somewhere else there appeared to be a fresh outbreak of Ross River fever – yet another previously unknown malady for me to worry about. Then there was Paul Keating, the former Prime Minister – he of the deeply expressive vocabulary, as you may recall from the Canberra chapter – standing on the steps of an office building answering questions from reporters and looking testy. It was impossible to determine what he was saying, but I imagined he was telling all those present that they were nongs and maggots. I decided I quite liked watching the news with the sound off.

Meanwhile, back in the Known World something was happening in Kosovo; convoys were rolling along country roads and mortars were throwing up puffs of smoke on distant hills. Bill Clinton was in some kind of moral hot water again, or so I assumed because he was shown strolling through the Rose Garden holding hands with Hillary and Chelsea, all of them looking mutually devoted. They had a lovable spaniel with them as well, which I took as a sign that the President had been very bad indeed. It hardly mattered. It all seemed so far away.

Then lots of sport, all of it featuring Australians performing commendably. Finally a weather chart came on and showed sun everywhere and then the newsreader tapped her papers square and smiled in a way that suggested that we could all go to bed happy because Greg Norman was winning the golf and everything else was a long, long way away and didn't really affect us.

It is amazingly easy in Australia to forget, or at least to reduce to a dim awareness, that there is a world out there. Australians work hard in their news coverage to overcome the handicap of distance, but even so sometimes around the margins of the news you get a curious sense of disconnectedness – little things that remind you that this is a far, far country. I had noticed, for instance, that Australian newspapers commonly run obituaries, particularly of foreign figures, weeks or even months after they die. That's fair enough in a sense, I suppose – these people are going to be dead for ever, after all – but it does lend the pages a curiously leisured air. Then the previous day on my flight from Melbourne to Sydney, while browsing through a copy of the *Bulletin*, the country's venerable news magazine, I read a section called 'Flashback', which recorded important events in history on that week's dates. For 22 January, it had this interesting entry: '1934: Actor Bill Bixby (died 1993) is born in Park Ridge, Illinois, US.'

Consider that just for a moment. In a column devoted to significant moments in world history, the birth date of an actor whose culminating achievement was to play the straight man in a 1960s' television series called *My Favorite Martian* is still being recalled in Australia *six years after his death*. Well, I think that's kind of spooky, frankly. I appreciate, of course, that this was a filler item at the back of a magazine and one shouldn't read too much into it, so let me offer a rather more compelling piece of temporal eccentricity.

As I sat at the bar now I pulled out my one-volume history of Australia by Manning Clark and dutifully ploughed into it. I had only about thirty pages left and I would be less than candid if I didn't tell you that I couldn't wait to have Mr Clark and his extravagant dronings out of my life for ever. Still, Australia's history is an interesting one and I had a comfy stool and the prospect of as much beer as I wanted, so I wasn't unhappy.

So I sat and read the rest of the book, and here's the thing. It finished in 1935. After 619 pages of the densest exposition, the book terminates with the appointment of John Curtin as leader of the Australian Labor Party on 1 October 1935. This is, let me stress, the standard, current, one-volume history of Australia – the one to which you will be directed in every bookshop in the land – and it finishes in 1935. That's sixteen Prime Ministers ago!

I was so dumbfounded that I actually lifted the book over my head to see if some pages had fallen out, then looked on the floor around my bar stool. But no. The book finished by design in 1935. Manning Clark died – or yielded the final tortured spark of life, as I am sure he would have wished me to put it – in 1991, so I was prepared to excuse him the last decade or so of Australia's eventful saga, but I would have thought he would find space for, let us say, the Second World War. Although his history was written long after the war (specifically, between 1962 and 1987 as a series of six books, of which I held the distilled essence), it contains not one mention of the most important event of the twentieth century. There is not even a hint of gathering storm clouds. Nor does the text find room for the Cold War, Aboriginal land reforms, the emergence of a multicultural society, the fall of the Whitlam government, the move to become a republic or the life and times of Bill Bixby, among rather a lot else.

To cover this troubling gap, the publishers had introduced into the present edition an afterword – a 'coda' – written by the book's editor and abridger. This condensed the last sixty-five years of Australian history into thirty-four pages, which, as you can imagine, gave the whole a somewhat breathless and incidental flavour. And until the 1995 edition, it didn't even have that.

Well, I find that extremely odd. That's all I'm saying.

Sighing, I closed my book and realized I was famished. According to a sign on a door across the room, the Nambucca had a restaurant, so I wandered over to investigate. The door wouldn't open.

'Dining room's closed, mate,' said one of the two guys at the bar. 'Chef's crook.'

'Must've ate some of his own cooking,' came a voice from the pokie alcove, and we all had a grin over that.

'What else is there in town?' I asked.

'Depends,' said the man, scratching his throat thoughtfully. He leaned towards me slightly. 'You like good food?'

I nodded. Of course I did.

'Nothin' then.' He went back to his beer.

'Try the Chinese over the road,' said his companion. 'It's not too bad.'

The Chinese restaurant was just across the road as

promised, but according to a sign in the window it was not licensed to serve alcohol and I couldn't face small-town Chinese food without the solace of beer. I have travelled enough to know that a chef does not, as a rule, settle in a place like Macksville because he has a lifelong yearning to share the subtleties of 3,500 years of Szechuan cuisine with sheep farmers. So I went off to see what else there might be in Macksville's compact heart. The answer was very little. Everything appeared to be shut except one small takeaway establishment called, not altogether promisingly, Bub's Hotbakes. I opened the door, briefly enlivening 5,000 flies that had dropped by to see what Bub and his team were up to, and stepped inside, knowing in my heart that this was almost certainly going to be a regretted experience.

Bub's had a substantial range of food, nearly all of it involving brown meat and gravy lurking inside pastry. I ordered a large sausage roll and chips.

'We don't do chips,' said the amply proportioned serving maiden.

'Then how did you get like that?' I wanted to say, but of course I suppressed this unworthy thought and revised my order to a large sausage roll and something called a 'continental cheesecake square' and went with them outside. I ate standing on the corner.

I take nothing away from Bub's culinary prowess, I trust, when I tell you that a large sausage roll and a continental cheesecake square was not the most satisfying possible culmination to a night on the town even in as remote and challenging a spot as Macksville. Besides, it was only seven thirty in the evening. I weighed my options – TV back in the motel, a sunset stroll along the highway or more beer in the Nambucca – and toddled back into the Nambucca.

The two men at the bar had departed, and their place had been taken by a lone woman who was engaged in some deep and earnest conversation with the barmaid. Judging from their pinched and animated faces, this clearly involved gossip. 'Aw, he's all right in his place – they just haven't dug it yet,' I heard one quip drily to the other.

I acquired another beer and retired with it to my favoured spot at the bar, where I cracked open my book of maps to see where exactly I stood. It had only begun to dawn on me in the last day or two just how much of this amazingly vast and ungainly country I had still to tackle. I had been driving around almost continuously now for four weeks and I had covered only the tiniest portion of it. What's more, I had done the easy parts – the parts that are well paved and reasonably inhabited. Altogether Australia has 180,000 miles of paved highway, enough to keep a dedicated driver occupied for about a year, but the great bulk of it is bundled into the populous eastern corridor. Elsewhere, over vast areas there is nothing. Not an inch of paved road exists along the nearly 2,000 miles of indented coastline from Darwin to Cairns, which must make it one of the longest, not to say comeliest, stretches of coastline in the world not touched by highway. Similarly, no road intrudes on the tropical lushness that stretches for 500 miles from just beyond Cairns to the tip of Cape York, Australia's northernmost point and another area of superlative beauty. In the whole of Queensland, an area into which you could comfortably fit most of Western Europe, just three paved roads venture into the state's vast and arid interior, and only one provides an outlet to the two-thirds of Australia that lies to the west. From Camooweal in the north to Barringun in the south, you could, if you were completely out of your mind, walk 1,400 miles of Queensland without once crossing a paved surface. Travel any distance into the interior and you are, with amazing swiftness, in an empty country.

The outback does have dirt tracks in relative abundance, 300,000 miles of them altogether, but standard rental cars aren't allowed on them and even in a fully equipped offroad vehicle it is a brave or foolhardy driver who ventures out on his own because it is so easy to get lost or stranded. Just recently a young couple from Austria, on a trip into the outback in a rented four-by-four, had sunk to their axles in sand on a lonely, nameless track in the Simpson Desert. When they realized they were hopelessly embedded, the woman decided to hike forty miles to the Oodnadatta Track, where rescue was more likely. Why the woman went and not the man I don't know. What is known is that she took nine of their twelve litres of water and set off into 140 degree F. heat.

For most of us it is not possible to conceive just how punishing such heat is. Under a full sun with temperatures that high, it is actually possible to begin to cook, rather as you would in a microwave oven, from the inside out. The poor woman didn't stand a chance. Even with a good supply of water, she lasted less than two days and covered just eighteen miles, less than half the distance required. (Her partner, sitting in shade, survived and was rescued.) In short, you don't want to be caught in the outback.

My more immediate problem was what I was going to do with my last couple of days. My original programme called for me to go to Brisbane, Surfers Paradise, and the Big Banana at Coff's Harbour. But I didn't really have time now to see Brisbane, at least in any meaningful way, and I wasn't all that excited about the Big Banana. I mean no disrespect to a national treasure, but my devotion to giant fruit goes only so far. So as I sat at the bar now I leafed idly through the pages looking at the alternative diversions – Byron Bay, Dorrigo National Park, the Darling Downs of south Queensland – when two words, printed small and attached to a pale and erratic blue line, leaped out at me. I had my destination. I was going to a place called Myall Creek.

It was time to consider Australia's forgotten people.

Chapter

THIRTEEN

One of the most momentous events in human history took place at a time that will probably never be known, for reasons that can only be guessed at, by means that seem barely credible. I refer, of course, to the peopling of Australia.

Until fairly recently accounting for the presence of human beings in Australia was not such a problem. At the beginning of the twentieth century, it was thought that Aborigines had been on the continent for no more than 400 years. As recently as the 1960s, the time frame was estimated to be perhaps 8,000 years. Then in 1969 a geologist named Jim Bowler from the Australian National University in Canberra was poking around on the shores of a long-dried lake bed called Mungo in a parched and lonely corner of western New South Wales when something caught his eye. It was the skeleton of a woman, obtruding slightly from a sandbank. The bones were collected and sent off for carbon dating. When the report came back, it showed that the woman had died 23,000 years ago, at a stroke almost tripling the known period of occupation of Australia. Since then, other finds have pushed the date back further. Today the evidence points to an arrival date of at least 45,000 years ago, but probably more like 60,000.

The first occupants of Australia could not have walked there because at no point in human times has Australia not been an island. They could not have arisen independently because Australia has no apelike creatures from which humans could have descended. The first arrivals could only have come by sea, presumably from Timor in the Indonesian archipelago, and here is where the problems arise.

In order to put *Homo sapiens* in Australia you must accept that, at a point in time so remote that it precedes the known rise of behaviourally modern humans, there lived in southern Asia a people sufficiently advanced that they were fishing inshore waters from boats of some sort, rafts presumably. Never mind that the archaeological record shows no one else on earth doing this for another 30,000 years. We have got to get these people waterborne.

Next we have to explain what led them to cross at least sixty miles of open sea to reach a land they could not know was there. The scenario that is invariably invoked is of a simple fishing raft – probably little more than a floating platform – accidentally carried out to sea, probably in one of the sudden squalls that are characteristic of this part of the world. This craft then drifted helplessly for some days before washing up on a beach in northern Australia. So far so good.

The question that naturally arises – but is seldom asked – is how you get breeding stock out of this. If it's a lone fisherman who is carried off to Australia, then clearly he must find his way back to his homeland to report his discovery and to persuade enough people to come with him to start a colony. This suggests, of course, the possession of nautical skills sufficient to shuttle back and forth between invisible land masses – a prowess few prehistorians are willing to grant. If, on the other hand, the trip was one-way and accidental, then it must necessarily have involved a community of people of both sexes swept out to sea, either all together on a large raft (thought very unlikely) or in a flotilla of small rafts, and after successfully weathering a storm and at least a few days at sea, they were washed up on proximate parts of the north Australian coast where they regrouped and established a society.

You don't need vast numbers of people to populate Australia. Joseph Birdsell, an American academic, calculated that a group of twenty-five founding colonists could have produced a society of 300,000 in a little over 2,000 years. But you still need to get those initial twenty-five people there – more than can be plausibly accounted for with a raft or two blown off course.

Of course all of this may have happened in any number of other ways, and it may have taken generations to get fully under way. No one can possibly say. All that is certain is that Australia's indigenous peoples are there because their distant ancestors crossed at least sixty miles of fairly formidable sea tens of thousands of years before anyone else on earth dreamed of such an endeavour, and did it in sufficient numbers to begin to start the colonization of a continent.

By any measure this is a staggeringly momentous accomplishment. And how much note does it get? Well, ask yourself when was the last time you read anything about it. When was the last time in any context concerning human dispersal and the rise of civilizations that you saw even a passing mention of the role of Aborigines? They are the planet's invisible people.

A big part of the problem is that for most of us it is nearly impossible to grasp what an extraordinary span of time we are considering here. Assume for the sake of argument that the Aborigines arrived 60,000 years ago (that is the figure used by Roger Lewin of Harvard in *Principles of Evolution*, a standard text). On that scale, the total period of European occupation of Australia represents about 0.3 per cent of the total. In other words, for the first 99.7 per cent of its inhabited history the Aborigines had Australia to themselves. They have been there an almost unimaginably long time. And here lies their other unappreciated achievement.

The arrival in Australia of the Aborigines is, of course, merely the start of the story. They also mastered the continent. They spread over it with amazing swiftness and developed strategies and patterns of behaviour to exploit or accommodate every extreme of the landscape, from the wettest rainforests to the driest deserts. No people on earth have lived in more environments with greater success for longer. It is generally accepted that the Aborigines have the oldest continuously maintained culture in the world. It is thought by some – the respected prehistorian John Mulvaney, for instance – that the Australian language family may be the world's oldest. Their art and stories and systems of beliefs are indubitably among the oldest on earth.

These are obviously important and singular achievements, too. They provide incontestable evidence that the early Aboriginal peoples spoke and cooperated and employed advanced technological and organizational skills at a time much earlier than anyone had ever supposed. And how much notice do these achievements get? Well, again, until recently, virtually none. I had this brought home to me with a certain unexpected forcefulness when, after leaving Alan and Carmel and flying to Sydney, I went for an afternoon to the State Library of New South Wales. There while browsing for something else altogether I came across a 1972 edition of the *Larousse Encyclopedia of Archaeology*. Curious to see what it had to say about the findings at Lake Mungo three years earlier, I took it down to have a look. It didn't mention the Mungo findings. In fact, the book contained just one reference to Australia's Aborigines, a sentence that said: 'The Aborigines also evolved independently of the Old World, but they represent a very primitive technical and economic phase.'

That was it – the entire discussion of Australia's indigenous culture by a scholarly volume of weight and authority, written in the last third of the twentieth century. When I say these are the world's invisible people, believe me these are the world's invisible people. And the real tragedy is that that is only the half of it.

From the first moment of contact the natives were a source of the deepest wonder to the Europeans. When James Cook and his men sailed into Botany Bay they were astonished that most of the Aborigines they saw sitting on the shore or fishing in the shallows from frail bark canoes seemed hardly to notice them. They 'scarce lifted their eyes from their employment', as Joseph Banks recorded. The creaking *Endeavour* was clearly the largest and most extraordinary structure that could ever have come before them, yet most of the natives merely glanced up and looked at it as if at a passing cloud and returned to their tasks.

They seemed not to perceive the world in the way of other people. No Aboriginal language, for instance, had any words for 'yesterday' or 'tomorrow' – extraordinary omissions in any culture. They had no chiefs or governing councils, wore no clothes, built no houses or other permanent structures, sowed no crops, herded no animals, made no pottery, possessed almost no sense of property. Yet they devoted disproportionate efforts to enterprises that no one even now can understand. All around the coast of Australia the early explorers found huge shell mounds, up to thirty feet high and covering at the base as much as half an acre. Often these were some distance inland and uphill. The Aborigines clearly had made some effort to convey the shells from the beach to the mounds – one midden was estimated to contain 33,000 cubic metres of shells – and they kept it up for an enormously long time: at least 800 years in one case. Why did they bother? No one knows. In almost every way it was as if they answered to some different laws.

A few Europeans – Watkin Tench and James Cook notably – viewed the Aborigines sympathetically. In the *Endeavour* Journal Cook wrote: 'They may appear to some to be the most wretched people on earth, but in reality they are far happier than we Europeans. They live in a tranquillity which is not disturbed by the inequality of condition: the earth and the sea of their own accord furnish them with all things necessary for life . . . they seemed to set no value upon anything we gave them, nor would they ever part with anything of their own.' Elsewhere, he added with a touch of poignancy: 'All they seem'd to want was for us to be gone.'

Unfortunately, few others were so enlightened. For most Europeans, the Aborigines were simply something that was in the way – 'one of the natural hazards', as the scientist and natural historian Tim Flannery has described it. It helped to regard them as essentially subhuman, a view that persisted well into the twentieth century. As recently as the early 1960s, as John Pilger notes, Queensland schools were using a textbook that likened Aborigines to 'feral jungle creatures'. When they weren't subhuman, they were simply inconsequential. In the same period, a Professor Stephen Roberts produced a fat and scholarly tome entitled *A History of Australian Land Settlement*, which managed to survey the entire period of European occupation and displacement without mentioning the Aborigines once. Such was the marginalization of the native peoples that until 1967 the federal government did not even include them in national censuses – did not, in other words, count them as people.

Largely for these reasons no one knows how many Aborigines were in Australia when Britons first settled it. The best estimates suggest that at the beginning of occupation the Aboriginal population was about 300,000, though possibly as high as a million. What is certain is that in the first century of settlement those numbers fell catastrophically. By the end of the nineteenth century the number of Aborigines was probably no more than 50,000 or 60,000. Most of this decline, it must be said, was inadvertent. Aborigines had almost no resistance to European diseases: smallpox, pleurisy, syphilis, even chickenpox and the milder forms of influenza often cut swathes through the native populations. But where Aborigines remained, they were sometimes treated in the most heartless and wanton manner.

In *Taming the Great South Land*, William J. Lines details examples of the most appalling cruelty by settlers towards the natives – of Aborigines butchered for dog food; of an Aboriginal woman forced to watch her husband killed, then made to wear his decapitated head around her neck; of another chased up a tree and tormented from below with rifle shots. 'Every time a bullet hit,' Lines reports, 'she pulled leaves off the tree and thrust them into her wounds, till at last she fell lifeless to the ground.' What is perhaps most shocking is how casually so much of this was done, and at all levels of society. In an 1839 history of Tasmania, written by a visitor named Melville, the author relates how he went out one day with 'a respectable young gentleman' to hunt kangaroos. As they rounded a bend, the young gentleman spied a form crouched in hiding behind a fallen tree. Stepping over to investigate and 'finding it only to be a native', the appalled Melville wrote, the gentleman lifted the muzzle to the native's breast 'and shot him dead on the spot'.

Such behaviour was virtually never treated as a crime – indeed was sometimes officially countenanced. In 1805, the acting judge-advocate for New South Wales, the most senior judicial figure in the land, declared that Aborigines had not the discipline or mental capacity for courtroom proceedings; rather than plague the courts with their grievances, settlers were instructed to track down the offending natives and 'inflict such punishment as they may merit' – as open an invitation to genocide as can be found in English law. Fifteen years later our old friend

Lachlan Macquarie authorized soldiers in the Hawkesbury region to shoot any group of Aborigines greater than six in number, even if unarmed and entirely innocent of purpose, even if the number included women and children. Sometimes, under the pretence of compassion, Aborigines were offered food that had been dosed with poison. Pilger quotes a mid-nineteenth-century government report from Queensland: 'The niggers [were given] . . . something really startling to keep them quiet . . . the rations contained about as much strychnine as anything and not one of the mob escaped.' By 'mob' he meant about one hundred unarmed men, women and children.

The wonder of all this is that the scale of native murders was not far greater. In the first century and a half of British occupation, the number of Aborigines intentionally killed by whites (including in self-defence, during pitched battles and in other rather more justifiable circumstances) is thought to be about 20,000 altogether – an unhappy total, to be sure, but much less than one-tenth the number of Aborigines who died from disease.

That isn't to say that violence wasn't casual or widespread. It was. And it was against this background, in June 1838, that a dozen men on horseback set off from the farm of one Henry Dangar, looking for the people who had stolen or driven off some of their livestock. At Myall Creek they happened on an encampment of Aborigines who were known among the white settlers of the district as peaceable and inoffensive. Almost certainly they had nothing to do with the rustled cattle. None the less their captors tied them together in a kind of great ball – twenty-eight men, women and children – led them around the countryside for some hours in an indecisive manner, then abruptly and mercilessly slaughtered them with rifles and swords.

In the normal course of things, that would almost certainly have been that. But in 1838 the mood of the nation was changing. Australia was becoming an increasingly urbanized society, and city dwellers were beginning to express revulsion for the casual slaughter of innocent people. When a campaigning Sydney journalist named Edward Smith Hall got hold of the story and began to bray for blood and justice, Governor George Gipps ordered the perpetrators tracked down and brought to trial. When arrested, two of the accused protested, with evident sincerity, that they hadn't known killing Aborigines was illegal.

Despite clearly damning evidence at the subsequent trial, it took a jury just fifteen minutes to acquit the defendants. But Hall, Gipps and the urban public were not lightly pacified and a second trial was ordered. This time seven of the men were found guilty and hanged. It was the first time that white people had been executed for the murder of Aborigines.

The Myall Creek hangings didn't end the slaughter of Aborigines so much as drive them underground. They went on sporadically for almost another century. The last was in 1928 near present-day Alice Springs when a white dingo hunter named Fred Brooks was murdered in uncertain circumstances and at least seventeen and perhaps as many as seventy Aborigines were chased down and killed by mounted constabulary in reprisal. (A judge in that case declared that the police had acted within the law.) But the Myall Creek case was undoubtedly a defining moment in Australian history. Though it gets at least a mention in almost all history books these days, I hadn't met anyone who had been there or even quite knew where it was, and it seemed apparent from the descriptions I had read that the authors had drawn exclusively from historical sources. I wanted to have a look.

It takes a little finding. From Macksville the next morning I drove sixty miles up the Pacific Highway to Grafton, then headed inland on a steep and lonely road up and through the Great Dividing Range. Four hours later, in hot and empty sheep country, I reached Delungra – a petrol station and a couple of houses with long views over mostly treeless plains – and there I turned down a back road that followed a twisting, sometimes nearly washed-out course on its way to the small town of Bingara twenty-five miles to the south. A couple of miles short of Bingara, I came to a small rickety-looking bridge over a half-dry creek. A little sign announced it as Myall Creek. I pulled the car into the shade of a river gum and got out to have a look. There was no memorial, no historical plaque. Nothing at all to indicate that here, or at least somewhere in the immediate vicinity, was where one of the most infamous events in Australian history took place. To one side of the bridge was a forlorn rest area with a pair of broken picnic tables and a good deal of shattered bottles in the stubby grass around the edge. In the sunny middle distance, perhaps a mile away, stood a large farmhouse, surrounded by fields of unusually verdant crops. In the other direction, and much closer, an overgrown track led to a white building. I walked along it to see what it was. A sign announced it as the Myall Creek Memorial Hall. It wasn't much of a monument to a terrible slaughter, but at least it was something. Then on a wall of the building I noticed a hand-painted sign and discovered that it had nothing to do with the slaughter; it was a memorial for the dead of two world wars.

I drove on the last couple of miles into Bingara (pop. 1,363), a hot and listless village with a dozing main street. It looked like a place that had once known prosperity, but most of the storefronts now were either empty or taken up with government enterprises – a health clinic, an employment advice centre, a tourist information office, police station, something called a 'Senior Citizens Rest Centre'. An old and improbably large movie house still announced itself as the Roxy, but clearly had been shut for years. In the tourist information centre I was received by a pleasant-looking middle-aged lady who bobbed to her feet at the sight of a customer. I asked her if they had any information about the massacre, and she gave me a crestfallen look.

'I'm afraid I don't know much about that,' she said.

'Really?' I said, surprised. The place was full of leaflets and books.

'Well, it was a long time ago. I believe the children study about it in school, but I'm afraid it's not something visitors ask about very often.'

'How often? Just out of interest.'

'Oh,' she said and clasped her chin as if that was a real poser. She turned to a colleague who was just emerging from a back room. 'Mary, when was the last time someone asked about Myall Creek?'

'Oh,' said the colleague, equally stumped. 'I couldn't say – no, wait, there was a man who asked about it maybe two months ago. I remember now. He had a little goatee. Looked a bit like Rolf Harris. I can't remember the last time before that.'

'Most visitors want to go fossicking,' the first lady explained.

Fossicking is to hunt for precious minerals.

'What do they find?' I asked.

'Oh, lots – gold, diamonds, sapphires. This used to be a big mining area.'

'But you have nothing at all on the massacre?'

'I'm afraid not.' She seemed genuinely regretful. 'I tell you who can help you and that's Paulette Smith at the *Advocate*.'

'That's the local paper,' added the colleague.

'She knows all about the massacre. She did some kind of study on it for college.'

'If anybody can help you, Paulette can.'

I thanked them and went off to find the *Advocate*. Bingara was an oddly interesting little town. It was small and half dead and on a road to nowhere, yet it had not only a tourist office but also its own newspaper. At the *Advocate* office I was told that Paulette Smith had popped out and that I should try back in an hour. Slightly at a loss, I went into a café and ordered a sandwich and a coffee, and was mindlessly consuming both when a lady, red-haired, late-thirtyish and looking faintly breathless, abruptly slid onto the seat facing me.

'I hear you're looking for me,' she said.

'News travels fast here.' I smiled.

She rolled her eyes ironically. 'Small town.'

Paulette Smith was rather intense but with a sudden, disarming smile that would flash at odd moments, like a broken sign, and then be lost at once in the greater intensity of what she was telling me.

'We didn't learn anything about the massacre when I was growing up,' she said. 'We knew it had happened – you know, that a long time ago some Aborigines were killed out by the creek and that some white people were hanged for it. But that was about it. We weren't taught about it in

274

school. We didn't, you know, make school trips out there or anything.' The smile came and went.

'Did people talk about it?'

'No. Never.'

I asked her where exactly it had happened. 'Nobody knows. Somewhere on Myall Creek Station.' (Station in the context means a farm or ranch.) 'It's all private property now, and they're not real friendly to trespassers.'

'So there's never been any kind of archaeological dig or anything? You don't get academics poking around?'

'No, there's not that kind of interest in it. Anyway, I don't think they'd know where to look. It's a big property.'

'And there's no memorial of any kind?'

'Oh no.'

'Isn't that odd?'

'No.'

'But wouldn't you expect the government to put up *something*?'

She considered for a moment. 'Well, you've got to understand there was nothing all that special about Myall Creek. Aborigines were slaughtered all over the place. Three months before the Myall massacre 200 Aborigines were killed at Waterloo Creek, near Moree.' Moree was sixty miles or so further west. 'Nobody was ever punished for that. They didn't even *try* to punish anybody for that.'

'I didn't know that.'

She nodded. 'No reason why you should. Most people have never heard of it. All that was different about Myall Creek was that white people were punished for it. It didn't stop them killing Aborigines. It just made them more circumspect. You know, they didn't boast about it in the pub afterwards.' Another flickering smile. 'It's kind of ironic when you think about it. Myall Creek's not famous

275

for what happened to the blacks here, but for what happened to the whites. Anyway, you wouldn't be able to move in this country for memorials if you tried to acknowledge them all.'

She stared dreamily for a moment at my notebook, then said abruptly: 'I have to get back to work.' She made an apologetic look. 'I'm afraid I haven't been much help.'

'No, you've been a great help,' I said, then I thought of another question.

'Are there any Aborigines here now?'

'Oh, no. They're long gone from round here.'

I paid for my lunch and returned to the car. On the way out of town, I stopped again by the bridge and wandered a little way up an overgrown lane that led on to part of the station property. But there was nothing to see and I was a little afraid of snakes in the tall grass. So I returned to the car and retraced my route across the dusty plain and on towards the distant blue slopes of the Great Dividing Range.

And so to Surfers Paradise, back on the Pacific Coast Highway and another hundred miles north. Surfers Paradise is just over the border in Queensland, and I was eager to dip a toe into that interesting and erratic state. In a country where states are both few and immense, the arrival in a new one is always an event. I wasn't going to come this far and not at least slip over the border.

One thing you find if you browse much through non-fiction works on Australia is that practically every book written about the country in the last forty years, possibly more, has in it somewhere an anecdote illustrating that Queenslanders are not like other people. In *Australian Paradox*, Jeanne MacKenzie relates the story of an

American guest at a rural Queensland hotel in the 1950s who was presented at dinner with a plate of cold meat and potatoes. He stared with private disappointment at the offering for a moment, then diffidently enquired whether he might have a little salad with it.

'The waitress', Ms MacKenzie reports, 'looked at him with astonishment and disdain and, turning to the other guests, remarked: "The bastard thinks it's Christmas."'

Here's another that I have seen twice. A visitor (French in one version, English in the other) is staying at a Queensland hotel during 'the wet', the rainy season that is a feature of life in northern Australia. The guest is startled, upon reaching his room, to discover that it is flooded to a depth of three or four inches. When he reports this at the front desk, the owner looks at him with pain and irritation and says: 'Well, the bed's dry, isn't it?'

All these stories have certain things in common. Generally they take place in the 1950s. Generally they involve a foreign visitor at a rural hotel. Generally they are presented as true. And always they make Queenslanders look like pricks. Most suggest that Queenslanders are just crazy, and the evidence does rather point in that direction. For almost two decades the state was under the control of Joh Bjelke-Peterson, an eccentric, right-wing state premier who at one time seriously entertained the notion of blowing up parts of the Great Barrier Reef with small atomic bombs to create shipping channels. Of late it had gained fame as the seat of a politician named Pauline Hanson, a fish-and-chip shop owner who had started a right-wing, anti-immigration party called One Nation, which had had a spell of striking success before it became evident even to her most ardent followers that Ms Hanson was a little, shall we say, cerebrally unpredictable. She wrote a book in which she suggested that Aborigines engaged in cannibalism, and produced an interestingly paranoid video which began: 'Fellow Australians, if you are seeing me now it means I have been murdered.' Her seat was the Brisbane suburb of Oxley, which inspired some genius to dub her the Oxley moron. In a word, Queensland has a reputation for being a place apart. I couldn't wait to get there.

In 1933 Elston, Queensland, was a remote and inconsequential seaside hamlet with an excellent beach, a few flimsy cottages, a popular but slightly raffish hotel and a couple of shops. Then the town fathers got a really good idea. Realizing that nobody was going to travel hundreds of miles to visit a place called Elston (and, more to the point, that nobody was travelling hundreds of miles to visit a place called Elston), they decided to give the place a peppier name, based on something novel and upbeat. Looking around, their gaze fell on the local hotel. It was called Surfers Paradise. The name had a certain ring. They decided to give it a try and see what happened. The town has never looked back.

Today Surfers Paradise is famous, while its neighbouring resort communities – Broadbeach, Currumbin, Tugun, Kirra, Bilinga – are scarcely known outside Queensland. It hardly matters because they have all coalesced into a single unsightly sprawl stretching for thirty miles from the Queensland–New South Wales border almost to Brisbane. The whole is called the Gold Coast. This is Australia's Florida.

You see it long before you get to it – shimmering towers of glass and concrete rising beside the sea and snaking off down the coastline to a distant, hazy vanishing point.

When Jeanne MacKenzie passed this way in 1959, not one bit of this glitziness existed. Surfers Paradise was still a low-key, low-rise, old-fashioned sort of place. In 1962 it got its first high-rise. Another followed a year or two later. By the end of the sixties, half a dozen ten- or twelve-storey buildings stood awkwardly and a little self-consciously along the front. Then in the early 1970s a development frenzy started. Where once there were just sandy quarter-acre plots, each holding a matchbox beach cottage, today stand hotels of Trump-like splendour, balconied apartment blocks, a domed casino, verdant golf courses, water parks, amusement parks, miniature golf courses, shopping malls and all the rest. Much of this, you are told in a confidential tone, was built and paid for with money of dubious pedigree. People outside Queensland will tell you that the Gold Coast is rife with unsavoury elements – Australian drug barons, Japanese yakuza, flashy linchpins of the Hong Kong triads. This is not, you are led to believe, a place to bump a Mercedes and start an argument.

Nearly everyone you meet elsewhere in Australia will tell you: 'Oh, you must see the Gold Coast. It's awful.'

'Really?' you say, intrigued. 'In what way?'

'I don't know exactly. I've never been there myself. Well, obviously. But it's like – have you seen *Muriel's Wedding*?'

'No.'

'Well, it's like that. Just like it. Apparently.'

So I was interested on many levels to see the Gold Coast, and disappointed on nearly every one of them. To begin with, it wasn't tacky at all. It was just another large, impersonal, well-provisioned international resort. I could have been in Marbella or Eilat or anywhere else developed in the last twenty-five years. The hotels were mostly big international names – Marriott, Radisson, Mercure – and of an unexceptionably respectable standard. I parked the car on a side street and walked along to the seafront. En route I passed stores of an unexpected glitziness – Prada, Hermès, Ralph Lauren. All perfectly fine. It just wasn't very interesting. I didn't need to travel 8,000 miles to look at Ralph Lauren bath towels.

The beach, however, was exceedingly splendid – broad, clean, sunny, with lazy, manageable-sized waves rolling in from an almost painfully blue and bright sea. The air was filled with salt tang and the ozone-enriched shrieks of pleasure and children shouting and a sense of people having fun. I took a seat on a bench and just watched people enjoying themselves. I had read somewhere that the Gold Coast beaches are actually quite treacherous for rips. As it happened, drownings were much in the news lately. The Australian media cover beach mishaps the way American papers cover blizzards and hurricanes – as a seasonal event involving lots of comparative statistics. According to the papers, there had been thirty-four drownings already this year, more than most years, and the summer wasn't yet half over. Much of it was blamed on tourists who didn't know how to read the water for rips or to stay calm when they were caught in one. But a lot of it was just down to lunacy. The *Sydney Morning Herald* cited the case of a 52-year-old man at a place called North Avoca Beach, who had sternly cautioned people not to swim at a particular spot, then went in himself and drowned. Just that morning, while packing up at my motel, I had paused to watch a lifeguard from here at Surfers Paradise being interviewed on a breakfast television programme. He said that he himself had rescued 100 people the previous week, including one tourist whom he had saved twice.

'Twice?' said the interviewer.

The lifeguard grinned at the ridiculousness of it. 'Yip.'

'What, you saved him and he went back in the water and you had to save him again?'

The grin broadened. 'Yip.'

I scanned the water for troubled swimmers. I couldn't imagine how any lifeguard could spot a drowning person among all the hundreds of happy, frolicking bodies, but they most assuredly do. Australian lifeguards are unquestionably the finest in the world. In the same period that thirty-four people drowned, more than 6,000 were saved – a commendable ratio, to say the very least.

Eventually I stopped for a cup of coffee and then wandered through the business district, but Surfers Paradise was mostly just a succession of stores selling the same stuff – painted boomerangs and didgeridoos, cuddly toy koalas and kangaroos, postcards and souvenir books, rack upon rack of T-shirts. In one of the shops I bought a postcard that showed a kangaroo surfing, and asked the young lady who served me if she knew where the original Surfers Paradise Hotel was.

'Oh, I don't know,' she said and looked guilty, as if she had forgotten a secret with which she had been entrusted. 'I haven't been in the area very long,' she added.

I nodded that it didn't matter and asked her where she was from.

'ACT.' Seeing my mind whirring to little effect, she added: 'Australian Capital Territory. Canberra.'

Of course. 'So which is better,' I asked, 'Canberra or Surfers Paradise?'

'Oh, Surfers by a mile.'

I raised an eyebrow. 'It's that good, is it?'

'Oh *no*,' she said emphatically, amazed that I had misread her. 'Canberra's that bad.'

I smiled at her solemnity.

She nodded with conviction. 'I reckon if you were going to rank things for how much pleasure they give – you know? – Canberra would come somewhere below breaking your arm.' I grinned and she grinned too. 'Well, at least with a broken arm you know it'll get better.' She talked with the rising intonation common to young people in Australia, which turns every statement into a question. It drives older Australians crazy, but personally I find it endearing, and sometimes, as here, charmingly sexy.

A supervisor-type person came over to make sure we weren't enjoying ourselves too much. 'Cahn I be of assistahnce?' she said in an odd accent that suggested long devotion to a book entitled *Elocution Self Taught*. She held her head at an odd angle too, tilted back slightly as if she were afraid that her eyeballs might fall out.

'I was looking for the original Surfers Paradise Hotel.'

'Ah, that was torn down some years ago.' She flashed a satisfied smile – it reminded me exactly of William F. Buckley – though whether the smile indicated that she was happy that it had been torn down or merely pleased to be able to convey disappointing news I couldn't say. She showed me on the map in my guidebook where it had stood.

I thanked them both and, clutching my directions, found my way to the site of the famous and now irretrievably lost Surfers Paradise Hotel. Today the spot is occupied by a shopping complex called the Paradise Centre, which was much more in keeping with the modern resort, in that it was ugly and filled with overpriced shit.

In the Surfers Paradise book I had consulted in Adelaide, a photograph from the late 1940s had shown a delightfully ramshackle hotel – a place that looked as if it had been built in phases with whatever materials had come to hand – with a terrace bar on which sat many people soaking up sunshine and alcohol in careless volumes and looking awfully pleased to be there. I walked all the way around the block, then stood on the opposite corner and stared at the site for a long time, but it wasn't possible to imagine it as it had been, any more than it was possible to imagine the Myall Creek massacre from its present peaceful situation. So I returned to the car and headed out of town through the dappled stripes of sun and shade created by the big hotels and lavish palm trees. At the edge of town I rejoined the Pacific Highway and headed south.

I had a long drive to Sydney ahead of me. For the moment, my trip was over. But I would be back, of course. I wasn't anywhere near finished with this place yet.

Part Three

AROUND THE EDGES

Chapter

FOURTEEN

'I just want you to know,' said a voice in my ear as Qantas flight 406 popped cork-like out of a tower of monsoonal cumulo-nimbus, presenting the window passengers with a sudden view of emerald mountains rising almost sheer from a pewter sea, 'that if it comes to it you may have all my urine.'

I turned from the window to give this remark the attention it deserved and found myself staring at the solemn and rested countenance of Allan Sherwin, my friend and temporary travelling companion. It would be incorrect to say that I was surprised to find him sitting beside me because we had met in Sydney by design and boarded the flight together, but there was none the less a certain residual measure of unexpectedness – a kind of pinch-me quality – in finding him seated there. Ten days earlier in London, where I had stopped on my way back to

America from my hike in the Middle East, I had met Allan to discuss some project he had in mind. (He is a television producer by profession; we had become friends while working together on a series for British television the previous year.) There, in a pub on the Old Brompton Road, I had told him of my experiences in Australia so far and mentioned my plans on the next trip to tackle the formidable desert regions alone and at ground level. In order to deepen his admiration for me, I had told him some vivid stories of travellers who had come unstuck in the unforgiving interior. One of these had pertained to an expedition in the 1850s led by a surveyor named Robert Austin, which grew so lost and short of water in the arid wastes beyond Mount Magnet in Western Australia that the members were reduced to drinking their own and their horses' urine. The story had affected him so powerfully that he had announced at once the intention to accompany me through the most perilous parts of the present trip, in the role of driver and scout. I had, of course, tried to dissuade him, if only for his own safety, but he would have none of it. Clearly the story was still much on his mind, judging by his kind offer to keep me in urine.

'Thank you,' I replied now, 'that's very generous of you.'

He gave me a nod that had a touch of the regal about it. 'It's what friends are for.'

'And you may have as much of mine as I can spare.'

Another regal nod.

The plan, to which he was now resolutely attached, was to accompany me first to northern Queensland, where we would relax for a day amid the fertile shoals of the Great Barrier Reef before setting off in a suitably sturdy vehicle along a bumpy track for Cooktown, a semi-ghost town in the jungle some way north of Cairns. This warm-up adventure completed, we would fly on to Darwin in the Northern Territory – the 'Top End' as it is fondly known to Australians – for the thousand-mile drive through the scorched red centre to Alice Springs and mighty Uluru. Having assisted me through the worst of the perils, the heroic Mr Sherwin would fly back to England from Alice, and leave me to continue on through the western deserts on my own. It wasn't that he thought I would be ready for this by then – for he had no confidence whatever in my survival capabilities – but that ten days was all he had to spare. For my part, I had no greater confidence in him, but I was glad of the company.

'You know,' I added reassuringly, 'I don't suppose it will actually be necessary to drink urine on this trip. The infrastructure of the arid regions is much improved since the 1850s. I understand they have Coca-Cola now.'

'Still, the offer is there.'

'And much appreciated, too.'

Another exchange of regal nods, and then I returned my gaze to the exotic verdure below our waggling wingtip. If you needed convincing that Australia is an exceptional part of the world, then tropical Queensland would be the place to come. Of the 500 or so sites on the planet that qualify for World Heritage status, only thirteen satisfy all four of UNESCO's criteria for listing, and of these thirteen special places, four – almost a third – are to be found in Australia. Moreover, two of these, the Great Barrier Reef and the wet tropics of Queensland, were right here. It is the only place in the world, I believe, where two such consummate environments adjoin.

We were lucky to be there at all. They were having a terrible wet season in the north. Cyclone Rona had recently buzzsawed along the coast, causing $300 million of havoc, and lesser storms had been teasing the region for weeks, disrupting travel. Only the day before all flights had been cancelled. It was evident from the dips and wobbles of our approach into Cairns that a lot of assertive weather was still about. The view as we came in was of palm trees, golf courses, seaside marinas, some big beachside hotels and lots and lots of red-roofed houses poking out of abundant foliage. Weather apart, it all looked very promising.

It is remarkable now, when over two million people a year come to the Great Barrier Reef and it is universally esteemed as a treasure, how long it took the tourism industry to discover it. In *Rum Jungle*, an account of a tour through northern Australia in the 1950s, the historian Alan Moorehead made venturing into northern Queensland sound like a journey to the headwaters of the Orinoco. Then, Cairns was a small, muggy coastal outpost hundreds of miles up a jungle road and occupied mostly by eccentric dropouts of a fugitive disposition. Today it is a bustling mini-metropolis of 60,000 inhabitants, in-distinguishable from any community of similar size in Australia except for the humidity that falls over you like a hot towel when you emerge from the airport terminal and a certain hale devotion to the tourist dollar. It has become a hugely popular stopoff point for backpackers and other young travellers for whom it has a certain reputation for tropical liveliness. On this day the whole was pressed under an oppressive weight of low grey skies of the sort that threatened rain in volume at any moment. We took a cab into town through a long, unbecoming sprawl of motels, petrol stations and fast food establishments. Central Cairns was somewhat snugger, but it had the feel of a place that had been built only recently, in haste. Every second business offered reef cruises or snorkelling expeditions, and most of the rest sold T-shirts and postcards.

We went first to pick up our hire car. Because I had been hiking in the Middle East, I had left the arrangements to a travel agent, and I was mildly surprised to find that the agent had plumped for an obscure local firm – Crocodile Car Hire or something similarly improbable and unpromising – whose office was little more than a bare counter on a side street. The young man in charge had a certain chirpy cockiness that was ineffably irritating, but he dealt with the paperwork in a brisk and efficient manner, chattering throughout about the weather. It was the worst wet in thirty years, he told us proudly. Then he led us out to the pavement and presented us with our vehicle – an aged Commodore Holden estate car that seemed to have a decided sag about the axles.

'What's this?' I asked.

He leaned towards me and said as you might to a dementia sufferer: 'It's your car.'

'But I asked for a four-wheel drive.'

He sifted through his paperwork and carefully extracted a fax from the travel agent, which he passed to me. It showed a request for a large, standard, high-polluting car with automatic transmission – an American car, in other words, or the nearest local equivalent. I sighed and handed back the paper. 'Well, do you have a four-wheel drive I can take instead?' I asked.

'Nope, sorry. We only do town cars.'

'But we were going to drive up towards Cape York.'

'Oh, you won't get up there in the wet. Not even in a four-wheel drive. Not at this time of year. They had a

291

hundred centimetres of rain at Cape Tribulation last week.'
I had no very clear idea what a hundred centimetres was,
but it was evident from his tone that it was considerable.
'You won't get beyond Daintree in anything less than a
helicopter.'

I sighed again.

'The road to Townsville's been cut off for three days,' he
added with yet more pride.

I looked at him again. Townsville is south of Cairns – in
the opposite direction from Cape York. It appeared we
were boxed in. 'So where *can* we go?' I asked.

He spread his hands in cheerful irony. 'Anywhere you
like in greater Cairns.'

Allan looked at me in the happily brainless way of
someone who doesn't realize disaster is afoot, irritating
me further. I sighed and hefted my bags. 'Well, can you
point us the way to the Palm Cove Hotel?' I asked.

'Certainly. You go back out past the airport to the Cook
Highway and take the road north. It's about twenty
kilometres up the coast.'

'Twenty kilometres?' I sputtered. 'I asked for a hotel in
Cairns.'

He scratched his chin thoughtfully. 'Well, it's sure not in
Cairns.'

'But the road is open?'

'So far.'

'You mean it might flood?'

'Always a possibility.'

'And if it floods we're stuck in the middle of nowhere?'

He looked at me with a touch of pity. 'Mister, you're
already in the middle of nowhere.' The point was
inarguable. Cairns was 1,100 miles from Brisbane, its own
state capital, and there was nothing in the other directions

but ocean, jungle and desert. 'But Palm Cove's real nice,' he added. 'You'll like it.'

And he was right. Palm Cove was lovely – really quite astonishingly so. It was a purpose-built village inserted with some care into a stretch of tropical luxuriance beside a curving bay. On one side of a beachside road stood low-rise hotels and apartments, a few cottages and a scattering of bars, restaurants and shops, all discreetly obscured by palms, spreading fronds and flowering vines, and on the other was a palm-lined walk overlooking a smooth, golden beach and the sea.

Our hotel was, in everything but name, setting and price, a motel, but it was friendly and overlooked the sea. We claimed our rooms, then went for a walk along the beach. A few other people were strolling over the sand, but no one was in the water and for a very good reason. It was the height of the season for box jellyfish, also known in Queensland as marine stingers, or just stingers. By whatever name they go, these little bubbles of woe are not to be trifled with. From October to May, when the jellyfish come inshore to breed, they render the beaches of the tropics useless to humans. It is quite an extraordinary thought when you are standing there looking at it. Before us stood a sweep of bay as serene and inviting as you would find anywhere, and yet there was no environment on earth more likely to offer instant death.

'So you're telling me,' said Allan, for whom all this was new, 'that if I waded into the water now I would die?'

'In the most wretched and abject agony known to man,' I replied.

'Jesus,' he muttered.

'And don't pick up any of the seashells,' I added, stopping him from leaning over to pick up a seashell. I explained to him about coneshells – the venomous creatures that lurk inside some of the handsomest shells, waiting for a human hand to sink their vile pincers into.

'Seashells will kill you?' he said. 'They've got lethal seashells here?'

'There are more things that will kill you up here than anywhere else in Australia, and that's saying a lot, believe me.'

I told him about the cassowary, the flightless, man-sized bird that lives in the rainforests, with a razor claw on each foot with which it can slice you open in a deft and appallingly expansive manner; and the green tree snakes that dangle from branches and so blend into the foliage that you don't see them until they are clamped on to a facial extremity. I mentioned also the small but fearsomely poisonous blue-ringed octopus, whose caress is instant death; and the elegant but irritable numb ray, which moves through the water like a flying carpet discharging 220 volts of electricity into anything that troubles its progress; and the loathsome, sluggish stonefish, so called because it is indistinguishable from a rock, but with the difference that it has twelve spikes on its back that are sharp enough to pierce the sole of a sneaker, injecting the hapless sufferer with a myotoxin bearing a molecular weight of 150,000.

'And what does that mean exactly?'

'Pain beyond description followed shortly by muscular paralysis, respiratory depression, cardiac palpitations and a severe disinclination to boogie. You might similarly be discommoded by firefish, which are easier to spot but no less hurtful. There's even a jellyfish called the snottie.'

'You're making all this up,' he said, but without conviction.

'Oh, but I'm not.'

Then I told him about the dreaded saltwater crocodile, which lurks in tropical lagoons, estuaries and even bays such as this one, leaping from the waters from time to time to snatch and devour unsuspecting passers-by. Just up the coast from where we now strolled, a woman named Beryl Wruck had been taken not so long before in a startling manner. 'Shall I tell you about it?' I offered.

'No.'

'Well, one day,' I went on, knowing that really he wanted to hear, 'a group of locals at Daintree got together for a festive pre-Christmas barbie when some of them decided to go for a cooling dip in the Daintree River. The river was known to be the home of crocodiles, but none had ever attacked anybody locally. So several of the party scampered down to the water's edge, stripped to their underwear and splashed in. Ms Wruck apparently thought better of leaping in, so she merely stepped a foot or so into the water. As she stood there watching the happy frolicking, she idly leaned over and trailed a hand through the water. Just at that instant the water split in a flash of movement and poor Ms Wruck was gone, never to be seen again. "There was no sound, no scream," reported one witness. "It was so quick that if you had blinked an eye you'd have missed the whole thing." That is what a crocodile attack is like, you see – swift, unexpected, extremely irreversible.'

'And you're telling me there are crocodiles here in this water?' Allan said.

'Oh, I don't know whether there are or not. But it's why I'm letting you walk on the inside.'

Just then from the restive skies there came a single startling crack of thunder. Abruptly the wind kicked up, sending the palm trees dancing, and a few fat splats of rain fell. Then the skies opened in a warm but soaking downpour. We hied back to our hotel where we took refuge under the veranda of the beachfront bar, ineffectually wrung out our steaming shirts and watched the rain beat down with a tumultuous fury. There was nothing so dainty as raindrops in this. It was just a cubic mass of falling water, filling the world with a fearful pounding din. I had thought that growing up in the American Midwest I was familiar with lively weather, but I am happy to concede that where the elements are concerned Australia plays in a league of its own. I had never seen anything like it.

'So let me get this straight,' Allan was saying. 'We can't go to Cooktown because we can't get through. We can't swim because the ocean's full of deadly jellyfish. And the road to Cairns might be cut off at any moment.'

'That's about the size of it.'

He blew out thoughtfully. 'Might as well have a few beers then.' He went off to get some. I took a seat at a small table on the veranda and watched the rain pour down.

One of the bar employees came and stood in the doorway. 'Worst wet in thirty years,' he said.

I nodded. 'What's the forecast?'

'Same.'

I nodded bleakly. 'We were supposed to be going out to the Great Barrier Reef tomorrow.'

'Oh, you've got no worries there. They don't cancel the reef tours unless it's a hurricane.'

'People go out to the reef in this kind of weather?'

He nodded. The water in the bay was sloshing around like a bath into which a fat man has just jumped.

'Why?'

'How much did you pay for your tickets?'

I had no idea – everything had been booked as part of a package – but I had the tickets with me and pulled them out of my wallet. 'A hundred and forty-five dollars each,' I squeaked in miserly disbelief.

He smiled. 'There you go.'

He went back in. A moment later Allan reappeared with the beers, looking unusually dejected. 'There is a jellyfish called the snottie,' he said in wonder. 'The barman told me.'

I gave him an apologetic smile. 'Told you.'

He stared for some minutes at the rain. On the table someone had left a copy of the local paper, the *Port Douglas and Mossman Gazette*. Allan started to move it to get at the ashtray, then something caught his eye. He read for a minute, with increasing absorption, then passed the paper to me, tapping the article he wished me to see. It was a small story at the bottom of the front page noting that the dengue fever epidemic in Port Douglas had slowed at last. The article said that since the epidemic had started 485 cases had been reported in the area. Although the pace was slowing, this was not grounds for complacency, a spokeswoman for the Tropical Public Health Unit warned.

'It's at the bottom of the page!' he said, his eyes just a trifle wild.

'That's where we're going tomorrow,' I noted with idle interest.

'Do you have any idea what a dengue epidemic would be like in Britain? People would be nailing boards over their windows. Ferries would have people hanging off the sides trying to get out of the country. The police would have to shoot people in the streets to restore order. Here they get 485 cases in a single community and it's two bloody inches on the bottom of the page! Where have you brought me, Bryson? What kind of country is this?'

'Oh, it's a wonderful country, Allan.'

'Yeah, right.'

We split up to shower and change, then reconvened in the bar for an aperitif before dinner. As the rain showed no sign of easing, we decided to dine at the hotel. At dinner, Allan ordered red snapper.

'You've not heard of ciguatera then?' I said casually.

'Of course I haven't bloody heard of it,' he replied through clenched teeth. 'What now?'

'It's nothing,' I said.

'Of course it must be something or you wouldn't have mentioned it. What is it? Am I sitting in it? Is it on my head? What?'

'No, it's a kind of toxin endemic to tropical waters. It accumulates in certain fish.'

'Like red snapper, for instance?'

'Well, especially red snapper, actually.'

He considered this with a kind of slow, catatonic nod. I think jet lag was kicking in. It can do terrible things to one's equilibrium.

'I'm sure there's nothing to worry about,' I added reassuringly. 'I mean, if there was an outbreak snapper wouldn't be on the menu, would it? Unless of course.' I stopped there.

'What?'

'Well, unless you were to be the first case. It has to start with somebody, after all. But, hey, what are the chances of that? One in a hundred? One in twenty?'

'I want you to stop this right now.'

'Of course,' I agreed at once. 'I'm sorry. Do you want to change your order?'

'No.'

'The symptoms include, but are not limited to, vomiting, severe muscle weakness, loss of motor control, paraesthesia of the lips, general lassitude, myalgia and paradoxical sensory disturbances – that is, feeling hot surfaces as cold and vice versa. Death occurs in about twelve per cent of cases.'

'I'm telling you to stop it right now.' The waitress came with our drinks. 'This snapper,' Allan said with forced casualness. 'It's all right, is it?'

'Oh, yeah. It's beaut.'

'I mean, it hasn't got – what is it, Bryson?'

'Ciguatera.'

She gave us a befuddled look. 'No, it comes with chips and salad.'

We exchanged glances.

'Would I be right in assuming you're not from around here?' I asked.

Her puzzlement deepened. 'No, I'm from Tassie. Why?'

'Just wondered.' I whispered to Allan: 'She's from Tasmania.'

He leaned to me and whispered back: 'Yes. So?'

'Their snapper are OK.'

'Is it possible to change my order, love?'

She stared at him heavily for a moment, the way young people do when they realize they are being asked to take twenty steps they hadn't budgeted for, and with a martyred air went off to find out. A minute later she reported back that permission had been granted to change his order.

'Excellent!' said Allan with sudden enthusiasm, perusing the menu anew. He considered the many alternative options. 'Do you do baked snottie?' he asked distantly.

She stared at him.

'Just joking!' he said, seeming much chirpier. 'I'll have the sirloin and chips,' he announced. 'Medium rare, please.' He turned to me. 'No horrid diseases I should know about with regard to beef? Queensland beef palsy or anything like that?'

'You should be fine with steak.'

'Steak it is then.' He handed her the menu. 'And easy on the ciguatera,' he called after her. 'And keep the beers coming,' he added further.

We had a lovely meal, and afterwards retired once more to the bar where, through the foolish wonders of alcohol, we managed to acquire nearly all the symptoms that we had so recently been at pains to avoid.

In the morning, the rain had stopped but the skies were dark and dirty and the sea full of chop. Just looking at it made me feel faintly ill. I am not enamoured of the ocean or anything within it, and the prospect of bouncing out to a rain-shrouded reef to see the sort of darting fish I could view in comfort at any public aquarium, or indeed dental waiting room, was not enticing. According to the morning paper, a 2.3-metre swell was expected. I asked Allan, who once owned a sailing boat and a captain's cap and thus fancies himself an accomplished mariner, how big this was and he lifted his eyebrows in the manner of one impressed. 'Oh, that's big,' he said. This led him to tell me many happy anecdotes of being pitched about in terrifying seas, some of them involving boats not tied to a dock. As we sat there, one of the members of the staff breezed past.

'Cyclone coming!' she said perkily.

'Today?' I asked in what was becoming a customary bleat. 'Maybe!'

Our reef tour included pick-up at our hotel and transfer by coach to the boat at Port Douglas, twenty miles up the coast. The bus drew up at eight fifty, on time to the minute. As we climbed aboard, the driver was giving a rundown on marine stingers, with vivid descriptions of people who had failed to their cost to heed the warning signs. He assured us, however, there were no jellyfish on the reef. Unaccountably, he failed to mention reef sharks, boxfish, scorpionfish, stinging corals, sea snakes or the infamous grouper, a 900-pound monster that occasionally, through a combination of testiness and stupidity, chomps off a swimmer's arm or leg, then remembers that it doesn't like the taste of human flesh and spits it out.

I can't tell you how pleased I was when we arrived at Port Douglas to find that the boat was huge – as big as an English Channel ferry or very nearly – and sleekly new. I was also pleased, for their sake and mine, that none of the crew seemed to be manifesting any of the more obvious signs of dengue fever. As we lined up with other arriving coach passengers I learned from a crew member that the ship held 450 and that 310 people were booked today. He also told me that the trip to the reef took ninety minutes and that the seas should be relatively benign. It was thirty-eight nautical miles to Agincourt Reef, where we would moor. This was, I noted with more than passing interest, the place where the American couple had gone missing.

When we got aboard they announced the free distribution of seasickness tablets to anyone who wanted. I was the first to the table.

'This is awfully thoughtful of you,' I said as I swilled down a handful.

301

'Well, it's better'n having people spewing up all over the shop,' said the girl brightly, and it was hard to argue with that.

The trip to the reef was smooth, as promised. What's more the sun came out, albeit weakly, turning the water from a leaden grey to an approximation of cobalt. While Allan went off to the sun deck to see if there were any women with large breasts to look at, I settled down with my notes.

Depending on which sources you consult, the Great Barrier Reef covers 280,000 square kilometres or 344,000 or something in between; stretches 1,200 miles from top to bottom, or 1,600; is bigger than Kansas or Italy or the United Kingdom. Nobody can agree really on where the Barrier Reef begins and ends, though everyone agrees it's awfully big. Even by the shortest measure, it is equivalent in length to the west coast of the United States. And it is of course an immensely vital habitat – the oceanic equivalent of the Amazon rainforest. The Great Barrier Reef contains at least 1,500 species of fish, 400 types of coral and 4,000 varieties of molluscs, but those are essentially just guesses. No one has ever attempted a comprehensive survey. Too big a job.

Because it consists of some 3,000 separate reefs and over 600 islands some people insist that it is not a single entity and therefore cannot accurately be termed the largest living thing on earth. That seems to me a little like saying that Los Angeles is not a city because it consists of lots of separate buildings. It hardly matters. It is fabulous. And it is all thanks to trillions of little coral polyps working with a dedicated and microscopic diligence over 18 million years, each adding a grain or two of thickness before expiring in a self-created silicate tomb. Hard not to be impressed.

As the ship began to make the sort of slowing-down noises that suggested imminent arrival, I went out on deck to join Allan. I had expected that we would be arriving at some kind of sandy atoll, possibly with a beach bar with a thatched roof, but in fact there was nothing but open sea all around, and a long ruff of gently breaking water, which I presumed indicated the sunken and unseen reef. In the middle of this scene sat an immense aluminium pontoon, two storeys high and big enough to accommodate 400 day trippers. It brought to mind, if vaguely, an oil platform. This was to be our home for the next several hours. When the boat had docked, we all filed happily off. A loudspeaker outlined our many options. We could loll in the sun in deckchairs, or descend to an underwater viewing chamber, or grab snorkels and flippers for a swim, or board a semisubmersible ship for a tour of the reef in comfort.

We went first on the semisubmersible, a vessel in which thirty or forty people at a time could crowd into a viewing chamber below the waterline. Well, it was wonderful. No matter how much you read about the special nature of the Barrier Reef, nothing really prepares you for the sight of it. The pilot took us into a shimmery world of steep coral canyons and razor-edged defiles, fabulously colourful and teeming with schools of fish of incredible variety and size – butterfly fish, damselfish, angelfish, parrotfish, the gorgeously colourful harlequin tuskfish, tubular pipefish. We saw giant clams and sea slugs and starfish, small forests of waving anemones and the pleasingly large and dopey potato cod. It was, as I had expected, precisely like being at a public aquarium, except of course that this was entirely wild and natural. I was amazed, no doubt foolishly, by what a difference this made. As I looked out a great turtle swam past, just a couple of yards from the window and quite indifferent to us. Then, furtively poking about on the bottom, was a reef shark – only a couple of feet long but capable of giving you a jolly good nip. It wasn't just the darting fish and other creatures, but the way the light filtered down from above, and the shape and texture and incredible variety of the coral itself. I was captivated beyond description.

Back on the pontoon, Allan insisted we go at once for a swim. At one side of the pontoon metal steps led into the water. At the top of the steps were large bins containing flippers, snorkels and masks. We kitted up and plopped in. I had assumed that we would be in a few feet of water, so I was taken aback – I am putting this mildly – to discover that I was perhaps sixty feet above the bottom. I had never been in water this deep before and it was unexpectedly unnerving – as unnerving as finding myself floating sixty feet in the air above solid ground. This panicky assessment took place over the course of perhaps three seconds, then my mask and snorkel filled with water and I started choking. Gasping peevishly, I dumped the water out and tried again, but almost immediately the mask filled again. I repeated the exercise two or three times more, but with the same result.

Allan, meanwhile, was shooting about like Darryl Hannah in *Splash*. 'For God's sake, Bryson, what are you doing?' he said. 'You're three feet from the pontoon and you're drowning.'

'I am drowning.' I caught a roll of wave full in the face and came out of it sputtering. 'I'm a son of the soil,' I gasped. 'This is not my milieu.'

He clucked and disappeared. I dipped my head lightly under to see him shooting off like a torpedo in the direction of a colourful Maori wrasse – an angelfish the size of a sofa cushion – and was consumed once more with a bubbly dismay at all the clear, unimagined depth beneath me. There were big things down there, too – fish half as big as me and far more in their element than I was. Then my mask filled and I was sputtering again. Then another small rolling wave smacked me in the face. I must confess that I liked this even less – quite a good deal less – than I had expected to, and I hadn't expected to like it much.

Interestingly, I later learned that this is quite a common reaction among inexperienced ocean swimmers. They get in the water, discover that they are way out of their comfort zone, quietly panic and faint (a Japanese speciality, apparently) or have a heart attack (a fat person speciality). Now here's where the second interesting aspect comes in. Because snorkellers lie on the water with their arms and legs spread and their faces just under the surface – that is, in the posture known as the dead man's float – it isn't actually possible (or so I am told) to tell which people are snorkelling and which are dead. It's only when the whistle blows and everyone gets out except for one oddly inert and devoted soul that they know there will be one less for tea.

Fortunately, as you will have deduced from the existence of this book, I escaped this unhappy fate and managed to haul myself back on to the pontoon. I took a seat on a deckchair in the mild sunshine and towelled off with Allan's shirt. Then I pulled out the newspaper files Alan Howe had given me on the American couple who had died out here. I had read them once before, but now that I could attach visible landmarks to the words I went through them again with particular interest.

The story, insofar as the known events are concerned, is

straightforward. In January 1998, Thomas and Eileen Lonergan, of Baton Rouge, Louisiana, who had recently completed a tour of duty as Peace Corps volunteers in the south Pacific, were holidaying in Australia before returning home when they went for a day's scuba diving on the reef with a company called Outer Edge. At the end of the afternoon, they failed to return to the dive boat at the time directed. Their absence was not noted and the boat left without them. Two and a half days passed before anyone reported them missing. No trace of them was ever found.

Why the Lonergans didn't return to the dive boat and what became of them when they realized they had been stranded are necessarily matters of conjecture.

From where I sat I could see the scuba-diving boat, which a passing crew member informed me was about three nautical miles away. (A nautical mile is about a hundred yards longer than a land mile.) It looked awfully small and distant, but the Lonergans, who were experienced divers and at home in the water, should have found the swim no terrible hardship. Conditions were perfect. The sea was calm, the water temperature was 29° C (84° F) and they had on wetsuits. In addition to the pontoon, they had the somewhat easier option of swimming to St Crispin Reef, just 1.2 nautical miles away, where there were some exposed coral outcrops onto which they could clamber to await rescue. The problem, as Alan Howe had so rightly recalled, was that to reach either of these refuges meant crossing a deep-water trench known to be a haunt of large pelagics – which is to say toothy sharks and the occasional blundering grouper.

From this point the mystery deepened. A few days after their disappearance, the Lonergans' flotation jackets washed up undamaged on a mainland beach. Why two people stranded at sea would take off their flotation devices would appear to be an unanswerable question. Moreover, the absence of damage to the flotation jackets suggested that they had not been attacked by sharks. Puzzlement grew further when police examined the belongings they had left behind at the backpackers' hostel in Cairns where they had been staying. There it became clear that the polite young American couple weren't as happy as they appeared to be. Eileen Lonergan had recorded in her diary that her husband had been depressed and had said he wanted 'to end it all' on a scuba-diving trip. (Whoa!) He had suggested that he would take her with him. (Double whoa!)

There was obviously more to this than met the eye.

Allan emerged at last, looking invigorated and holding in his stomach in a manner that recalled Jeff Chandler in some of his later films, chattering with tedious gusto about what a brilliant experience it had been and what an egregious wimp I was. He slipped on his shirt and fell into the chair beside me, looking very happy. Then he sat up and patted himself extravagantly.

'This shirt's wet,' he announced.

'Is it?' I said, frowning with concern.

'It's wringing wet.'

I touched it lightly. 'Why, yes it is,' I agreed.

They were losing people all over the place in Queensland these days, it appeared. The papers the next day were full of reports of an inquest that had been convened to examine the disappearance of a young British backpacker named Daniel Nute on the Cape Tribulation promontory almost two years earlier. Nute had set off alone on a six-hour hike to a place called Mount Sorrow and had dutifully filled out the safety forms bush hikers are asked to complete to help searchers in the event that they fail to return. Unfortunately, no one from the national park staff collected or checked the safety sheets that day. In fact, it turned out that the national park staff seldom collected or checked the safety sheets. So when Nute failed to return no one noticed and no alarm call went out. Even more puzzling was that although Nute had left a tent pitched on the grounds of a backpackers' lodge in Daintree, the staff at the lodge did not notify the authorities that he was missing for twenty-three days. An employee at the lodge told the inquest that it was 'common for people to abandon their tents and leave without telling management'.

But of course.

The upshot was that by the time a search was organized almost a month had passed. Nute's body has never been found.

All this took on a certain relevance the next morning when Allan and I drove into Cairns to run a couple of errands. Something in the window of a sportswear shop caught his eye so we went in. While he was off trying on items of clothing, I chatted pleasantly with the two middle-aged ladies who worked there. I mentioned for no reason – just making conversation really – that Cairns had been much in the news lately.

'Oh?' said one of the ladies, a little coolly.

'You know, the Lonergan case and the Chinese boat people and this poor kid who went missing at Daintree.'

'Oh, all that,' said the lady with a dismissive air. 'They always blow these things out of proportion down south.'

Her colleague nodded vigorously. 'Whenever there's a chance to make Queensland look bad, they leap on it. It was just the same with the cyclone. I was in Sydney that week visiting my sister and, do you know, they had pages of articles about it.'

'Well, it was a big story,' I pointed out.

'But they wouldn't have covered it like that if it had been in Western Australia.'

'Oh?'

'No. They do it to discourage people from coming up here, you see.'

'You really think so?'

'Oh yes. They don't want visitors to leave Sydney. They want to keep them down there. So they take any story that makes Queensland look, you know, dangerous or backward and they twist the facts about to frighten people.'

They both nodded in the sincerest agreement.

'It was the same with that young couple out on the reef. It's quite evident that it was suicide, but they blew it all out of proportion—'

'All out of proportion,' seconded her friend.

'—so that they could make it look like it wasn't safe to go out on the reef.'

'And the boy at Daintree?' I ventured.

'They don't know that he's dead at all,' she said in the tone of one who has unimpeachable sources.

'But he's been missing for two years.'

'Yes, but he's been sighted all over the Cape York peninsula.'

'All over,' agreed her friend.

'I'm sorry, are you saying the papers falsely reported his death to make Queensland look dangerous?'

'I'm just saying that all the facts aren't in.' She nodded primly and crossed her arms. Her partner did likewise.

And I thought: madder than cut snakes.

As it happened, we were heading to Daintree ourselves. It was as far north as you could get on a paved road in this part of Australia, so we decided to go and have a look. By mid-morning all traces of rain had abated and the sun began to come out – tentatively at first, but then with sumptuous gusto. Queensland was transformed. Suddenly we were in Hawaii – tropical mountains running down to sparkling seas, sweeping bays, flawless beaches guarded by listing palms, little green and rocky islands standing off the headlands. From time to time we drove through sunny canefields, overlooked by the steep, blue eminence of the Great Dividing Range.

At Daintree we parked and got out to have a look around. We walked down to the edge of the Daintree River, where both the road and Beryl Wruck came to their respective abrupt terminations. We couldn't see any sign of crocodiles. Then we got back in the car and drove off down a winding side road that leads to a ferry across the Daintree to Cape Tribulation. The ferry had been shut for a week by the rains, so there wasn't much point in going down there, but I wanted to see the cape at least from across the river, and there was the off chance that we might glimpse a crocodile. To our surprise, the ferry was operating. We had been assured in Daintree that it was still shut.

'Reopened yesterday,' said the ferryman, a man of few words.

So we took the ferry across and set off on the twenty-mile drive to Cape Tribulation through Daintree National

Park. The road wound up and through a mountainous and intensely beautiful rainforest. We had at last made it into the wet tropics, and I couldn't have been more pleased.

The Daintree forest is a remnant of a time when the world was a single land mass, the whole covered in steamy growth. As time passed, continents split up and drifted off to the far corners of the globe, but the Daintree, through some tectonic fluke, escaped the more dramatic transformations of climate and orientation that spurred ecological change elsewhere. In consequence, there are plants out there – whole families of plants – that survived as nowhere else. In 1972, scientists began to appreciate just how ancient and exceptional Australia's northern rainforest is when some cattle mysteriously sickened and died after grazing in the jungle's lower slopes. The cows, it turned out, had been poisoned by the seeds of a tree called *Idiospermum australianse*. What was unexpected about this was that *Idiospermum* was thought to have vanished from the earth 100 million years ago. In fact, it was doing very well in the Daintree, as were eleven other members of its family, a primitive outpost of botany called the angiosperms, from which all flowering plants are descended. That's the kind of place Daintree National Park is – dark, dense, seeming to belong to some remote epoch. It's a landscape in which it wouldn't entirely surprise you to see pterosaurs gliding through the trees or velociraptors sprinting across the road ahead.

In fact, there is quite a lot of odd life out there. This is one of the few remaining areas where you can hope to see cassowaries. They look much like emus except that they have a bony growth on their head called a casque and the infamous murderous claw on each foot. They attack by jumping up and striking out with both feet together.

Fortunately, this doesn't happen very often. The last fatal attack was in 1926, when a cassowary charged a sixteen-year-old boy who had been taunting it and sliced open his jugular as it bounded across him. The reason attacks are so few is that cassowaries are exceedingly reclusive and now, alas, very few in number. No more than a thousand of them survive. The Daintree is also one of the last homes of the celebrated tree kangaroo – which, as its name suggests, is a kangaroo that lives in trees – but it is even shyer than the cassowary and almost never seen. So dense is the jungle, and so remote from the centres of academia, that much of it remains unstudied. The first scientific study of cassowaries, for instance, was begun only about a decade ago.

At length the road ended at a sunny clearing in the jungle with, incongruously, a takeaway food stand and a phone booth. Tucked away in the extravagant foliage was a campground, and beside it an arrowed sign pointed the way to the beach. This led to a boardwalk through mangroves. Little creatures plinked unseen into the swampy water as we approached. After a few minutes we emerged onto the beach. It was remarkably beautiful – a great sweep of soft white sand strewn with driftwood, palm fronds and other natural clutter, standing before a very bright blue bay. Ahead of us loomed a towering headland cloaked in green.

The spot was sunnily pristine, exactly as it must have appeared to James Cook when he first laid eyes on it more than two centuries ago. He called it Cape Tribulation because it was here that the *Endeavour* disastrously lodged on coral some twelve miles off the coast. Severely holed, it was in imminent danger of sinking, but Cook had with him a seaman who had once been in similar straits on a ship that had been saved by an unusual process known as fothering – in effect bandaging its underside by running a sail beneath it and pulling it tight to cover the hole. It was a desperate and improbable measure, but miraculously it worked.

Cook nursed the ship to shore a few miles around the headland from where we were now. The crew spent seven weeks making repairs before sailing off to England and glory. Had the *Endeavour* sunk, and Cook failed to get home, history would of course have been very different. Australia would very likely have become French – an eerie thought, to say the least – and Britain would have had to adjust its colonial ambitions accordingly. No part of the world would have escaped the effects. Melbourne might now stand on African plains. Sydney could be the capital of the Royal Colony of California. Who can possibly say? What is certain is that the global balance of power would have changed in ways beyond imagining. On the other hand, we would almost certainly have been spared *Home and Away*, so it's not as if it would have been an unmitigated disaster.

Allan and I explored along the beach for half an hour or so, then walked back to the clearing where the food stand was, and had a look at where the road continued on to Cooktown. Beyond the food stand it became at once a rough and rocky track, which climbed steeply up into the lush hills. It looked like something Harrison Ford would struggle to negotiate in an adventure movie. I had learned only the day before that the track is dangerously and unnervingly tippy even in good weather, so perhaps it was as well that Allan and I hadn't been let loose on it. In any case, it was impassable now.

Still, it did look awfully inviting in an adventuresome

sort of way. Cooktown, a former gold-mining town that had once had a population of 30,000 and has just 200 now, lay seventy-five kilometres away on the other side of the mountains. It is the last town in eastern Australia. Beyond it there is nothing but a scattering of Aboriginal settlements along the 600-kilometre track to Cape York, Australia's northernmost point. But this was as far as I was going to get here.

I turned around to discover that Allan had slipped off. He reappeared after a minute from the direction of the food stand bearing two cans of Coke, one of which he passed to me.

'They didn't have urine,' he said, and we both had a good laugh over that.

Chapter

FIFTEEN

And so to the top end. We bounced into Darwin through the outer strands of two minor cyclones that were bumping along the north coast, and acquired another rental car – a sleek and powerful Toyota sedan that looked as if it could cover the 1,500 kilometres to Alice Springs in a single rocket-like burst. We dubbed it the Testosterone.

The Northern Territory has always had something of a frontier mentality. In late 1998, the inhabitants were invited to become Australia's seventh state and roundly rejected the notion in a referendum. It appears they quite like being outsiders. In consequence, an area of 523,000 square miles, or about one-fifth of the country, is in Australia but not entirely of it. This throws up some interesting anomalies. All Australians are required by law to vote in federal elections, including residents of the Northern Territory. However, since the Northern Territory is not a state, it has no seats in Parliament. So the Territorians elect representatives who go to Canberra and attend sessions of Parliament (at least that's what they say in their letters home) but don't actually vote or take part or have any consequence at all. Even more interestingly, during national referendums the citizens of the Northern Territory are also required to vote, but the votes don't actually count towards anything. They're just put in a drawer or something. Seems a little odd to me, but then, as I say, the people seem content with the arrangement.

Personally, I feel that the Territorians should not be permitted to take full part in national affairs until they get friendlier hotel staff in Darwin. This might seem a curious basis on which to found a political philosophy, but there you are. Darwin's hoteliers are seriously deficient in the charm department and if it takes the withholding of certain civil liberties to get them to address the problem then I think that is a small charge to exact, frankly.

Our troubles began when we went looking for our hotel. We were booked into a place called the All Seasons Frontier Hotel, but no such establishment appeared to exist. The guidebook mentioned a Top End Frontier Hotel, and a tourist leaflet I acquired at the airport listed a Darwin City Frontier Hotel, and yet another listed an All Seasons Premier Darwin Central Hotel. All of these we spied, distantly, as we drove around for the next forty minutes, squabbling quietly in the manner of a fractious married couple. We stopped about half a dozen pedestrians, but none had heard of an All Seasons Frontier Hotel, except one man who thought it was at Kakadu, 200 kilometres to the east. With the aid of a small, inadequate map I directed Allan down a series of streets which proved always to end at a pedestrianized zone or a cul de sac of loading bays, to his increasing exasperation.

'Can you not read a simple map?' he asked in the peevish tone of a man whose happy-hour needs are going unmet, reversing into cardboard boxes and wheelie bins.

'No,' I replied in kind, 'I cannot read a simple map. I can read a good map. This map, however, is useless. Less than useless. It is the print equivalent of your driving, if I may say so.'

Eventually we stopped outside a large hotel on the seafront and Allan ordered me to go inside and seek professional guidance. At the front desk a young man who had evidently invested a recent pay cheque in a very large tub of hair gel stood with his back to me regaling two female colleagues with some droll anecdote. I waited a long minute, then went: 'Ahem.'

He turned his head to give me a look that said, without warmth: 'What?'

'Could you point me to the All Seasons Frontier Hotel?' I asked politely.

Without preamble he reeled off a series of complex directions. Darwin is full of strange street names – Cavenagh, Yuen, Foelsche, Knuckey – and I couldn't begin to follow. On the counter was a pad of maps, and I asked him if he could show me on that.

'It's too far to walk,' he said dismissively.

'I don't want to walk. I've got a car.'

'Then ask your driver to take you.' He rolled his eyes for the benefit of the girls, then continued with his story.

How I longed for a small firearm or perhaps a set of industrial tongs with which to clamp his reedy neck and draw his head close to me, the better to hear what I next had to say. It was: 'Do you think if I had a driver I would be asking directions of you? It's a rental car, you snide, irksome, preposterously glossy little shit.' I may not have said the words precisely in that order, or indeed at all, but that was certainly the emotional gist of it.

With sullen gaze and a long sigh, he took a pen and rapidly but vaguely sketched the route on the map, tore it from the pad and handed it over as if giving me a voucher to which I had no right. Ten minutes later we pulled up outside a hotel that announced itself, in large letters, as the Darwin City Frontier Hotel. We had passed it several times already, but I had confidently rejected it on each occasion. I stalked through the front doors.

'Is this the All Seasons Frontier Hotel?' I barked from an unsocial distance.

The young woman behind the counter looked up, and blinked. 'Yes,' she said.

'Then' – I came much closer – *'why don't you put a sign up saying so?'*

She regarded me levelly. 'It says it on the side of the building.'

'Well, it doesn't.'

She favoured me with a thin, metallic, supremely condescending smile. 'Yes, it does.'

'Well, it doesn't.'

Torn between her training in customer relations and her youthful certitude, she hesitated, and in a soft voice said: 'Does.'

I held up a finger in a way that said: 'Don't move. Don't go anywhere. I'm going to check this out and then come back and throttle someone. You, actually.'

I went out and ranged around the hotel in the manner of a demented building inspector, examining it from every angle and from various distances, held up a silencing

318

finger to Allan, who watched bewildered from the driver's seat, then came back in and announced: 'It doesn't say All Seasons on it anywhere.'

She looked at me and said nothing, but I could see she was thinking: 'Does.'

I am happy to let the record show that by whatever name it goes, the Darwin City Frontier Hotel was a wondrously disappointing establishment. It was overpriced, charmless and inconveniently sited. The TV in my room didn't work, the pillows were concrete slabs and the receptionist was irritating. This was not the Australia I had come to respect and adore.

To get to the hotel bar, we discovered after much blind experimentation and a further interview with our young friend at the front desk, it was necessary to descend by a back stairway to the basement, find our way through some storage areas, leave the building and present ourselves at a pair of automatic sliding doors, which weren't working. Allan, who is not a man to let any impediment stand between him and his evening beverage, yanked them open with a vehemence that was impressive, and we squeezed through. The bar was liberally, not to say unexpectedly, arrayed with rough, boisterously drunk and dangerous-looking fellows, all with copious tattoos, long hair and beards like mattress ticking – not exactly the patrons you would expect to find drinking in the bar of a business hotel.

'Like a fucking ZZ Top convention,' Allan muttered darkly but correctly.

We procured a couple of beers and sat primly in a corner, like two old maids at an inner city bus station, and watched as two of the burlier fellows played a game of pool in which each disappointing shot – and there seemed to be almost no other kind – was accompanied by a whack of cue across something metallic or unyielding: the pool table, a chairback, the swinging light above the table. It seemed only a matter of time before flesh and bone came into the equation. We decided to repair to the rooftop restaurant on the seventh floor in search of a more serene and composed environment. The restaurant was a large room with big windows giving expansive views over Darwin by twilight. Of the perhaps fifty tables in the room no more than three or four were occupied, so it came as a surprise when the hostess informed us, with a look of stark panic, that no tables were available at the moment.

'But it's practically empty,' I pointed out.

'I'm sorry, but we've got a terrible rush on.' As if to underline the urgency of the situation she flew off.

We took a seat at the bar and had two more beers, which we coaxed out of a cheerful Indonesian fellow who sometimes wandered past, and may actually have been an employee. After another thirty minutes and further enquiries we were finally granted a table by a far window. There we sat for ten minutes more until a waitress came out and plonked in front of each of us a small standard terracotta flowerpot in which had been baked a little loaf of bread.

'What's this?' I asked.

'It's bread,' she replied.

'But it's in a flowerpot?'

She gave me a look that I was beginning to think of as the Darwin stare. It was a look that said: 'Yeah? So?'

'Well, isn't that kind of unusual?'

She considered for a moment. 'Is a bit, I suppose.'

'And will we be following a horticultural theme throughout the meal?'

Her expression contorted in a deeply pained look, as if she were trying to suck her face into the back of her head. 'What?'

'Will the main course arrive in a wheelbarrow?' I elaborated helpfully. 'Will you be serving the salad with a pitchfork?'

'Oh no. It's just the bread that's special.'

'I'm so pleased to hear it.'

Before we could take our relationship to the next stage and ask for drinks or perhaps a menu, she was gone, announcing as she went that she would be back when she could but there was a bit of a rush on.

There then followed the most extraordinary evening in which, each time we hankered for food or additional refreshment or just the sound of an Australian voice, we had to go off and stand by the kitchen doors until we caught someone emerging. Some of the other few diners were doing likewise. During one foray I asked a man with an empty beer glass if he dined here often.

'Wife likes the view,' he explained, and we looked across the room to a plump little woman who gave us a small but cheery wave.

'Service is a bit slow, don't you think?'

'Bloody hopeless,' he agreed. 'They've got some kind of a rush on apparently.'

In the morning a new man was behind the front desk. 'And how did you enjoy your stay, sir?' he asked smoothly.

'It was singularly execrable,' I replied.

'Oh, *excellent*,' he purred, taking my card.

'In fact, I would go so far as to say that the principal value of a stay in this establishment is that it is bound to make all subsequent service-related experiences seem, in comparison, refreshing.'

321

He made a deeply appreciative expression as if to say: 'Praise indeed,' and presented my bill for signature. 'Well, we hope you'll come again.'

'I would sooner have bowel surgery in the woods with a stick.'

His expression wavered, then held there for a long moment. 'Excellent,' he said again, but without a great show of conviction.

We went into town to look around. Darwin is in the steamy heart of the tropics, which to my mind imposes certain stylistic requirements – white buildings with verandas, louvred windows, potted palms, lazy ceiling fans, cool drinks in tall glasses presented by obsequious houseboys, men in white suits and Panama hats, ladies in floral-print cotton dresses, a little mahjong to pass the sultry afternoons, Sydney Greenstreet and Peter Lorre in evidence somewhere looking hot and shifty. Anything that falls short of these simple ideals will always leave me disappointed, and Darwin failed in every respect. To be fair, the place has been knocked about a good deal – it was bombed repeatedly by the Japanese in the Second World War and then devastated by Cyclone Tracy in 1974 – so much of it is necessarily new. Even so, there was almost nothing to suggest a particular climatic affiliation. We could have been in Wollongong or Bendigo or any other moderately prosperous provincial city. The one small local peculiarity was that there seemed to be no one about of professional demeanour. Nearly every person on the streets was bearded and tattooed and scuffed along with a wino shuffle, as if some very large mission had just turned everyone out for the day. Here and there, too, were scatterings of Aborigines, shadowy and furtive, sitting quietly on the margins of sunny plazas as if in a waiting room. While Allan went off to get some money out of a bank machine, I drifted into the vicinity of three Aboriginal people, two men and a woman, all staring at nothing. I gave them a nod and respectful g'day smile as I passed, but failed signally to establish eye contact. It was as if they were somewhere else, or I was transparent.

We had breakfast in a small Italian café, the only customers, then drove out to the Museum and Art Gallery of the Northern Territory because I had read that it had a box jellyfish on display. I had expected the museum to be small and dusty, and to detain us for no longer than it took to find and briefly examine the jellyfish display, but in fact it was sleek and modern and quite wonderful. It was improbably large for a provincial museum and chock-full of interesting stuff thoughtfully presented.

One area was devoted to Cyclone Tracy, still the most devastating natural event in Australian history. It all but blew away the town on Christmas Eve 1974. According to a recorded commentary, most people didn't expect the storm to come to much. A weaker cyclone had passed through a few weeks earlier without doing significant damage, and the leading edge of Tracy brushed over the town without leaving any hint of particular ferocity to come. Most people turned in as if it were a normal night. It wasn't until Darwin was hit by the back end of the storm system, about 2.30 a.m., that people realized they were really in for it. As the winds whipped up to 160 miles an hour Darwin's frail tropical houses began to shed pieces and then to disintegrate. Most of the housing was post-war fibreboard homes of a type called the D series, which were cheap and quick to build but could not stand up to a real hurricane. Before the night was out Tracy had blown away 9,000 homes and killed more than sixty people.

Just off the main display area was a small, darkened chamber in which you could listen to a tape recording of the storm that had been made on the night by a Roman Catholic priest. A sign on the door warned that people who had lived through the storm might find the recording distressing, which I thought perhaps a trifle overwrought until I heard it myself. Well, it was an amazingly effective way of making you realize how powerful and terrifying such a storm can be. The recording began with various lively but clearly preliminary wind noises – branches knocking, gates banging – and then rose and rose again till it was a continuous, howling, unearthly fury, with sounds of metal roofs being wrenched from their moorings and other weighty debris flying murderously through the night. Experiencing it in pitch darkness, as the locals would have done, gave it an immediacy that was inexpressibly effective. I actually found myself ducking whenever anything crashed nearby. When it finished, Allan and I exchanged impressed and drained looks, and proceeded on to the visual part of the display with a new appreciation.

On a wall outside, a television endlessly showed the original Australian Broadcasting Corporation footage of what the town woke up to the next day – namely, total devastation. The film, taken from a slow-moving car, showed street after street in which every structure was flattened.

Much of the rest of the museum was given over to cases of stuffed animals illustrating the Northern Territory's extraordinary biological diversity. Pride of place was given to an enormous stuffed crocodile named Sweetheart, who was for a time the most famous in Australia. Sweetheart – who was, despite the effeminate name, a male – had a passionate dislike for outboard engines and used to attack any boats that disturbed his peace. Unusually for a crocodile, he never harmed a person, but he crunched at least fifteen boats and their motors, bringing a certain unexpected liveliness to many a fisherman's afternoon. In 1979 when it was feared that he would do himself some serious harm – he was constantly being clobbered by propellers – wildlife officials decided to move him somewhere safer. Unfortunately, the capture was botched when a cable snagged and Sweetheart drowned. So he was stuffed and put on display in the Darwin museum, where he has been impressing visitors ever since with his very substantial heft: he stretches almost seventeen feet and in life weighed over 1,700 pounds.

Another case answered a question that must have occurred to nearly everyone at one time or another: namely, how exactly do they stuff the animals? I had always assumed they filled them with sawdust or old socks or something. Well, here I learned, by means of a small stuffed animal shown in cross-section, that in fact a mounted specimen is empty but for a spare interior framework of styrofoam balls and wooden dowels. I was touched and grateful that some curator had taken the trouble to provide this insight. Also on display were lots of snakes and reptiles, many of them quite severely murderous, which Allan regarded with particular absorption.

Perhaps the most admirable quality about the museum – and I suspect this is a real Northern Territory thing – is that it didn't mince words about the dangers of the world outside. Most museums in Australia are at pains to stress the unlikelihood of anything happening to you. The Darwin museum makes it quite obvious, with cold facts and figures, that if something does happen to you out there, you are really going to regret it. This was most potently displayed in the aquatic creatures section – and here at last we found what we had come to see: a large glass cylinder containing a preserved box jellyfish, the deadliest creature on earth.

It was remarkably unprepossessing – a translucent box-shaped blob, six or eight inches high, with threadlike tentacles several feet long trailing off beneath it. Like all jellyfish, it is all but brainless, but its lethality is unbelievable. The tentacles of a box jellyfish carry enough wallop to kill a roomful of people, yet they live exclusively on tiny krill-like shrimp – creatures that hardly require a great deal of violent subduing. As ever in the curious world of Australian biology, no one knows why the jellyfish evolved such extravagant toxicity.

Alongside were displays of other dangerous sea creatures, of which the Northern Territory has an impressive plenitude – five types of stingray, two of blue-ringed octopus, thirty varieties of sea snake, eight types of coneshell, and the usual roguish assortment of stonefish, scorpionfish, firefish and others too numerous to list and too depressing to dwell on. All these are found in shallow coastal waters, in rock pools and even sometimes on the beaches themselves. It is a wonder to me that anyone goes within a hundred feet of the sea in northern Australia. The sea snakes are especially unnerving, not because they are aggressive, but because they are inquisitive. Stray into their territory and they will come to check you out, all but rubbing against you in the manner of cats seeking affection. They are the most sweet-tempered creatures in existence. But cross them or alarm them and they can hit you with enough venom to kill three grown men. Now *that*'s scary.

As we were studying the display, a man, lean and lavishly bearded in the Darwinian style, said g'day and asked how we were going. He identified himself as Dr Phil Alderslade, curator of coelenterates. 'Jellyfish and corals,' he added at once, seeing our expressions of frank ignorance. 'I noticed you taking notes,' he added further.

I told him of my devotion to box jellyfish and asked him if he worked with them himself.

'Oh, sure.'

'So how do you keep from getting stung?'

'Basic precautions really. You wear a wetsuit, of course, and rubber gloves, and you just take a good deal of care when handling them because if even a tiny piece of tentacle is left on a glove and you accidentally touch it to bare skin – wiping sweat from your face or brushing away a fly or something – you can get a *very* nasty sting, believe me.'

'Have you ever been stung?'

'Once. My glove slipped and a tentacle touched me just here.' He showed us the soft underside of his wrist. It bore a faint scar about half an inch long. 'Just touched me, but jeez it bloody hurt.'

'What'd it feel like?' we asked together.

'The only thing I can compare it to is if you took a lit cigarette and held it to your skin – held it there a goodish long while, maybe thirty seconds. That's what it felt like. You get stung from time to time by various things in my line and I can tell you I've never felt anything like it.'

'So what would a couple of yards feel like?' I wondered.

He shook his head at the thought of it. 'If you tried to imagine the worst pain possible, it would be beyond that. You're dealing with pain of an order of magnitude well past anything most people have ever experienced.'

He did something you don't often see a scientist do: he shivered. Then he smiled cheerfully through his extravagant facial hair and excused himself to get back to his corals.

We left the museum and headed out of town through Darwin's sunny, orderly suburbs – white bungalows on tidy lawns – and at the edge of town passed a sign that said: 'Alice Springs 1479 kilometres'. Ahead, along the lonely Stuart Highway, lay nearly a thousand miles of largely unrelieved emptiness all the way to Alice Springs. We were on our way into the famous and forbidding Never Never, a land of dangerous heat and bone-white sunshine.

The road – the Track, as it is still sometimes called – was nearly empty but straight and well maintained. Ask ten people in Sydney or Melbourne whether the highway from Darwin to Alice Springs is paved or not and most will have no idea. In fact, it was paved long before most other outback roads: during the Second World War when northern Australia became a principal staging post for the Pacific campaign. These days it carries a small but growing number of tourists, a very little local traffic and lots of road trains – multi-trailered lorries up to a hundred and fifty feet long, which haul freight between the most distant outposts of Australia. To meet a barrelling road train coming at you at full throttle on a two-lane highway on which it desires all of its lane and some of yours is a reliably invigorating experience – an explosive *whoomp* as you hit its displaced air, followed at once by a consequent lurch onto the shoulder, several moments of hypermanic axle action sufficient to loosen dental fillings and empty your pockets of coins, an enveloping shroud of gritty red dust and the metallic dinks and savage thumps of flying rocks, some involuntary oral emissions on your part as the dust clears and you spy a large boulder dead ahead; and a sudden, miraculous return to tranquillity and smoothness as the car regains the highway, entirely of its own volition, and continues on its way to Alice Springs.

The only time that this part of the world had any life at all was during the Second World War, when sixty airfields and thirty-five hospitals were built along the highway between Darwin and Daly Waters, and a hundred thousand American troops were stationed in the area. The sites are still indicated with historical markers, and a couple of times we pulled off to have a look. When Alan Moorehead passed this way for *Rum Jungle*, a decade after the war's end, most of the buildings were still standing. Sometimes he came across abandoned planes and stacks of munitions quietly decomposing in the desert. I naturally hoped we would as well, but there was nothing out there now – nothing but stillness and oppressive heat and a sense of being on the edge of a boundless nullity.

In every direction for as far as the eye could see the earth was covered with spinifex, a brittle grass, which grew in clumps so closely packed as to give an appearance of verdure. It looked like land that could support a thousand head of cattle an acre. In fact, spinifex is useless – the only wholly non-edible grass in the world apparently. It is also murder to travel through because its needle-sharp points, tipped in silica, break off when brushed and become embedded in the skin, where they fester into small but horrible sores. Scattered among the spinifex were turpentine bushes and man-sized termite mounds, which stood in the desert like ancient dolmens. And that was it.

After about three hours we passed through Katherine, a dusty, inoffensive little community, and the last town worthy of the name for 400 miles. Beyond it, the landscape grew more visibly impoverished, and the traffic thinned out from little to almost none. For much of the way the highway was simply a taut line connecting impossibly distant horizons, the landscape on either side a monumental emptiness punctuated by spinifex, low bushes, lunar rocks and almost nothing else. The sky everywhere was huge, and brilliantly blue.

We had been driving for perhaps ninety minutes in a largely mindless silence when at last Allan spoke. He said: 'How are you off for urine?'

'I have all I need, thank you. Why do you ask?'

'It's just that I notice we're nearly out of petrol.'

'Truly?' I leaned over to confirm that Allan could indeed interpret a petrol gauge – if not perhaps quite as frequently as one might wish.

'Interesting time to notice, Allan,' I observed.

'This thing just seems to suck up fuel,' he replied, perhaps just a trifle inadequately. 'So where are we?' he asked after a moment's further reflection.

'We're in the middle of nowhere, Allan.'

'I mean in relation to the next town.'

I looked at the map. 'In relation to the next town, we are' – I looked again, just to confirm – 'in the middle of nowhere.' I did some measurements with my fingers. 'We appear to be about forty kilometres from a dot on the map called Larrimah.'

'And do they have petrol there?'

'One sincerely hopes so. And do you think we have enough to get there?'

'One sincerely and, if I may just say, bloody well hopes so.'

We chugged into Larrimah on the last vapour of gas. It

was an all but dead hamlet, but it did have a petrol station. While Allan fuelled up, I went in and purchased a stock of bottled water and snack foods for future emergencies. We vowed that henceforth we would jointly keep a steady eye on the fuel gauge and not let it dip below the halfway mark. There were even greater stretches of emptiness to come.

Still, the very slight brush with crisis buoyed our spirits, and we were in a triumphant frame of mind when in late afternoon we rolled into Daly Waters, our destination for the day. Daly Waters – 370 miles from Darwin, 570 from Alice Springs – was off the Stuart Highway a couple of miles down an unpaved side road and over a small ford, which added to its already palpable sense of remoteness. If you were looking for a classic outback spot, you could not improve upon it. It consisted of a few small houses, a tumbledown and obviously long-closed general store, two petrol pumps unattached to any particular building beneath a sign saying 'Outback Servo' and a utilitarian pub with a tin roof. All the rest was heat and dust.

We parked outside the pub. It had signs hung all over it. One said: 'Est. 1893. Australia's oldest licensed public house.' Nearby another sign said: 'Est. 1930. Northern Territory's Oldest Pub.' The heat when we stepped from the car was stifling. The temperature must have been pushing 110 degrees. A tourist brochure I had picked up in Darwin hinted, without actually saying, that the Daly Waters pub provided accommodation. I certainly hoped so as we were 230 miles from the next town, with nothing but a scattered and uncertain assortment of roadhouses in between. Anyway, it's dangerous to drive through dusk in the outback. That's when kangaroos come bounding out of the gloaming and into the paths of passing vehicles, to the frequent regret of both. Trucks sweep them aside, but they can make a mess of cars, and sometimes the cars' occupants.

We stepped into the gloomy interior – gloomy because the world outside was so painfully bright and we had been out in it all afternoon. I could hardly see a thing.

'Hello,' I said to a face behind the bar that might, for all I could tell, have been a ping-pong paddle, 'do you do rooms?'

'Finest rooms in Daly Waters,' responded the paddle. 'Also the only rooms in Daly Waters.' As the form spoke, it transmogrified before my eyes into a cheerfully sweaty, bespectacled, slightly harassed-looking man of late middle years. He was sizing us up with a look that was very slightly askance. 'You want two rooms,' he said, 'or are you bunking up together?'

'Two,' I said at once.

This seemed to please him. He rummaged in a drawer and produced two keys with unmatching tags. 'This one's a single,' he said, laying a key on my palm, 'and this one's got a double bed in it – in case one of yers gets lucky tonight.' He bounced his eyebrows in a slightly salacious manner.

'And do you think that's likely?'

'Hey, miracles happen.'

The rooms were in a separate block that stood alongside the pub, ten or so of them ranged on either side of a central corridor. I insisted Allan take the double as he was far more likely to get lucky than I was.

'Out here?' He gave a hollow laugh.

'There's eighty million sheep in the outback, Allan. They can't all be picky.'

We parted to examine our rooms. Basic was the word

332

that leaped to mind. Mine consisted of an ancient bed, a battered dresser and a raffia wastebasket. There was no TV or phone, and the illumination consisted of a bare yellow bulb dangling from the ceiling, but the solitary window held an ancient air conditioner, which shook and juddered violently when switched on but did actually seem to generate a little cool air. The bathroom was at the end of the corridor and was a touch insalubrious, with rust stains in the sink and a shower that looked actively infectious.

I went to visit Allan, who was sitting on his bed grinning inanely. 'Come in!' he cried. 'Come in. I'd offer you something from the minibar, but I don't seem to have one. Pull up a chair – oh, no! There is no chair. Well, please make full use of the wastebasket.'

'It is a little basic,' I conceded.

'Basic? It's a bloody cell. I'd show you the light, but it's burnt out.'

'I'm sure we can get a replacement for you.'

'No, no, no. I think I'll like it better in full darkness.' He pursed his lips. 'Is it too early to start drinking?'

I looked at my watch. It was only four forty-five. 'It is a bit. There's actually something I wanted to see.'

'An attraction? In Daly Waters? What can it be? Someone getting petrol? The evening sheep shag?'

'It's a tree.'

'A *tree*. Of course it is. Please lead the way.'

We went out to the car and drove a couple of miles down a hot dirt track. There on the edge of a large, barren clearing beside the road stood a sign announcing that we had found our way to the Stuart Tree, commemorating John McDouall Stuart, perhaps the greatest of all Australian explorers. A Scottish soldier of bantamweight dimensions (he barely topped five feet), Stuart led three epic expeditions through the interior, and all but killed himself in the process. The bright light of the outback severely disagreed with his vision, and on at least two of his trips he was soon seeing double – not perhaps the most encouraging affliction in someone choosing a route through an uncharted wilderness. ('So, boys, which of those twin peaks do you think we should head for? I say we go for the one under the left-hand sun.') Generally he would finish the trips effectively blind. On his second expedition, he also became crippled with scurvy, for which he seemed to have a particular susceptibility. His body became 'a mass of sores that will not heal'. The skin, one of his lieutenants noted, 'hung from the roof of his mouth, his tongue became swollen and he was incapable of talking'. Virtually insensible, he was carried on a stretcher for the last 400 miles and each day his colleagues lifted him down from his mount expecting to find him dead. Yet within a month of returning to society he was on his feet again and setting off once more into the punishing void.

His final attempt, in 1861–2, seemed fated to end in failure as well. His horses 'were much distressed' for want of water, and both men and beasts were tormented by bulwaddy, a treacherous shrub with thorny spikes. But at Daly Waters they found a stream with potable water. It was the moment that saved the venture. The men rested, rewatered and pushed on. In July 1862, nine months after setting off from Adelaide, they reached the Timor Sea and in so doing became the first to find a practical route through the heart of the continent. Within a decade, a telegraph line had been strung from Adelaide to what would eventually become Darwin, putting Australia at last in direct touch with the world.

In his delight at finding the stream at Daly Waters, Stuart carved an S into a big gum tree. It was this that we had come to see. The tree, it must be said, was not much – a fifteen-foot-high chunk of gum tree, lopped of its upper branches and long dead. Every guidebook tells you the S is clearly visible, but we couldn't find it. Still, there was a certain pleasure in being at a famous spot that few Australians visit. As we stood there, a flock of galahs, a noisy pinkish parrot, came and settled on the surrounding trees. It was a scene almost entirely without feature – a barren plain, a fat setting sun, a scattering of ragged gum trees – and yet, in a wholly uncharacteristic way, I was captivated by it. I don't know why, but I loved it out here.

We regarded it for quite a time, then Allan turned to me and asked in a respectful voice if we could go for a drink now.

'Yes we can,' I said.

Daly Waters' fame did not begin and end with the fleeting visit of Stuart and his band. In the 1920s a rather shadowy couple by the name of Pearce came to Daly Waters and opened a shop with a borrowed twenty pounds. Amazingly, they did pretty well. Within a few years they had a shop, a hotel, a pub and an aerodrome. Daly Waters became a stopoff point between Brisbane and Darwin on the run to Singapore and on to London in the early days of Qantas and the old Imperial Airways. Lady Mountbatten was among the first overnight guests at the hotel. Goodness knows what she made of the place – though I dare say she was just awfully glad to be on solid ground. In the early days a commercial flight from London involved, in addition to nerves of steel, forty-two refuelling stops, up to five changes of aircraft and a train journey through Italy because Mussolini wouldn't allow flights through Italian air space. It took twelve days. As well as the seasonal monsoons, the flights were subject to dust storms, mechanical failures, navigational confusion and occasional pot-shots from hostile or impish bedouins. Crashes were not infrequent.

The perils of aviation in the period are neatly encapsulated in the experience of Harold C. Brinsmead, the head of Australia's Civil Aviation Department in the first days of commercial aviation. In 1931, Brinsmead was on a flight to London, partly for business and partly to demonstrate the safety and reliability of modern air passenger services, when his plane crashed on takeoff in Indonesia. No one was seriously hurt, but the plane was a write-off. Not wanting to wait for a replacement aircraft to be flown in, Brinsmead boarded a flight with the new Dutch airline, KLM. That flight crashed while taking off in Bangkok. On this occasion, five people were killed and Brinsmead suffered serious injuries from which he never recovered. He died two years later. Meanwhile, the surviving passengers carried on to London in a replacement plane. That plane crashed on the return trip.

Daly Waters claims to be Australia's oldest international airport, though I suspect many other venerable airstrips make a similar boast. It is certainly true that it was used as a stopoff point on some international flights and more regularly on cross-country flights from Queensland to Western Australia, so it was a kind of crossroads. The airport stayed open until 1947. The pub opened in 1938, so it is not by any stretch the oldest in the outback or the Northern Territory, but it is certainly one of the most extraordinary.

As with most outback pubs every inch of interior surface

– walls, rafters, wooden support posts – was covered with mementos left by earlier visitors: college ID cards, drivers' licences, folding money from many nations, bumper stickers, badges from various police and fire departments, even a generous and arresting assortment of underwear, which dangled from rafters or was nailed to walls. The rest was nicely spartan: a large but basic central bar, concrete floor, bare tin roof, an assortment of tables and chairs of different vintages and styles, a battered pool table. At the bar, seven or eight men, all in shorts, T-shirts, boots and bush hats, stood drinking stubbies – squat bottles of beer – served in insulated foam holders to keep them cold. They all looked hot and dusty, but then everything in Daly Waters was hot and dusty. The atmosphere in the pub can best be described as convivially sweltering. Even standing still, the sweat dripped off us. The windows had screens, but most were full of holes and anyway the doors were wide open so flies came in freely. The men at the bar gave me compact but friendly nods as I bellied up to the bar, and obligingly made space for me to stand to order, but showed no special interest in me as an outsider. Clearly, as the souvenirs attested, visitors were not a novelty.

I acquired a pair of chilled stubbies and conveyed them to the table where Allan sat beneath a bumper sticker commemorating a visit by the 'Wheredafukarwi Touring Club'. Allan was suffused with a strange happiness.

'You like it here?' I said.

He shook his head with a kind of speechless delight. 'I do. I actually do.'

'But I thought you hated it.'

'I did,' he said. 'But then I was sitting here looking out the window at the setting sun, and it was lovely – I mean really quite astoundingly lovely – and then I turned and saw the bar with all these outback characters, and I thought: "Bugger me, I like it here."' He looked at me in the frankest wonder. 'And I do. I really like it.'

'I'm so pleased.'

He drained his beer and rose. 'You ready for another?'

Now it was my turn to be filled with wonder. I started to point out that it was a touch early to be setting such a blistering pace, but then I thought: what the hell. We had come a long way and this place was, after all, built for drinking.

I drained my bottle and handed it over. 'Sure,' I said, 'why not?'

Well, I can't pretend I remember a great deal of what followed. We drank huge amounts of beer – huge amounts. We ate steaks the size of catcher's mitts (they may actually have been catcher's mitts) and washed them down with more beer. We made many friends. We circulated as if at a cocktail party. I talked to ranchers and sheep shearers, to nannies and cooks. I met fellow travellers from around the world, and talked for some time to the proprietor, one Bruce Caterer, who told me the complicated story of how he had come to own a pub in this lonely and far-flung spot, of which confidence I have not the tiniest recollection and certainly nothing approximating a note. As the evening wore on, the bar grew almost impossibly crowded and lively. Where all the people were coming from I couldn't guess. What was certain was that there were at least fifty cheerfully committed drinkers tucked away in the bush in the vicinity of Daly Waters and at least as many visitors like us. I got comprehensively beaten at pool by at least fourteen people. I bought rounds for strangers. I called my wife and professed my lasting devotion. I giggled at any story told me and radiated uncritical affection in all directions. I would have gone anywhere with anyone. I awoke the next morning, fully clothed and on top of the bedding, with no clear memory past the catcher's mitt portion of the evening and a head that felt like a train crash.

I pressed my watch to an eyeball and groaned at the discovery that it was nearly ten o'clock. We were hours late if we were ever going to get to Alice Springs. I stumbled down to the bathroom and put myself through some cursory ablutions, then found my way blearily into the pub. Allan sat propped against a wall with his eyes closed, a cup of black coffee steaming untouched before him. There was no one else around.

'Where coffee where?' I croaked in a tiny voice.

He indicated vaguely with a weak hand. In a side room I found an urn of hot water and containers of instant coffee, tea bags, powdered milk and sugar with which to make a hot beverage. I loaded a cup half full with instant coffee powder, dribbled in some water, and rejoined Allan.

Weakly, in the manner of an invalid, I lifted the cup and introduced a little coffee to my lips. After a couple of more sips, I began to feel a little better. Allan, on the other hand, looked terminally wretched.

'How late were we up?' I asked.

'Late.'

'Very late?'

'Very.'

'Why are you sitting with your eyes closed?'

'Because if I open them I'm afraid I'll bleed to death.'

'Did I disgrace myself?' I peered around the room to see if my boxer shorts were draped from any rafters.

'Not that I recall. You were shit at pool.'

I nodded without surprise. I often use alcohol as an artificial check on my pool-playing skills. It's a way for me to help strangers gain confidence in their abilities and get in touch with my inner wallet.

'Anything else?' I asked.

'You're doing a house swap next summer with a family from Korea.'

I pursed my lips thoughtfully. 'North or South?' I asked.

'Not sure.'

'You're making this up, aren't you?'

He reached over and plucked from my shirt pocket a business card, which he presented to me. It said: 'Park Ho Lee, Meat Wholesaler' or something and gave an address in Pusan. Underneath it, in my own handwriting, it said: 'June 10–August 27. No worries.'

I placed the card, folded once, in the ashtray.

'I think I'd like to get out of here now,' I said.

He nodded and with an effort of will rose from the table, wobbled ever so slightly, and went off to gather up his things. I hesitated a long moment and followed.

Ten minutes later we were on our way to Alice Springs.

Chapter

SIXTEEN

Now here's a story to ponder.

In April 1860, during the second of his heroic attempts to cross Australia from south to north, John McDouall Stuart reached the almost waterless centre of the continent, roughly halfway between the present sites of Daly Waters and Alice Springs. A thousand miles from anywhere, the spot was the very 'climax of desolation', as Stuart's fellow explorer Ernest Giles once nicely put it, and Stuart and his men went through hell to get there. They were sick and ragged and half starved, and it had taken months, but at least they had the satisfaction of knowing that they had become the first outsiders to penetrate to the brutal heart of the continent.

So you may imagine Stuart's surprise when, in the middle of this baking nowhere, he and his party encountered three Aboriginal men who greeted them by making a secret sign of the Freemasons. Stuart didn't say in his journal what the sign was, but it was clear from his amazed description that it was unlikely to have been coincidental. Then a few days later Stuart and his men found horse tracks following a natural course across the plains. Finally, some distance further on, the explorers were setting up camp for the night when some people from the Warramunga tribe approached. One of Stuart's party, a young man named W. P. Auld, was sitting with his boots off rubbing his aching feet when one of the Warramunga men knelt before him. While Auld watched bemusedly, the man replaced the boots on Auld's feet and carefully but deftly tied the laces for him, then sat back with a big pleased smile. It was painfully evident to Stuart that he and his men were not in fact the first white people to reach the empty centre of the country. So who preceded them? No one has ever had the faintest idea.

I mention this to make the point that the outback is an odd and unfathomable place. There is something about all that emptiness that exerts a strange hold on people. It is an environment that wants you dead, yet again and again in the face of the most staggering privations, for the meagrest of rewards, explorers ventured into it. Sometimes, as Stuart found, they didn't even bother to leave their names. It is almost not possible to exaggerate the punishing nature of Australia's interior. For nineteenth-century explorers, it wasn't just the inexpressible heat and constant scarcity of water, but a thousand other miseries. Stinging ants swarmed over them wherever they rested. Natives sometimes attacked with spears. The landscape was full of thorny bushes and merciless spinifex whose silicate pricks nearly always grew infected from sweat and dirt. Scurvy was a constant plague. Hygiene was impossible. Pack animals grew frequently crazed or lost the will to go on. Ernest Giles recorded in his memoirs how his horse once grew so delirious after an unsuccessful search for water that when they returned to camp at the end of the day the animal plunged its nose into a fire in the deluded hope that it would provide relief. In pity, Giles gave the injured animal a drink from his own meagre supplies, but it died anyway. Even camels could barely cope with the desert conditions. In *Beyond Leichhardt*, a history of Australian exploration, Glen McLaren notes how blowflies doted on the wounds of camels, laying eggs in any raw lesions, which soon erupted in horrible swarms of wriggling maggots. On one expedition, a camel's wound grew so infected that the maggots 'were scooped out daily with a pint pot'. Eventually the animal just lay down and died. When even camels can't manage a desert, you know you've found a tough part of the world. For human and animal alike, nearly every breathing moment was a living hell.

And yet over and over the explorers returned. Nearly every expedition of the nineteenth century started off with some ostensible practical purpose – to find a route for a telegraph line, to look for gold, to uncover some zone of hidden promise – but almost without exception the explorers soon became transfixed by the emptiness. Unable to resist its allure, they just pushed on and on.

Perhaps no one suffered privations more willingly and repeatedly, to less effect, than Ernest Giles. In 1874, while he was travelling with a companion named Alfred Gibson through the barren wastes of Western Australia, Gibson's horse died. Giles gave Gibson his own mount with instructions to follow their tracks 120 miles back to a place called Fort McKellar to fetch another. Gibson lost his way in the emptiness and was never seen again. (The area is now called the Gibson Desert.) Left to find his own way back on foot, Giles staggered for days over exhausting sandhills, the last sixty miles with almost no water. It was while in this desperate state, tormented by flies and half dead with hunger, that he famously spotted a baby wallaby and fell upon it, devouring it raw, fur, skin and all.

These were not exceptional experiences, you understand. This is what awaited you when you went into the outback. When Robert Austin and his men, lost in the featureless wastes of Western Australia, drank their own and their horses' urine, there was nothing terribly unusual about that. Lots of people did likewise in the desert. When Giles found and devoured the baby wallaby, he thought himself exceedingly lucky – not just at that moment but for years afterwards. 'The delicious taste of that creature I shall never forget,' he wrote with sincere and telling enthusiasm in his memoirs. Stuart and his men retained equally fond memories of a time when, on the brink of starvation, they found a clutch of dingo puppies and boiled them up in a pot. They were, he wrote, 'delicious!'

Why people repeatedly subjected themselves to such ordeals is a mystery that surpasses understanding. Despite the extreme travails he experienced on the fatal expedition with Gibson, Giles returned almost at once to his compulsive wanderings. Stuart did likewise; almost continuously for four years he hurled himself at the unyielding interior until he succeeded in breaking through. Worn out by the effort, he retired to London and died soon after.

It is impossible to say who endured the greater hardships, Stuart or Giles, but there is no question that Giles did it for less reward. No explorer was ever unluckier. In the same year that he lost Gibson in the desert and stumbled 120 miles through appalling heat, Giles also explored the central regions around the area known as Yulara. One day, he struggled up a small rise and was confronted with a sight such as he could never have dreamed of finding. Before him, impossibly imposing, stood the most singular monolith on earth, the great red rock now known as Uluru. Hastening to Adelaide to report the find, he was informed that a man named William Christie Gosse had chanced upon it a few days ahead of him and had already named it Ayers Rock in honour of the South Australia governor.

Eventually, too old to explore, Giles ended up working as a clerk in the gold fields of Coolgardie, where he died in obscurity in 1891. Today he is almost entirely forgotten. No highway bears his name.

And so the doughty Mr Sherwin and I proceeded through the hot and inexhaustible desert. As we travelled south from Daly Waters, the landscape became more sparsely vegetated. It began to feel eerily as if we had left Planet Earth. The soil took on a reddish glow, more Martian than terrestrial, and the sunlight seemed to double in intensity, as if generated by a nearer, larger sun. Even on a smoothly paved highway, in the comfort of air conditioning, you are not entirely robbed of the sense of what the explorers must have gone through. The discomforts can't be fully imagined but the scale can, and it was awesome.

To the left were several thousand square miles of stubbled nothingness called the Barkly Tableland, which eventually merges into the Simpson Desert, probably the toughest ranching country in the world. So unyielding is the land that ranches have to be vast to support a single operation; the largest of them, at a place called Anna

Creek, is bigger than Belgium. To the right, unbelievably, the land was even harsher. This was the infamous Tanami Desert, an area of hellish dryness that even now is largely uncharted. On my map, not a feature was indicated – not a dried creekbed or old dirt track – for 300 miles to the Western Australia border. Beyond that, it was virtually as bleak for 600 miles more.

Even along the Stuart Highway, with its life-bearing traffic, the 550-odd miles between Daly Waters and Alice Springs could boast just one small town, an old gold-mining community called Tennant Creek, three or four clustered habitations that made Daly Waters look cosmopolitan, and a roadhouse perhaps once every eighty miles. And that was it. I had never been out in such a boundless blank. Eventually, some hills began to rise in the middle distance: the MacDonnell Ranges. Very occasionally – once or twice an hour – a road train would bomb past. Once we saw an approaching car, the driver evidently sedated by monotony, leave the road and bang wildly along the rough shoulder for perhaps two hundred feet, pulling in its wake a long speed ramp of dust. As he neared us – stirred possibly by Allan's honking – the driver jerked to startled wakefulness and veered reflexively, but much too sharply, for the pavement and thence, to our shrill amazement, into our path. It was absurd: in an area of inexpressible emptiness the only two pieces of moving metal were about to bang together in a very big way. There passed an instant made up in equal parts of horn blare, muted shrieks and wild, tight swerves. For the strangest moment, time went into arrest and I could see perfectly our unwitting assailant, frozen as if in a candid photograph, looking at us with a mixture of bewilderment and apology. I shouldn't wonder that it's a moment all people are given when they are about to die suddenly. Then all was blurred swiftness again. The cars passed without hitting – goodness knows how – and I turned full in the seat to watch our adversary shooting away into the distance behind us, soberly attentive to his lane. I watched until he was a dot at vanishing point, then turned to Allan.

'Well, I don't know about you,' he said brightly, 'but I'm ready for a cup of coffee and a change of underpants.'

'Excellent plan,' I agreed, and I joined him in scanning the horizon for a lonely but welcoming roadhouse.

The great virtue about driving through emptiness is that when you come to anything – anything at all – that might be called a diversion you get disproportionately excited. In mid-afternoon we saw a signpost for something called the Devils Marbles and, with the briefest exchange of glances, followed a side road a mile or so to a parking area. And there we saw something really quite fabulous – enormous piles of smooth granite boulders, many as big as houses, stacked in jumbled piles or scattered over an immense area (1,800 hectares, according to a signboard). Every one brought to mind something else: a jelly bean, a bread roll, a bowling ball – except that they were immense and often perched on impossibly fine points. Imagine a boulder maybe thirty feet high and nearly spherical standing on a base little larger than, say, a manhole cover. Needless to say, there wasn't a soul around. Put these stones anywhere in Europe or North America and they would be world famous. In every family album would be a photograph of mom and the kids having a picnic against a backdrop of fantastic rocks. Here they were a lost wonder, off the road in the middle of a boundless nowhere. We wandered around for half an hour, as amazed by the solitude as much as by the rocks, then congratulated ourselves on our good fortune and good sense in stopping, and returned to the road in a state of elevated contentment.

Ten hours and 903 kilometres after leaving Daly Waters we arrived, dry and dusty, in Alice Springs, a grid of ruler-straight streets set like an enormous helipad on a plain beside the golden slopes of the MacDonnell Ranges. Because it is so bang in the middle of nowhere, Alice Springs ought to seem a miracle – an actual town with department stores and schools and streets with names – and for a long time it was a sort of antipodean Timbuktu, a place tantalizing in its inaccessibility. In 1954, when Alan Moorehead passed through, Alice's only regular connection to the outside world was a weekly train from Adelaide. Its arrival on Saturday evening was the biggest event in the life of the town. It brought mail, newspapers, new pictures for the cinema, long-awaited spare parts and whatever else couldn't be acquired locally. Nearly the whole town turned out to see who got off and what was unloaded.

In those days, Alice had a population of 4,000 and hardly any visitors. Today it's a thriving little city with a population of 25,000 and it is full of visitors – 350,000 of them a year – which is of course the whole problem. These days you can jet in from Adelaide in two hours, from Melbourne and Sydney in less than three. You can have a latte and buy some opals and then climb on a tour bus and travel down the highway to Ayers Rock. The town has not only become accessible, it's become a destination. It's so full of motels, hotels, conference centres, campgrounds and desert resorts that you can't pretend even for a moment that you have achieved something exceptional by getting yourself there. It's crazy really. A community that was once famous for being remote now attracts thousands of visitors who come to see how remote it no longer is.

Nearly all guidebooks and travel articles indulge the gentle conceit that Alice retains some irreproducible outback charm – some away-from-it-all quality that you must come here to see – but in fact it is Anywhere, Australia. Actually, it is Anywhere, Planet Earth. On our way into town we passed strip malls, car dealerships, McDonald's and Kentucky Fried Chicken outlets, banks and petrol stations. Only a scattering of Aborigines strolling along the dried bed of the Todd River gave any hint of exoticism. We took rooms in a motor inn on the edge of the modest town centre. My room had a balcony where I could watch the setting sun flood the desert floor and burnish the golden slopes of the MacDonnell Ranges beyond – or at least I could if I looked past the more immediate sprawl of a K-Mart plaza across the road. In the two million or more square miles that is the Australian outback, I don't suppose there is a more unfortunate juxtaposition.

Allan was evidently held by a similar thought, for a half hour later when we met out front he was staring at the same scene. 'I can't believe we've just driven a thousand miles to find a K-Mart,' he said. He looked at me. 'You Yanks have a lot to answer for, you know.'

I started to protest, in a sputtering sort of way, but what could I say? He was right. We do. We have created a philosophy of retailing that is totally without aesthetics and totally irresistible. And now we box these places up and ship them to the far corners of the world. Visually, almost every arrestingly regrettable thing in Alice Springs was a product of American enterprise, from people who couldn't know that they had helped to drain the distinctiveness from an outback town and doubtless wouldn't see it that way anyway. Nor come to that, I dare say, would most of the shoppers of Alice Springs, who were no doubt delighted to get lots of free parking and a crack at Martha Stewart towels and shower curtains. What a sad and curious age we live in.

We strolled through the centre of town looking for somewhere to eat. Alice's central business district was sufficiently compact that it took little time to exhaust its modest possibilities for sustenance and diversion. When we realized that we were walking the same streets twice, we repaired more or less by default to a Chinese restaurant we had passed a few minutes earlier from the other direction. It was nearly empty.

While we waited for our food, Allan gazed critically at the flock wallpaper and gaudy fixtures as if these alone might explain Alice's disappointing inadequacies. For a moment he seemed even to be gazing at the background music. 'So how long are we here for?' he asked at last.

'Well, we're here tomorrow. And then we go to Uluru. And then we come back here for a day. And then you fly back to England.'

He nodded thoughtfully. 'So two days here altogether?'

'Yup.'

'And what is there to do for two days in Alice Springs?'

'Quite a lot, in fact,' I said encouragingly, and pulled out a brochure I had taken from a rack in the motel. I flipped through it. 'There's the Alice Springs Desert Park, for one thing.'

He inclined his head a fraction. 'What's that?'

'It's a nature reserve where they've carefully recreated a desert environment.'

'In the desert?'

'Yes.'

'They've recreated a desert in the desert? Have I got that right?'

'Yes.'

'And you pay money for this?'

'Yes.'

He nodded contemplatively. 'What else?'

I turned the page. 'The Mecca Date Garden.'

'Which is?'

'A garden where they grow dates.'

'And they charge money for this as well?'

'I believe so.'

'Is that it or is there more?'

'Oh, much more.' I went through the list of other attractions – the old telegraph station, Frontier Camel Farm, Old Timers' Folk Museum, National Pioneer Women's Hall of Fame, Road Transport Hall of Fame, Minerals House, Chateau Hornsby Winery, Sounds of Starlight Theatre, Strehlow Aboriginal Research Centre.

Allan listened intently, sometimes requesting a soupçon of elaboration, and considered all this for some moments. Then he said: 'Let's go to Ayers Rock.'

I thought for a moment. 'Yeah, all right,' I said.

And so in the morning we rose early and set off for mighty Uluru. Alice Springs could wait.

Uluru and Alice Springs are so inextricably linked in the popular imagination that nearly everyone thinks of them as cosily proximate. In fact, it is almost 300 miles across a largely featureless tract to get from the one to the other. Uluru's glory is that it stands alone in a boundless emptiness, but it does mean that you have to really want

351

to see it; it's not something you're going to pass on the way to the beach. That is as it should be, of course, but it is equally a fact that when you have just completed a thousand-mile passage through barren void, you don't really require another five hours of it to confirm your impression that much of central Australia is empty.

Well into the 1950s Ayers Rock was inaccessible to all but the most dedicated sightseers. As late as the late 1960s, the number of annual visitors was no more than 10,000. Today Uluru gets that many every ten days on average. It even has its own airport, and the resort that has sprung up to serve it, called Yulara, is the third largest community in the Territory when full. Yulara stands a discreet and respectful dozen or so miles from the rock itself, so we stopped there first to get rooms. It consists essentially of a lazy loop road along which are tucked a range of accommodations, from campgrounds and a youth hostel up to the most sumptuously de luxe of resort hotels.

With nothing better to do, we had passed much of the five-hour drive working out a programme for ourselves for our stay. Essentially this had established that we would spend the afternoon studying the rock in a calm and reflective manner, then divide whatever remained of the day between a cooling dip in the hotel pool, drinks on a terrace while watching the setting sun gorge the rock with the red glow for which it is famed, a little stroll through the desert to stretch our legs and look for dingoes, wallabies and kangaroos, and finally a dinner of refinement and quality beneath a sky of twinkling stars. We had, after all, just driven 1,300 miles in two and a half days. If ever anyone was entitled to a little desert R&R it was us. So there was a certain real excitement as we turned off the highway and entered the cosseted confines of Yulara.

We went first to the Outback Pioneer Hotel, which sounded moderately priced if dangerously likely to have chandeliers made of waggon wheels and an all-you-can-eat buffet for people in baseball caps. In fact, it proved on approach to be rather grand and clearly very nice, but unexpectedly busy. Stacks of luggage were being unloaded from two tour buses out front and there were people everywhere, nearly all white-haired and pear-shaped, standing around squinting or fiddling with cameras and video recorders. Allan dropped me out front and I trotted inside to enquire about rates. I was amazed at the amount of hubbub in the lobby. It was early afternoon on a weekday out of season and the place was a circus. The check-in area brought to mind a mustering station on a foundering cruise ship. I asked a guy at the concierge desk what was going on.

'Nothing in particular,' he said, joining me in considering the unattractive chaos. 'It's always like this.'

'Really?' I said. 'Even out of season?'

'There is no out of season here now.'

'Are there any rooms here, do you know?'

'Afraid not. The only place with rooms left is the Desert Gardens.'

I thanked him and hied back to the car.

'Problem?' said Allan as I climbed in.

'Very poor dessert selection,' I said, not wishing to alarm him. 'Let's try the Desert Gardens Hotel. It's much nicer.'

The Desert Gardens was vastly more swank than the Pioneer Outback, and mercifully less crowded. Only one person, a man of about seventy, stood between me and the check-in clerk. I arrived just in time to hear the clerk say to him: 'It's three hundred and fifty-three dollars a night.'

I swallowed hard at this.

'We'll take it,' said the man in an American accent. 'How big is it?'

'I beg your pardon?'

'How big is the room?'

The clerk looked taken aback. 'Well, I'm not sure of its dimensions exactly. It's a fair size.'

'What's that mean? "Fair size".'

'It's amply proportioned, sir. Would you like to see the room?'

'No, I want to sign in,' the man said shortly, as if the clerk were needlessly delaying him. 'We want to get to the rock.'

'Very good, sir.'

As he signed in he asked a million subsidiary questions. Where was the rock exactly? How long did it take to get there? Was there a cocktail lounge in this hotel? Where was that exactly? What time was dinner served? Could you see the rock from the dining room? Was it worth seeing the rock from the dining room? Where was the pool? Through which doors? *Which* doors? And what about the elevator – where was that? *Where?*

I looked at my watch unhappily. It was getting on for two o'clock, and we didn't even have rooms yet. Time was speeding away.

'So is it good, this rock?' the man was saying in what might have been an attempt at levity.

'I beg your pardon, sir?'

'The rock. Is it worth coming all this way?'

'Well, as rocks go, sir, I think you could say it's first class.'

'Yeah, well, it'd better be,' the man said darkly.

Then his wife joined him and to my dismay *she* began asking questions. Was there a hairdresser's? How late was it open? Where could they mail postcards? Did the gift shop accept travellers' cheques? These were US dollar travellers' cheques; was that OK? And how much are postage stamps for America? Is there an iron and ironing board in the room? Where'd you say the gift shop is? And what about my brain? Have you seen that anywhere? It's about the size of a very small walnut and never been used.

Eventually they shuffled off and the clerk turned to me. With a regretful air, he informed me that the gentleman ahead of me had taken the last room. 'There might be dormitory space at the youth hostel,' he said, and allowed this deeply unappealing proposition to sit there for a moment. 'Shall I check?'

'Yes, please,' I murmured.

He consulted his computer and looked suitably doleful. 'No, I'm afraid even that's full now. I'm sorry.'

I thanked him and went out. Allan was leaning against the car with a hopeful face, which fell when he saw mine. I explained to him the situation. He looked crushed.

'So no swim?' he said.

I nodded.

'No wine on the terrace? No sunset over the rock? No elegant room with downy pillows? No complimentary fluffy dressing gown and tinkling mini-bar?'

'The dressing gowns never fit anyway, Allan.'

'Not quite the point.' He fixed me with a frank gaze. 'And instead of these things we will be . . . ?'

'Driving back to Alice Springs.'

He removed his focus to the wider world while he allowed this thought to settle. 'Well,' he said at last, 'I suppose we'd better go and see if this bloody rock is worth a 600-mile round trip.'

* * *

It was.

The thing about Ayers Rock is that by the time you finally get there you are already a little sick of it. Even when you are a thousand miles from it, you can't go a day in Australia without seeing it four or five or six times – on postcards, on travel agents' posters, on the cover of souvenir picture books – and as you get nearer the rock the frequency of exposure increases. So you are aware, as you drive to the park entrance and pay the ambitiously pitched admission fee of $15 a head and follow the approach road around, that you have driven 1,300 miles to look at a large, inert, loaf-shaped object that you have seen photographically portrayed a thousand times already. In consequence, your mood as you approach this famous monolith is restrained, unexpectant – pessimistic even.

And then you see it, and you are instantly transfixed.

There, in the middle of a memorable and imposing emptiness, stands an eminence of exceptional nobility and grandeur, 1,150 feet high, a mile and a half long, five and a half miles around, less red than photographs have led you to expect but in every other way more arresting than you could ever have supposed. I have discussed this since with many other people, nearly all of whom agreed that they approached Uluru with a kind of fatigue, and were left agog in a way they could not adequately explain. It's not that Uluru is bigger than you had supposed or more perfectly formed or in any way different from the impression you had created in your mind, but the very opposite. It is exactly what you expected it to be. You *know* this rock. You know it in a way that has nothing to do with calendars and the covers of souvenir books. Your knowledge of this rock is grounded in something much more elemental.

In some odd way that you don't understand and can't begin to articulate you feel an acquaintance with it – a familiarity on an unfamiliar level. Somewhere in the deep sediment of your being some long-dormant fragment of primordial memory, some little severed tail of DNA, has twitched or stirred. It is a motion much too faint to be understood or interpreted, but somehow you feel certain that this large, brooding, hypnotic presence has an importance to you at the species level – perhaps even at a sort of tadpole level – and that in some way your visit here is more than happenstance.

I'm not saying that any of this is so. I'm just saying that this is how you feel. The other thought that strikes you – that struck me anyway – is that Uluru is not merely a very splendid and mighty monolith, but also an extremely distinctive one. More than this, it is very possibly the most immediately recognizable natural object on earth. I'm suggesting nothing here, but I will say that if you were an intergalactic traveller who had broken down in our solar system, the obvious directions to rescuers would be: 'Go to the third planet and fly around till you see the big red rock. You can't miss it.' If ever on earth they dig up a 150,000-year-old rocket ship from the Galaxy Zog, this is where it will be. I'm not saying I expect it to happen; not saying that at all. I'm just observing that if I were looking for an ancient starship this is where I would start digging.

Allan, I noted, seemed similarly affected. 'It's weird, isn't it?' he said.

'What is?'

'I don't know. Just seeing it. I mean, it just feels weird.'

I nodded. It does feel weird. Quite apart from that initial shock of indefinable recognition, there is also the fact that Uluru is, no matter how you approach it, totally arresting.

357

You cannot stop looking at it; you don't want to stop looking at it. As you draw closer, it becomes even more interesting. It is more pitted than you had imagined, less regular in shape. There are more curves and divots and wavelike ribs, more irregularities of every type, than are evident from even a couple of hundred yards away. You realize that you could spend quite a lot of time – possibly a worryingly large amount of time; possibly a sell-your-house-and-move-here-to-live-in-a-tent amount of time – just looking at the rock, gazing at it from many angles, never tiring of it. You can see yourself in a silvery ponytail, barefoot and in something jangly and loose-fitting, hanging out with much younger visitors and telling them: 'And the amazing thing is that every day it's different, you know what I'm saying? It's never the same rock twice. That's right, my friend – you put your finger on it there. It's awesome. It's an awesome thing. Say, do you by any chance have any dope or some spare change?'

We stopped at several places to get out and have a look, including the spot where you can climb up it. It takes several hours and much exertion, which comfortably eliminated it from our consideration, and in any case the route was closed for the afternoon. So many people have collapsed and died on the rock that they close it to climbers when the weather is really warm, as it was this day. Even when it's not too hot, lots of people get in trouble from fooling around or taking wrong turns. Just the day before a Canadian had had to be rescued after getting himself onto some ledge from which he could not get either up or down. Since 1985, ownership of the rock has been back in the hands of the local Aboriginal people, the Pitjantjatjara and Yankunyjatjara, and they deeply dislike visitors (whom they call 'minga', or ants) clambering all over it. Personally I don't blame them. It is a sacred site to them. I think it should be for everyone, frankly.

We stopped at the visitors' centre for a cup of coffee and to look at the displays, which were all to do with interpretations of the Dreamtime – the Aborigines' traditional conception of how the earth was formed and operates. There was nothing instructive in a historical or geological sense, which was disappointing because I was curious to know what Uluru is doing there. How do you get the biggest rock in existence onto the middle of an empty plain? It turns out (I looked in a book later) that Uluru is what is known to geology as a bornhardt: a hunk of weather-resistant rock left standing when all else around it has worn away. Bornhardts are not that uncommon – the Devils Marbles are a collection of miniature bornhardts – but nowhere else on earth has one lump of rock been left in such dramatic and solitary splendour or assumed such a pleasing smooth symmetry. It is a hundred million years old. Go there, man.

Afterwards we had one last drive around the rock before heading back to the lonely highway. We had been at the site for barely two hours, obviously not nearly enough, but I realized as I turned around in my seat to watch it shrinking into the background behind us that there never could be enough, and I felt moderately comforted by that thought.

Anyway, I'll be back. I have no doubt of that. And next time I'm bringing a really good metal detector.

Chapter

SEVENTEEN

So we drove all the way back to Alice Springs. To compensate for our setback at Uluru, we decided to stay at one of Alice's fancy outlying resort hotels and hang the expense. Imagine then our surprise and gratification when we pulled into the oasis-like splendour of the Red Centre Resort and discovered that it was $20 a night less than we had paid for much less at the town-centre Best Western the night before. This alone, we agreed at once, was almost worth a 600-mile drive.

The Red Centre was really just a very large motel with a bit of landscaping, but it was friendly and welcoming and at its heart was a pool with a terrace and an adjoining bar and restaurant. Needless to say, this is where we were to be found thirty seconds after arrival. There we were told by the kindly staff that we were too late for dinner, but that they could probably rustle us up a couple of steak sandwiches or something. We told them we would be grateful for whatever they could give us, particularly if it was accompanied with drink, then took a table by the pool's edge, where we sat watching the tranquil shimmer of the water and savouring the delightfully warm and wholesome desert air, under a sky spread with stars.

Suddenly life seemed pretty good. Our driving was behind us now. We had seen Uluru – too briefly, perhaps, but sufficient to appreciate its wonders. And here at the Red Centre we appeared to have landed on our feet.

Allan announced his intention to spend his final day in Australia sitting in a lounger beside the pool, reading inferior fiction and working on his tan.

'How very shallow of you,' I said.

He accepted the criticism with imperturbable equanimity.

'So you're not coming to see the desert park?' I said.

'Nope. Nor the telegraph station, nor the sand dune hall of fame, nor the fig farm . . .'

'It's a date garden.'

A pause to stand corrected. 'Nor anywhere else. I'm going to sit right here beside this pool and pass my day in a vain and idle manner. And you?'

'I'm going to see the sights, of course.'

'Well, then I will meet you afterwards and you can tell me all about it, no doubt in excruciatingly boring detail.'

'You can count on it.'

And so the following morning I emerged from my room in a clean summer shirt, clutching a notebook with a pen tucked into the spiral, and went off in a dutiful frame of mind to see what Alice had to offer. I called first at the telegraph station, on a patch of sunny high ground a mile or so outside town. In its early days Alice Springs was a repeater station, one of twelve between Darwin and Adelaide, which were needed to boost signals on their way across the country. What a forlorn and tedious existence that must have been, stuck in the middle of a suffocating nowhere, endlessly tapping out second-hand messages involving people you would never see or know, living in places you could only dream about. Outside the station was the reedy pool of water from which Alice Springs takes its name. The Alice in question was the wife of the director of telegraphs in Adelaide, and originally it was only the station that was called Alice Springs. The town that slowly rose in the valley below was called Stuart, after the explorer. For some reason people found this confusing, and in 1933 the whole became known as Alice Springs. So the most famous town in the outback is named for a woman who had no connection with it and, as far as I know, never saw it.

This done, I made a tick beside 'Telegraph Station' on my list of things to do, then drove on to the Alice Springs Desert Park. My expectations frankly were not high, but in fact it was splendid. It's run by the Parks and Wildlife Commission of the Northern Territory. What they have done is recreate over a large area three primary desert habitats – one that is very dry, one that gets a little moisture, and one that is normally dry but occasionally is swept by flash floods. This alone provided a worthwhile lesson – it makes you realize that deserts in their quiet, arid way are as varied as other environments – but I was also grateful to find various shrubs and other plants labelled and explained. It was a pleasure to be able to say: 'Ah, so *that*'s kangaroo paw. Well, I never. And let's see if this spinifex really does hurt as much as Ernest Giles said. Why, yes, it does!'

Scattered at intervals were large walk-in enclosures containing birds and other small desert animals – bandicoots and bush-tailed possums and so on – with labels detailing their habits. Best of all was a large nocturnal house where all manner of night creatures endlessly prowled and hopped and sniffed the air in a succession of night-time dioramas. The display area was so faintly illuminated that it was actually possible to walk into walls and glass panels, but as my eyes slowly adjusted I was able to pick out an amazingly diverse and rewarding range of small marsupials – potoroos and bettongs and bilbies and numbats and quolls and much more.

Because Australia is so vast and arid and difficult a landscape to study, and because the modest population base produces comparatively few scientists for the amount of ground to be covered, and because, above all, the animals within it are often small, furtive, nocturnal and sometimes mysterious, even now nobody really knows quite what is out there. Any list of Australian wildlife is arrestingly punctuated with qualified comments like 'possibly extinct' or 'thought to be endangered' or 'may survive in some remote areas'. The difficulties are well illustrated, I think, by the uncertain fate of the oolacunta, or desert rat kangaroo. Nearly everything that is known about this interesting creature is owed to two men. The first was a nineteenth-century naturalist named John Gould, who studied and described the animal in 1843. It had, according to Gould, the shape and manner of a kangaroo but was only about the size of a rabbit. What particularly distinguished it was that it could move at very high speeds for unusually long distances. Since that one initial report, however, the oolacunta had not been seen. Enter Hedley Herbert Finlayson.

Finlayson was a chemist by profession, but devoted much of his life to searching for rare native animals. In 1931 he led an expedition that travelled on horseback deep into the interior, to the perpetual furnace that is Sturt's Stony Desert. Upon arriving, Finlayson was surprised to discover that the little desert rat kangaroo, far from being on the verge of extinction or possibly gone altogether, was both visible and clearly thriving. The animal's speed and endurance were just as Gould had reported. Once when Finlayson and his colleagues gave chase on horseback a desert rat kangaroo ran twelve miles without pause through the searing heat of day, exhausting three horses in the process. Ounce for ounce, the little oolacunta may well have been the greatest runner (or bouncer, actually) the animal kingdom has ever produced. Returning to society, Finlayson reported his exciting find and naturalists and zoologists everywhere dutifully amended their texts to account for the desert rat kangaroo's rediscovery. Over the next three years Finlayson made further expeditions, but in 1935 when he returned once more he was nonplussed, as you may imagine, to discover that the little desert rat kangaroo had quietly vanished – as utterly as it had after Gould's single sighting in 1843. It hasn't been seen since.

The chronicles of Australian fauna are amazingly full of stories such as this – of animals that are there one moment and gone the next. A more recent casualty of the phenomenon was a frog called *Rheobatrachus silus*, which was around for such a short time that it didn't even manage to attract an informal name. What was extraordinary about *R. silus* (and it almost goes without saying that there would be something) was that it gave birth to live young through its mouth – something never before seen in nature inside Australia or out. It was discovered by biologists in 1973 and by 1981 it had disappeared. It is listed as 'probably extinct'.

My favourite animal disappearance story, however, harks back to a somewhat earlier age. It concerns a nineteenth-century naturalist named Gerard Krefft, who in 1857 caught two very rare pig-footed bandicoots. Unfortunately for science and for the bandicoots, Krefft soon afterwards grew hungry and ate them. They were, as far as anyone can tell, the last of the species. Certainly none has been seen since. Krefft, incidentally, was later appointed head of the Australian Museum in Sydney, but was invited to seek alternative employment when it was discovered that he was supplementing his salary by selling pornographic postcards. I am sure there must be a moral in there somewhere.

From the Desert Park, I went to the Strehlow Aboriginal Research Centre. This was a quietly boring display concerning a man born on the Hermannsburg Mission, an Aboriginal reserve outside Alice, who devoted his life to studying Aborigines. He collected a huge stock of spiritual artifacts, but because they are sacred and not allowed to be seen by the uninitiated, they cannot be put on display. What you get instead are lots of old photographs of life at Hermannsburg and more detail on the life and work of Theodore Strehlow than a reasonable person could wish.

However, as I was walking back to the car, I noticed a small aviation museum in an old hangar next door. Curiously, no one was in attendance, but the door was open so I stepped inside and had a look around. The museum had a fairly predictable assortment of old engines and walls of yellowing photographs, but in a separate building there was something I had no idea still existed and certainly never expected to see. No guidebook I have ever seen draws attention to it; even the local tourism literature contained no hint that it is there. But for a few fretful days in 1929 it was the most famous and sought-after object in Australia – and here it was in a small aviation museum in Alice Springs, of all places. I refer to the remains of a light aircraft known as the Kookaburra, which went down in the desert while searching for a lost pilot named Charles Kingsford Smith.

Kingsford Smith was not only the greatest Australian aviator of his age, but possibly the greatest aviator ever. He held more records than anyone else and tackled infinitely more daring challenges. Just a year after Charles Lindbergh made his historic solo flight across the Atlantic, Kingsford Smith became the first to cross the Pacific – a far more ambitious enterprise, not simply because the scale was greater but because flying conditions were much, much tougher and far less well understood. At the time of his Pacific attempt, only ten months had passed since the first aeroplane had successfully flown to Hawaii in a race sponsored by a Hawaiian pineapple magnate – and that event had claimed the lives of ten airmen. So when, in 1928, Kingsford Smith set off with a crew of three from San Francisco aiming to reach Brisbane by way of Honolulu and Suva in Fiji, the undertaking was widely held to be impossible and insane, and so it nearly proved. Six hundred miles out from Hawaii, Kingsford Smith flew into a belt of meteorological liveliness known as the intertropical convergence zone – an expanse of boiling clouds, towering storms and the sort of winds that could blow a moustache off. As his small craft began to bounce about like some kind of elasticated toy, Kingsford Smith had no idea what to expect, or when it might end, because no pilot had ever flown into such a system before.

This was, bear in mind, in a frail, spruce-framed, cloth-covered 1920s Fokker so elemental in design that the seats weren't even bolted down. For hours Kingsford Smith fought to hold the plane steady and in one piece. When at last it popped into clear air, he and his men were perilously low on fuel and faced with the problem of finding Fiji – a dot in an all but infinite ocean – before their engine ran dry and they fell into the sea. This and a hundred other alarming obstacles Kingsford Smith tackled with courage, skill, resolution and wit. Crossing the Pacific was possibly the most daring organized feat of aviation ever.

Kingsford Smith always flew with a co-pilot, and generally with a navigator and radioman as well, so it is unfair to compare his achievements with the solitary heroics of Charles Lindbergh. None the less it is fair to observe that Lindbergh never flew through anything as ferocious as Kingsford Smith's Pacific storm. Indeed, after 1927 Lindbergh scarcely made another notable flight. Kingsford Smith, on the other hand, flew on and on, establishing records all over. He became the first to fly the Atlantic from east to west (again much tougher because it was against the jet stream), first to fly from Australia to New Zealand and back again, and first to cross the Pacific in the other direction. He also held a fistful of records for fastest flights between Australia and England, and for various legs along the way.

Which brings us to the Kookaburra. In March 1929, with a crew of three, Kingsford Smith set off to fly from

Sydney to England. Over north-west Australia, along the Kimberley coast, they hit bad weather, grew hopelessly lost (not altogether surprisingly: for guidance they had only a couple of admiralty charts and a map of Australia torn from a standard *Times Atlas*) and made a forced landing on a coastal mudflat, with almost no fuel left and hopelessly short of supplies. Almost all they had was a flask of coffee and some brandy, which could be combined to make a drink called a coffee royal. Thus what followed became known, somewhat darkly, as the Coffee Royal Affair.

Luckily for Kingsford Smith, he and his men were in an area with plentiful fresh water and some adequate if unappealing sources of food (mud snails mostly). However, because the plane's radio was broken, they had no way of telling the outside world where they were. When news of the disappearance reached Sydney, two of Kingsford Smith's associates, Keith Anderson and Bob Hitchcock, decided to mount a rescue. In the little Kookaburra they took off from Mascot Airport in Sydney, flew by stages to Alice Springs, and finally set off from there on what was supposed to be the final leg early on the morning of 12 April 1929. Soon afterwards, while crossing the parched emptiness of the Tanami Desert – the area that Allan and I had skirted in the car on our drive from Daly Waters to Alice Springs – the engine began to sputter and backfire and they were forced to make an emergency landing in the desert. In their haste to depart they had packed no food and only three litres of water. Unlike Kingsford Smith, they landed in a place that offered no succour.

They were dead by the third day. That is how unimaginably murderous the outback is. I don't wish to seem obsessive about this, but they drank their own urine, too. Nearly everybody does who gets stuck in the outback. (It's actually counterproductive because the salts in urine accelerate thirst.)

At almost the moment when Anderson and Hitchcock were wretchedly expiring, Kingsford Smith and his cronies were rescued by someone else. They returned to civilization looking so fit and rested that some people began to suspect (and some newspapers to speculate) that it had all been a publicity stunt. The whole thing grew rather ugly. Kingsford Smith was subjected to the humiliation of a public inquiry into his character (he was ultimately exonerated). Meanwhile, the nation waited breathlessly for news that Anderson and Hitchcock had been found alive. Alas, they were not. In late April, a search plane spotted the downed Kookaburra with their bodies nearby, and a few days later a rescue party recovered the remains and brought them back to civilization. Hitchcock's family opted for a quiet funeral in Perth, but Anderson was given a state funeral of the most grave and magnificent pomp in Sydney. For days beforehand people in their thousands stood in line for hours to view the coffin. On the day of the funeral, thousands more lined the streets to watch the cortège or gathered at the burial site. It was the biggest funeral in Sydney to that time, possibly the biggest ever.

Today, it almost goes without saying, Anderson and Hitchcock are completely forgotten, inside Australia as well as out. So, too, for a long time was the Kookaburra. It sat in the desert, rusting and unnoted, for half a century before it was finally collected and taken to Darwin for restoration. About ten years ago, it was placed in a special small building at the aviation museum at

Alice Springs, where it appears to attract no attention whatever.

Kingsford Smith returned to flying, setting yet more records. In 1935, while flying home from England, his plane crashed into the sea off Burma, taking him with it. Today, he is fitfully remembered in Australia (Sydney's airport is named after him) and not at all elsewhere. In 1998, the American writer Scott Berg produced a 600-page doorstop biography of Charles Lindbergh, which naturally ranged over the whole story of aviation's early days. Of Charles Kingsford Smith it contained not a mention.

Allan and I dined that evening on the patio of the Red Centre, where I told him in great detail about my many exciting discoveries of the day. As we sat enjoying the warm evening and lazily finding our way to the bottom of our second bottle of very nice Western Australia Cabernet Sauvignon, as if on cue a wallaby hopped up to the perimeter fence on the far side of the swimming pool, regarded us for a moment with a general air of unconcern, and began nibbling the shrubs that were planted there. It was the first time since my crossing of the country on the Indian Pacific many weeks earlier that I had seen a distinctive Australian animal in the wild. It was the first time Allan ever had, and he was thrilled.

Whether for this reason or some other, he announced that he thought Australia a very fine place.

'Do you?' I said, pleased, but just a little surprised for he had seen little of it but desert.

He leaned towards me very slightly and said, as if sharing a confidence: 'It's very roomy.'

I looked at him. 'Yes, it is.'

'It's a very roomy country.'

On reflection, I think it may have been our third bottle.

In the morning I drove him to Alice's small but handsome airport, where we had a cup of coffee and sat quietly, for we were both a trifle hung over. I saw him to his gate, where we exchanged the usual rushed and fatuous expressions of thanks and goodwill, and he disappeared down the walkway. I watched him go, then turned and walked back to the car. I had a day to kill before flying on to Western Australia, and I wasn't at all certain how I was going to fill it. I headed into town for the business district to find a bank machine and buy a newspaper, but en route I passed a sign for the School of the Air, down a side street, and impetuously I decided to have a look.

I didn't expect a great deal, but it was terrific. What a lot of nice surprises Alice Springs was throwing up. The School of the Air was in an anonymous building on a residential street. It consisted of a reception area where the children's work was displayed on tables and around the walls, two small studios, a large meeting room and that was about it. Although there are seventeen schools of the air in Australia now, Alice Springs is the grandmother of them all and still covers the largest and emptiest area. It was a Saturday, so no lessons were in progress, but a very nice man was happy to show me around and tell me how it worked.

The idea was simple enough: to provide formal schooling and some sense of classroom experience for kids growing up on cattle stations or other lonely spots – something it has been dutifully doing since 1951. Lonely is certainly the key word here. With a catchment area of 468,000 square miles – that is an area roughly twice the size of France – the Alice Springs school has just 140 pupils spread between kindergarten and the early teens. I retain a strangely vivid and influential memory of watching a film about it at school when I was eight or nine, and of being extremely taken with the notion of being hundreds of miles from your teacher, entrusted with your own microphone and shortwave radio set, and free to sit there buck naked with a plate of cookies if you chose since no one could see you. All of these seemed incalculable improvements on the situation that prevailed at Greenwood Elementary in Des Moines, Iowa. So the romance of radio learning has never quite left me. I was disappointed, therefore, to discover that the radio portion has only ever been a tiny and incidental part of the programme. The School of the Air is and always has been essentially a correspondence course, which doesn't sound anything like as appealing.

Even so, the place had a very real charm and air of goodwill. The noticeboards were filled with illustrated essays from kids of about eleven describing life on their stations and what a typical day was like for them. I read every one with absorption.

'Would you like to listen to a lesson?' the man in charge asked me.

'Very much,' I said.

He took me into a side room and put on a tape recording of a day's lesson for five-year-olds. It consisted mostly of a perky teacher going through the roll-call, saying: 'Good morning, Kylie. Can you hear me? Over.'

After a moment there would be a faint crackle, as of a transmission from a very distant galaxy, and sounds almost recognizable as human speech but much too indistinct to be deciphered.

'I say good morning, Kylie. Are you there? Can you hear me? Over.'

This time there would be a pause and no response at all, just a rather poignant interval of dead air. Then: 'Well, let's try Gavin then. Good morning, Gavin. Are you there? Over.'

More crackle and then a small, tinny voice would come back: 'Good morning, Miss Smith!'

And so it went, with some voices coming in loud and clear, but many others fading in or out or proving totally unreachable. As I listened to this, I also read a little booklet I had bought where I was frankly taken aback to discover that each child spends only half an hour a day (actually, 'up to half an hour a day') on the radio, plus ten minutes a week in a private tutorial with their teachers – hardly a lavish amount of personal attention. For the rest, they are expected to spend five to six hours a day working under the supervision of a parent or nanny. The students also make use of televisions, VCRs and personal computers, but I didn't see any sign of them. The conclusion to which you are reluctantly but inescapably drawn is that it is forever 1951 at the School of the Air.

The real surprise, however, was that there seemed to be no Aboriginal children involved – certainly none were evident in the photographs. The population of the Northern Territory is about 20 per cent Aboriginal overall, but in the far outback the proportion is much higher. I asked the man about that on my way out.

'Oh, there are some,' he said. 'I'm not sure how many just at the moment, but there are a few. The problem is that the pupils have to be supervised by a competent adult, you see.'

I waited a moment, then said: 'I'm sorry, I don't see.'

'They need a reliable, conscientious adult with core language and reading skills.'

'And Aboriginal parents don't have that?'

He looked unhappy, as if this was a route we really shouldn't be travelling down. 'No, I'm afraid not. Not always.'

'But if you're not giving the kids the lessons because the parents can't help them, then those kids, when they become parents, won't have the core skills either, will they?'

'Yes, it's a problem.'

'And so it will just go on for ever?'

'It's a very big problem.'

'I see,' I said, though of course I didn't really see at all.

Afterwards, I continued into town. I bought a newspaper and took it to an open-air café on Todd Street, a pedestrian mall. I read for a minute or two, but then found myself just watching the passing scene. It was quite busy with Saturday shoppers. The people on the street were overwhelmingly white Australians but there were Aborigines about, too – not great numbers of them, but always there, on the edge of frame, unobtrusive, nearly always silent, peripheral. The white people never looked at the Aborigines, and the Aborigines never looked at the white people. The two races seemed to inhabit separate but parallel universes. I felt as if I was the only person who could see both groups at once. It was very strange.

A very high proportion of the Aborigines looked beaten up. Many had puffy faces, as if they had wandered into a hornet's nest, and an almost absurdly high number sported bandages on shins, elbows, foreheads or knees. A label at the Strehlow exhibition which I had seen the day before had been at pains to stress that the most ruined Aborigines were those one saw in towns. The idea, I guess, was to inform visitors like me that one shouldn't judge all Aborigines by these mild wrecks seen shuffling through the streets. Nonetheless, it struck me as an odd and paternalistic thing to say, in that it seemed to imply that Aborigines had two choices in their lives: to stay on the missions and prosper, or come into town and fall into penury and dereliction.

It made me think of a line I had seen penned by a famous outback character named Daisy Bates, who came to Australia from Ireland in 1884 and for years lived among and studied the indigenous peoples of Western Australia. In *The Passing of the Aborigines*, published in 1938, she wrote: 'The Australian native can withstand all the reverses of nature, fiendish droughts and sweeping floods, horrors of thirst and enforced starvation – but he cannot withstand civilization.' In 1938 that may have qualified as sympathetic and enlightened comment, but it was disheartening to see it presented in modified form at an Aboriginal research centre in 1999.

You don't have to be a genius to work out that Aborigines are Australia's greatest social failing. For virtually every indicator of prosperity and well-being – hospitalization rates, suicide rates, childhood mortality, imprisonment, employment, you name it – the figures for Aborigines range from twice as bad to up to twenty times worse than for the general population. According to John Pilger, Australia is the only developed nation that ranks high for incidence of trachoma – a viral disease that often leads to blindness – and it is almost exclusively an Aboriginal malady. Overall, the life expectancy of the average indigenous Australian is twenty years – *twenty years* – less than that of the average white Australian.

In Cairns, quite by chance, I had been told about a lawyer named Jim Brooks who has worked for years for and with Aborigines, and I had managed to meet him for a cup of coffee in town just before Allan and I had flown on to Darwin. A calm, easygoing, immediately likeable man with just a hint of the earnestness that must have led him to devote his working life to fighting for the disaffiliated rather than piling up money in private practice, he runs the Native Title Rights Office in Cairns, which helps native peoples with land issues, and was one of the members of a human rights commission set up in the mid-1990s to investigate an unfortunate experiment in social engineering popularly known as the Stolen Generations.

This was an attempt by government to lift Aboriginal children out of poverty and disadvantage by physically distancing them from their families and communities. No one knows the actual numbers, but between 1910 and 1970 between one-tenth and one-third of Aboriginal children were taken from their parents and sent to foster homes or state training centres. The idea – thought quite advanced at the time – was to prepare them for a more rewarding life in the white world. What was most amazing about this was the legal mechanism that enabled it to be done. Until the 1960s, in most Australian states Aboriginal parents did not have legal custody of their own children. The state did. The state could take children from their homes at any time, on any basis it deemed appropriate, without apology or explanation.

'They did everything they could to eliminate contact between the parents and children,' Jim Brooks told me when we met. 'We found one woman whose five children were sent to five different states. She had no way of keeping in touch with them, no way of knowing where they were, whether they were sick or well or happy or anything. Have you got kids?'

'Four,' I said.

'Well, imagine if a government van turned up at your house one day and some inspector came to the door and told you they were taking your children. I mean seriously imagine how you would feel if you had to stand by and watch your children taken from your arms and put into a van. Imagine watching the van driving off down the road, with your kids crying for you, looking at you out the back window, and knowing that you will probably never see them again.'

'Stop,' I said with an uneasy stab at jocularity.

He smiled sympathetically at my discomfort. 'And there is not a thing you can do about it. Nobody you can turn to. No court that will take your side. And this went on for decades.'

'Why did they do it in such a heartless way?'

'They didn't see it as heartless. They thought they were doing a good thing.' He passed me a précis of the rights commission's report, which he had brought for me, and showed me a quotation from early in the twentieth century by a travelling inspector named James Isdell, who wrote of the dispossessed parents: 'No matter how frantic [their] momentary grief might be at the time, they soon forget their offspring.'

'They sincerely believed that indigenous peoples were somehow immune to normal human emotions,' Brooks said. He shrugged at the hopelessness of such thinking. 'Very often the children were told that their parents were dead; sometimes that the parents no longer wanted them. That was their way of helping them cope. Well, you can imagine the consequences. There was a lot of grief-related alcoholism, stratospheric levels of suicide, all that kind of stuff.'

'What became of the kids?'

'Well, the kids, meanwhile, were kept in care until they were sixteen or seventeen, and then turned out into the community. They had a choice of staying in the cities and trying to cope with the inevitable prejudices, or returning to their traditional communities and resuming a way of life that they could barely remember with people they no longer really knew. The conditions for dysfunction and dislocation were bred into the system. You don't get rid of that overnight. You know, some people will tell you that the removal of children only affected a small proportion of indigenous families. That is both wrong – there was scarcely a family in the land that wasn't affected at some profound and immediate level – but even more tragically to miss the point. Taking children away destroyed a whole continuity of relationships. Just because you stop that practice doesn't mean that all that damage is going to be magically undone and everything will be fine.'

'So what can you do for them?' I asked.

'Help to give them a voice,' he said. 'That's all I can do.' He shrugged, a little helplessly, and smiled.

I asked him if there was still much prejudice in Australia and he nodded. 'Huge amounts,' he said. 'Really quite huge amounts, I'm afraid.'

Over the past twenty years, successive governments have done quite a lot – or quite a lot compared with what was done before. They have restored large tracts of land to Aboriginal communities. They have returned Uluru to

Aboriginal stewardship. They have spent more money on schools and clinics. They have introduced the usual initiatives for encouraging community projects and helping small businesses get started. None of this has made any difference at all to the statistics. Some have actually got worse. At the end of the twentieth century, an Aboriginal Australian was still eighteen times more likely to die from an infectious disease than a white Australian, and seventeen times more likely to be hospitalized as a result of violence. An Aboriginal baby remained two to four times more likely to die at birth depending on cause.

Above all, what is perhaps oddest to the outsider is that Aborigines just aren't *there*. You don't see them performing on television; you don't find them assisting you in shops. Only two Aborigines have ever served in Parliament; none has held a Cabinet post. Indigenous peoples constitute only about 1.5 per cent of the Australian population and they live disproportionately in rural areas, so you wouldn't expect to see them in vast numbers anyway, but you would expect to see them *some*times – working in a bank, delivering mail, writing parking tickets, fixing a telephone line, participating in some productive capacity in the normal workaday world. I never have; not once. Clearly some connection is not being made.

As I sat now on the Todd Street Mall with my coffee and watched the mixed crowds – happy white shoppers with Saturday smiles and a spring in their step, shadowy Aborigines with their curious bandages and slow, swaying, knocked-about gait – I realized that I didn't have the faintest idea what the solution to all this was, what was required to spread the fruits of general Australian prosperity to those who seemed so signally unable to find their way to it. If I were contracted by the Commonwealth of Australia to advise on Aboriginal issues all I could write would be: 'Do more. Try harder. Start now.'

So without an original or helpful thought in my head, I just sat for some minutes and watched these poor disconnected people shuffle past. Then I did what most white Australians do. I read my newspaper and drank my coffee and didn't see them any more.

Chapter

EIGHTEEN

Consider the platypus. In a land of improbable creatures, it stands supreme. It exists in a kind of anatomical netherworld halfway between mammal and reptile. Fifty million years of isolation gave Australian animals the leisure to evolve in unlikely directions, or sometimes scarcely to evolve at all. The platypus managed somehow to do both.

When word reached England in 1799 that there existed in Australia a toothless, venomous, fur-covered, egg-laying, semi-aquatic animal with a duck-like bill, the tail of a beaver, feet that were both webbed and clawed, and a strange orifice called a cloaca, which served both reproductive and excretory purposes (a feature, as one taxonomist delicately noted, that was 'highly curious but not well adapted for popular details'), it was received, not altogether surprisingly, as a hoax. Even after a careful examination of a shipped specimen, the British Museum's anatomist, George Shaw, found it 'impossible not to entertain some doubts as to the genuine nature of the animal, and to surmise that there might have been practised some arts of deception in its structure'. According to the natural historian Harriet Ritvo, the original specimen still bears the scissor scars where Shaw snipped and fiddled to determine whether a hoax had been perpetrated.

For most of the next century, scientists argued – and argued heatedly, for it was an age obsessively devoted to exactitude – over how to classify the animal before putting it and its cousin the echidna (a creature similar to a hedgehog) in a family of their own: the monotremes. (The name means 'one hole', in reference to the distinguishing cloaca.) Unresolved, however, was the question of whether the monotremes were to be regarded as primarily mammal or reptile. It was evident from their peculiar anatomy that monotremes laid eggs, a reptilian trait, but it was equally evident that they suckled their young, a mammalian characteristic. A further vexation was that for almost a century nobody could find a monotreme egg. So we may envision the murmur and buzz that swept the auditorium when, in 1884, at a meeting of the British Association, the delegates were read a cable just arrived from a young British naturalist in Australia named W. H. Caldwell.

Caldwell's message in full read: 'Monotremes oviparous, ovum meroblastic.'

Well, the murmurs were prodigious, the buzz electric. What Caldwell was announcing with such elegant pith was that he had found platypus eggs and they were unquestionably reptilian in nature. In the end, Caldwell's find didn't make a lasting difference. The monotremes ended up in the mammalian camp, though for a while it was a close-run thing.

I mention all this to give a little context to the very real excitement I felt the following day when, freshly arrived in Perth, I happened upon a monotreme of my own: an echidna crossing a path in a lonely corner of Kings Park. I was already, I have to say, in pretty high spirits. Perth is a lovely city and one of my favourites in Australia. I have perhaps an inflated fondness for it because on my first visit there, in 1993, I arrived by way of Johannesburg, where I had just been robbed in a fairly hair-raising manner, in broad daylight in the city centre, by a party of cheerfully menacing youths with twitchy knives, and it was such a relief to find myself in a city where I could wander without fear that I might be bundled into an alley, liberated of my possessions and liberally incised with sharp instruments.

Even without arriving fresh from an incident of criminal excitement, Perth is a cheery and welcoming place. There is first of all the delight in finding it there at all, for Perth is far and away the most remote big city on earth, closer to Singapore than to Sydney, though not actually close to either. Behind you stretches 1,700 miles of inert red emptiness all the way to Adelaide; before you nothing but a featureless blue sea for 5,000 miles to Africa. Why 1.3 million members of a free society would choose to live in such a lonely outpost is a question always worth considering, but climate explains a lot. Perth has glorious weather, *good-natured* weather – the kind that sets the postman to whistling and puts a spring in the step of delivery people. Architecturally, Perth has no particular distinction – it is a large, clean, modern city: Minneapolis down under – but its sharp and radiant light makes it a beauty. You will never see bluer city skies or purer sunlight bouncing off skyscrapers than here.

But what especially sets Perth apart is the possession of one of the world's largest and finest parks, Kings Park. Spread across a thousand comely acres on a bluff above the broad basin of the Swan River, Kings is all those things a city park should be – playground, sanctuary, strolling area, botanical garden, vantage point, memorial – and so big that you can never feel as if you have seen it all. Most of it is arrayed in a conventional manner – undulant lawns, paths, flower beds – but a substantial corner, constituting perhaps a quarter of the whole, has been left as unimproved bush. It was while strolling down a sunny path through this little-visited zone that I saw a small furry hemisphere, rather like the brush portion of a floor polisher, emerge from the undergrowth on one side of the path and proceed with a stately lack of haste towards identical undergrowth on the other side.

Sensing me, it stopped. It had glossy black quills pointing straight back and had curled itself roughly into a ball so I couldn't see its pointy snout, but it was clearly an echidna. It could be nothing else. I couldn't have been more thrilled. It was a little pathetic, I grant you, when you consider that this was my most exciting moment of engaging a creature in the wild in Australia. In a country filled with exotic and striking life forms my high point was finding a harmless, animated pincushion in a city park. I didn't care. It was a monotreme – a physiological anomaly, a wonder of the reproductive world, an oddity from the loneliest branch on the mammalian tree. When the echidna sensed that I had retreated to a respectful distance, it unfurled and continued on its waddling way into the bush.

Thrilled to my cloaca, I followed the path around and back into the park proper, where I came after some time to a long, lovely avenue of tall white gum trees planted long ago to commemorate the fallen of the First World War. Each tree bore a small plaque giving bare details – unexpectedly moving when read one after another down a long walk – of an abbreviated life. 'In honour of Capt. Thomas H. Bone, 44th Batt.,' said one. 'Killed in action Passchendaele 4th October 1917 aged 25. Dedicated by his wife and daughter.' It is a fact little noted outside Australia – and I think worth at least a mention here – that no other nation lost more men as a proportion of population in the First World War than Australia. Out of a national population of under five million, Australia suffered a staggering 210,000 casualties – 60,000 dead, 150,000 injured. The casualty rate for its soldiers was 65 per cent. As John Pilger has put it: 'No army was as decimated as that which came from farthest away. And all were volunteers.' Only a few days earlier, in one of the weekend papers I had read a review of a new history of the First World War by the British historian John Keegan. In passing, the reviewer had noted, with an all but palpable sigh, that Keegan's 500 pages of densely observed text had failed to include a single mention of the Australian forces.

Poor Australia, I thought. Other countries produce unknown soldiers. It produces unknown armies.*

Beyond this sombre avenue lay the much perkier and sunnier realm of the botanical gardens, and this I approached now with unusual devotion, for Australia's

* Weeks later, in London, I checked the Keegan book, and it was full of references to the Australian army. The conclusion to draw from this, I guess, is that Australians so expect to be overlooked that they sometimes overlook not being overlooked, so to speak.

plants are exceptional and there is no place where you will find them more handsomely displayed. Australia really is the most amazingly fecund country. It is thought to contain something of the order of 25,000 species of plants (Britain, for purposes of comparison, has 1,600 species) but that's really only a guess. At least a third of what is out there has never been named or studied, and new stuff is turning up all the time, often in the most unlikely places. In 1989 in Sydney, for instance, scientists found an entirely new species of tree called *Allocasuarina portuensis*. People had been living around these trees for 200 years, but because they weren't very numerous – just ten have been found – no one had noticed them before. In much the same way, in 1994 in the Blue Mountains some botanist out for a walk happened on another of those unexpected relic species long presumed to be extinct. Called wollemi pines, these were not modest shrubs hidden among tall grasses but stout and imposing trees up to 130 feet tall and ten feet around. It's just that with such a lot of land to survey and only so many botanists to go round, it took a while for the two to intersect. Nobody can guess, of course, what else might be out there awaiting discovery. This is what makes Australia such a fundamentally exciting place to engage in the natural sciences. In Britain or Germany or America, you might with great luck find a new strain of mountaintop lichen or some sprig of previously overlooked moss, but in Australia take a stroll through the bush and you can find half a dozen unnamed wildflowers, a grove of Jurassic angiosperms and probably a ten-kilo lump of gold. I know where I'd be working if I were in science.

The question that naturally occurs in all this is why Australia, which so often seems singularly hostile to life, has produced such an abundance of it. Paradoxically, half the answer lies in the very poverty of the soil. In the temperate world, most plants can prosper in most places – an oak tree can grow as productively in Oregon as it can in Pennsylvania – and so a relatively few generalist species tend to predominate. In poor soils, on the other hand, plants are driven to specialize. One species will learn to tolerate soils containing, say, high concentrations of nickel, an element that other plants find distasteful. Another will become tolerant of copper. Yet another might learn to tolerate nickel *and* copper, and perhaps prolonged drought as well. And so it goes. After a few million years, you end up with a landscape filled with a great variety of plants each favouring very specific conditions and each master of a patch of ground that few other plants could abide. Specialized plants lead to specialized insects, and so on up the food chain. The result is a country that seems on the face of it hostile to life but in fact is wonderfully diversified.

The second, more obvious factor in Australia's variety is isolation. Fifty million years as an island clearly sheltered indigenous life forms from a great deal of competition and allowed certain of them – eucalypts in the plant world, marsupials in the animal world – to prosper uncommonly. But no less important in terms of species diversity is the isolation that has long existed *within* Australia. In general terms, Australia comprises scattered pockets of life separated by great zones of harshness. And nowhere is all of this more true than in south-western Australia. According to David Attenborough (in *The Private Life of Plants*), this one corner of Australia 'contains no less than twelve thousand different plant species and 87 per cent of them grow nowhere else in the world'.

Which makes it alarming to report that many of these singular plants are in trouble from a terrible and little-understood malady called 'dieback'. Dieback comes from a fungus family called *Phytophthora*, which is related to the fungus that caused the potato blight in Ireland. It has been in Australia for a century and has affected plants all over the country, though the source wasn't identified by science until 1966. It is especially a worry in south-west Australia, partly because it thrives there as nowhere else and partly because the south-west has such a density of rare and vulnerable plants. I discovered now, from an informative signboard, that even banksias are under threat. The banksia (named for its discoverer, Joseph Banks) is perhaps the most adored flower in Australia. It's a bit of an oddity – the flowers look uncannily like toilet brushes – but Australians love it because it is striking and it is everywhere and it is theirs alone. So it was discouraging to read that seven species of banksia are on the endangered list and could well become extinct in the wild in the next few years. Twelve more species are under threat. Perhaps it's my natural pessimism, but it seems that an awfully large part of travel these days is to see things while you still can. The most disturbing thought of all, I suppose, is that with so much still unrecorded many plants could disappear before they are even found.

All of this was of some moment because I was about to go off on a small botanical quest of my own. First, however, I had a day at leisure in Perth. I had nothing very particular in mind, but a few minutes later as I sat on the shady terrace of the park's central café, decorating my face with a chocolatey froth of cappuccino and reading the *West Australian* newspaper, I came upon a news article that planted the possibility of an idea.

The article was to do with a man named Lang Hancock, about whom I had lately been reading. Hancock was a rancher in the remote north of Western Australia who had the exceptional good fortune to be at the heart of one of the greatest mineral booms in modern history. Anyone who doubts that Australia truly is a lucky country has only to review the story of the country's mineral discoveries in the 1950s and a little beyond. Up until that time, conventional wisdom held that Australia was deficient in almost all natural resources. Iron ore, for instance, was considered to be in such short supply that for two decades it was illegal to export it. Then in 1952 Lang Hancock made an important discovery. While piloting a light aircraft over the trackless emptiness of the Hamersley Range near the north coast he lost his bearings in a sudden storm and made a forced landing in a zone of flat rock known to geology as the Western Shield. Stepping from his aeroplane, he realized that he was standing on almost solid iron. Looking into the matter further, he discovered that he owned a 100-kilometre-long block of nearly solid iron ore. From almost nothing in 1950, Australia's estimated reserves of iron ore rose to 20 billion tonnes in 1960. By the end of the 1960s, Hancock alone controlled iron ore reserves greater than those of the United States and Canada combined. That is a lot of iron ore.

But it was only the beginning. In dizzying succession mineral deposits were found all over the place – bauxite, nickel, manganese, uranium, copper, lead, diamonds, tin, zinc, zircon, rutile, ilmenite and many others that most of us have never heard of. Almost overnight, people with mining interests made fortunes that were embarrassing to contemplate and impossible to spend. The stock markets went crazy as investors scrambled to grab a piece of the action. In Sydney one broker lost an ear – an ear! – in the frenzied trading that accompanied the constant reports of new discoveries. It was a heady period, and it transformed Australia's fortunes. From a sleepy, good-natured producer of wool, it became a mining colossus, the world's biggest exporter of minerals. As many of the biggest finds were in Western Australia, much of the wealth settled in Perth, the state capital, which is what accounts for all its skyscrapers.

Lang Hancock, the man who started it all, was called to the great iron mountain in the sky in 1992 but in his dotage, it appears, he did that thing that brings dread to the hearts of rich children everywhere: he married his housekeeper, a lady from the Philippines named Rose. According to the morning paper, Hancock's daughter had filed a lawsuit alleging that the widow Rose and the late Mr Hancock had 'lavishly and improperly spent money that was not their own'. Helpfully the article provided a sidebar in which Mrs Hancock's principal assets were listed. These included a $35-million house in a Perth suburb called Mosman Park, complete with the address. It was apparently the grandest residence in the city; the chandeliers alone had cost $3 million. Looking at my map of the city, I realized that Mosman Park was at the far end of a clutch of famously well-heeled suburbs running all the way to Fremantle, and as it was a fine day and I was feeling perky, I decided to walk out.

Well, it's a long way from central Perth to Mosman Park and beyond, that's all I'm saying. I walked for hours, through the leafy sprawl of the University of Western Australia campus and around the sunny foreshore of the Swan River estuary, tracing the sweep of sunny bays and yacht-cluttered coves, and made my way at length into residential zones of startling, showy wealth – Nedlands,

Dalkeith, Peppermint Grove – where palatial houses basked in the penetrating sunshine. These neighbourhoods went on for miles – just street after foot-wearying street of trophy homes, with big gates beside broad drives, patios adorned with Grecian urns on ornate plinths and garages for fleets of cars. It was a stunning demonstration of the proposition that money and taste don't always, or even often, go together. These were the houses of lottery winners, of retailers of the sort who appear in their own television commercials, of people for whom the words 'Peppermint Grove' in an address would not be an embarrassment. I would not suggest for a moment that Australia's nouveaux riches are more distant from refinement than the people of other lands, but the absence of a distinctive architectural vernacular in Australia does mean that people can take their styles from a wider range of sources – principally drive-in banks, casinos, upmarket nursing homes and ski lodges. To see it massed over a spread of miles as in the western suburbs of Perth is certainly an absorbing experience.

I had been walking for nearly three hours when I arrived at a landmark called Chidley Point and realized I had found Mosman Park. I delved in my bag for the newspaper to check the address, and discovered that I had evidently left it on the table at the café in Kings Park. Never mind. I had walked eight or nine miles by now and had seen enough extravagant real estate to last me a lifetime. I vaguely recalled the Hancock house as being on Wellington Street, so I found my way to this sedate thoroughfare and strolled along it. En route I saw perhaps eight houses that looked as if they might contain many million dollars' worth of bricks, mortar, garden ornaments and tinkling chandeliers, but nothing that announced itself unequivocally as the grandest pile in the metropolis. As I stood there, a young woman in shorts and a matching top – a professional dog walker, I supposed – came along behind a frisky dog not much smaller than a pony. She wasn't so much walking the dog as skiing behind it on the soles of her shoes. I stepped into the street to keep from being eaten, but asked as she passed if she knew the Hancock house and she pointed to a place about three doors up. I went and had a look. Considering the cost, I have to say I had expected rather more – a sort of San Simeon meets Liberace's dream mausoleum is what I believe I had in mind – but this was on a smallish lot and was neither particularly tacky nor outstandingly ornate. I studied it for a few minutes, struck by the somewhat tardy thought that although I had voluntarily invested a good deal of exertion to get here, I didn't actually care in the tiniest degree where Rose Hancock dwelled. This notion absorbed, I turned with a thoughtful countenance and continued on my long march to the sea.

Fremantle is an interesting and likeable place. In gold-rush days it was a port of cosmopolitan liveliness, but then it sank into a long period of decrepitude. In the 1970s, it underwent a gentrifying revival as people realized the commercial potential of its large stock of neglected Victorian buildings. So today it is a trendy hangout, a place of latte and gelato and little shops selling things of an arty nature. Everybody is fond of Freo, as they call it. So am I normally, though my enthusiasm was wilting swiftly this day. The afternoon was uncomfortably warm, with no sign of the ameliorating ocean breeze they call the Fremantle Doctor (because it makes you feel better, of course). I had already walked far enough to make my feet smoke when I realized that I still had a good four miles to go, nearly all of it along the busy, charmless, mercilessly shadeless Stirling Highway.

By the time I flopped into central Fremantle, it was late afternoon and I was comprehensively bushed. I went into a pub and downed a beer for medicinal purposes.

'You all right?' said the barmaid.

'Yeah,' I replied. 'Why?'

'Seen your face?'

I knew at once. 'Am I sunburned?' I asked bleakly.

She gave a frank, sympathetic but essentially deeply amused nod.

I peered past her into the mirror behind the bar. Looking back at me, mockingly attired in clothes to match my own, was a cartoon character called Mr Tomato Head. I allowed myself a small sigh. For the next four days, I would be a source of concern to every elderly Western Australian and of amusement to all else. Then for three days more, as my skin flaked and peeled and I took on the look of someone just escaped from a leprosarium, the mood would change to universal horror and revulsion. Waitresses would drop trays; gawkers would walk into lamp-posts; ambulance drivers would slow as they passed and look me over carefully. It would, as always, be a quiet ordeal. In another three or four hours I would be in tender pain. Meanwhile, I was already a small wreck. My feet and legs hurt so much that I wasn't sure they would ever be of service to me again. I was as dirty as a street urchin and rank enough to be buried. And all of this so that I could see a house I had no actual interest in seeing and then walk on to a place that I was now too tired to explore.

But I hardly minded at all. And do you know why? I had seen a monotreme. Life could throw nothing at me that would diminish the thrill of that. Sustained by this thought, I drained my beer, lowered myself gingerly from the bar stool and limped through the staring crowds to see if I could find a taxi to take me back to the city.

In the morning, I took custody of another rental car and set off on the penultimate of my Australian quests. I was on my way to the great jarrah and karri forests of the south-west peninsula. If that sounds a trifle dull, then bear with me please, for these are exceptional trees. They are to the Australian arboreal world what the giant worm of Gippsland is to invertebrates: large, under-appreciated, and mysteriously occurring in only one small area, the south-west corner of Western Australia below Perth. Karris are Australia's sequoias. They attain heights of over 250 feet, but it is their amazing girth – they can be up to fifty feet around and scarcely taper on their climb to their distant crowns – that gives them their majesty. Think of the mightiest, most graceful sycamore you have ever seen, then triple it in every dimension and you have pretty well got a karri.

The dominant species of the region, however, is the handsome and noble jarrah, slightly less massive than the karri, but still enormous and arresting. It is something of a miracle that jarrahs are left at all, for it is just about the unluckiest tree alive. The specialization that allowed it to flourish in the first place was also its tragic undoing, for jarrah has the poor luck to thrive in soils rich in bauxite, and bauxite is a very valuable mineral. In the 1950s mining companies discovered the connection and came almost simultaneously to the exhilarating realization that they could knock down and sell the jarrah for quite a lot of money, then dig out all that gorgeously commercial bauxite underneath, thus getting two lots of income from

one plot of land. Life doesn't get much better than that –
so long, of course, as your conscience can bear the thought
of removing large stands of prime forest of a type that
occurs nowhere else and replacing them with large,
unsightly gashes. Mining engineers – these people are so
ingenious – got around this problem by having no
consciences at all. Brilliant!

In this they were long aided by their colleagues in the
forestry industry. Australian foresters, it must be said, do
rather like to chop down a tree. You can't entirely blame
them – it is after all how they make their livelihood – and
unquestionably they are less reckless than in former times,
but they were allowed to get away with so much for so
long that they still need the most attentive watching. These
are people, you must understand, who could describe
clear-cutting as 'the full sunlight method of regeneration'
and not blush. Just to ease you into a sense of perspective
here, Australia is the least wooded continent (Antarctica
excluded, of course) and yet it is also the world's largest
exporter of woodchips. Now I am no authority, and for all
I know this is all managed with the most exacting care
(that is certainly the impression the Australian
Department of Conservation and Land Management
strives to create), but it does seem to me that there is a
certain mathematical discrepancy between having very few
trees on the one hand and the world's liveliest chip-
exporting industry on the other. Anyway, there is much
less jarrah forest than there once was, and even a good deal
less of the rare and clearly irreplaceable karri forests.
According to William J. Lines, between 1976 and 1993
Australia lost a quarter of its karri forests to woodchipping.
To woodchipping! I repeat: these people need watching.

Even without its singular forests, the south-west corner

of Australia would be an area of interest. Stretching for about 180 miles from Cape Naturaliste on the Indian Ocean to Cape Knob on the Southern Ocean, it is another of those unexpected intrusions of comparative lushness that occur in Australia from time to time. It's rather like the Barossa Valley of South Australia, but so obscure and unassuming that it doesn't even have a name. Nearly everywhere you go in Australia you are provided with a handy label to fix your bearings – Sunshine Coast, Northern Tropics, Mornington Peninsula, Atherton Tablelands – but the zippiest appellation I saw for this region was 'the Southern corner of Western Australia'. I think they need to work on that a little. However, of the land itself and the seas beyond, no improvements are necessary.

Perhaps it was because my Australian adventure was nearly at an end and I was feeling consequently affectionate, or maybe because I had spent so much of the previous couple of weeks at large in arid landscapes, or perhaps simply because I knew almost nothing of the area (hardly anyone outside Western Australia does) and thus had no expectations to disappoint, but I was charmed at once. It was as if it had been assembled from the most pleasant, least showy parts of Europe and North America: lowland Scotland, the Meuse Valley of Belgium, Michigan's upper peninsula, Wisconsin's dairyland, Shropshire or Herefordshire in England – nice parts of the world but nothing you would normally travel vast distances to savour. This wasn't a world-class landscape, but it was an engagingly snug and wholesome one. I dubbed it – and offer it here for free pending the invention of something better – the Pleasant Peninsula. ('Where everything is . . . *rather nice!*')

So I spent an agreeable day – a pleasant day – motoring through woods and rolling fields, past orderly orchards and bottle-green vineyards, on winding country roads forever running down to a blue and sunny sea. It was a blessed little realm. I stopped often in the country towns – Donnybrook, Bridgetown, Busselton, Margaret River – to sit with a cup of coffee or browse through stacks of second-hand books or take a walk along a wooden pier or duney foreshore.

I stayed the night in Manjimup, on the edge of the southern woodlands, and in the morning rose early and refreshed, and set off without delay in the direction of Shannon and Mount Frankland National Parks. Within minutes I was in cool, green forests of erect and stately grandeur. This was very promising indeed. I was headed for a place called the Valley of the Giants, to a recently developed tourist attraction that I had been told not to miss. It's called the Tree Top Walk, and as the name suggests it is an elevated walkway that wanders through the canopy of a grove of tingle trees – yet another of the rare outsized species of eucalypts unique to the region. I had assumed it was essentially a gimmick, but in fact I discovered that tingle trees, for all their immensity, are quite delicate and reliant on the few nutrients to be found in the soil at their bases, and that the constant trampling of visitors' feet was interfering with the breakdown of organic matter, imperilling their well-being. The Tree Top Walk thus not only provided visitors with a novel diversion and an unusual perspective, but also kept them conveniently out of harm's way.

The Tree Top Walk stands a mile or two into coastal forest near the small town of Walpole. I arrived at opening time, but already the car park was crowded and filling fast.

A lot of people were gathered by the entrance and milling around in the little shop. The whole thing is run by the Department of Conservation and Land Management and, like the Desert Park at Alice Springs, it was an impressive example of a government department doing something innovative and doing it extremely well. We could do with these people back in the Known World.

Well, all I can say is that the Tree Top Walk deserves to be world famous. It consists of a series of cantilevered metal ramps, like industrial catwalks, wandering at exhilarating heights through the uppermost levels of some of the world's most beautiful and imposing trees. The Tree Top Walk is an impressive erection. It runs for almost 2,000 feet and at its highest point stands 120 feet above the ground – a goodly height, believe me, when you are peering over the edge of a waist-high railing. Since the walkway surface is an open grid that lets you look straight down – indeed, more or less compels you to – there is a certain element of rakishness and daring in proceeding along it. I loved it. There are larger trees than the tingle (even the ashes of eastern Australia grow a little higher) and doubtless there are more beautiful trees than the tingle, but I cannot believe that there are any trees in the world that are both. Redwoods may reach giddier heights, but their canopy is nothing – like a broom handle with nails hammered into it. Tingles, because they are broad-leafed, spread out with luxuriant profusion. Makes all the difference. You simply won't find a better tree.

I went around twice, charmed and appreciative. It wasn't until I was halfway around the second time that I realized that actually it was quite crowded and that, like everyone else, I was sharing the experience with those around me, pointing out things to strangers and in turn allowing them to point things out to me. I am seldom drawn to strange children but I found myself now talking to two young boys – bright young brothers, about ten and twelve, on holiday from Melbourne with their parents – trying to decide between us whether there were koalas in Western Australia and whether we might therefore spy any up here in the treetops. Then their father joined us and we discussed it with him. Then the mother came along and took one look at me. 'You know, you're awfully sunburnt,' she said with concern, and offered me some cream from her bag. I declined, but was touched nonetheless.

It was oddly heart-warming to realize that we were all having this experience together, sharing our observations and pharmaceutical products. It reminded me very much of my stroll through the parks of Adelaide on Australia Day when hundreds of people seemed to be – effectively were – picnicking together. This had that same spirit of shared undertaking. In the most interesting and elemental anthropological sense, this was a social occasion.

Even then, it didn't quite register with me how important a component this is in Australian life until I descended to ground level and strolled through an area called the Ancient Empire. This consisted of a protective boardwalk path that made a large and inviting loop through another part of the same woods. It was in its way nearly as diverting as the Tree Top Walk – to stand at the foot of a circle of tingle trees, head craned to take in their impossibly remote heights, is an experience almost as dizzying as wandering on foot through the leafy canopy – but because the boardwalk wasn't novel and lofty, no one came here. I had it entirely to myself, but rather than feeling pleased to have found solitude, as I normally would, I felt suddenly quite lonely. 'Hey, everybody!' I wanted to call. 'Come down and see this! It's great. Come down and be with me! Somebody! Please!!'

But of course I said no such thing. Instead I had a long and respectful look around. It struck me in a moment's idle thinking that this forest was quite an apt metaphor for Australia. It was to the arboreal world what Charles Kingsford Smith was to aviation or the Aborigines were to prehistory – unaccountably overlooked. It seemed amazing to me, in any case, that there could exist in this one confined area some of the rarest and mightiest broad-leafed trees on earth, forming a forest of consummate and singular beauty, and hardly anyone outside Australia has even heard of them. But that is the thing about Australia, of course – that it is packed with unappreciated wonders.

And with that thought in mind, I set off now for what was, in its quiet way, one of the most amazing wonders of all.

Chapter

NINETEEN

Earlier on this trip, while driving back to Sydney from Surfers Paradise, I stopped for coffee in a pleasant college town called Armidale in north-eastern New South Wales. Indulging myself in a brief amble through its attractive streets, I happened on an official-looking building called the Mineral Resources Administration and – I don't know why exactly – I went in. I had long wondered why there is such an abundance of mineral wealth in Australia and not, say, in my back garden, and I went in thinking maybe somebody could tell me. One of the delights of poking about journalistically in a cheerful and open society like Australia's is that you can just turn up in places like the Mineral Resources Administration with nothing very particular in mind, and people will invite you in and answer any questions you care to put to them.

The upshot is that I spent a half hour with an obliging

geologist named Harvey Henley who told me that in fact Australia is not really fantastically overendowed with mineral resources – at least not on the basis of mineral wealth per square metre. It's just that Australia has a lot of square metres, relatively few people and a short history, so that much of the country is still unexplored and unexamined. To put matters in perspective for me, he took me through to his work area to show me what he does for a living. He makes geological maps, large, impressively detailed ones, rolled like blueprints, which he spread across a table with a certain respectful care, as if they were old prints. Even an untrained eye could see that they recorded every lump and ruffle on the landscape, with particular emphasis on pools of mineralogical splendour. Each, he explained, covered a portion of New South Wales sixty kilometres long by forty wide and took ten to fifteen man-years to produce. The Armidale team was in the process of surveying eighty such blocks.

'Big job,' I said, impressed.

'You bet. But we're finding new stuff all the time.' He drew back one map to expose the one beneath. 'That,' he said, tapping a portion of the map shaded in a restful pastel tone, 'is a new mine at a place called Cadice Hill near Orange. It contains about 200 million tonnes of mineral-bearing sands.'

'And that's good, is it?'

'That's very good.'

'So,' I said thoughtfully, trying to get a grasp on all this, 'if it takes ten to fifteen man-years to produce one map covering a block of land sixty kilometres by forty, and if there are eight million square kilometres in Australia, then how much of the country has been properly surveyed?'

He looked at me as if I had asked a very basic question.

'Oh, hardly any.'

I found this quite an arresting thought. 'Really?' I said.

'Sure.'

'So,' I went on, still thoughtful, 'if you parachuted me into some random spot in the outback, into the Strzelecki Desert or something, I would be landing on a patch of land that had never been surveyed?'

'Formally surveyed? Almost certainly.'

I gave a moment to taking this aboard. 'So just how much mineral wealth might be left out there to be discovered?'

He looked at me with the happy beam of a man whose work will never be completed. 'No one knows,' he said. 'Impossible to say.'

Now hold that thought just for a moment while I take you with me onto the lonely coastal highway from Perth north towards Darwin, 4,163 kilometres away. Here, near the coast, there are a very few towns and quite a lot of visible farming, but head inland over the low, pale green hills to the right and with amazing swiftness you will find yourself in a murderous and confusing emptiness. And nobody really knows what is out there. I find that a terribly exciting thought. Even now people still sometimes make the sort of stupefying, effortless finds that can only happen in uncharted country. Just recently, some beaming fellow had come in from the western deserts cradling a solid gold nugget weighing sixty pounds. It was nearly the largest such nugget ever found, and it was just lying in the desert. Goodness!

Mining experts may study satellite images and the sort of charts generated by repeated aeroplane passes at low altitudes ('fantasy maps' as Harvey Henley termed them for me, just a touch dismissively), but up-close investigations, the kind that involve wandering through dried riverbeds and taking rocks away for later analysis, have barely begun. The problem lies not just in the vastness of Australia – though that is daunting enough, goodness knows – but in the risks involved in wandering into unknown country. As the British palaeontologist Richard Fortey has written: 'Tracks appear briefly, only to disappear into ambiguous washes, where the bewildered and anxious passenger is instructed to hang out the window to look for broken twigs which might indicate where a vehicle has passed before . . . It is appallingly easy to get lost.'

In such an environment rumours of fabulous, unexploited finds naturally proliferate. The most famous story concerns a man named Harold Bell Lasseter, who in the 1920s claimed to have stumbled on a gold reef some ten miles long in the central deserts thirty years before, but for various reasons beyond his control had neglected to return to claim it. Although it seems an unlikely tale, the story evidently had greater plausibility than a bare description would suggest. In any case, Lasseter managed to persuade several sceptical businessmen and even some large corporations (General Motors, for one) to underwrite an expedition, which set off from Alice Springs in 1930. After several weeks of confused and fruitless tramping around, Lasseter's backers began to lose confidence. One by one his team members abandoned him, until Lasseter was on his own. One night his two camels bolted. Lost and on foot, he died a lonely and wretched death. I dare say he drank some urine. In any case, he never found the gold. People are searching for it yet.

Although Lasseter was almost certainly either sorely deluded or a charlatan, the idea of there being a vast reef of gold just sitting in the desert is not at all beyond the bounds of reasonable possibility. Nor is it as implausible as it seems that people might make such a fabulous find and then, as it were, mislay it. Others far more meticulous and attentive than Lasseter have misplaced important discoveries in the desert. Such was the case of Stan Awramik, a geologist who was poking about in the low, irregular, exceedingly hot hills of the Pilbara, a region of north-western Australia still largely unexplored, when he came upon an outcrop of rocks bearing tiny fossilized organisms called stromatolites dating back to the dawn of life some 3.5 billion years ago. At the time of Awramik's discovery they were the most ancient fossils yet found on earth. From a scientific point of view, these rocks were the equivalent of Lasseter's elusive gold reef. Awramik collected some samples and made his way back to civilization. But when he returned to the Pilbara to pursue his searches, he couldn't find the rock outcrop again. It had just vanished into an endless sameness of low hills. Somewhere out there those original stromatolites still wait to be rediscovered. It could as easily have been gold.

Since that time other stromatolite beds of similar or greater venerability have been found elsewhere, both in Australia and further afield. Meanwhile, however, in the warm, shallow waters of Shark Bay, on a lonely stretch of the Western Australian coast, scientists found something no less extraordinary, and even more unexpected. They found a community of *living* stromatolites – colonies of lichen-like formations that quietly but perfectly replicate the conditions that existed on earth when life was in its infancy. It was this that I was on my way to see.

It's about an eight-hour drive from Perth north to Shark Bay. In early afternoon, near a place called Dongara, the road curved down towards the sea and I began at last to get glimpses of blue ocean. This section of Western Australia is called the Batavia Coast, which, as it happens, was something else I was interested to look into. At Geraldton, the only town worthy of the name (certainly the only place with more than one set of traffic lights) for 600 miles, I stopped for coffee and parked by chance outside a small maritime museum in the town centre. I hesitated by the door, torn between the need to keep moving and a curiosity to see what was in there, then impulsively stepped in, and how glad I was I did, for the museum was devoted in large part to the little-known story of the ship that gave the coast its name – a forgotten merchant vessel called the *Batavia*, which blundered onto Australian shores in 1629 and in so doing set in motion one of the more bizarre and unlikely episodes in the annals of maritime affairs. Most Australian histories give it no more than a footnote (Manning Clark does not mention it at all), which is a little surprising because it was the first sojourn by Europeans on Australian soil, and it remains the greatest slaughter of white people in Australian history. But I get ahead of myself.

In 1629, when our story begins, Dutch mariners had only recently discovered that the swiftest way to the East Indies from Europe was not to make a beeline across the Indian Ocean after rounding Africa's Cape of Good Hope, but to drop down to the fortieth parallel – the famous Roaring Forties – and let those lively winds convey you eastward. The approach worked well so long, of course, as you managed not to crash into Australia. Alas, this was the fate that befell Captain Francisco Pelsaert, two hours before dawn in early June 1629, when the *Batavia* ran aground on some sandy impediments called the Abrolhos Islands off Australia's west coast. Almost at once the ship began to break up.

Many of the 360 people aboard drowned in the confusion, but 200 or so managed to struggle ashore. As the sun came up, they found themselves on a desolate sandbar with a few salvaged provisions and exceedingly dim prospects. They were 1,500 miles from Batavia (now Jakarta). Pelsaert ruminated for a while, then announced that he would take a party of men in a longboat and try to row to Batavia – a faint hope but their only one.

He left in charge a man named Jeronimus Cornelisz. What happened next is not entirely certain, but it appears that Cornelisz was both a madman and a religious fanatic – always a dangerous combination. What is certain is that over the next few days he and a few faithful followers slaughtered the bulk of the survivors – 125 men, women and children in all. The few they spared became their slaves – the women to cook and provide sexual favours, the men to fish and toil – except for a small group who escaped to another sandbar a couple of hundred yards away across a difficult channel. There they made such weapons as they could fashion from shells and driftwood, and built a fort to stave off the attacks that Cornelisz and his men occasionally flung at them.

Pelsaert, unaware of the turmoil he had left behind and with quite a lot on his mind already – he had, after all, wrecked a brand new ship, the pride of the Dutch merchant fleet – rowed on to the Timor Sea and miraculously reached Batavia. There his dumbfounded superiors listened to his tale, gave him another ship and ordered him to return at once for survivors.

Five months after all his troubles started, Pelsaert arrived back at the Abrolhos Islands. There, the ever-blundering captain, finding the survivors engaged in a civil war, came within a whisker of supporting the wrong side and losing his ship to the crazed Cornelisz and his desperate band. Eventually, however, he managed to sort out what had happened and to introduce order and justice to the murderous little sandbar. Cornelisz and six henchmen were swiftly hanged. Most of the others were whipped or keelhauled and clapped in chains to be taken back to Batavia for further corrective treatment. But for reasons unknown, Pelsaert decided to go to the considerable trouble of having two of the miscreants – a marine named Wouter Looes and a cabin boy named Jan Pelgrom – rowed to the mainland and marooned there.

On 16 November 1629, they were set down at a place called Red Bluff Beach. What became of the two Dutchmen after that no one knows, but two things are certain. They were the remotest Europeans in the world and the first white Australians.

Red Bluff Beach, I learned from the helpful museum staff, is at a place called Kalbarri, a couple of hours further up the coast, and since it was on the way to Shark Bay I decided to stop there for the night. Kalbarri lies about forty miles down a side road off the North West Coastal Highway, across a green plain covered to every horizon in heathery scrub. It was getting on for evening when I arrived – too late to go looking for the Dutchmen's landing place – so I got a room in a motel near the beach and contented myself with a stroll around the town. Kalbarri was an appealing little place. It dates only from

1952, when some fishermen discovered that the waters offshore teemed with lobster. Until the mid-1970s, when the road in from the North West Coastal Highway was paved, it was essentially cut off from the outside world except by sea. Today fishing remains at the heart of community life, but it has also grown into a small resort. The two seem to coexist very well.

The setting could hardly be bettered. It stands on a big bay, sheltered by long white sandbars. I walked to the front through warm end-of-day sunshine. The Abrolhos Islands were sixty kilometres out to sea – well out of sight of the mainland – but I could clearly see, only a couple of miles down the coast, the headland called Red Bluff, where the two mutineers were marooned.

As I strolled along the front, two things caught my notice – that a few hundred yards out in the bay a boat, half sunk, was being towed very slowly into the harbour through a narrow channel between the sandbars, and that crowds of people were gathering to have a look. The biggest cluster of onlookers was on the jetty at what appeared to be the commercial side of the harbour about a mile away. Here on the resort side of the harbour there were lots of people, too – sitting on the bonnets of cars parked along the beach, gazing from the balconies of seafront homes and apartment houses, coming out of shops and pubs to stand and watch. About it all, there was a strange, almost eerie silence.

I asked a man sitting on a car bonnet what was going on. 'Oh, it's a fishing boat that got holed on a reef last night,' he explained. The accident had happened at two thirty in the morning, far out to sea, and for a time it looked as if the boat might be in serious peril. To add to the tension, the skipper had his seven-year-old son with him – evidently taken out with him as a treat. Three other local fishing boats had gone out to rescue them. I looked at my watch. They'd have been at it for sixteen hours by now. I remarked on this to my informant and he gave a small smile, as if in apology. 'It's been a long day for the town,' he said. 'We've been on a bit of a knife-edge. Still, it seems to have turned out all right.'

Kalbarri has a year-round population of 1,500, and I would guess that two-thirds of the town was there. As the boat came through the sandbars and its safety seemed assured at last, people from all sides of the harbour clapped warmly, as if welcoming home the winner of a regatta, and called encouragement. I thought that was wonderful – that a whole town would turn out to watch a stricken local fishing boat brought in. If I handed out fivers, I'm sure I couldn't find a thousand people to watch me limp into port after a night of peril. I decided I liked Kalbarri very much.

In the morning, I rose early and drove the couple of miles along the coast to Red Bluff Beach where I had been told I would find a cairn marking the spot where the two naughty Dutchmen had been left to their lonely fate. It was a dramatic spot – a very large rock platform bashed by waves, which threw spray everywhere. Leading off to one side was a long duney beach marked at intervals with signs saying: 'Caution – Dangerous Rips'. The ocean was a bright turquoise, and the long beach was being pounded by a fury of big waves.

I had a good hunt around the area but couldn't find the cairn anywhere, and there was no one out at this hour to ask except for a couple way down the beach exercising a bouncy dog. It hardly mattered. Whoever built the cairn had to have done so long after the fact and was almost certainly guessing. So I just enjoyed the sunshine and sea-freshened air, and realized with a touch of surprise that the idea of being stranded here wasn't entirely without appeal. It was a lovely spot. The sea was lavishly fruitful and the hills behind abounded in materials for building. Looes and Pelgrom – again for mysterious reasons – were quite generously endowed by Pelsaert. They were left with a small boat, some food and water, a few tools and some trinkets with which to trade with the natives, if any could be found. There were certainly far worse places in the world to see out your days – not least a fetid and malarial dungeon in Batavia, which was their alternative fate. Assuming cordial relations with the natives, you could make quite a nice life for yourself here.

I was quite taken with the notion – not least because it was so patently a real possibility here. The coastline of Western Australia north from Perth is astoundingly beautiful and almost entirely untouched by development. Beyond Kalbarri there is not a single town for some 200 miles to Carnarvon, and just one side road to the sea – the one I was heading for at Shark Bay. Beyond Carnarvon, it's much the same for another 1,800 miles to Darwin – just a coastline of undisturbed splendour dotted at distant intervals with small communities. Altogether, Western Australia has some 7,800 miles of coastline and only about three dozen coastal communities, even including those along the south-western peninsula from which I had just come.

That is, of course, why it took so long to discover the stromatolites at Shark Bay. Though they are there on the edge of an accessible shell beach, for any fool to see, they weren't noticed by anyone until 1954, and not identified by science for another decade. But then with almost 23,000 miles of Australian coastline to investigate, it takes time to get to it all.

From Kalbarri it was forty miles back to the North West Coastal Highway – there is still just the one road in and out – and then another hundred or so miles on to Shark Bay. In two and a half hours I passed just three other cars and a solitary barrelling road train. At one point I saw a couple of mysterious dots in the road far ahead. It turned out to be two workmen, digging a hole in the middle of the highway and protected from either direction by a single orange plastic cone placed in the centre of the road about five feet from where they worked. This was, you understand, the main west coast highway. It was an arresting reminder of just how far from anywhere I was. This was about as far from the main population centres as you can get in Australia. By road from where I was now, it was over 4,000 kilometres to Sydney and nearer 5,000 to Brisbane. Even Alice Springs, the nearest town to the east, was 4,000 highway kilometres away, because of the way the roads ran. At length, in the middle of a featureless nowhere, I came to the turnoff for Shark Bay. I followed a newly paved side road for a few miles to another, unpaved side road, which passed through a marshy landscape for another mile or so. It ended at an old telegraph repeater station at a place called Hamelin Pool – a complex of white wooden buildings, one of which now announced itself as a museum, another as a café and gift shop.

The car park had only two or three other cars in it, but as I stood reading an information board two coaches pulled up in convoy, wheezed to a pneumatic halt and almost at once began disembarking streams of passengers – all white-haired, camera-toting and blinking confusedly under the impossible glare of sun. They appeared to be from all over – America, Britain, Holland, Scandinavia. Having come this far, I didn't wish to share the experience with a hundred twittering strangers, and I set off for the beach in a brisk stroll along a chalky track. It was amazingly hot. A breeze was running in from the sea, but it seemed only to bring more heat. After about half a mile the track brought me to a sumptuously sunny bay, flat calm and of the deepest aquamarine. At some distance across the water a long sandbar ran in a lazy curve out to sea. This, I gathered, was the Fauré Sill – a thirty-mile-long dune barrier that nearly encloses the bay and gives it its special character, namely warm, shallow, very saline waters of the sort that once prevailed across the planet when stromatolites were king.

Nowhere in any direction was there a sign of human intrusion except directly ahead where a nifty wooden walkway zigzagged for 150 feet or so out into the bay over some low, dark, primeval-looking masses that didn't quite break the water's calm surface. I had found my living stromatolites. Eagerly I boarded the walkway and followed it out to the first cluster of shapes. The water was as transparent as glass and only three or four feet deep.

Stromatolites are not easy to describe. They are of so primitive a nature that they don't even adopt regular shapes in the way, say, crystals do. Stromatolites just, as it were, blob out. Nearer the shore they formed large, slightly undulant platforms – rather like very old asphalt. Further out they were arrayed as individual clumps that brought to mind very large cow-pats, or perhaps the dung of a particularly troubled elephant. Most books refer to them as club-shaped or cauliflower-shaped or even columnar. In fact, they are shapeless grey-black blobs, without character or lustre.

It has to be immediately conceded that a stromatolite formation is not a handsome or striking sight. I can almost guarantee that your reaction upon seeing a bed of living stromatolites for the first time will be to say 'Hmm' in the vague, ruminative, cautiously favourable tone you would use if you were given a canapé that tasted better than it looked but not so good that you wanted another right away, or possibly ever. It is a sound that says: 'Well, I'll be.'

So it's not the sight of stromatolites that makes them exciting. It's the *idea* of them – and in this respect they are peerless. Well, imagine it. You are looking at living rocks – quietly functioning replicas of the very first organic structures ever to appear on earth. You are experiencing the world as it was 3.5 billion years ago – more than three-quarters of the way back to the moment of terrestrial creation. Now if that is not an exciting thought, I don't know what is. As the aforementioned palaeontologist Richard Fortey has put it: 'This is truly time travelling, and if the world were attuned to its real wonders this sight would be as well-known as the pyramids of Giza.' Quite right.

Stromatolites are rather like corals in that all of their life is on the surface, and that most of what you are looking at is the dead mass of earlier generations. If you peer, you can sometimes see tiny bubbles of oxygen rising in streams from the formations. This is the stromatolite's only trick and it isn't much, but it is what made life as we know it possible. The bubbles are produced by primitive algae-like micro-organisms called cyanobacteria, which live on the surface of the rocks – about three billion of them to the square yard, to save you counting – each of them capturing a molecule of carbon dioxide and a tiny beat of energy from the sun and combining them to fuel its unimaginably modest ambitions to exist, to live. The by-product of this very simple process is the faintest puff of oxygen. But get enough stromatolites respiring away over a long enough period and you can change the world. For two billion years this is all the life there was on earth, but in that time the stromatolites raised the oxygen level in the atmosphere to 20 per cent – enough to allow the development of other, more complex life forms: me, for instance. My gratitude was real.

The chemical process involved in this makes the little cells very slightly sticky. Tiny motes of dust and other sediments cling to their surfaces and these slowly bind and accrete into the rocks I was looking at now. The stromatolites thrive here not so much because the conditions are particularly amenable to them as because they are discouraging to other creatures. The reason stromatolites don't exist elsewhere is that they would either be washed away by stronger tides or eaten. Here nothing else can survive the bitter salt waters, so there is nothing to graze the stromatolites away.

That stromatolites gave rise to life on earth, then became a food themselves and were eaten out of existence has a certain irony, of course. Something not entirely unlike that happened to me now, for as I stood studying the crystalline waters the elderly day trippers could be heard coming down the track, and a few minutes later the spryer among them began to arrive on the boardwalk. A woman in a Miami Dolphins eyeshade took a position beside me, stared at the water for some moments, waved away a couple of flies, then regarded her husband and in a voice that would have drowned the clang of a steelworks said: 'Are you telling me we just crossed a *continent* for *this*?'

I was feeling charitably disposed, so I turned to her with an understanding smile and with all the gentleness and tact I could muster I endeavoured to ease her into a position of appreciation for this marvel that lay at our feet. I saluted her perceptiveness in recognizing that stromatolites were not much to behold, but explained how their diligent, infinitesimal chemical twitchings, over a span of unimaginable duration, made the world the green and lovely place it is. I pointed out too that at only two other places on earth have such living formations been found – one elsewhere in Australia, the other off a remote coral cay in the Bahamas, both much smaller and practically inaccessible – so that this was the only place in the world where visitors could with relative ease examine these singular creations in their full understated glory. So in fact, I concluded – and here I offered my warmest, most ingratiating smile – this really *was* worth crossing a continent for.

She listened with what I can only call an air of startled submissiveness, never taking her gaze from my face. Then she touched a hand to my forearm and said: 'Did you know that you have the most terrible sunburn?'

I took a walk along the neighbouring shell beach until the flies made it impossible to persevere, then wandered back to the telegraph station. The museum was locked and in darkness, so I went to the café. The trippers, I gathered, had stopped for refreshments because the lady in charge was busy rounding up cups and plates. I wondered in passing how she managed out here to feed coachloads of people 140 miles from the nearest supermarket.

'Yes, love?' she said brightly as she passed.

'I was wondering if it's possible to see the museum.'

'Course it is. I'll get Mike to take you.'

Mike was Mike Cantrall, an equally cheery middle-aged fellow with a raffish earring and an easygoing manner, who emerged from the kitchen wiping his hands on a tea towel and looking pleased to be excused dishwashing duty. He took me to the museum and with some difficulty unlocked the door. The museum was small and airless and felt as if it hadn't been opened for months – he told me that not many visitors asked to see it – but entirely charming. One room was devoted mostly to stromatolites. It had a fish tank with a stromatolite quietly bubbling away in it – the only one in the world in captivity, apparently. On an old TV and VCR he showed me a four-minute video, which gave a concise rundown on what stromatolites were and how they were formed. Then he picked up a brick-sized fragment of old stromatolite and passed it to me and I made the appropriate expressions of surprise at how heavy it was.

The rest of the museum was given over to its days as a telecommunications outpost – first for telegraph and then for telephones. It was a great deal more appealing than I had expected it to be, not least because one of the walls was dominated by a large photograph of a linesman, Adgee Cross by name, standing at the top of a ladder buck naked, repairing a telegraph line and looking for all the world as if this were absolutely the correct attire for telegraph repairs in the outback. He was naked, Mike told me, because he had just swum the Murchison River with his ladder and didn't want to get his clothes wet. I didn't say anything, but the thought crossed my mind that wet clothes would dry out in minutes in the desert, whereas boots – the one thing he had kept on – would stay wet for hours. My suspicion is that Adgee Cross did his line repairs naked because he liked to. To which I say: why not?

I also learned the happy story of Mrs Lillian O'Donahue who was a telephone operator here in the days before automated telephone exchanges. At Carnarvon up the road was a big satellite dish that NASA used until the 1970s to track spacecraft as they passed over the Indian Ocean. During a mission in 1964 the communications link between the Carnarvon dish and a tracking station near Adelaide broke down, and all messages had to be routed through Mrs O'Donahue and her ancient equipment. Through one long, hot night Mrs O'Donahue sat at her switchboard, carefully recording strings of coded messages from one outpost and passing them on to the other. Each time the Gemini craft passed over southern skies the fate of the mission – I just love this – was in the devoted hands of an unassuming little old lady sitting in a small white building miles down a dusty track on the west Australian coast. She made $6 in overtime money, Mike told me. I loved that, too.

When we emerged and Mike had locked the door, we walked together across the car park. I asked him how he had come to be in this lonely place. He told me that he and his wife, Val – the cheery lady behind the counter – had been there just three weeks. They were novice grey nomads – retirees (often these days early retirees) who sell up, buy a motorhome of some description and spend their lives on the open road, stopping from time to time to earn a little money, but never tied to anywhere and essentially ever on the move. Six months earlier this would have seemed to me the dreariest punishment imaginable – endlessly driving across a landscape that is mostly hot and dry and empty. But now I understood completely. All that emptiness and dazzling light has a seductive quality that you might actually never tire of – an amazing thought. Besides, Australia is just so full of surprises. There is always something just down the road – a treetop walk, a beach harbouring ancient life forms, museums celebrating improbable Dutch shipwrecks or naked telegraph repairmen, really nice people like Mike and Val Cantrall, a fishing village turning out to see a stricken ship limp home. You never know what it's going to be but it is nearly always pretty good. Maybe it was just my mood at the time, but I felt I could keep this up for a good long while yet.

So I thanked Mike for showing me around and returned to my glinting vehicle. Even from a distance I could see it was going to be unbearably hot inside, so I opened the doors to air it a little and went with my book of maps to the shade of a bent tree beside the track to the beach. I don't know why I bothered exactly because the only way back to Perth was the way I had come, along the long and empty North West Coastal Highway. But as I stood there, I flipped idly through the other pages of Western Australia – it's so big it needs several – and my eye was caught by a patch of highlighted landscape very near the Northern Territory border. It was a range of hills called, with un-improvable melody, the Bungle Bungles. I had only lately read about these. The Bungle Bungles are an isolated sandstone massif where eons of harsh, dry winds have carved the landscape into weird shapes – spindly pinnacles, acres of plump domes, wave walls. The whole extends to about a thousand square miles, yet, according to the book *Australia: A Continent Revealed*, these extraordinary formations 'were not generally known until the 1980s'. Think of it. One of the natural wonders of the world, covering an area the size of an English county, was unvisited and essentially unknown until less than twenty years ago.

I had a sudden powerful impulse to go there. When would I be this close again? Besides, it would be a chance to drive into the Pilbara and visit little Marble Bar, famous as the hottest town in Australia. I could see the landscape where Stan Awramik found and lost his fossilized stromatolites. From there it was but a hop along the Victoria Highway to Darwin. The wet season would be over soon, so I could go to Kakadu National Park – said to be a wonder, but a virtual lake when I had been in the area – and maybe even cross Queensland to visit Cooktown at last. Why, I could do this for ever.

But of course this was just a fantasy, born of perhaps a little too much sun, a natural longing not to have to retrace my steps along 450 miles of lonely highway back to Perth, and a genuine reluctance to bring this adventure to a close just yet. I made callipers of my fingers to measure the distance and was both appalled and hardly surprised at all to find that it was 1,600 miles to the turnoff for the Bungle Bungles – plus another hundred miles or so over rough back-country tracks on which I was neither insured nor safe. Here I was halfway up the west Australian coast, on the very edge of the world, and there was still 1,600 miles of emptiness to an attraction in the same state. What a preposterously outsized country this was.

But that is of course the thing about Australia – that there is such a lot to find in it, but such a lot of it to find it in. You could never see the half of it. Idly I wondered what my wife would say if I called home and announced: 'Honey, we're selling the house and buying an Australian motorhome. We're off to see the Bungle Bungles!' I didn't think it would fly, frankly, so I shut the car doors, climbed into the driver's seat and began the long journey back to Perth.

I drove in the gloomy frame of mind that overtakes me at the end of every big trip. In another day or two I would be back in New Hampshire and all these experiences would march off as in a Disney film to the dusty attic of my brain and try to find space for themselves amid all the ridiculous accumulated clutter of half a century's disordered living. Before long, I would be thinking: 'Now what was the name of that place where I saw the Big Lobster?' Then: 'Didn't I go to Tasmania? Are you quite sure? Let me see the book.' Then finally: 'The Prime Minister of Australia? No, sorry. No idea.'

It seemed a particularly melancholy notion to me that life would go on in Australia and I would hear almost nothing of it. I would never know who ended up with the Hancock millions. I would never learn if anyone found out what became of that poor American couple stranded on the Great Barrier Reef. Chinese immigrants might wade ashore and ask for cabs, and I would never hear of it. Crocodiles would attack, bush fires would rage, ministers would depart in shame, amazing things would be found in the desert, and possibly lost again, and word of none of this would reach my ears. Life in Australia would go on and I would hear nothing, because once you leave Australia, Australia ceases to be. What a strange, sad thought that is.

I can understand it, of course. Australia is mostly empty and a long way away. Its population is small and its role in the world consequently peripheral. It doesn't have coups, recklessly overfish, arm disagreeable despots, grow coca in provocative quantities or throw its weight around in a brash and unseemly manner. It is stable and peaceful and good. It doesn't need watching, and so we don't. But I will tell you this: the loss is entirely ours.

You see, Australia is an interesting place. It truly is. And that really is all I'm saying.

Bibliography

Attenborough, David, *The Private Life of Plants*. Princeton: Princeton University Press, 1995.

Bates, Daisy, *The Passing of the Aborigines*. New York: Pocket Books, 1973.

Berndt, R. M. and C. H., *The World of the First Australians*. Sydney: Lansdown Press, 1981.

Berra, Tim, *A Natural History of Australia*. Sydney: University of New South Wales Press, 1998.

Blainey, Geoffrey, *Triumph of the Nomads: A History of Ancient Australia*. Sydney: Pan Macmillan Australia, 1982.

——, *A Land Half Won*. Melbourne: Sun Books, 1983.

——, *A Shorter History of Australia*. Sydney: Random House Australia, 1997.

Bowden, Tim, *Penelope Goes West: On the Road from Sydney to Margaret River and Back*. Sydney: Allen & Unwin, 1999.

Boyd, Robin, *The Australian Ugliness*. Melbourne: Penguin Books, 1980.

Charles-Picard, Gilbert (ed.), *Larousse Encyclopaedia of Archaeology*. London: Hamlyn, 1972.

Clark, Manning (abridged by Michael Cathcart), *Manning Clark's History of Australia*. Ringwood, Victoria: Penguin Books, 1995.

Diamond, Jared, *Guns, Germs, and Steel: The Fates of Human Societies*. New York: W. W. Norton, 1997.

Edwards, Hugh, *Crocodile Attack in Australia*. Marleston, South Australia: J. B. Books, 1998.

Fagan, Brian M. (ed.), *The Oxford Companion to Archaeology*. New York: Oxford University Press, 1996.

Flannery, Tim, *The Future Eaters: An Ecological History of the Australasian Lands and People*. Sydney: Reed New Holland, 1997.

—— (ed.), *1788: Comprising a Narrative of the Expedition to Botany Bay and a Complete Account of the Settlement at Port Jackson by Watkin Tench*. Melbourne: Text Publishing, 1996.

—— (ed.), *The Explorers*. Melbourne: Text Publishing, 1998.

Fortey, Richard, *Life: An Unauthorised Biography*. London: HarperCollins, 1997.

Gould, Stephen J., *Bully for Brontosaurus: Reflections in Natural History*. London: Hutchinson Radius, 1991.

Gunn, John, *The Defeat of Distance: Qantas 1919–1939*. St Lucia, Queensland: University of Queensland Press, 1985.

Gunther, John, and William H. Forbis, *Inside Australia*. New York: Harper and Row, 1972.

Hall, Timothy. *Flying High: The Story of Hudson Fysh. Qantas and the Trail-Blazing Days of Early Aviation*. Melbourne: Methuen of Australia, 1979.

Hermes, Neil, and Anne Matthews, *Australia: A Continent Revealed*. London: New Holland (Publishers) Ltd., 1996.

Hiddins, Les, *Bush Tucker Man: Stories of Exploration and Survival*. Sydney: ABC Books, 1996.

Hornadge, Bill, *The Australian Slanguage: A Look at What We Say and How We Say It*. Melbourne: Mandarin Books, 1986.

Hough, Richard, *Captain James Cook: A Biography*. New York: W. W. Norton, 1995.

Hughes, Robert, *The Fatal Shore: A History of the Transportation of*

Convicts to Australia, 1787–1868. London: Pan Books, 1988.

James, Clive, *Flying Visits: Postcards from the Observer, 1976–1983*, London: Picador, 1984.

Keneally, Thomas, *Outback*. Sydney: Hodder and Stoughton, 1983.

Lacour-Gayet, Robert, *A Concise History of Australia*. London: Penguin Books, 1976.

Laseron, Charles Francis, *The Face of Australia: The Shaping of a Continent*. Sydney: Angus and Robertson, 1953.

Lewin, Roger, *Principles of Evolution*. Oxford: Blackwell Science, 1997.

Lines, William J., *Taming the Great South Land: A History of the Conquest of Nature in Australia*. Sydney: Allen and Unwin, 1991.

——, *A Long Walk in the Australian Bush*. Athens, Georgia: The University of Georgia Press, 1998.

Low, Tim, *Feral Future: The Untold Story of Australia's Exotic Invaders*. Sydney: Viking, 1999.

Luck, Peter, *Australian Icons: Things That Make Us What We Are*. Melbourne: William Heinemann Australia, 1992.

McGregor, Craig, *Profile of Australia*. London: Penguin Books, 1968.

McIntyre, K. G., *The Secret Discovery of Australia*. London: Souvenir Press, 1977.

MacKenzie, Jeanne, *Australian Paradox*. Melbourne: F. W. Cheshire, 1961.

Mackersey, Ian, *Smithy: The Life of Sir Charles Kingsford Smith*. Sydney: Little, Brown and Co., 1998.

McLaren, Glen, *Beyond Leichhardt: Bushcraft and the Exploration of Australia*. Fremantle: Fremantle Arts Centre Press, 1996.

Malouf, David, *A Spirit of Play: The Making of Australian Consciousness*. Sydney: ABC Books, 1998.

Marshall, Sam, *Luna Park: Just for Fun*. Sydney: Luna Park Reserve Trust, 1995.

Moorehead, Alan, *Rum Jungle*. New York: Charles Scribner's Sons, 1954.

——, *Cooper's Creek*. London: Hamish Hamilton, 1963.

——, *The Fatal Impact: An Account of the Invasion of the South Pacific, 1767–1840*. New York: Harper and Row, 1966.

Moorhouse, Geoffrey, *Sydney*. Sydney: Allen and Unwin, 1999.

Morris, Jan, *Sydney*. London: Viking, 1992.

Morrison, Reg, *Australia: The Four Billion Year Journey of a Continent*. Sydney: Weldon Publishing, 1988.

Mulvaney, John, and Johan Kamminga, *Prehistory of Australia*. Sydney: Allen and Unwin, 1999.

Nile, Richard, and Christian Clerk, *Cultural Atlas of Australia, New Zealand and the South Pacific*. Oxford: Andromeda Books, 1996.

O'Connor, Siobhan (ed.), *The Book of Australia*. Sydney: Watermark Press, 1997.

Pilger, John, *A Secret Country: The Hidden Australia*. New York: Alfred A. Knopf, 1991.

Powell, Alan, *Far Country: A Short History of the Northern Territory*. Melbourne: Melbourne University Press, 1982.

Rich, P. Vickers, *Wildlife of Gondwana*. London: Reed, 1993.

Ritvo, Harriet, *The Platypus and the Mermaid and Other Figments of the Classifying Imagination*. Cambridge, Massachusetts: Harvard University Press, 1998.

Rolls, Eric, *They All Ran Wild: The Animals and Plants That Plague Australia*. Sydney: Angus and Robertson, 1969.

Sampson, Anthony, *Empires of the Sky*. London: Hodder and Stoughton, 1985.

Seal, Graham, *The Lingo: Listening to Australian English*. Sydney: University of New South Wales Press, 1999.

Sheehan, Paul, *Among the Barbarians*. Sydney: Random House Australia, 1998.

Spearritt, Peter, *Sydney's Century: A History*. Sydney: University of New South Wales Press, 2000.

Terrill, Ross, *The Australians*. New York: Simon and Schuster, 1987.

Vizard, Steve, *Two Weeks in Lilliput: Bear-Baiting and Backbiting at the Constitutional Convention*. Sydney: Penguin Books, 1998.

Ward, Russell, *The History of Australia: The Twentieth Century*. New York: Harper and Row, 1977.

White, Mary E., *Australia's Prehistoric Plants*. Sydney: Methuen, 1984.

——, *The Greening of Gondwana: The 400 Million Year Story of Australia's Plants*. Sydney: Reed Australia, 1994.

Bill Bryson is one of the funniest writers alive. For the past two decades he has been entertaining readers with bravura displays of wit and wisdom. His first book, *The Lost Continent*, in which he put small town America under the microscope, was an instant classic of modern travel literature. Although he has returned to America many times since, never has he been more funny, more memorable, more acute than in his most recent book, *The Life and Times of the Thunderbolt Kid*, in which he revisits that most fecund of topics, his childhood. The trials and tribulations of growing up in 1950s America are all here. Des Moines, Iowa, is recreated as a backdrop to a golden age where everything was good for you, including DDT, cigarettes and nuclear fallout. This is as much a story about an almost forgotten, innocent America as it is about Bryson's childhood. The past is a foreign country. They did things differently then . . .

Chapter 1
HOMETOWN

SPRINGFIELD, ILL. (AP) – The State Senate of Illinois yesterday disbanded its Committee on Efficiency and Economy 'for reasons of efficiency and economy'.

– *Des Moines Tribune*, 6 February 1955

IN THE LATE 1950S, the Royal Canadian Air Force produced a booklet on isometrics, a form of exercise that enjoyed a short but devoted vogue with my father. The idea of isometrics was that you used any unyielding object, like a tree or wall, and pressed against it with all your might from various positions to tone and strengthen different groups of muscles. Since everybody already has access to trees and walls, you didn't need to invest in a lot of costly equipment, which I expect was what attracted my dad.

What made it unfortunate in my father's case was that he would do his isometrics on aeroplanes. At some point in every flight, he would stroll back to the galley area or the space by the emergency exit and, taking up the posture of someone trying to budge a very heavy piece of machinery, he would begin to push with his back or shoulder against the outer wall of the plane, pausing occasionally to take deep breaths before returning with quiet, determined grunts to the task.

Since it looked uncannily, if unfathomably, as if he were trying to force a hole in the side of the plane, this naturally drew attention. Businessmen in nearby seats would stare over the tops of their glasses. A stewardess

432

would pop her head out of the galley and likewise stare, but with a certain hard caution, as if remembering some aspect of her training that she had not previously been called upon to implement.

Seeing that he had observers, my father would straighten up, smile genially and begin to outline the engaging principles behind isometrics. Then he would give a demonstration to an audience that swiftly consisted of no one. He seemed curiously incapable of feeling embarrassment in such situations, but that was all right because I felt enough for both of us – indeed, enough for us and all the other passengers, the airline and its employees, and the whole of whatever state we were flying over.

Two things made these undertakings tolerable. The first was that back on solid ground my dad wasn't half as foolish most of the time. The second was that the purpose of these trips was always to go to a big city like Detroit or St Louis, stay in a large hotel and attend ballgames, and that excused a great deal – well, everything, in fact. My dad was a sportswriter for the *Des Moines Register*, which in those days was one of the country's best papers, and often took me along on trips through the Midwest. Sometimes these were car trips to smaller places like Sioux City or Burlington, but at least once a summer we boarded a silvery plane – a huge event in those days – and lumbered through the summery skies, up among the fleecy clouds, to a proper metropolis to watch Major League baseball, the pinnacle of the sport.

Like everything else in those days, baseball was part of a simpler world, and I was allowed to go with him into the changing rooms and dugout and on to the field before games. I have had my hair tousled by Stan Musial. I have handed Willie Mays a ball that had skittered past him as he played catch. I have lent my binoculars to Harvey Kuenn (or possibly it was Billy Hoeft) so that he could scope some busty blonde in the upper deck. Once on a hot July afternoon I sat in a nearly airless clubhouse under the left field grandstand at Wrigley Field in Chicago beside Ernie Banks, the Cubs' great shortstop, as he autographed boxes of new white baseballs (which are, incidentally, the most pleasurably aromatic things on earth, and worth spending time around anyway). Unbidden, I took it upon myself to sit beside him and pass him each new ball. This slowed the process considerably, but he gave a little smile each time and said thank you as if I had done him quite a favour. He was the nicest human being I have ever met. It was like being friends with God.

I can't imagine there has ever been a more gratifying time or place to be alive than America in the 1950s. No country had ever known such prosperity. When the war ended the United States had $26 billion worth of factories that hadn't existed before the war, $140 billion in savings and war bonds just waiting to be spent, no bomb damage and practically no competition. All that American companies had to do was stop making tanks and battleships and start making Buicks and Frigidaires – and boy did they. By 1951, when I came sliding down the chute, almost 90 per cent of American families had refrigerators, and nearly three quarters had washing machines, telephones, vacuum cleaners and gas or electric stoves – things that most of the rest of the world could still only fantasize about. Americans owned 80 per cent of the world's electrical goods, controlled two-thirds of the world's productive capacity, produced over 40 per cent of its electricity, 60 per cent of its oil and 66 per cent of its steel. The 5 per cent of people on Earth who were Americans had more wealth than the other 95 per cent combined.

I don't know of anything that better conveys the happy bounty of the age than a photograph (reproduced in this volume as the endpapers at the front and back of the book) that ran in *Life* magazine two weeks before my birth. It shows the Czekalinski family of Cleveland, Ohio – Steve, Stephanie and two sons, Stephen and Henry – surrounded by the two and a half tons of food that a typical blue-collar family ate in a year. Among the items they were shown with were 450 pounds of flour, 72 pounds of shortening, 56 pounds of butter, 31 chickens, 300 pounds of beef, 25 pounds of carp, 144 pounds of ham, 39 pounds of coffee, 690 pounds of potatoes, 698 quarts of milk, 131 dozen eggs, 180 loaves of bread, and 8½ gallons of ice cream, all purchased on a budget of $25 a week. (Mr Czekalinski made $1.96 an hour as a shipping clerk in a Du Pont factory.) In 1951, the average American ate 50 per cent more than the average European.

No wonder people were happy. Suddenly they were able to have things they had never dreamed of having, and they couldn't believe their luck. There was, too, a wonderful simplicity of desire. It was the last time that people would be thrilled to own a toaster or waffle iron. If you bought a major appliance, you invited the neighbours round to have a look at it. When I was about four my parents bought an Amana Stor-Mor refrigerator and for at least six months it was like an honoured guest in our kitchen. I'm sure they'd have drawn it up to the table at dinner if it hadn't been so heavy. When visitors dropped by unexpectedly, my father would say: 'Oh, Mary, is there any iced tea in the Amana?' Then to the guests he'd add significantly: 'There usually is. It's a Stor-Mor.'

'Oh, a Stor-Mor,' the male visitor would say and raise his eyebrows in the manner of someone who appreciates quality cooling. 'We thought about getting a Stor-Mor ourselves, but in the end we went for a Philco Shur-Kool. Alice loved the E-Z Glide vegetable drawer and you can get a full quart of ice cream in the freezer box. *That* was a big selling point for Wendell Junior, as you can imagine!'

They'd all have a good laugh at that and then sit around drinking iced tea and talking appliances for an hour or so. No human beings had ever been quite this happy before.

People looked forward to the future, too, in ways they never would again. Soon, according to every magazine, we were going to have underwater cities off every coast, space colonies inside giant spheres of glass, atomic trains and airliners, personal jetpacks, a gyrocopter in every driveway, cars that turned into boats or even submarines, moving sidewalks to whisk us effortlessly to schools and offices, dome-roofed automobiles that drove themselves along sleek superhighways allowing Mom, Dad and the two boys (Chip and Bud or Skip and Scooter) to play a board game or wave to a neighbour in a passing gyrocopter or just sit back and enjoy saying some of those delightful words that existed in the Fifties and are no longer heard: *mimeograph, rotisserie, stenographer, ice box, rutabaga, panty raid, bobby sox, sputnik, beatnik, canasta, Cinerama, Moose Lodge, pinochle, daddy-o.*

For those who couldn't wait for underwater cities and self-driving cars, thousands of smaller enrichments were available right now. If you were to avail yourself of all that was on offer from advertisers in a single issue of, let's say, *Popular Science* magazine from, let's say, December 1956, you could, among much else, teach yourself ventriloquism, learn to cut meat (by correspondence or in person at the National School of Meat Cutting in Toledo, Ohio), embark on a lucrative career sharpening skates door to door, arrange to sell fire extinguishers from home, end rupture troubles once and for all, build radios, repair radios, perform on radio, talk on radio to people in different countries and possibly different planets, improve your personality, get a personality, acquire a manly physique, learn to dance, create personalized stationery for profit, or 'make $$$$' in your spare time at home building lawn figures and other novelty ornaments.

My brother, who was normally quite an intelligent human being, once invested in a booklet that promised to teach him how to throw his voice. He would say something unintelligible through rigid lips, then quickly step aside and say, 'That sounded like it came from over there, didn't it?' He also saw an ad in *Mechanics Illustrated* that invited him to enjoy colour television at home for 65 cents plus postage, placed an order and four weeks later received in the mail a multi-coloured sheet of transparent plastic that he was instructed to tape over the television screen and watch the image through.

Having spent the money, my brother refused to concede that it was a touch disappointing. When a human face moved into the pinkish part of the screen or a section of lawn briefly coincided with the green portion, he would leap up in triumph. 'Look! Look! *That's* what colour television's gonna look like,' he would say. 'This is all just experimental, you see.'

In fact, colour television didn't come to our neighbourhood until nearly the end of the decade, when Mr Kiessler on St John's Road bought an enormous RCA Victor Consolette, the flagship of the RCA fleet, for a lot of money. For at least two years his was the only known colour television in private ownership, which made it a fantastic novelty. On Saturday evenings the children of the neighbourhood would steal into his yard and stand in his flowerbeds to watch a programme called *My Living Doll* through the double window behind his sofa. I am pretty certain that Mr Kiessler didn't realize that two dozen children of various ages and sizes were silently watching the TV with him or he wouldn't have played with himself quite so enthusiastically every time Julie Newmar bounded on to the screen. I assumed it was some sort of isometrics.

Every year for nearly forty years, from 1945 until his retirement, my father went to the baseball World Series for the *Register*. It was, by an immeasurably wide margin, the high point of his working year. Not only did he get to live it up for two weeks on expenses in some of the nation's most cosmopolitan and exciting cities – and from Des Moines all cities are cosmopolitan and exciting – but he also got to witness many of the most memorable moments of baseball history: Al Gionfriddo's miraculous one-handed catch of a Joe DiMaggio line drive, Don Larsen's perfect game in 1956, Bill Mazeroski's series-winning home run of 1960. These will mean nothing to you, I know – they would mean nothing to most people these days – but they were moments of near ecstasy that were shared by a nation.

In those days, World Series games were played during

the day, so you had to bunk off school or develop a convenient chest infection ('Jeez, Mom, the teacher said there's a lot of TB going around') if you wanted to see a game. Crowds would lingeringly gather wherever a radio was on or a TV played. Getting to watch or listen to any part of a World Series game, even half an inning at lunchtime, became a kind of illicit thrill. And if you did happen to be there when something monumental occurred, you would remember it for the rest of your life. My father had an uncanny knack for being present at such moments – never more so than in the seminal (and what an apt word that can sometimes be) season of 1951 when our story begins.

In the National League (one of two principal divisions in Major League baseball, the other being the American League) the Brooklyn Dodgers had been cruising towards an easy championship when, in mid-August, their crosstown rivals the New York Giants stirred to life and began a highly improbable comeback. Suddenly the Giants could do no wrong. They won thirty-seven of forty-four games down the home stretch, cutting away at the Dodgers' once-unassailable lead in what began to seem a fateful manner. By mid-September people talked of little else but whether the Dodgers could hold on. Many dropped dead from the heat and excitement. The two teams finished the season in a perfect dead heat, so a three-game playoff series was hastily arranged to determine who would face the American League champions in the World Series. The *Register*, like nearly all distant papers, didn't dispatch a reporter to these impromptu playoffs, but elected to rely on wire services for its coverage until the Series proper got under way.

The playoffs added three days to the nation's exquisite torment. The two teams split the first two games, so it came down to a third, deciding game. At last the Dodgers appeared to recover their former poise and invincibility. They took a comfortable 4–1 lead into the final inning, and needed just three outs to win. But the Giants struck back, scoring a run and putting two more runners on base when Bobby Thomson (born in Glasgow, you may be proud to know) stepped to the plate. What Thomson did that afternoon in the gathering dusk of autumn has been many times voted the greatest moment in baseball history.

'Dodger reliever Ralph Branca threw a pitch that made history yesterday,' one of those present wrote. 'Unfortunately it made history for someone else. Bobby Thomson, the "Flying Scotsman," swatted Branca's second offering over the left field wall for a game-winning home run so momentous, so startling, that it was greeted with a moment's stunned silence.

'Then, when realization of the miracle came, the double-decked stands of the Polo Grounds rocked on their 40-year-old foundations. The Giants had won the pennant, completing one of the unlikeliest comebacks baseball has ever seen.'

The author of those words was my father – who was abruptly, unexpectedly, present for Thomson's moment of majesty. Goodness knows how he had talked the notoriously frugal management of the *Register* into sending him the one thousand one hundred and thirty-two miles from Des Moines to New York for the crucial deciding game – an act of rash expenditure radically out of keeping with decades of careful precedent – or how he had managed to secure credentials and a place in the press box at such a late hour.

But then he had to be there. It was part of his fate, too. I am not *exactly* suggesting that Bobby Thomson hit that home run because my father was there or that he wouldn't have hit it if my father had not been there. All I am saying is that my father was there and Bobby Thomson was there and the home run was hit and these things couldn't have been otherwise.

My father stayed on for the World Series, in which the Yankees beat the Giants fairly easily in six games – there was only so much excitement the world could muster, or take, in a single autumn, I guess – then returned to his usual quiet life in Des Moines. Just over a month later, on a cold, snowy day in early December, his wife went into Mercy Hospital and with very little fuss gave birth to a baby boy: their third child, second son, first superhero. They named him William, after his father. They would call him Billy until he was old enough to ask them not to.

* * *

Apart from baseball's greatest home run and the birth of the Thunderbolt Kid, 1951 was not a hugely eventful year in America. Harry Truman was President, but would shortly make way for Dwight D. Eisenhower. The war in Korea was in full swing and not going well. Julius and Ethel Rosenberg had just been notoriously convicted of spying for the Soviet Union, but would sit in prison for two years more before being taken to the electric chair. In Topeka, Kansas, a mild-mannered black man named Oliver Brown sued the local school board for requiring his daughter to travel twenty-one blocks to an all-black school when a perfectly good white one was just seven blocks away. The case, immortalized as *Brown v. the Board of Education*, would be one of the most far-reaching in modern American history, but wouldn't become known outside jurisprudence circles for another three years when it reached the Supreme Court.

America in 1951 had a population of one hundred and fifty million, slightly more than half as much as today, and only about a quarter as many cars. Men wore hats and ties almost everywhere they went. Women prepared every meal more or less from scratch. Milk came in bottles. The postman came on foot. Total government spending was $50 billion a year, compared with $2,500 billion now.

I Love Lucy made its television debut on 15 October, and Roy Rogers, the singing cowboy, followed in December. In Oak Ridge, Tennessee, that autumn police

443

seized a youth on suspicion of possessing narcotics when he was found with some peculiar brown powder, but he was released when it was shown that it was a new product called instant coffee. Also new, or not quite yet invented, were ball-point pens, fast foods, TV dinners, electric can openers, shopping malls, freeways, supermarkets, suburban sprawl, domestic air conditioning, power steering, automatic transmissions, contact lenses, credit cards, tape recorders, garbage disposals, dishwashers, long-playing records, portable record players, Major League baseball teams west of St Louis, and the hydrogen bomb. Microwave ovens were available, but weighed seven hundred pounds. Jet travel, Velcro, transistor radios and computers smaller than a small building were all still some years off.

Nuclear war was much on people's minds. In New York on Wednesday 5 December, the streets became eerily empty for seven minutes as the city underwent 'the biggest air raid drill of the atomic age', according to *Life* magazine, when a thousand sirens blared and people scrambled (well, actually walked jovially, pausing upon request to pose for photographs) to designated shelters, which meant essentially the inside of any reasonably solid building. *Life*'s photos showed Santa Claus happily leading a group of children out of Macy's, half-lathered men and their barbers trooping out of barber shops, and curvy models from a swimwear shoot shivering and feigning good-natured dismay as they emerged from their studio, secure in the knowledge that a picture in *Life* would do their careers no harm at all. Only restaurant patrons were excused from taking part in the exercise on the grounds that New Yorkers sent from a restaurant without paying were unlikely to be seen again.

Closer to home, in the biggest raid of its type ever undertaken in Des Moines, police arrested nine women for prostitution at the old Cargill Hotel at Seventh and Grand downtown. It was quite an operation. Eighty officers stormed the building just after midnight, but the hotel's resident ladies were nowhere to be found. Only by taking exacting measurements were the police able to discover, after six hours of searching, a cavity behind an upstairs wall. There they found nine goose-pimpled, mostly naked women. All were arrested for prostitution and fined $1,000 each. I can't help wondering if the police would have persevered quite so diligently if it had been naked men they were looking for.

The eighth of December 1951 marked the tenth anniversary of America's entry into the Second World War, and the tenth anniversary plus one day of the Japanese attack on Pearl Harbor. In central Iowa, it was a cold day with light snow and a high temperature of 28°F/−2°C but with the swollen clouds of a blizzard approaching from the west. Des Moines, a city of two hundred thousand people, gained ten new citizens that day – seven boys and three girls – and lost just two to death.

Christmas was in the air. Prosperity was evident

445

everywhere in Christmas ads that year. Cartons of cigarettes bearing sprigs of holly and other seasonal decorations were very popular, as were electrical items of every type. Gadgets were much in vogue. My father bought my mother a hand-operated ice crusher, for creating shaved ice for cocktails, which converted perfectly good ice cubes into a small amount of cool water after twenty minutes of vigorous cranking. It was never used beyond New Year's Eve 1951, but it did grace a corner of the kitchen counter until well into the 1970s.

Tucked among the smiling ads and happy features were hints of deeper anxieties, however. *Reader's Digest* that autumn was asking 'Who Owns Your Child's Mind?' (Teachers with Communist sympathies apparently.) Polio was so rife that even *House Beautiful* ran an article on how to reduce risks for one's children. Among its tips (nearly all ineffective) were to keep all food covered, avoid sitting in cold water or wet bathing suits, get plenty of rest and, above all, be wary of 'admitting new people to the family circle'.

Harper's magazine in December struck a sombre economic note with an article by Nancy B. Mavity on an unsettling new phenomenon, the two-income family, in which husband and wife both went out to work to pay for a more ambitious lifestyle. Mavity's worry was not how women would cope with the demands of employment on top of child-rearing and housework, but rather what this would do to the man's traditional standing as breadwinner. 'I'd be ashamed to let my wife work,' one man told Mavity tartly, and it was clear from her tone that Mavity expected most readers to agree. Remarkably, until the war many women in America had been unable to work whether they wanted to or not. Up until Pearl Harbor, half of the forty-eight states had laws making it illegal to employ a married woman.

In this respect my father was commendably – I would even say enthusiastically – liberal, for there was nothing about my mother's earning capacity that didn't gladden his heart. She, too, worked for the *Des Moines Register*, as the Home Furnishings Editor, in which capacity she provided calm reassurance to two generations of homemakers who were anxious to know whether the time had come for paisley in the bedroom, whether they should have square sofa cushions or round, even whether their house itself passed muster. 'The one-story ranch house is here to stay,' she assured her readers, to presumed cries of relief in the western suburbs, in her last piece before disappearing to have me.

Because they both worked we were better off than most people of our socio-economic background (which in Des Moines in the 1950s was most people). We – that is to say, my parents, my brother Michael, my sister Mary Elizabeth (or Betty) and I – had a bigger house on a larger lot than most of my parents' colleagues. It was a white clapboard house with black shutters and a big screened porch atop a shady hill on the best side of town.

My sister and brother were considerably older than I – my sister by six years, my brother by nine – and so were effectively adults from my perspective. They were big enough to be seldom around for most of my childhood. For the first few years of my life, I shared a small bedroom with my brother. We got along fine. My brother had constant colds and allergies, and owned at least four hundred cotton handkerchiefs, which he devotedly filled with great honks and then pushed into any convenient resting place – under the mattress, between sofa cushions, behind the curtains. When I was nine he left for college and a life as a journalist in New York City, never to return permanently, and I had the room to myself after that. But I was still finding his hand-kerchiefs when I was in high school.

The only downside of my mother's working was that it put a little pressure on her with regard to running the home and particularly with regard to dinner, which frankly was not her strong suit anyway. My mother always ran late and was dangerously forgetful into the bargain. You soon learned to stand aside about ten to six every evening, for it was then that she would fly in the back door, throw something in the oven, and disappear into some other quarter of the house to embark on the thousand other household tasks that greeted her each evening. In consequence she nearly always forgot about dinner until a point slightly beyond way too late. As a rule you knew it was time to eat when you could hear potatoes exploding in the oven.

We didn't call it the kitchen in our house. We called it the Burns Unit.

'It's a bit burned,' my mother would say apologetically at every meal, presenting you with a piece of meat that looked like something – a much-loved pet perhaps – salvaged from a tragic house fire. 'But I think I scraped off most of the burned part,' she would add, overlooking that this included every bit of it that had once been flesh.

Happily, all this suited my father. His palate only responded to two tastes – burned and ice cream – so everything was fine by him so long as it was sufficiently dark and not too startlingly flavourful. Theirs truly was a marriage made in heaven, for no one could burn food like my mother or eat it like my dad.

As part of her job, my mother bought stacks of housekeeping magazines – *House Beautiful*, *House and Garden*, *Better Homes and Gardens*, *Good Housekeeping* – and I read these with a certain avidity, partly because they were always lying around and in our house all idle moments were spent reading something, and partly because they depicted lives so absorbingly at variance with our own. The housewives in my mother's magazines were so collected, so organized, so calmly on top of things, and their food was perfect – their *lives* were perfect. They dressed up to take their food out of the oven! There were no black circles on the ceiling above their stoves, no mutating goo climbing over the sides of their forgotten saucepans. Children didn't have to be ordered to stand back every time they opened *their* oven doors. And their foods – baked Alaska, lobster Newburg, chicken cacciatore – why, these were dishes we didn't even dream of, much less encounter, in Iowa.

Like most people in Iowa in the 1950s, we were more cautious eaters in our house.* On the rare occasions when we were presented with food with which we were not comfortable or familiar – on planes or trains or when invited to a meal cooked by someone who was not herself from Iowa – we tended to tilt it up carefully with a knife and examine it from every angle as if determining whether it might need to be defused. Once on a trip to San Francisco my father was taken by friends to a Chinese restaurant and he described it to us afterwards in the sombre tones of someone recounting a near-death experience.

'And they eat it with sticks, you know,' he added knowledgeably.

'Goodness!' said my mother.

'I would rather have gas gangrene than go through that again,' my father added grimly.

In our house we didn't eat:

---

*In fact like most other people in America. The leading food writer of the age, Duncan Hines, author of the hugely successful *Adventures in Eating*, was himself a cautious eater and declared with pride that he never ate food with French names if he could possibly help it. Hines's other proud boast was that he did not venture out of America until he was seventy years old, when he made a trip to Europe. He disliked much of what he found there, especially the food.

- pasta, rice, cream cheese, sour cream, garlic, mayonnaise, onions, corned beef, pastrami, salami or foreign food of any type, except French toast;
- bread that wasn't white and at least 65 per cent air;
- spices other than salt, pepper and maple syrup;
- fish that was any shape other than rectangular and not coated in bright orange breadcrumbs, and then only on Fridays and only when my mother remembered it was Friday, which in fact was not often;
- soups not blessed by Campbell's and only a very few of those;
- anything with dubious regional names like 'pone' or 'gumbo' or foods that had at any time been an esteemed staple of slaves or peasants.

All other foods of all types – curries, enchiladas, tofu, bagels, sushi, couscous, yogurt, kale, rocket, Parma ham, any cheese that was not a vivid bright yellow and shiny enough to see your reflection in – had either not yet been invented or were still unknown to us. We really were radiantly unsophisticated. I remember being surprised to learn at quite an advanced age that a shrimp cocktail was not, as I had always imagined, a pre-dinner alcoholic drink with a shrimp in it.

All our meals consisted of leftovers. My mother had a seemingly inexhaustible supply of foods that had already been to the table, sometimes repeatedly. Apart from a few perishable dairy products, everything in the fridge was older than I was, sometimes by many years. (Her oldest food possession of all, it more or less goes without saying, was a fruit cake that was kept in a metal tin and dated from the colonial period.) I can only assume that my mother did all her cooking in the 1940s so that she could spend the rest of her life surprising herself with what she could find under cover at the back of the fridge. I never knew her to reject a food. The rule of thumb seemed to be that if you opened the lid and the stuff inside didn't make you actually recoil and take at least one staggered step backwards, it was deemed OK to eat.

Both my parents had grown up in the Great Depression and neither of them ever threw anything away if they could possibly avoid it. My mother routinely washed and dried paper plates, and smoothed out for reuse spare aluminium foil. If you left a pea on your plate, it became part of a future meal. All our sugar came in little packets spirited out of restaurants in deep coat pockets, as did our jams, jellies, crackers (oyster *and* saltine), tartare sauces, some of our ketchup and butter, all of our napkins, and a very occasional ashtray; anything that came with a restaurant table really. One of the happiest moments in my parents' life was when maple syrup started to be served in small disposable packets and they could add those to the household hoard.

Under the sink, my mother kept an enormous collection of jars, including one known as the toity jar. 'Toity' in our house was the term for a pee, and throughout my early years the toity jar was called into service whenever a need to leave the house inconveniently coincided with a sudden need by someone – and when I say 'someone', I mean of course the youngest child: me – to pee.

'Oh, you'll have to go in the toity jar then,' my mother would say with just a hint of exasperation and a worried glance at the kitchen clock. It took me a long time to realize that the toity jar was not always – or even often – the same jar twice. In so far as I thought about it at all, I suppose I guessed that the toity jar was routinely discarded and replaced with a fresh jar – we had hundreds after all.

So you may imagine my consternation, succeeded by varying degrees of dismay, when I went to the fridge one evening for a second helping of halved peaches and realized that we were all eating from a jar that had, only days before, held my urine. I recognized the jar at once because it had a Z-shaped strip of label adhering to it that uncannily recalled the mark of Zorro – a fact that I had cheerfully remarked upon as I had filled the jar with my precious bodily nectars, not that anyone had listened of course. Now here it was holding our dessert peaches. I couldn't have been more surprised if I had just been handed a packet of photos showing my mother *in flagrante* with, let's say, the guys at the gas station.

'Mom,' I said, coming to the dining-room doorway and holding up my find, 'this is the *toity* jar.'

'No, honey,' she replied smoothly without looking up. 'The toity jar's a *special* jar.'

'What's the toity jar?' asked my father with an amused air, spooning peach into his mouth.

'It's the jar I toity in,' I explained. 'And this is it.'

'Billy toities in a jar?' said my father, with very slight difficulty, as he was no longer eating the peach half he had just taken in, but resting it on his tongue pending receipt of further information concerning its recent history.

'Just occasionally,' my mother said.

My father's mystification was now nearly total, but his mouth was so full of unswallowed peach juice that he could not meaningfully speak. He asked, I believe, why I didn't just go upstairs to the bathroom like a normal person. It was a fair question in the circumstances.

'Well, sometimes we're in a hurry,' my mother went on, a touch uncomfortably. 'So I keep a jar under the sink – a special jar.'

I reappeared from the fridge, cradling more jars – as many as I could carry. 'I'm pretty sure I've used all these too,' I announced.

'That can't be right,' my mother said, but there was a kind of question mark hanging off the edge of it. Then she added, perhaps a touch self-destructively: 'Anyway, I always rinse all jars thoroughly before reuse.'

My father rose and walked to the kitchen, inclined over the waste bin and allowed the peach half to fall into it, along with about half a litre of goo. 'Perhaps a toity jar's not such a good idea,' he suggested.

So that was the end of the toity jar, though it all worked out for the best, as these things so often do. After that, all my mother had to do was mention that she had something good in a jar in the fridge and my father would get a sudden urge to take us to Bishop's, a cafeteria downtown, which was the best possible outcome, for Bishop's was the finest restaurant that ever existed.

Everything about it was divine – the food, the understated decor, the motherly waitresses in their grey uniforms who carried your tray to a table for you and gladly fetched you a new fork if you didn't like the look of the one provided. Each table had a little light on it that you could switch on if you needed service, so you never had to crane round and flag down passing waitresses. You just switched on your private beacon and after a moment a waitress would come along to see what she could help you with. Isn't that a wonderful idea?

The restrooms at Bishop's had the world's only atomic toilets – at least the only ones I have ever encountered. When you flushed, the seat automatically lifted and retreated into a seat-shaped recess in the wall, where it was bathed in a purple light that thrummed in a warm, hygienic, scientifically advanced fashion, then gently came down again impeccably sanitized, nicely warmed and practically pulsing with atomic thermoluminescence.

Goodness knows how many Iowans died from un-explained cases of buttock cancer throughout the 1950s and '60s, but it was worth every shrivelled cheek. We used to take visitors from out of town to the restrooms at Bishop's to show them the atomic toilets and they all agreed that they were the best they had ever seen.

But then most things in Des Moines in the 1950s were the best of their type. We had the smoothest, most mouth-pleasing banana cream pie at the Toddle House and I'm told the same could be said of the cheesecake at Johnny and Kay's, though my father was much too ill-at-ease with quality, and far too careful with his money, ever to take us to that outpost of fine dining on Fleur Drive. We had the most vividly delicious neon-coloured ice creams at Reed's, a parlour of cool opulence near Ashworth Swimming Pool (itself the handsomest, most elegant public swimming pool in the world, with the slimmest, tannest female lifeguards) in Greenwood Park (best tennis courts, most decorous lagoon, comeliest drives). Driving home from Ashworth Pool through Greenwood Park, under a flying canopy of green leaves, nicely basted in chlorine and knowing that you would shortly be plunging your face into three gooey scoops of Reed's ice cream is the finest feeling of well-being a person can have.

We had the tastiest baked goods at Barbara's Bake Shoppe, the meatiest, most face-smearing ribs and crispiest fried chicken at a restaurant called the Country Gentleman, the best junk food at a drive-in called George the Chilli King. (And the best farts afterwards; a George's chilli burger was gone in minutes, but the farts, it was said, went on for ever.) We had our own department stores, restaurants, clothing stores, supermarkets, drug stores, florist's, hardware stores, movie theatres, hamburger joints, you name it – every one of them the best of its kind.

Well, actually, who could say if they were the best of their kind? To know that, you'd have had to visit thousands of other towns and cities across the nation and taste all their ice cream and chocolate pie and so on because every place was different then. That was the glory of living in a world that was still largely free of global chains. Every community was special and nowhere was like everywhere else. If our commercial enterprises in Des Moines weren't the best, they were at least ours. At the very least, they all had things about them that made them interesting and different. (And they were the best.)

Dahl's, our neighbourhood supermarket, had a feature of inspired brilliance called the Kiddie Corral. This was a snug enclosure, built in the style of a cowboy corral and filled with comic books, where moms could park their kids while they shopped. Comics were produced in massive numbers in America in the 1950s – one billion of them in 1953 alone – and most of them ended up in the Kiddie Corral. It was *filled* with comic books. To enter the Kiddie Corral you climbed on to the top rail and dove in, then swam to the centre. You didn't care how long your mom took shopping because you had an infinite supply of comics to occupy you. I believe there were kids who lived in the Kiddie Corral. Sometimes when searching for the latest issue of *Rubber Man*, you would find a child buried under a foot or so of comics fast asleep or perhaps just enjoying their lovely papery smell. No institution has ever done a more thoughtful thing for children. Whoever dreamed up the Kiddie Corral is unquestionably in heaven now; he should have won a Nobel prize.

Dahl's had one other feature that was much admired. When your groceries were bagged (or 'sacked' in Iowa) and paid for, you didn't take them to your car with you, as in more mundane supermarkets, but rather you turned them over to a friendly man in a white apron who gave you a plastic card with a number on it and placed the groceries on a special sloping conveyor belt that carried them into the bowels of the earth and through a flap into a mysterious dark tunnel. You then collected your car and drove to a small brick building at the edge of the parking lot, a hundred or so feet away, where your groceries, nicely shaken and looking positively refreshed from their subterranean adventure, reappeared a minute or two later and were placed in your car by another helpful man in a white apron who took back the plastic card and wished you a happy day. It wasn't a particularly efficient system – there was often a line of cars at the little brick building if truth be told, and the juddering tunnel ride didn't really do anything except dangerously overexcite all carbonated beverages for at least two hours afterwards – but everyone loved and admired it anyway.

It was like that wherever you went in Des Moines in those days. Every commercial enterprise had something distinctive to commend it. The New Utica department store downtown had pneumatic tubes rising from each cash register. The cash from your purchase was placed in a cylinder, then inserted in the tubes and noisily fired – like a torpedo – to a central collection point, such was the urgency to get the money counted and back into the economy. A visit to the New Utica was like a trip to a future century.

Frankel's, a men's clothing store on Locust Street downtown, had a rather grand staircase leading up to a mezzanine level. A stroll around the mezzanine was a peculiarly satisfying experience, like a stroll around the deck of a ship, but more interesting because instead of looking down on empty water, you were taking in an active world of men's retailing. You could listen in on conversations and see the tops of people's heads. It had all the satisfactions of spying without any of the risks. If your dad was taking a long time being fitted for a jacket, or was busy demonstrating isometrics to the sales force, it didn't matter.

'Not a problem,' you'd call down generously from your lofty position. 'I'll do another circuit.'

Even better in terms of elevated pleasures was the Shops Building on Walnut Street. A lovely old office building some seven or eight storeys high and built in a faintly Moorish style, it housed a popular coffee shop in its lobby on the ground floor, above which rose, all the way to a distant ceiling, a central atrium, around which ran the building's staircase and galleried hallways. It was the dream of every young boy to get up that staircase to the top floor.

Attaining the staircase required cunning and a timely dash because you had to get past the coffee-shop manageress, a vicious, eagle-eyed stick of a woman named Mrs Musgrove who hated little boys (and for good reason, as we shall see). But if you selected the right moment when her attention was diverted, you could sprint to the stairs and on up to the dark eerie heights of the top floor, where you had a kind of gun-barrel view of the diners far below. If, further, you had some kind of hard candy with you – peanut M&Ms were especially favoured because of their smooth aerodynamic shape – you had a clear drop of seven or eight storeys. A peanut M&M that falls seventy feet into a bowl of tomato soup makes one *heck* of a splash, I can tell you.

You never got more than one shot because if the bomb missed the target and hit the table – as it nearly always did – it would explode spectacularly in a thousand candy-coated shards, wonderfully startling to the diners, but a call to arms to Mrs Musgrove, who would come flying up the stairs at about the speed that the M&M had gone down, giving you less than five seconds to scramble out a window and on to a fire escape and away to freedom.

Des Moines's greatest commercial institution was Younker Brothers, the principal department store downtown. Younkers was enormous. It occupied two buildings, separated at ground level by a public alley, making it the only department store I've ever known, possibly the only one in existence, where you could be run over while going from menswear to cosmetics. Younkers had an additional outpost across the street, known as the Store for Homes, which housed its furniture departments and which could be reached by means of an underground passageway beneath Eighth Street, via the white goods department. I've no idea why, but it was immensely satisfying to enter Younkers from the east side of Eighth and emerge a short while later, shopping completed, on the western side. People from out in the state used to come in specially to walk the passageway and to come out across the street and say, 'Hey. Whoa. Golly.'

Younkers was the most elegant, up to the minute, briskly efficient, satisfyingly urbane place in Iowa. It employed twelve hundred people. It had the state's first escalators – 'electric stairways' they were called in the early days – and first air conditioning. Everything about it – its silkily swift revolving doors, its gliding stairs, its whispering elevators, each with its own white-gloved operator – seemed designed to pull you in and keep you happily, contentedly consuming. Younkers was so vast and wonderfully rambling that you seldom met anyone who really knew it all. The book department inhabited a shadowy, secretive balcony area, reached by a pokey set of stairs, that made it cosy and club-like – a place known only to aficionados. It was an outstanding book department, but you can meet people who grew up in Des Moines in the 1950s who had no idea that Younkers *had* a book department.

But its *sanctum sanctorum* was the Tea Room, a place where doting mothers took their daughters for a touch of elegance while shopping. Nothing about the Tea Room remotely interested me until I learned of a ritual that my sister mentioned in passing. It appeared that young visitors were invited to reach into a wooden box containing small gifts, each beautifully wrapped in white tissue and tied with ribbon, and select one to take away as a permanent memento of the occasion. Once my sister passed on to me a present she had acquired and didn't much care for – a die-cast coach and horses. It was only two and a half inches long, but exquisite in its detailing. The doors opened. The wheels turned. A tiny driver held thin metal reins. The whole thing had obviously been hand-painted by some devoted, underpaid person from the defeated side of the Pacific Ocean. I had never seen, much less owned, such a fine thing before.

From time to time after that for years I besought them to take me with them when they went to the Tea Room, but they always responded vaguely that they didn't like the Tea Room so much any more or that they had too much shopping to do to stop for lunch. (Only years later did I discover that in fact they went every week; it was one of those secret womanly things moms and daughters did together, like having periods and being fitted for bras.) But finally there came a day when I was perhaps eight or nine that I was shopping downtown with my mom, with my sister not there, and my mother said to me, 'Shall we go to the Tea Room?'

I don't believe I have ever been so eager to accept an invitation. We ascended in an elevator to a floor I didn't even know Younkers had. The Tea Room was the most elegant place I had ever been – like a state room from Buckingham Palace magically transported to the Middle West of America. Everything about it was starched and classy and calm. There was light music of a refined nature and the tink of cutlery on china and of ice water carefully poured. I cared nothing for the food, of course. I was waiting only for the moment when I was invited to step up to the toy box and make a selection.

When that moment came, it took me for ever to decide. Every little package looked so perfect and white, so ready to be enjoyed. Eventually, I chose an item of middling size and weight, which I dared to shake lightly. Something inside rattled and sounded as if it might be die cast. I took it to my seat and carefully unwrapped it. It was a miniature doll – an Indian baby in a papoose, beautifully made but patently for a girl. I returned with it and its disturbed packaging to the slightly backward-looking fellow who was in charge of the toy box.

'I seem to have got a *doll*,' I said, with something approaching an ironic chuckle.

He looked at it carefully. 'That's surely a shame because you only git one try at the gift box.'

'Yes, but it's a *doll*,' I said. 'For a girl.'

'Then you'll just have to git you a little girl friend to give it to, won'tcha?' he answered and gave me a toothy grin and an unfortunate wink.

Sadly, those were the last words the poor man ever spoke. A moment later he was just a small muffled shriek and a smouldering spot on the carpet.

Too late he had learned an important lesson. You really should never fuck with the Thunderbolt Kid.